Additional Praise for *The Dick Davis Dividend*
(*continued from back cover*)

"Dick Davis has been around longer than you or I; he has seen it all, heard it all, and absorbed the lessons of a life in investing with finesse and skill. *The Dick Davis Dividend* distills down this wisdom into a smooth, satisfying, and profitable brew that all investors would do well to imbibe."
—William Bernstein, author of *The Four Pillars of Investing*

"One heck of a book. Three things surprised me about Dick Davis' new book. Surprise number one, Davis, unlike most people in this business, is a very good writer. Surprise number two, his book contains an absolutely staggering amount of useful and well-researched information. Davis really knows the investment business. Surprise number three, Dick Davis and I attended the same high school in NYC, Horace Mann."
—Richard Russell, Publisher of Dow Theory Letters

"The year 1982 witnessed two great events: The great bull market in stocks took off, and Dick Davis launched the most successful newsletter digest in the world. Over the years, Dick has sifted through the wisdom (and lack thereof) of more financial advisors than anyone. In *The Dick Davis Dividend*, he distills the best of it and brings it to you in one handy reference."
—Robert Prechter, ElliottWave.com.

"I found *The Dick Davis Dividend* to be a very comprehensive, broad-based explanation of the financial universe. For the novice it is simply explained, easy to understand, and balanced. It also gives investors a good understanding of active vs. passive investing."
—Ned Davis, President, Ned Davis Research

"A fine book and an insightful resource for investors."
—The Motley Fool

Public Acclaim for Dick Davis On the Air

Dick Davis provided daily radio and television reports on the financial markets for many years (Chapter 1: Personal Background). Here are the responses from some of his listeners and viewers:

"You are rendering a truly remarkable service in providing an astonishing wealth of helpful information. I travel a great deal and feel acutely deprived when I'm away from your broadcasts."

— Karl King, Miami

"Your TV and radio broadcasts are superb. They are the best, most comprehensive, most intelligent, most meaningful . . . well, the MOST! Your performance is impeccable and I thank you for your talent."

—Ernest Frank, Riviera Beach

"I tape your programs and listen to them a second time so I can absorb everything. They are wonderful. Please don't retire."

—J. Clay, Miami

"Without a doubt, this is the best market review I have ever heard at any time or anywhere in my 20 years experience as an investor. The service you render to the public is immeasurable."

—Arthur de Ponceau, Miami

"When my neighbor gets home from the office he sits in his car in his circular driveway until you are through imparting your wisdom. His wife, friends, and cocktails all must wait. Why aren't you on a national hookup? As a traveler, I ask this for selfish reasons, not just so millions of other investors can profit."

—S.B. Jaquith, Marquesas Keys

"For investors who are baffled and befuddled by the vagaries of the market, your down to earth explanations are truly a 'beacon in the wilderness.'"

—Harriet Lapidus, Miami

"I was the national Financial Editor for the Hearst newspapers. Your radio and TV reports are almost better than reading *The Wall Street Journal*. I don't recall anything as good on the New York airwaves. You should be heard nationally."

—Julius Berens, Miami Beach

"I think half the tenants in my condominium would sell their radio and TV sets if they couldn't hear Dick Davis."

—Irma Muskin, Bal Harbour

"I have traveled all over the United States. I know of no city in the country that has an in-depth market report either on radio or TV that comes anywhere close to matching yours."

—Bert Jones, Lake Worth

"I deeply appreciate and greatly admire your reporting. Never in 30 years as an investor have I heard anyone who can say so much so clearly, so succinctly, in such limited time on a complex and many-faceted subject."

—William Golden, Orlando

"I listened to your broadcast while in Nassau. It is the best reporting I have ever heard anywhere in New York or elsewhere. You have my enthusiastic congratulations."

—Samuel Kingsley, Kingsley, Boye & Co., Member NYSE

"Yours is a priceless service."

—Marion Blue, North Miami

"A group of us Palm Beach widows get together for dinner and bridge several evenings a week. We stop everything, even chatter, when your TV and radio shows come on. We wouldn't miss it."

—Marylou Hardy, Palm Beach

"I don't think you can fully realize how much you are appreciated by novice and sophisticated investors alike."

—Henry Hill, Miami

"I listened to you while vacationing in Jamaica. Yours is by far the best financial program I have ever heard—and I'm in the business."

—Les Pollack, Reynolds & Co., NY

"Your commentary on the market is just fabulous. My whole family is geared to mom listening to Dick Davis. Everyone knows to be quiet while you're on."

—Grace Sewers, Miami

"Your broadcasts are the greatest—which is why Dick Davis is a household word all over Florida. Everyone with any interest in the market listens to you."

—Eve Cassady, Surfside

"I am an ardent admirer of your splendid broadcasts and your painstaking research. No one compares with you."

—Bunny St. Ivan, North Bay Village

"The organization and presentation of your broadcasts is superb. They represent a vital service to thousands of investors like myself."

—Fred Garlick, III, Stuart

"Yours is an invaluable service—the best in the country. How did we get along without you?"

—L. Schoch, Fort Lauderdale

"You are doing a magnificent job."

—Mrs. John Boccafogli, Fort Lauderdale

"Yours are the best organized and meatiest reports I have listened to anywhere, either radio or TV."

—Thomas Wells, Hobe Sound

The Dick Davis Dividend

Straight Talk on Making Money from 40 Years on Wall Street

Dick Davis

BICENTENNIAL
1807
WILEY
2007
BICENTENNIAL

John Wiley & Sons, Inc.

For general information on our other products and services or for technical support, please contact our Customer Care Department within the United States at (800) 762-2974, outside the United States at (317) 572-3993 or fax (317) 572-4002.

Wiley also publishes its books in a variety of electronic formats. Some content that appears in print may not be available in electronic formats. For more information about Wiley products, visit our Web site at www.wiley.com.

Library of Congress Cataloging-in-Publication Data

Davis, Dick, 1928–
    The Dick Davis dividend : straight talk on making money from 40 years on
Wall Street / Dick Davis.
        p. cm.
    Includes index.
    ISBN 978-0-470-09903-2 (cloth)
        1. Investments. 2. Stocks. 3. Portfolio management. 4. Investment
analysis. I. Title.
    HG4521.D137 2008
    332.63'22—dc22

                                                                    2007023237

Printed in the United States of America.

10 9 8 7 6 5 4 3 2 1

If she's not bringing me her homemade applesauce with raisins, meatloaf, or a Costco rotisserie chicken, she's thinking of other ways to make the life of her live-alone brother happier, healthier, and easier. This book is dedicated to my unwavering twin sister, Ellie, the one person on this planet who is thinking of my welfare every single day. She sweated out this book with me for three years. One of her happiest days was when I finished: "Now you can go out and have some fun." Happy when I'm happy and sad when I'm sad, my twin sister has been a lifelong blessing.

Contents

Preface

There are thousands and thousands of books on investing, a century of scholarship by brilliant students of the market. It may seem presumptuous of me to think, as I do, that there are still important basic truths that have not been widely discussed. Not that everything in this book is groundbreaking. But some of it is not being heard.

I think it should be. My conviction comes after 40 years of interaction with the investment public as a radio and TV broadcaster, teacher, speaker, newsletter editor, and columnist.

My dealing with investors is ongoing and up-to-the-minute. Every week I teach a stock market class open to the public. It's not the usual basic, Stock Market 101 format. Instead, I give my perspective on what's currently happening in the market and what we can learn from it. I do this voluntarily because it enables me to use what I know to help others. That makes me feel good, but it's also frustrating. There are some 95 million stock owners in this country and I want them all to know what my students know. During class I make no stock recommendations or market forecasts (nor have I during my career). What I mostly do is pound the table about the universal but seldom-discussed truths of investing that are reflected in the market events of the day. In my view, these are truths all investors need to know if they are to put the odds in their favor.

If I am asked in class for an opinion on what a stock or the market will do, my answer is always twofold: First, "I don't know" and second, "Here's a list of all the positives, all the reasons the stock or market should go up; and here's a list of all the negatives, all the reasons the stock or market should go down. There's always a column A and there's always a column B." Perplexing, yes. The very essence of the market is ambiguity and contradiction. I end each of my classes with this: "If you are not confused and frustrated after these two hours, then I haven't done my job. That's what the market is—confusing and frustrating." My students tell me that a lot of what I talk about, they're hearing for the first time and they wish they had heard sooner. They have encouraged me to write this book.

Obviously, reading Dick Davis is not required for making money in the stock market. In my view, however, whatever your approach to the market, it should begin with knowing the type of truths found in this book. Your odds for success will increase. Without such awareness, luck will have to play a bigger role. Also, all brokers and investment advisers, all those in the media, especially on TV, whose job is to inform investors, as well as those in and out of government who may try to reform the markets and perhaps securitize Social Security—in other words, all those in a position to influence investors—should be keenly aware of the salient points in this book. That's not very humble on my part, but I believe it with enough passion to have devoted seven days a week for over three years to setting it all down. (I am painfully slow. It takes me forever to think out what I want to say and then endless long rewritings by hand before I find the right words to convey my thoughts.)

Emphasizing the Obvious

A logical question would be this: "If some of the material found in this book is so basic and so important, why hasn't it been given more attention elsewhere?" The obvious answers are (1) my judgment is wrong—it's not that important; or (2) it is important but it has been discussed and people know about it. My sense is that others have come to the same conclusions long before me but simply haven't felt compelled to discuss or write about them. (The key concept of the durability of major trends, discussed in Chapter 3, is one example.)

I'm sure other points made in this book have been neglected because, apparently, they are so glaringly obvious that they seemingly need no discussion. My decades-long experience with investors has convinced me otherwise. They *do* need discussion, and lots of it. What may sound too obvious or too basic to mention is far from it. Think of the hundreds of thousands of complaints filed with the SEC by naive investors who thought everything their advisers told them was gospel. There is probably no investment truth that would appear more obvious and yet is less understood than the fact that absolutely no one has the answers and everybody is guessing, with some guesses more educated than others. Financial columnist Ben Stein (Sunday *New York Times* Business Section and Yahoo Finance online) says, "Basic advice for being a better investor is so commonplace it doesn't make for great TV programming or speeches. But if followed over a long period, it is life-changing." (From *Your Money,* NYTimes.com, February 27, 2005.)

Many market truisms appear to be self-evident. What advice can be more obvious than "Buy low, sell high"? But many investors do not fully realize just how crucial it is to buy at a reasonable price. Failure to do so is by far the biggest reason for losses in the market. What you buy is probably less important than what you pay for it. You can buy the highest-quality stock but if you buy it high, you can sit with it for a decade before getting your money back (case in point: IBM, 1987–1997). So yes, "Buy low . . ." is not a breakthrough concept. It's a truism that every investor has in the back of his mind. But instead, it should be in the forefront of his thinking. Proper entry level should be driven home with focus and clarity because it is so critical to chances for success. It is a question of emphasizing the obvious.

There are many other market truisms that would appear too obvious for discussion that in fact need vigorous verbal reinforcement. If for every opinion there is an exact opposite opinion by someone equally knowledgeable; if, by our nature and emotions, we are predisposed toward failure in the stock market; if the single biggest contributor to success in the market is luck, and so on (I elaborate on these and many other basics in this book), why aren't these facts of investment life seared into the consciousness of every investor?

A Different Level of Professionalism

I have the questions but not the answers, except to say that this book is an attempt to fill in some of the gaps. Wall Street and the financial media that feeds off it are not going out of their way to alert the public about the limitations of their knowledge. On the contrary, Wall Street firms aggressively promote the image of being expert in providing answers to the problem of what to do with your money.

As a result, there is a popular perception that professionals in the securities business offer the same level of professionalism as lawyers, doctors, accountants, engineers, and the like, when it comes to providing correct answers. (This, despite the fact that it takes many more years of training to be a licensed doctor or lawyer than it does to be a broker.) The fact is money managers are mostly using educated guesses to make decisions. Professionals in other fields do some guessing but, more often than not, they also provide authoritative, definitive, correct answers. Professionals in the securities business also give authoritative, definitive answers but they do so (or should do so) with fingers crossed. The widespread perception that a security adviser's expertise is on a par with professionals in other fields leads to unrealistic expectations and misplaced confidence.

There is a myth, fostered by slick advertising in the industry, that all the investor has to do is to bring his money to a Wall Street firm and they will have the answers and make everything right. Just explain your situation and goals and they'll know just what to do to make your future secure. It's not that the adviser is not genuine in his desire to help the client. It's just that the perverse nature of the entity he's dealing with, the stock market, precludes consistently correct answers. In fact, it's hard to be *mostly* right or even more right than wrong. This is a fact the industry is reluctant to share with its customers.

Coping With Mood Swings

The industry, then, has done a poor job educating the investor about just what he's up against. The market's many moods are unpredictable, but the fact that they will occur and that investors will have to cope with them is certain.

To prepare for a contest, athletes routinely study game film of their adversary. To prepare for the care of a patient suffering from sudden mood swings and irrational behavior, caretakers are trained. Why shouldn't investors be equally prepared, at least to the extent that the arbitrary action of the securities market is not going to cause surprise or shock. When surprises do come, the news is usually in harmony with the major trend of the market. In bear markets, surprises are likely to be negative; in bull markets, the surprise is likely to be good news.

It behooves the investor, as in any long-term relationship, to be familiar with the market's mercurial personality. He should know that the market goes to extremes in both directions, that it can be both the supportive, caring, seductive lover and the cruel, cold, insidious antago-nist; that it can cause euphoria and exhilaration or anger, fear, and despair. He should know that the market can change its mood on a dime; that it can be capricious, enigmatic, and ornery; and that mostly it can be dull, listless, and boring. Most investors have little grasp of these complexities, and Wall Street is not about to focus on them. Such knowledge would only diminish the credibility of advisers and increase public awareness that the job of predicting the unpredictable is simply not doable.

No Pictures

This book has evolved because of a unique set of circumstances that shaped my thinking, my choices, and my values. The circumstances involved my family and my summer-camp upbringing, my one-of-a-kind job in the securities business, and my long-standing unaffiliated status that gives me the flexibility to say what I want. I represent no company, product, or service; I have no personal agenda; I can be bluntly

> "I've never seen a situation where having money made it worse."
> —*Woody Allen*

honest since I am beholden to no one. I have nothing to sell. Yes, I can profit from this book but, trust me, financial gain has nothing to do with the reasons for writing this book. For years, I've been explaining my core convictions to a few. Now I can reach many. That's my motivation, along with the hope that on some rainy day, my children and/or grandchildren will pick it up and read more than the title. Since there are no pictures, that's probably wishful thinking.

Acknowledgments

To write a book, an author has to believe he's saying something that matters. How does he come to that conclusion? Usually, it's through strong personal conviction and an extra helping of ego. In my case, I needed a little extra push; I needed some outside validation. I got it in small but important ways from *Barron's* when they published an article I submitted, from columnists Andrew Tobias and Humberto Cruz when they said some nice things about my work, and from the students in my class who thought my teachings would be helpful to others.

I have done a lot of writing, but this is my first book. It has taken me three years. I received important help along the way. Lori Davis, a gifted writer, a blunt critic, and my niece, provided key support in the early stages when I needed it the most. Charles Kirk, a professional trader and friend, asked John Wiley to call me, thus solving the sticky problem of first-time authors finding a publisher. Kirk was supportive throughout. Virginia Ramirez, a crackerjack typist, converted 20 writing pads of scribbled longhand into book-ready copy. Her dedication and skills are extraordinary, as was my luck in finding her.

During my career in the media I have stuck to the same formula of exposing the reader/listener to the best investment thinking out there. I've done the same in this book, but this time I have made my own beliefs central and used the opinions of others to supplement my own. Sometimes the opinion of others agrees with mine, oftentimes it does not. Since no one is even close to being consistently right in this business, giving both sides of the story is the only approach that makes sense to me.

In seeking other opinions, I have leaned heavily on certain sources. These are islands of excellence that I come back to again and again. Wisdom is not a common trait. I focus on those who have it (admittedly a subjective call) and quote them extensively. I am grateful that great teachers like Warren Buffett and John Bogle are around for me to quote and make this book better. The same goes for exceptional writers, researchers, and web sites. Their contribution is major and I am in their debt.

The list of oft-repeated sources includes William Bernstein, Henry Blodget, John Bogle, Warren Buffett, Jonathan Clements, Jim Cramer, Ned Davis, John Dorfman, Paul Farrell, Benjamin Graham, Joel Greenblatt, Mark Hulbert, Roger Ibbotson, David Jackson, Doug Kass, Charles Kirk, Peter Lynch, Burton Malkiel, Paul Merriman, Bill Miller, Charles Munger, Harry Newton, William O'Neil, Don Phillips, Richard Russell, Michael Santoli, Charles Schwab, Jeremy Siegel, Ben Stein, Sue Stevens, Andrew Tobias, and Marty Whitman.

My thanks to the 28 index fund gurus featured in Part Two. The inclusion of their model portfolios makes for what is probably the most valuable part of the book. I am beholden to the best minds in the field of indexing for making Chapter 7 possible.

I have also made liberal use of a few outstanding publications and their web sites. They include the American Association of Individual Investors (AAII), *Bloomberg, BusinessWeek, Dick Davis Digest, Forbes,* Investopedia, *Investors Business Daily,* MarketWatch, Morningstar, *Motley Fool,* MSN Money, *New York Times,* SeekingAlpha, TheStreet, *Wall Street Journal,* Wikipedia, and Yahoo! Finance. I am especially grateful to *Barron's.* I have been excerpting it for over 40 years and review its contents each week in class. I feel like *Barron's* is almost part of my family. Writers like Michael Santoli, Andrew Barry, and the dean, Alan

Abelson, are superb at their craft. I have taken full advantage of their talents on these pages.

I tap into the best thinking on Wall Street for another reason. If my judgments are found wanting, the reader is still left with a book that is eminently worthwhile.

Annoyed on Oscar Night? This is Worse

I feel like I'm making an acceptance speech at the Academy Awards when I thank my family for their support. My daughter, Ellen Davis, encouraged me; her husband, Alex, edited me; my son, Jeff Davis, counseled me; and my twin sister, Ellie Eisenberg, sustained me—literally. Since I live alone and was often housebound, it was Ellie's shopping, cooking, and caring that nourished my body and spirit. If you or your children are planning to have children, make sure they're boy-girl twins. It's the quintessential sibling arrangement.

My father, William Davis; mother, Florence Davis; and brother, Robert "Skip" Davis have passed on, but not their influence. My father's active interest in the stock market triggered my own. My mother's support was unending and unconditional. I was close to my brother, Skippy. With a bigger-than-life presence and a zest for life, he loved people, golf, food, and telling funny stories—and he was always there for his younger brother.

I suggest you skip the following paragraph. It is little more than blatant self-indulgence. I list the people in my life, who, over the years, have made an indelible imprint. No one on the planet cares. But to me, next to helping the investor, being able to express my gratitude and affection in this way is the biggest bonus I'll get from writing this book. With profuse apologies to the reader, the following are some of the special people (in no particular order) that enable me to say, "I have lived a rich life."

Vesta Gillon, Myra Davis, "Nursie" Kubler, Laura Jerabek, Rebecca Gault, Prudence Reeves, Shirley Greene, Billie Breiner, Jane Avrach, Elsie Stein, Marshall Eisenberg, Fred Zimmerman, Carolyn Zimmerman, Henry Foster, Herb Cohen, Lucille Cohen, Arnold Ganz, Craig Donoff, David Wachs, Matt Greenwald, Dan Blatman, Biff Kogan, Steve Halpern,

Carla Neufeld, Cap Girden, Irwin Fleischner, Joe Stein, Dick Bower, Fred Rothman, Danny Barnhard, Ted Greenfield, Manny Greenfield, Adele Greenfield, Risa Davis, Alex Goncalves, Eleanor and Sam Aaron, Lois Kempler, Dotty Fox, Sue Eisenberg, Richy Eisenberg, Billy Davis, Lori Davis, Benjamin Davis, Joshua Davis, Zachary Davis, Jonathan Davis, Daniel Goncalves, and Gabrielle Goncalves.

I am grateful to many fellow investment newsletter writers and financial columnists who have brought this book to the attention of their readers.

My special thanks to the team at John Wiley & Sons, who magically managed to make a book out of 574 double-spaced pages of raw copy. Kevin Commins, Emilie Herman, and Laura Walsh are true professionals. Their guidance, patience, and encouragement for this first-time author was invaluable.

> "Man will occasionally stumble over the truth, but most of the time he will pick himself up and continue on."
> —*Winston Churchill*
>
> "An economist's guess is liable to be as good as anybody else's."
> —*Will Rogers*

Finally, and not to sound maudlin, how can a 79-year-old author writing acknowledgments fail to give thanks to the good Lord for keeping him around long enough to complete this three-year journey? Let's face it, little else matters without His endorsement.

About the Author

Dick Davis is one of the most widely known and highly respected market commentators of his time. He founded the *Dick Davis Digest* in 1982, one of the nation's most successful investment newsletters, with subscribers in 50 states and 50 foreign countries. (He no longer has an affiliation.) Based in south Florida, Davis was the nation's only nonsalesman employee of a member firm of the New York Stock Exchange (Merrill Lynch, Walston, Drexel Burnham) to work full-time as a broadcaster.

He pioneered in-depth stock market reporting on radio and television in the mid-1960s through the mid-1980s. On radio, he broadcast as often as five times a day for 20 years. On television, he broadcast twice a day for 20 years. His was television's first daily in-depth market report. It won the Janus award for the nation's best business reporting. And it laid the groundwork for the popular PBS *Nightly Business Report,* launched from the same TV station in Miami in the late 1970s. Davis also wrote a three-times-a-week stock market column for the *Miami Herald* which was syndicated by Knight Ridder to some 100 newspapers for over 10 years.

Born in 1928 and raised in Yonkers, New York, Davis attended Horace Mann School for Boys, Hobart College, Syracuse University, and the University of Miami, with majors in English literature and accounting. He served in the Army Counter Intelligence Corps in Japan during the Korean War. His investment career started in 1958 in the Miami Beach office of Merrill Lynch. He first went on the air for Merrill in 1965, and he broadcast uninterruptedly for the next 20 years. He resides in Boca Raton, Florida, where he looks forward to visits from his six perfect grandchildren.

Introduction

Making money in the market is incredibly difficult to do with any consistency. This is a basic truth about investing that's often swept under the rug. Most of those who try have a negative experience. After 40 years in the business, I'm convinced that the individual investor either loses money or, at best, earns an annual return that's lower than the roughly 3 percent rate of inflation.

How is that possible if, as is widely recognized, the average annual return in the stock market for the past zillion years has been just over 10 percent (a figure that includes reinvested dividends)? It's an important question. The answer is because we're comparing apples with oranges. The 10 percent figure is based on the performance of broad-based market *indexes,* mainly the S&P 500. The much lower figure is based on the real-time performance of people, not indexes. And the results of real people often do not mirror the full-year performances of an index. Emotionally motivated, investors typically buy high and sell low, give back their profits and more over time, and fail to hold stocks for the long term. There are exceptions, of course, and some are able to do better, but they are few in number. The vast majority of investors, the millions for whom this book is written, struggle to come out ahead. What they make in good markets they more than give back in bad ones.

Can 95 Million Investors Be Wrong?

The reason why investors perform poorly is because they're dealing with a phenomenon, the stock market, that's unknowable, unpredictable, and unsolvable to *everybody,* including the most erudite. It's also because human beings are saddled with deeply ingrained emotions (fear, hope, greed, etc.) that, when activated, trigger wrong investment moves. And it's because investors think they know more than they do.

It's also because investors get mostly poor advice. The myth has been created over many years that like doctors, lawyers, engineers, and the like, Wall Street salespeople are professionals with definitive answers that will make your money grow. Some do (those who focus on the long term, proper entry level, and asset allocation) but most do not. The myth of knowledgeability is a deception—a pervasive, self-perpetuating fiction that endures because the market, when it decides to do so, bails out Wall Street and makes everybody look good.

Finally, most investors do poorly because they are surrounded daily by an intensely short-term oriented media. The perception is reinforced constantly on TV, in newspapers, magazines, and the Internet, that the excitedly reported news of the day actually matters to investors and requires action. As I explain in this book, to the long-term investor, 99 percent of the news is irrelevant. The scary part is that most reporters innocently believe that what they're saying matters. It is a big stumbling block for the long-term investor whose emotions are constantly and needlessly being tested.

For all these reasons the odds are against the investor. Most are not likely to do well. This is a fundamental tenet that, understandably, is not widely acknowledged. Obviously, it is not in the interest of the billion-dollar financial services industry to dwell on the formidable task investors face, nor on the industry's poor record in helping them. Most within the securities business realize the situation but adopt an "Emperor wears no clothes" approach: They see but they don't say.

> "I've never bought a stock unless, in my view, it was on sale."
> —*John Neff*
>
> "Invest at the point of maximum pessimism."
> —*John Templeston*

What to Do about It

There's little point in detailing the obstacles that confront investors without offering solutions. This book focuses on an easily doable answer to the problem. It offers actionable advice to all investors on how to invest like so many of the professionals secretly do. It's the one way I know that turns negatives into positives and skeptics into optimists.

I'm talking about indexing. Many of the best minds on Wall Street have embraced index fund investing: Warren Buffett, Charles Schwab, Andrew Tobias, Charles Ellis, Peter Lynch, Jonathan Clements, William Bernstein, Paul Merriman, Burton Malkiel, Jeremy Siegel, Michael Steinhardt, Arthur Levitt, Ben Stein, and many others.

One of the most impressive endorsements of passive index fund investing comes from the legendary Bill Miller. It carries added weight because it comes from, arguably, the best active fund manager in the business. No one has neared the performance of his Legg Mason Value Trust (LMVTX), which beat the S&P 500 Index for 15 years in a row, ending in 2006. Critics of passive investing via index funds point to Bill Miller as shining, living, walking proof that active investing works.

So you may be surprised to hear that Bill Miller is a strong advocate of indexing. "I think index funds ought to constitute, just from the broad standpoint of prudence, a significant portion of one's assets in equities. The evidence is that over any substantial period of time— 10 years, 15 years, 20 years—the odds that you will get a money manager who can outperform that period of time are about one in four. So unless you're very lucky, or extremely skillful in the selection of managers, you're going to have a much better experience by going with index funds" (CNNMoney.com, "Bill Miller: What's Luck Got To Do With It," July 18, 2007). Miller does go on to say he believes the investor should have some part of his money in active management as a means of moderately diversifying risk. (This combined passive/active strategy is the same approach recommended in this book.)

Institutions such as state pension funds are also big believers in indexing. Bill Schultheis, in his book *The Coffeehouse Investor* (Palouse Press, 2005), says that the administrators of state pension funds are "some of the largest and most sophisticated investors in our country. These people invest billions of dollars and have a fiduciary responsibility to do the right thing for the thousands of state employees who are counting on their pension funds when they retire. The state of Washington invests 100 percent of its stock market money in index funds, California 86 percent, Kentucky 67 percent, Florida 60 percent, New York 75 percent, and Connecticut 84 percent."

Investors and Pros Split on Indexing

Most individual investors, on the other hand, shun direct investment in index funds (they *are* being used increasingly in 401(k)s). Only about 8 percent of all the money that goes into stock mutual funds is invested in passive index funds. It is a striking dichotomy. The savviest veterans who have studied the market for a lifetime concede, in effect, that the odds are against beating the market. According to Schultheis, "Only 20 percent of all managed mutual funds beat the stock market averages in each of the last three-, ten-, and fifteen-year periods." Fees are the killer. Most active managers simply can't do well enough to offset the fees they charge. So with their own money, or a big chunk of it, many buy diversified, long-term portfolios of low-cost, no-load index funds like the ones featured in this book.

In contrast, the vast majority of the 95 million unsophisticated investors in this country continue to try and best the market. Everywhere they turn, they are encouraged to do so. According to repeated studies, the results are not pretty. Individual investors mostly buy and sell at the wrong time. When they take profits, they give them back, and then some, the next time around, or the time after that. Hope and greed work well in up-markets but offer little defense against the mean-spiritedness of down-markets. Because of the proclivity to buy high and sell low, the average equity investor has earned a scant 2.6 percent annual return over the past 19 years (*Your Retirement* monthly newsletter, January, 2006, page 4).

Closet Indexers

Many Wall Street executives, aware of their limitations in trying to predict an unpredictable market, put their own money in buy-and-hold index funds or alternative investments available only to the wealthy. The rest of us, thinking that we know more than we do, play a game with the odds stacked against us.

It is not unlike another common situation in corporate America. Employees of rival companies are often whipped up to an intense level of competition, bad-mouthing each other's products and services, while their CEOs are playing golf together. There's no way of knowing how many Wall Street CEOs are exhorting their salespeople to sell securities that they themselves avoid. Probably a lot. My sense is that if it were widely known how many really, really smart people on Wall Street are personally investing in the type of model index portfolios featured in this book, it would be a huge eye-opener.

What propels most investors down the wrong path more than anything else is the inability to control emotions. If by nature we were all cool, deliberate, and stoic, we'd all be far better investors. Ego is a big stumbling block. Neither advisers nor advisees want to admit their limitations. Success is credited to skill, while failure is blamed on bad luck or bad advice. Few can suppress their ego and employ a strategy (index funds) that recognizes the market is unknowable. This book hopefully will help add to the few.

Business Exploits Human Flaws

The exploitation of flaws in human nature to generate profit is common in the business world. The diet industry is a good example. It is built around the 100 percent dependable desire of all humans to look and feel good and the equally dependable inability of the dieter to maintain weight loss (which guarantees repeat business).

In similar manner, Wall Street firms are able to build financial empires based on the greed, fear, hopes, and naiveté of their customers. These are human qualities that do not change with the seasons, with evolving musical tastes or changing political parties. They are immutable and eternal. So the financial community creates a wide range of greed-satisfying products that offer the promise of future profit. Wall Street's mass marketing machine creates the perception that money managers, brokerage firms, media gurus, and the like all know the answers and that if you come to them with your money, they will make everything right.

In Greek mythology the singing of the sea nymphs lured unwary sailors onto the rocks. In like manner, investors are lured by the sirens of Wall Street with their hard-to-resist message: "Trust our expertise; we will show you the path to profits and a secure and prosperous retirement." The myth that Wall Street has the answers has been well entrenched for decades; it is only by painful experience that the investor learns otherwise.

> "Wall Street has become fabulously successful at separating capital from its owners."
>
> —*Ted Aronson*

The Blind Leading the Blind

What he learns is that a perverse market will do whatever it has to do in order to make the majority of people wrong. That majority includes both amateurs and professionals. So the ugly reality is that a massive group that doesn't know, is being led by an elite group that doesn't know—the blind leading the blind.

The way the game is played by most investors is a losing battle, but it doesn't have to be. How to win is spelled out in detail in Part Two of this book. Suffice it to say here that my focus is on index funds and target funds because they largely remove emotion from the investment process. Regardless of how wise the advice—or erudite or insightful or whatever glowing adjectives appear on a book cover—it is of little use if only robots can apply it successfully.

I recommend a combination of a mostly passive index fund strategy (80 percent of assets) along with some active management choices (20 percent). It's the best way I know to overcome the human predisposition toward making wrong decisions and, at the same time, fill the need for some fun and challenge. It's a practical approach that's easy to implement (with the help of a wide selection of model portfolios) and that can make 95 million investors right.

There Are Always Exceptions

Of course, there are investors who do well. You may know people who have had ongoing success in the market (i.e., you've seen their Schedule D on their 1040 tax return). It is unfair to characterize a huge group of 95 million with a broad brush. There are exceptions to everything I've written in this introduction. There *are* individual investors who outperform the market and see their portfolio grow each year. There *are* a handful of traders and professional money managers who do the same. And there *are* brokers who verbalize their limitations, explain the negatives as well as positives, and make money for their accounts. All of these represent a small minority. Maybe I should change the first heading in this Introduction to, "Can *94* Million Investors Be Wrong?" But you get the point.

My Own Fallibility

My personal experience in the market has helped to shape my index fund bias. I am a poor stock picker. Gains have been more than offset by losses. Like many other financial commentators, my net worth comes not from beating the market but from writing about it. That's why the *Dick Davis Digest* newsletter was filled with the recommendations of others, not mine. It's also why during all my years in the securities business, I've never recommended a stock.

Forty years of interaction with investors as a broker, full-time radio and TV broadcaster, syndicated columnist, newsletter publisher, speaker, and teacher has made me sensitive to the failings of investors. I have witnessed their reactions to the same situation in the same way with the same negative results. The combination of my own fallibility and that of those around me has been important in leading me toward index funds.

Chances for Success

It may be presumptuous for me to ask myself this question but I often do: "If someone like myself who has followed the market so closely for so many years, and who is keenly aware of all the emotional stumbling blocks, has problems buying and selling stocks, what chance has the less informed investor?"

The answer is a very good chance, with the help of this book. That's a bold statement, especially from someone who espouses humility. I wince a little when I say it. There are so many advice books by brilliant scholars filled with wise counsel. Yet most investors continue to do what they've always done: Act on emotion instead of reason. I think the combined 80 percent passive, 20 percent active strategy detailed in this book can break that pattern by putting the investor on automatic pilot with most of his/her money. The variety of recommended buy-and-hold portfolios featured in this book make the 80/20 approach easy to implement.

I am one of many pushing index funds. Twenty-eight leading proponents and their favorite index fund portfolios are featured in Chapter 7. Vanguard's John Bogle has been a staunch advocate since 1976. Advances have been made in the interim and today we're able to put together a diversified portfolio with the potential of doing *better* than the market, not just mirroring it.

Many have climbed aboard the indexing bandwagon and many more will follow. Most of the volume in ETF index funds, however, comes from the institutions who use them for sophisticated hedge fund strategies and program trading. As you might expect, Wall Street retail firms have given the no-load buy-and-hold index fund product a lukewarm reception.

A Different Index Fund Approach

The approach to index funds in this book is different from others in three respects:

1. A look at the Contents reveals that the subject of index funds does not dominate it. What does are the conclusions about successful investing that I feel most strongly about after a lifetime on Wall Street. Included are basic truths about active investing, many seldom discussed, that will help put the investment odds in the reader's favor.

2. In Part Two, dealing with "What should I do with my money?" the answer is not limited to passive index funds. It is also suggested that some money be invested actively, with specific recommendations on how to do that. This option provides a challenge to do-it-yourself investors and makes the whole approach more palatable. The stock market insights in the earlier part of the book are mostly applicable to active investing.

3. In the spirit of the *Dick Davis Digest* newsletter (where all stock recommendations were made by others, not me), both passive and active investors get the benefit of selections picked by a wide cross section of elite advisers, not just by one author.

Some investment products, like top-performing hedge funds, are only accessible to the super rich. Index funds are available to everybody. The fact that they may not be aggressively promoted by the Fidelities or Merrill Lynches of the world is simply another reason to buy them. If some of the nation's smartest financial advisers are putting at least a portion of their personal money in index

> "I recommend index funds for people who don't want to spend time studying the market. They are good for 95 percent of the population."
>
> —*Warren Buffett*

funds, why shouldn't all investors do the same? If they do, it's likely that a sequel to this book, say 10 years from now, will have a slightly different heading in the Introduction: "How 95 Million Investors Got It Right."

A Challenge: Blunt Honesty without Turning Off the Investor

When doctors recommend a hospital procedure, they will often minimize the unpleasant aftereffects. They'll either avoid the topic completely or brush it aside with "There's not much to it." Invariably, there *is* much to it. Many patients prefer to be told exactly what to expect so that they are mentally and emotionally prepared for whatever happens. The doctor, however, may feel justified in downplaying possible post-treatment difficulties. He or she knows that in the long run the patient will be better off and that the discomfort will be temporary. If the doctor were to be completely candid and graphic, the patient might be scared off, to the detriment of his or her long-term health.

I can empathize with the doctor. If I'm completely truthful in discussing the difficulties involved in investing, I'm likely to lose readers. Bad news may sell newspapers and lead the nightly newscast but, understandably, it's not what the investor wants to hear.

I believe that it is essential for all investors to have certain basic truths ingrained in their psyche. These include concepts that are unsettling and disconcerting. Any honest discussion about stocks must address the issue of just how difficult the market is to deal with. There's no way of getting around it. The fact that the market is confusing, illogical, complex, and unfathomable should be understood right off. Everything else comes after that.

Like the boxer, the investor's first step toward winning is knowing what to expect from his adversary. A book about the stock market that doesn't include plain talk about the potential for frustration, disappointment, and anger is simply incomplete. But once it's understood that the bad that happens in the market is what makes the good possible, and that it's an integral part of the process, the investor is ready to move on. We can't have bull markets without bear markets and we can't take profits without also taking losses. Once this realization is firmly fixed in the investor's mind, he is far better equipped to make good things happen.

Wall Street downplays the negatives and focuses almost exclusively on the good stuff. Doing so helps make the sale. And the more assertive, the more definitive, the more confident the recommendation, the more likely the sale.

I want to make the sale, too. That is, I want the investor to read this book. It's a challenge; I have to walk a fine line. On the one hand, I want to describe the unvarnished truth about what the investor is up against without turning him off in the process. On the other hand, I want to convince the reader that investing along the lines suggested in this book will make good things happen.

I'm a strong proponent of the stock market as a long-term means of growing money. I own stocks, my kids own stocks, my sister owns stocks, my father and brother owned stocks, and I buy stocks for my grandchildren. I dwell on the big picture, warts and all, because once you know the pitfalls, you can learn to minimize them and focus on ways to win.

In these pages you'll learn how to put the investment odds in your favor, whether you invest through a brokerage firm, online, in an IRA, or through your 401(k) at work. And you'll come to understand that investing can be a fulfilling, profitable pursuit. Stay with me through the bad stuff and I promise you an eminently happy ending.

> "I have enough money to last me the rest of my life, unless I buy something."
>
> —*Jackie Mason*

Where I'm Coming From

I remember something I read on how to write a good book: Tell the reader what you're going to do, do it, and then tell the reader what you did. Sounds more repetitive than riveting, but at least it's a game plan.

What I intend to do in the pages that follow is share with you the beliefs I feel most strongly about after 40 years on Wall Street. Many are seldom discussed even though, in my opinion, they should be. They are basic concepts and widely applicable. Investors should know them if they are to make truly informed judgments and put the odds in their favor.

When it came to organizing the contents of this book, the challenge was to reduce a lifetime of convictions about how to help investors into a concise, logical format. Luckily my beliefs fall easily into a few distinct categories. First are the things I'd like my kids to have going for them before they even think about investing. Second is what I see as the six carved-in-stone truths about investing that should never be forgotten. Third are the seven core convictions that I consider, by far, the most essential maxims to follow for achieving success. Fourth is everything else I feel strongly about investing, totaling 35 insights, many of them seldom discussed. And fifth is the answer to this likely question from the reader: Now that I know your deepest convictions about how to become a better investor, what specifically do I do with my money? So much for a thumbnail summary of how the book is divided.

My goal has been to write with clarity, brevity, and insight with an emphasis on complete candor. For starters, I believe that many who invest in the stock market do not belong there. The market can be a treacherous arena. Savings accumulated over years of hard work can be decimated. If the investor is aware of this possibility and can afford to take the risk, so be it. But if he depends on his investments to put food on the table or pay the rent, he should not be in stocks, at least not unless they are properly divided among different asset classes. If a sudden decline in the value of his holdings will force a change in lifestyle, he should not be in stocks. If a big hit is likely to cause emotional or physical illness, he should not be in stocks. He should be aware that there are some who go so far as to describe the investment arena as "a field where [investors] are condemned almost by mathematical law to lose" (Benjamin Graham, *The Intelligent Investor,* Harper Business, 1949. 4th revision 2003; 623-page paperback updated by Jason Zweig).

The stock market can be a formidable adversary. It can give munificently and then take away unmercifully. The gifts are too often fleeting, the erosion too often permanent. Young investors with job income have a big advantage. If their investments go bad, their current standard of living supported by their salary is still unaffected and they have time to recover in the market. But for those of moderate means who live off their investments, the risks are too high. I offer suggestions on what they should do with their money in the pages ahead. What they clearly should *not* do is expose themselves to the following type of situation, which occurs all the time.

The Bad That Can Happen

TXU Corp. (formerly Texas Utilities Corp.) is not a speculative highflier. It's a relatively conservative electric utility that's been a favorite income stock. On October 1, 2002, a major brokerage firm downgraded it from "buy" to "neutral," rated its volatility risk as "medium," and said that the $41.76 price of the stock already reflected much of the risk.

Just six days later, on October 8, TXU lowered its earnings forecast and the stock plummeted to a low of $13.85. A major firm called the $2.40 dividend secure and the CEO of the company appeared on CNBC and unequivocally stated that the dividend was safe. He expressed the same confidence to the *New York Times* on Friday, October 11. Bargain hunters pushed the stock back up to $18. Then on Monday, October 14, just days after the CEO's declaration, TXU slashed its dividend 80 percent from $2.40 to $.50. The stock immediately sank to an all-time low of $10.10. A highly recommended utility favorite, bought mostly for its safe dividend, had plunged from 41 to 10 in two weeks. With no advance warning and with lightning speed, the conservative investor's savings and income were dealt a crippling blow.

The TXU debacle turned out to be a giant whipsaw. Those able to hold on saw the stock rebound to a 2 for 1 split adjusted high of 136 four years later. The rise was helped by news in February 2007 of a proposed $69.25 per share take-over (equivalent to a presplit price of $138.50) by a private equity firm, the largest-ever leveraged buyout. But that didn't negate the damage suffered by those who felt betrayed and sold their shares near the bottom in disgust.

In situations like this the innocent investor is helpless. Like a leaf in the wind, he is at the mercy of analysts who fail to ask probing questions and CEOs who keep both analysts and the public in the dark and misrepresent the truth.

> "Time is the great healer. It is the investor's most powerful ally. You may be without luck or wealth, but stay healthy and you will always have time. Unless, of course, you buy a bad stock in which case an eternity won't help."
>
> —*Unknown*

The Inept Handling of Stock Market News

Another challenge faced by the investor is dealing with misleading information. The financial media's inept handling of news is a constant irritant to me. Perhaps I'm overly sensitive because, unlike most business reporters, my background is in stocks, not news. I give vent to my frustrations in Chapter 3, "The Market Is King—News Is Mostly Irrelevant." However, a telling event occurred a few days before the submission deadline for this book. I'm glad I can share it with you.

The media's lack of insight in reporting financial news is on display 24/7, but it is most glaring on big move days. On Thursday, July 26, 2007, the Dow Jones industrial average fell 450 points. It had been on a tear most of the prior year, climbing over 3,000 points from mid-July of 2006 to mid-July of 2007. During that steady rise, stocks climbed the typical "wall of worry"—growing weakness in the subprime lending and housing markets, worsening borrowing conditions, slowing economic growth, and so on. The Dow reached an historic high of 14,000 on July 16, 2007 but in the following week, reversed itself with a vengeance. It suffered one day losses of 149, 226, and 208 points. But the big hit came on July 26 when it plunged 450 points to its low, closing down 311 on huge volume. It was a scary time.

Why was it that by 2:40 P.M on Thursday, July 26, the Dow had lost 450 points—when the news background was exactly the same as it had been a week earlier when the Dow topped 14,000? In fact, the same bad news on the credit and housing markets had been dogging the market, not for days or weeks, but for months. What was there about this particular hot summer day in July that suddenly caused frenzied selling with news that had been ignored for so long?

The answer, of course, is that no one knows. But since the news that day was "old hat," it's reasonable to assume something else was going on. Based on behavioral studies, if not just plain common sense, it's likely that investor emotions played a role—probably a dominant one. Fear and greed are highly contagious. Both are quickly activated by sudden, extreme price moves. The intensity of the selling and the steepness of the decline make investors believe that their worst fears are about to become a reality. As prices plunge and momentum accelerates, their instinct is to sell to protect profits and limit losses. In other words, a major catalyst for the carnage is the unnerving action of the market itself.

But Why Did It Happen Today?

On the evening of the market's 450-point collapse, the media struggled with explanations. *The News Hour* with Jim Lehrer on PBS is among the most prestigious, reliable, news sources on the air. I rarely miss it. Jim Lehrer, Gwen Ifill, Ray Suarez, Margaret Warner, Judy Woodruff, and Jeffrey Brown are all consummate professionals. (I miss Robert McNeil, Charlayne Hunter-Gault, and don't get enough of Roger Rosenblatt.) On the night of July 26, award-winning 30-year veteran reporter Ray Suarez asked his two guest experts to explain why the stock market plummeted that day.

The choice of guests—two economists—negated from the get-go any insightful answers. It reflected the misguided thinking of all media everywhere, that a meltdown in the market must be tied to the news of the day. Interviewed were Thomas Lawler, a housing market consultant, and Diane Swonk, chief economist for a financial services firm. Since the news that day revolved around housing and credit problems, these were logical choices. But the market is illogical. For a full 10 minutes, both guests spoke eloquently about what they know, which is not the stock market (PBS.org/News Hour/Video; go to archives for full interview). Nothing that they said could not have been said the day before, the week before, or the month before. They were never asked, "But why today?"

This same inadequate explanation was repeated by media outlets throughout the country. Reasons were given by everyone *except* those who have insight into investor behavior, the complexities and randomness of the stock market, and the futility of trying to reduce explanations for the market's actions to one or two factors. Reporters who didn't know were asking analysts who didn't know. The result was a public that didn't know. But none of the parties knew that they didn't know.

This is the way the stock market has been covered by the media forever: Tie the event to whatever news makes it plausible. Completely ignored is the independent force that controls everything: the market itself and the emotions of those who respond to it. This media treatment of the stock market is so routine, so accepted, and so entrenched, that its validity is never questioned. Millions ask "What happened in the market today?" and millions respond with what they hear/read in the media, as if it were fact.

Stock market news is reported by news organizations, not by behavioral scientists, psychologists, or students of the subtleties of the market. The business of news organizations is to report news. They are trained to answer the "why" of things with logical explanations that make for neatly packaged, complete stories. They are well-intentioned, with little awareness their

> "The typical 30-second sound bite explaining the market's action that day is an affront to the sovereignty, mystery, and complexity that is the stock market."
> —*Unknown*

market stories are misguided. There is far less excuse for advisers and brokers in the securities business who often give the same vapid explanations. They should know better, but most don't.

The Media Wears No Clothes

I feel very alone in discussing this subject. The emperor has worn no clothes for such a long time, no one seems to care. But this is important. We're talking about people's money. If our net worth suddenly drops sharply, aren't we entitled to an honest, knowledgeable explanation of what is known and, more importantly, what isn't known? Why is truth in advertising more important than truth about our money? It is a myth that what's reported on market behavior in the media is fact. It's a myth that such behavior can be explained by knowable, identifiable reasons (surprises like invasions, tsunamis, and assassinations are exceptions). Correcting such a long-entrenched, widely-held misconception is difficult. It's unlikely to happen. I'm hoping those media sources with the most air-time and print space will try. Here are my suggestions.

I think Ray Suarez should have had another guest the night of July 26. In response to the question—which should always be asked—"Why today?," the stock-market savvy guest would present the following six points:

1. The stock market itself is the all-powerful final arbiter. The day, hour, or minute it feels the rubber band has been stretched too far, it'll do something about it, not before.
2. Human emotions, responding to the markets' gyrations, triggered by fear and greed, likely play a key role.
3. Worries over a wide range of overlapping factors, both fundamental and technical, may or may not be additional influences. (Future market historians may well cite long-standing housing and credit worries as major factors in shaping the market's trend. The significance of their role on July 26, however, is unknowable.)
4. A market that acts randomly and irrationally cannot be explained logically.
5. Except in cases of surprise, most news is irrelevant in explaining the market's action on a particular day. The stock market leads; the news follows.

6. The answer to the question, "Why today?," is: "I don't know—nor does anyone else." The markets are complex and perverse. They defy definitive answers.

In my view, every discussion on TV, radio, newspaper, magazine, or the Internet which gives reasons for a big move in the market is unbalanced, incomplete, and misleading—unless it alludes to the points listed above. Time and space restrictions may make that difficult, but unless some effort is made, the investor is short changed.

In all likelihood, things will stay as they are. So it is up to you, the informed individual investor, to rise above the misinformed media. If you are looking to the stock market to grow your net worth, you should be aware of the enigmatic nature of the phenomenon you're dealing with—even if your news provider is not. When you're watching or reading the whys of what happened in the market that day, know that the reporter is innocent and well-intentioned but clueless. What he presents as facts are guesses which may or may not be pertinent.

I know this sounds terribly arrogant. I don't mean to be. On the contrary, if there ever was a situation that calls for humility, it's dealing with the stock market. I hope investors develop a respect for the perplexity and primacy of the market itself and remember it is autocratic, not democratic. When it acts as you predicted, it is mostly coincidence.

The media's daily ineptness is of less concern to the long-term investor. Big market moves may be inexplicable, but a long-term or dollar-cost-averaging approach precludes the need for explanations. What can be said with confidence is that the *one* thing that is *not* random and irrational about the market's performance is its basic, underlying, 100-year entrenched uptrend. Focus on the long term and you can ignore the media's distortions.

> "When packing, lay out all your clothes and all your money. Then take half your clothes and twice the money.
> —*Susan Butler Anderson*

The irrelevance of news is discussed in greater detail in Chapter 3.

Know the Risks

The risks to the investor who cannot afford losses posed by a perverse stock market would seem obvious. Yet the ongoing flood of horror stories from uninformed investors indicates a pervasive problem, especially among the elderly.

Almost everything good that happens in the market requires the passage of time, often lots of time. The retiree or approaching retiree (including hordes of today's baby boomers) often doesn't have the luxury of letting things play out. He has to be luckier and smarter. He can gradually allocate his assets more conservatively as he gets older or he can buy life-cycle or targeted maturity mutual funds that will shift the asset mix for him. To the extent that his other asset classes go up (primarily bonds) when his stocks go down, he has some protection. But if he cannot afford the risks that go with owning common stocks, his focus should be on less risky assets like short- and medium-term bonds, and no-risk investments like immediate annuities and laddered CDs. If he is in stocks, he should sell not because he has to but because he wants to.

This book is written for those who can assume the risk of being in the stock market. It is for those who own or plan to own securities either directly or indirectly through mutual and index funds, annuities, 401(k)s, IRAs, and so on. This group represents almost one third of the U.S. population but only a tiny fraction of the people on this planet (it doesn't hurt to be aware of the big picture). Sadly, almost half the people on earth don't have clean water and live on less than $2 a day; a billion go to bed hungry every night. They have no investment problems. At the other extreme, there are over 1,000 billionaires in the world. They also have no investment problems.

Somewhere in between are the rest of us, and, fortunately, we do have a problem—namely, what do we do with our money? There are some who put it to work in a savings bank or in real estate, in collectibles or in a business. And some 95 million people in this country look to stocks or a combination of stocks and bonds as a way to grow their money. They make that choice because of one compelling fact: For over one hundred years the underlying bias of the stock market and the economy has been up.

Housekeeping Notes

There are a few things you should know about what you will and won't find in this book. You will not find it crowded with footnotes, charts, graphs, tables, and detailed historical references. The fact is that you can find statistics to support almost any conclusion. What you will find is lots of anecdotal evidence—conclusions formed from personal experience over the years, as well as the experience of others.

As I did on radio, on TV, in newspapers, and in the *Dick Davis Digest,* I make liberal use of other people's brains throughout this book. I have deep convictions and I express them—that's why I wrote the book. But I also include opposite views because they could be right. The goal is to expose the reader to the best investment thinking (always a subjective call). I often quote the same source again and again. If a person is wise, he is wise about a lot of things. If a quote from Warren Buffett is the best I can find to illuminate a subject (often the case), I will not skip it just because I've quoted him before.

In addition to sources, I also repeat ideas, themes, and conclusions. If it's something I feel strongly about, you're apt to find it in more than one place in the book. This is by design. It's done for the same reason an advertiser puts a phone number three times in a 30-second commercial: I want it to sink in.

Then there's the matter of how much attention should be paid to the obvious. Often, basic market truths are not addressed because it's assumed everybody knows about them (like "buy low, sell high"). Their self-evidence seemingly precludes any need for discussion. I don't believe that. Some of the most important truths about successful investing are glaringly uncomplicated. But because they are seldom mentioned, they are not in the forefront of investors' thinking. They retreat to the back recesses of the mind where they get dusty and forgotten. My goal is to help revive investor awareness of the unspoken obvious. In Chapters 3 and 4, I pound the table on oft-neglected stock market absolutes that are imperative for investors to understand.

My brother, Skippy, had weight and heart problems most of his life. I believe he may have lived longer if his doctor had warned him that if he didn't lose weight, he would likely die. The doctor didn't do so because he felt my brother already knew that. It was obvious. Of course, my brother *did* know that, but in my view, he would have been more motivated to do something about it if the doctor had emphatically verbalized what was left unsaid. When we are not reminded, the apparent

> "By working faithfully 8 hours a day you may eventually get to be boss and work 12 hours a day."
> —*Robert Frost*

often fades and is replaced by more immediate concerns. A jolt is required to restore awareness. There are times when it is crucial to vigorously state the obvious and then keep repeating it. This applies especially to the world of investing.

Truth Can Be Simply Expressed

Invariably, the best investment advice is basic, unadorned, and uncomplicated. "Buy good stocks at cheap prices and hold on" is not rocket science but, if followed, could largely do away with the multibillion-dollar stock advisory business. A profound truth is no less profound because it is obvious. Harry Markowitz won a Nobel Prize in economics because he found that to reduce risk, a portfolio needs securities that don't go up and down together. It's a simple concept that also happens to be crucial.

If what's most helpful to the investor is also obvious and covered elsewhere, should I still include it here? With me it was an easy question to answer. First, much of the material in this book is either original or discussed with a fresh approach. Second, my overriding mission is to put in the book *everything* I feel strongly about after observing people and markets for a long time. My priority is to include what's most important for my children and grandchildren to know when I'm no longer here. If some of these long-held convictions coincide with what's already known or written about, so be it. It probably means they're worth repeating.

A good book on investing should hold up over the years. The great books listed in Chapter 10 have all stood the test of time. The concepts they espouse have endured. By definition, timeless investment truths, the kind I deal with in this book, are always relevant, but the examples used to illustrate those truths soon fade from the headlines and are replaced by others. I mention this only to emphasize to future readers that the immediacy of the examples is unimportant. One is as good as another. It's the underlying truth that matters. A crash in the Dow in October 1987 or 20 years later in February 2007, or countless other examples, illustrate equally well an ageless market truism: The market is king and final arbiter; it will do what it wants when it wants, regardless of the news.

Confused Is Better than Certain

One of this book's fresh approaches is its insistence on telling both sides of the story. Even in instances where I hold strong opinions, I include the opposite viewpoint. It's a format well suited for a debate but not for an investment book. Investors want clear direction, not confusion. They want definitive, no-hedge answers, not choices. TV investment guru Jim Cramer says his viewers want strong opinions on what to do, not evenhandedness. The latter, he says, is a turnoff.

I agree. But does it help the investor to imply that the market is predictable and subject to unequivocal answers? I don't think so. If nothing else, the market *is* confusing. Suggesting otherwise creates unrealistic expectations.

Can an author write a successful book on investing using this blunt approach, or is it too much of a turnoff? I'm gambling that I can (as is my publisher), based in part on the favorable feedback from my students. Authors write investment books to give advice and opinion. But despite the passion behind it, it's still just one man's opinion. It's not gospel. When the reader finishes the book, as convincing as it may be, he should be left with a sense of where that book fits in the big picture. He should know there are other equally convincing books with opposite opinions. Most of all, he should know he's dealing with an irrational market that may not be convinced at all and has its own agenda. I prefer the reader be confused, aware, and prepared rather than certain, unaware, and unprepared.

Above all, my goal is to try and keep things simple. My inclination is to do the opposite—write long sentences with long words because it is much easier to do. Growing up, my favorite writers were people like Sidney Harris, Walter Lippman, James Reston, and Red Smith. All of them tackled weighty issues with concise, lucid, elegant prose. I learned that the most profound thoughts can be conveyed with simple language. And I learned the best way to write effectively is to get to the point quickly. Gifted finance writers like Andrew Tobias and Jonathan Clements do this all the time. I fall far short but it's a goal to which I aspire.

Because we live in a world of hype, simply expressed ideas are sometimes dismissed as lacking substance. Jeremy Siegel, the highly regarded author and professor of economics at the University of Pennsylvania (see Chapter 9), advises investors to "buy quality dividend-paying companies, hold them for a long time, and reinvest the dividends." Those 15 words reflect a lifetime of research. The same can be said of this deceptively terse conclusion from best-selling author, teacher, and money manager Joel Greenblatt: "Buy good stocks cheap" (see Chapter 9). The simplicity and brevity of thoughts like these belie their wisdom. It is folly to think that what is plain cannot also be profound.

A Word about Quotations

A picture is worth a thousand words. But sometimes just a few words can capture a profound truth so eloquently, so succinctly, and so graphically that it surpasses any picture in its ability to communicate. I often struggle to find the right words to convey an idea. Then I'll come across a great quotation. Not only does it say what I want to say, but it adds still more meaning to it, and with fewer words. With wisdom and clarity, a memorable quotation can capture the essence of a whole chapter or even a whole book in just a few sentences.

I make liberal use of quotations throughout this book. Some are found within the text; others are grouped together in Chapter 10. They are sayings I've cut out and saved over the years. They are stand-alone, independent thoughts that may or may not relate to the adjoining content. Some may express an opinion directly opposite that which is found in the text. Multiple quotes come from the same author—wise people say lots of wise things. The selection of quotations is a very subjective process. From my experience telling jokes, I am keenly aware that what strikes a responsive chord in one person may cause another to scratch his head. I'm hoping that we're mostly on the same wavelength.

One Final Note

One final note regarding upcoming content. I am keenly aware of the clear superiority of women in all areas of human endeavor (my twin sister being the better half). But to keep the prose less cumbersome, and with sincere apologies, "he" is used instead of the proper "he/she" throughout the text.

> "Unless you can watch your stock holding decline by 50 percent without becoming panic-stricken, you should not be in the stock market."
>
> —*Warren Buffett*

Chapter 1

Personal Background

This chapter deals with those influences during my early years and during my career on Wall Street that directly impacted the underlying themes expressed in this book. This is not completely an exercise in ego. It is an attempt to explain how and why a particular set of beliefs has become so important to me. As you read this background material you'll note one underlying theme: I've always attempted to break new ground.

I've tried to do the same with some of the content in this book, including this mini-bio. To those who say, "Let's get to the meat; who cares about all the personal stuff?" I say, "No one cares about an author's background if he has little of importance to say. But if what he says matters and is helpful, then knowing something about his background should add meaning to his words. I'm hoping I fall into the latter category."

Pre–Wall Street

My childhood growing up in Yonkers, New York, was a happy one. We were a close family with loving, indulgent parents. In junior high I was president of the student council and won the Westchester County oratorical contest. My best friend was Biff Kogan, an awkward, sickly, shy boy who was unathletic and unpopular. I liked him because he was bright, caring, irreverent, funny, and sensitive. He kept a diary, which was published after his early death.

I was especially close to my twin sister, Ellie, a closeness that is even stronger today. Being boy/girl twins gave us lots of advantages. Without trying, we were thrust in the spotlight and given special status by peers and family. My parents encouraged me to always look after my sister, which I have tried to do. However, Ellie does far more for me, which truly makes her "the better half" (part of my e-mail moniker is "Eleanorstwin").

I was a serious student, too much so. I remember my mother admonishing me, "Don't study so much. So you'll get a 'B' instead of an 'A.'" What she didn't understand was that the reason I studied hard was not to get an "A." The reason had to do with a personal trait that has characterized most everything I've done during my lifetime, including the writing of this book.

I recognized early on that the world is full of people smarter than me, a lot smarter, but that I can achieve what they can, maybe even more, if I'm willing to work longer and harder. I realized that most people work nowhere near their full potential and that if I do, I can accomplish what they can't. So in school and throughout my career, I put in a lot more hours than the next guy, not to get an "A" but to make sure that the result was the absolute best I was capable of. Like a horse with blinkers on, I was completely focused. I knew I could compete with higher IQs if they were operating on 50 percent and I was giving an all-out 100 percent. (I may hold the record for having the lowest IQ among straight-A students.)

In competition with more naturally gifted people, the best I could do might not be good enough. But that was something I had no control over. Everything I could do, I did without regard to the time it took. I could get away with this essentially selfish attitude during my career because I've lived alone most of my life. The beauty of this

focused approach is that knowing you've left nothing in the
tank leaves you with a deep feeling of satisfaction, regardless of
the outcome. Whatever happens,
happens. You've done your very
best. But I could never make my
mother understand.

> "No one traveling on a business
> trip would be missed if he failed
> to arrive."
> —*Unknown*
>
> "Our business in this world is to
> fail in good spirits."
> —*Unknown*

Summer Camp

Summer camp was a major influence on all that came later. It helped
shape my character and values. It instilled in me the self-confidence to
think differently, to pioneer, and to persevere. Some 60 years after the
fact, fellow campers are still among my closest friends. The camp has
been closed for decades but we still hold annual reunions. We reminisce
and sing camp songs arm-in-arm (to hold each other up).

The catalyst that made camp such a powerful and enduring experience for all of us was the founder and director, Barney "Cap" Girden. Cap
was a bigger-than-life, rugged outdoorsman who came from the Henry
Street settlements in lower Manhattan. He was a man's man, a charismatic
leader, teacher, and legend in his own time. A terrible businessman, he was
always in debt because he was lenient with poor families. He was a physical
fitness buff who wrestled and defeated the few counselors willing to challenge him. He was a student and lover of nature, a hypnotic storyteller, an
inventor, and a dreamer. He instilled in us all a respect for nature, for ourselves, and for each other. He deemphasized athletics and focused on good
fellowship and good sportsmanship.

I spent 15 summers at Camp Mooween (near Colchester,
Connecticut), the last two as head counselor. I was picked by Cap to
plan the daily activities for some 140 boys and supervise a staff of 35
counselors. I worked directly under Cap and was probably closer to
him than anyone in camp. The camp itself was in an isolated, rustic but
beautiful, wooded area on a large, pristine private lake with numerous
islands and lots of fish. In the evening, I remember all of us taking the
war canoe and paddling out to Dream Island in the middle of Red
Cedar Lake under starry skies. The island was crowded with tall cedar

trees, the ground was covered with a thick cushion of pine needles, and the air was punctured by the fragrance of pinewood and the croaking of bullfrogs. We would sit on logs that formed an Indian council ring and listen to Cap as he stood in front of the campfire under the stars and told us riveting stories of Indian chiefs and their brave deeds.

The powwow would end with various campers rising to recite the laws of the Mooween tribe. They included, among others: "Word of honor is sacred. Play fair; foul play is treachery. Be true to your ideals and respect the ideals of others. Be fearless. Courage is a noble attainment. Be not troubled by fears of the future; they are groundless. Listen well to your elders; they have much to offer you. Be kind. Do acts of unbargaining service. Understand and respect your body; it is the temple of the spirit. . . ."

Our daily activities in camp helped to instill these qualities. Tests of courage would include sleeping out on Dream Island alone at night. To encourage a respect for nature, during thunderstorms, Cap would have us do a snake dance on the campus and ask us to clap in appreciation after each crack of thunder, calling it "the greatest show on earth." The motto of the camp was "S-A-T-F" ("strong at the finish") and the lyric of a camp song was, "Don't give in, win all that you begin."

> "Borrow money from pessimists— they don't expect it back."
> —*Steven Wright*

Legion of Honor

Character development was so central to camp life that it was the basis for an evening activity once a week. On "Legion of Honor" night, we would get into bed early, turn out the light, and, in the dark, critique each other's behavior. Each kid would be discussed by his bunkmates and by his two counselors and then have a chance to respond. Qualities discussed included pitching in; helping others, especially the poorer athletes; responsibility; initiative; sharing; telling the truth; and so on. If a kid showed improvement, the counselor would make sure it was mentioned. The tone was upbeat, not accusatory.

Following the discussion, the counselors decided which kids were put on the list for that week. Standards were high and most did not make it. Being a member of the Legion of Honor was prized more than making the first team. Those who were on the list for every one of the eight weeks were strong candidates for the camp's biggest honor: the end of summer, all-around camper award. Cap was very careful in hiring his counselor staff (juniors and seniors in college). The Legion of Honor program worked only because the counselors genuinely cared about their kids.

Why couldn't the face-to-face critique of each other's behavior that we used so successfully in camp be used equally effectively in adult situations? Why couldn't the Legion of Honor format be utilized, for example, by small groups of employees and their bosses to create a happier, more productive workplace, or by sports teams, military units, students living in college dorms, or even family groups? I used to wonder about this until I happened upon an article that contained one of my favorite insights about human nature by one of my favorite writers, essayist Roger Rosenblatt (a sometimes guest on PBS's *Evening News Hour*). He wrote an article titled "Rules for Aging" in the May–June 1999 *Modern Maturity* magazine. Included was this nugget of wisdom:

> *Give honest, frank, and open criticism to nobody never.* The following situation will present itself to you over and over: There is a friend, a relative, an employee, an employer, a colleague, whose behavior flaws are so evident to everyone but themselves, you just know that a straightforward, no-punches-pulled conversation with them will show them the error of their ways. They will see the light at once, and forever be grateful that only as good and candid a person as yourself would have sufficient kindness and courage to confront them.

> Better still: From the moment you inform them about their bad table manners, their poor choices in clothing, their hygiene, their loudness, their deafness, their paranoia, they will reform on the spot. Their lives will be redeemed, and they will owe their renewed selves and all future happiness to you—honest, frank and open you.

I implore you: forgetaboutit. When the muse of candor whispers in your ear, swat it, take a long walk, a cold shower, and clear your head. Nobody is thinking about you, unless you tell them about their faults. Then you can be sure they are thinking of you. They are thinking of killing you.

I hope the reader, in response to the advice offered in this book, will have a less assertive reaction.

The Camp Mooween campsite, along with scenic Red Cedar Lake, was made into a state park by the state of Connecticut in 2000, a singular honor for a summer boys camp. These words are inscribed on the plaque that appears at the entrance to Mooween State Park: ". . . this was a place of magic, care-free summers, balmy days among the cedars and golden hours on Red Cedar Lake; a place for building character, lifelong friendships and sweet memories; a place of endless summer and eternal youth . . ."

Along with Edwin Land, founder of Polaroid, Mooween's most famous alumnus is lyricist Yip Harburg. I have to believe that when he wrote, "Somewhere over the rainbow, way up high, there's a land that I heard of, once in a lullaby . . ." he may have been inspired, in part, by nostalgia for Camp Mooween. My older brother, Skippy, spent 21 summers at camp, both as a camper and then as head water counselor. In 2002, while driving his car, he had a heart attack and died. It had been over 50 years since his last summer in camp. The license plate on his car that day read "Mooween."

Camp had a lifelong, profound influence, yet it only lasted eight weeks each year. The other 44 weeks I traded a clipboard and whistle for textbooks and homework.

One-of-a-Kind Career on Wall Street

My father's jewelry manufacturing business prospered during World War II and we moved from Yonkers to Park Avenue in Manhattan. I went to Horace Mann School for Boys, a private school in Riverdale. My classmates included James Schlessinger, later Secretary of State; Sy Newhouse, head of the Newhouse publication empire; and Saul Zabar of New York's Zabar's Food Market. Then I went to Hobart

College in upstate New York with my sister, but I transferred to Syracuse University in my junior year because I wanted to experience both a small and a big school. I remember I didn't stick around for the graduation ceremony. I didn't think it was fair to ask my folks to make a long trip just to see what would likely look like a dot among thousands of other dots crossing the stage to receive a diploma.

My father's poor health brought us to Florida. With a useless-for-getting-a-job degree in English literature (my major because I disliked it least of all), my first job was in a cafeteria on Miami Beach as an assistant steward (a glorified bus boy). I made up my mind I would think of some business I could start on my own that had not been done before. I had no practical work skills but I had a creative mind. I spent hours every day conjuring up ideas, starting out with the thought, "Find a need and fill it." In the evening after work, I would take long walks along the beach and just let my mind wander. I came up with some wild ideas, three of which I actually implemented.

We lived across the street from a long row of beachfront hotels. My first venture was a mail piece souvenir that I called a "TV-Gram," which I hoped to sell to hotels as a giveaway promotion for their guests. Television was in its infancy and still a novelty. The TV-Gram was a greeting card with a picture of the hotel and an image of a TV set with the screen cut out. The guest put his picture on the screen and mailed it. The hotels agreed it was good PR but not worth the cost. I sold one hotel.

I thought my next idea had great potential. I had seen an ad for a floating golf ball. Why not set up a golf range on a hotel's private beach for guests wanting to practice by driving golf balls into the ocean? It would be a first-time ever amenity for vacationers. The hotel would pay me to set up and run the operation, including the putt-putt boat retrieval service. The Fountainbleau showed an interest but the U.S. Coast Guard killed the idea before it ever got off the sand. They said it violated the three-mile limit for interference with maritime traffic.

My third idea met with more success. Would hotel guests rent books on the best-seller list? There were no rental libraries in the hotels, probably because it didn't sound like something someone on vacation would want to do. I wasn't sure. I convinced the newsstand operator at the Saxony Hotel to give it a shot. I bought the books and we split the revenues. The idea proved to be a winner, helped by a rainy stretch of weather in the early going. Guests from nearby hotels heard about the service and we ended up with waiting lists for the more popular books. Within a year I had a chain of rental libraries in the newsstands of a dozen of the leading hotels. I was labeled "the only legitimate bookie on Miami Beach." In 1950 I was drafted into the Army and sold the business.

My quest for innovative, breakthrough ideas has never stopped. Some ideas have fizzled, some have worked out. Most remain in my notebook for another day (or because they just don't sound that great on second look). Since retiring in 1989, I've continued to work on pioneering projects. It doesn't cost any more to think on a grand scale, so my ideas are bigger now. Perhaps my most ambitious project was to write this book. I had never made an attempt before because I am so painfully slow.

> "Prayer is your biggest tool when dealing with investments that are managed by someone else."
> —*Harry Newton*

Career: Radio

During the Korean War I served in the Counter Intelligence Corp. After Japanese language school, I was sent to Tokyo where I worked undercover. As with others who were lucky enough not to see combat, the service was an enlightening experience that I look back on with pleasant memories.

After discharge, I decided to go back to school to acquire a skill I could use to make money. I enrolled as an accounting major at the University of Miami. When I finished there, I worked briefly for a CPA firm but didn't like the work.

My next job was selling cigars (though I've never been a smoker). My father's friend was a director of the Bayuk Cigar Company out of Philadelphia. He got me a job as a factory representative calling on retail cigar outlets in Florida to promote Phillies and Websters. The overriding problem in the cigar business at the time was a scarcity of younger customers to replace the older smokers who were dying off.

It was an interesting challenge. Why not focus on a cigar that was more appealing aesthetically, a short, slim cigarillo shape instead of the traditional big fat cigar identified with the older smoker? There were a few such shapes but they weren't promoted. Why not have celebrity athletes and rock stars endorse this new cool, stylish look? Supported by charts and statistics that took months of evenings and weekends to research, I submitted a lengthy report to the Cigar Institute of America with the presumptuous title, "How to Revitalize the Industry." But then an opportunity came up in the securities business and I left Bayuk. In subsequent years, the use of cigarillos gained in popularity and even spread to women, helped by the promotion of plastic tips and the provocative TV ads for Muriel cigars by Edie Adams ("Hey, big spender, spend a little dime with me"). I like to think that my report had something to do with this, but it probably didn't.

My father's passion was the stock market and I became interested. When Merrill Lynch opened a new branch office in Miami Beach, I applied for a job. I was one of five that they hired out of 500 applicants.

What I remember most about my years as a Merrill stockbroker were my dealings with Maurice Gusman. He was a philanthropist/investor who made his money in the rubber business in Akron, Ohio, selling prophylactics to the U.S. Army. He later was involved with Coppertone and sold it to Abe Plough. Mr. Gusman's office was in the DuPont building, downtown Miami. One day when I was cold-calling the offices in the building, I knocked on his door. He agreed to see me, saying he admired a go-getter. He talked to me about his portfolio and gave me an order to sell a big block of Plough stock, easily the biggest order I ever handled. I couldn't believe my luck—and from a cold call! But what I remember most about Mr. Gusman, aside from his being a gentleman, was his investment savvy. He was not greedy and he was not out to get the last dollar. He would say to me, "Dick, I hope the person who buys this from me makes as much money with it as I did."

Sex and Stocks As a broker I grew frustrated saying "I don't know" over and over again. The customer wanted definitive opinions and I didn't have them. It became apparent that, by nature, I was not cut out to sell securities. To relieve my frustration at the office and to give vent to my creative juices, I worked on a wild idea. After a compliant day following the company line, I spent the evening and weekends putting together a magazine which I called *Sex and Stocks*. To think that there was a need for such a magazine was a stretch, but it served as a great outlet for my imagination.

The challenge was to create content that was clever, entertaining, and in good taste. One feature was a calendar of upcoming events in the market with a Vargas or Petty girl from *Playboy* and *Esquire* as the calendar girl for that month. Another feature was cut-out pictures of sexy women who were posing appropriately to illustrate market sayings ("The market has formed a round bottom," "The rally proved a huge bust," "ahead of the curve," "bare market," "asset turnover," "public offering,""full disclosure,""straddle," etc.). I included a crossword puzzle with only stock market–related words and I made liberal use of funny business-related cartoons. Other sections were devoted to personal finance, model portfolios, naked calls, and so on. I wrote a *Twilight Zone* type short story titled "The Moving Ticker" about a janitor cleaning up in a broker's office in the evening. He looks up and sees the stock ticker start to move. He writes down the prices and discovers they are the next day's closing prices. Each evening the same thing happens—he has tomorrow's prices today. The story goes on to tell how he uses this information and what happens to him.

I cut and pasted and printed the entire magazine by hand. It took me a year. It's the only major project I've worked on that I don't still have. At some point over the past 40 years, I misplaced it. The result is that I have nothing to show for a lot of work. I remember I was pleased with the results, both graphics and content. I approached a few magazine publishers but they dismissed it as a frivolous, less than compelling format. They were probably right—but I did get it out of my system.

> "The nicest thing about money is that it never clashes with anything I wear."
>
> —*Unknown*

Dial Dick Davis Back at the office I was not a happy camper. For me to be content, I needed to do something that gave me more control and more answers. So I put my thinking cap on and resumed my long meditative walks in the evening. The challenge was to create a job for myself that involved something I liked, something I could do well, and something that would permit me to stay with the firm (I thought the securities business itself was exciting).

I had always been struck by the inadequacy of stock market reporting on radio. It was usually done by an announcer in the studio reading copy off a newswire. It was obvious he knew little about what he was reading. Sometimes it was done by a broker from his office. He would read the latest quotes and averages and hoped the on-air exposure would bring in some business. In neither case was there an attempt at depth. Why not have someone knowledgeable in the business offer more than just prices? I called on the general managers of the top local radio stations. I quickly learned that radio in the 1960s and 1970s had little appreciation of the widespread public interest in the stock market (later on I found the same to be true of television).

I convinced WGBS (Storer Broadcasting) to give me 10 full minutes of drive time (soon expanded to 15 minutes) so I could include commentary, the alleged reasons behind the moves, and the opinions of well-known experts (never my own). My first broadcast was from a small studio above a movie theatre on Biscayne Blvd during a hurricane. The date was September 14, 1965. I broadcast uninterruptedly for the next 20 years, both on radio and TV.

The next step was to convince Merrill Lynch to let me stop selling and work exclusively on radio. The firm liked the idea of free prime time exposure and the fact that the name Merrill Lynch would be identified with a unique public service for investors. But they had not done this before and they were skeptical, so they insisted I do both selling and broadcasting. It was up to me to prove that my 100 percent focus on radio would be to their clear advantage. The immediate popularity of the program exceeded everybody's expectations except mine (because I knew there was a need that was not being filled).

I decided to offer Merrill Lynch research over the air as a means of measuring my audience. I received hundreds and hundreds of requests in the mail. I remember receiving over 1,500 responses for a report on Sperry Rand and 3,400 requests for a sample of the *Wall Street Transcript*. I had to increase the size of the post office box to handle the overflow mail.

The big bonus in all of this for the firm was the number and value of the leads I was able to distribute to the salesmen in the seven south Florida Merrill offices. These were quality leads because the salesman knew the prospect had an interest not only in the stock market but in a particular stock. If the Merrill broker kept the prospect continually informed on that stock, more than his current broker did, there was a good chance of opening the account. The leads I received each week via radio outnumbered the leads generated by Merrill Lynch newspaper ads by some 10 to 1. The firm soon let me give up my selling duties as a broker.

In effect, I created a one-of-a-kind job for myself. I became the only employee of a New York Stock Exchange member firm in the United States devoted full-time to in-depth reporting on the stock market via radio and soon on television and in newspapers in south Florida. To my knowledge and to this day, no employee of a member firm has done the same thing. (Closest is sage veteran Larry Wachtel, consultant to Wachovia Securities, who has done a great job of summarizing market activity three times a day for over 50 years.)

Instead of the Merrill Lynch branch manager, I reported directly to Louis Engel, the director of marketing, and Don Regan, board chairman (who later became Secretary of Defense under President Reagan). They called me to New York once a year to have lunch in the executive dining room and pat me on the back. In effect, they let me do my own thing.

The Professional Opinion Corner I expanded my radio reports to as many as five a day, broadcast direct from my office at Merrill in downtown Miami. I received thousands of complimentary letters from listeners. Because they were so intensely enthusiastic (not just "I enjoy your report"), I saved them in a big, fat, red notebook (which I still have) in case I needed ammunition for Merrill. There was a waiting list of sponsors for the radio show. To further impress the radio station and the advertiser, I would sometimes ask the listener to come into the sponsor's premises to pick up the report being offered. A flow of traffic into the Cadillac showroom, for example, did not make the local dealer unhappy.

The most popular feature of the radio report was "The Professional Opinion Corner." I received permission from the leading investment newsletters like those of Granville, Prechter, and Zweig to quote their market opinions and stock recommendations as long as I clearly identified the source. Thus, the listener received free what otherwise would have cost thousands of dollars in subscriptions. Later, I did the same thing on television, in my newspaper column, and eventually in my newsletter. In print I had the advantage of being able to include additional source information, including the address and special trial subscription rates. The popularity of the "Professional Opinion Corner" feature led to the creation of the *Dick Davis Digest* investment newsletter later on.

The format of reporting other people's opinions was a natural outgrowth of my own stock-picking insecurities. I knew there were many who felt no such restraints and who offered opinions with great conviction. I focused on those with the better track records and the most notoriety. I knew what the listener wanted most was to know what the popular gurus of the day were saying, especially if it included a $5 stock that was going to $50.

So it was someone else's opinion, not mine. I was off the hook. It was strictly a chicken approach but it fit my temperament. Most brokers, understandably, want to be perceived by their customers as *the* authority —the expert with the answers. For me it is just the opposite. I'm happy to be the conduit.

I have been dealing with investment advice on and off for some 50 years (since 1958 when I joined Merrill). During that time, I cannot remember ever personally recommending a stock, either via my radio and TV reports, my newspaper column, my newsletter, or my speeches. It's a policy I follow to this day, evidence that at least part of my ego is under control. It's always been easy for me to say, "I don't know"—first, because it's true, I really *don't* know; second, because then I can't hurt anybody; and third, because it often gives me an advantage. A display of complete candor and humility, because it is unusual in the advisory business, can prove far more impressive than the definitive opinion that's commonplace.

I usually try to follow up my chicken response, "I don't know," with an attempt to give both sides of the story. As best I can, I will list all those reasons why a stock or the market may go up and all the reasons why they may go down. There's always a column A and a column B, the positives and the negatives. An awareness of both sides of the story leads to wiser decisions and fewer surprises.

> "Never invest in any idea you can't illustrate with a crayon."
> —*Peter Lynch*

Career: TV

Because we developed such a large following on radio, I was encouraged to tackle television. My target was the number one rated station in south Florida, Channel 4 (CBS). But I knew I had to get my feet wet first. My first exposure was on closed circuit television. From a studio on the 79th Street causeway, my report was beamed into the rooms of Miami Beach hotel guests. Then I moved to PBS. The public broadcasting station in south Florida was Channel 2 WPBT in Miami. They had never had a daily financial show but they knew of my radio success and agreed to give me 10 minutes in the early evening. They were skeptical and programmed me immediately after *Mr. Rogers' Neighborhood*. This meant I had no lead-in audience and, in effect, was starting from zero. Using the proven format from radio, I quickly built a following. The mail response was heavy and Channel 2 gave me more time on-air.

I began to think of doing something nationally. There was nothing local about my report. In theory, if it was well-received in south Florida, it should be equally successful in New York, Chicago, or Des Moines. There was no daily, in-depth market report on network television. Why not the *Dick Davis Stock Market Report* (which included the day's business news) each night on PBS following *The MacNeil-Lehrer News Hour*? Louis Rukeyser had recently started *Wall Street Week* on PBS but that was weekly. It appeared to be a need waiting to be filled, and I had the filler.

I put together a 30-minute demo tape. It took me a long time to prepare because I wanted it just right (it's been almost 40 years, but I still have the tape). I sent it to PBS and their initial response was favorable. They said they would submit the tape to their affiliates around the country for approval. The fly in the ointment was they told me that I had to sever my relationship with Merrill. Public broadcasting rules at the time prohibited the mentioning or identification of any commercial entity on the air. That killed the PBS idea for me since I was raising a family and couldn't deal with a two-thirds cut in pay.

My three-year stint on Channel 2 started a long career on television but it was important for another reason. It laid the groundwork for the national program on PBS that is heard today and still originates in Miami. The same management team of Dooly and Felton that I had worked with asked Linda O'Brien seven years later to put together a daily business report that could be viewed nationally on PBS. For the anchor spot they recruited Paul Kangas, who was not saddled with a company affiliation. Linda, Paul, and Susie Gharib have done an excellent job and the *Nightly Business Report* (*NBR*) has been seen by millions for almost 30 years. I get satisfaction knowing that the seed I planted led to the *NBR,* enjoyed by so many investors over the years.

Fired Twice In 1971, as I was going full-steam on radio and television, without warning I was fired by Merrill Lynch. I was stunned. The firm claimed I had not told them I was getting a talent fee from the radio station. As I later explained in a letter to the NYSE, I had not only informed two executives in New York but on one occasion, the local branch manager had actually handed me my radio pay check. Merrill made no attempt to corroborate any of this and insisted that I leave at once, meaning within 30 minutes of their phone call. This, after 14 years of being the voice of the firm and distributing thousands of leads to the salesmen. It's a cold business.

I believe Merrill got rid of me because my four or five daily broadcasts were completely unsupervised and represented too much of a potential compliance problem. Unlike Merrill Lynch research reports, no one reviewed my scripts for possible violation of SEC rules. My broadcasting from south Florida instead of New York and writing copy for immediate airing did not allow for the control they needed.

Immediately upon being fired by Merrill and ushered out the front door, I walked across the street to the office of Walston & Co. Buck Peterson, the regional manager, was a regular listener and hired me the same day to do the same radio and TV work I had done for Merrill. A few nights later on my Channel 2 (PBS) TV show, I thanked Walston on the air for enabling me to continue my report without interruption. It was a brief mention but enough to trigger a telegram the next day from Channel 2 notifying me that I was fired (three years on the air, not even a phone call). I had violated the PBS rule that prohibited identification of my commercial affiliation.

In less than a week I had been fired twice. In both cases I was charged with breaking the rules. As far as I was concerned, a 10-second "thank you" to Walston was appropriate and harmless, although technically, I *was* guilty. It was almost as if management was looking for an excuse to discharge me. People like myself who are constantly pushing the envelope can easily irritate others and cause discomfort on the part of management. In the case of Merrill, my being a media personality was not consistent with being a company man. My broadcast had exceeded all expectations and, for investors in south Florida, Dick Davis had become a household name.

I was still employed by Walston doing radio. Business tycoon Ross Perot had bought DuPont, the brokerage firm, and was in talks to acquire Walston. A former naval officer, the word was that Perot ran a tight ship. I wondered how secure my one-of-a-kind job would be. Luckily, I didn't have to wonder long. Drexel Burnham came along and I was able to continue my broadcasts without interruption.

> "You can be young without money but you can't be old without it."
> —*Tennessee Williams*

Tubby Burnham and Ralph Renick I. W. "Tubby" Burnham had been listening to me for years during his annual trips to south Florida. He was chairman of the board for Drexel Burnham. One day he called me and invited me to lunch aboard his yacht at Bahia Mar in Fort Lauderdale. He told me Drexel planned to open a number of offices in south Florida and thought exposure of the firm's name via my broadcast would help them get off the ground. He made me an attractive offer and for the next 17 years I signed off each of my radio and TV broadcasts with "Dick Davis, Drexel Burnham Lambert."

My target was still to get on Channel 4, CBS, the kingpin in south Florida. So when Channel 2 let me go, I called Ralph Renick at Channel 4. Renick was the pioneer TV news anchorman who later ran for governor of Florida. He said he had been watching me and might be interested but that I needed more seasoning. So I went on a cable TV station that required a long drive to North Miami Beach every afternoon in between radio broadcasts. Then followed a stint on Channel 10, the ABC outlet in south Florida, which I thought would give me the experience I needed for CBS.

In addition to the evening news, Channel 10 agreed to let me try out a new format that I had not seen done before. Early every morning at 5:30 A.M., I drove out to the Miami airport to pick up the

Wall Street Journal and the *New York Times*. I returned to the studio and wrote my script, which included business news highlights and a summary of those articles in both papers that were likely to have an impact on the market (remember, this was the early 1970s when there was no Internet or CNBC). I also highlighted the contents of whatever major financial publications had just hit the newsstands. I went on the air at 7:30 A.M. The result was that the viewer not only had a concise summary of the *Journal* and the *Times* but also of the important articles from the very latest financial magazines—all before the market opened. Also, the viewer did not have to buy the source newspapers and magazines; it was all free. The 5:30 A.M. drive to the airport started my day; the 6:30 P.M. TV report ended it, and in between were three or four in-depth radio reports. It was a grinding routine, so I was not unhappy when I finally got a call from Ralph Renick.

"You're ready," he said, and the next week I started on Channel 4, CBS, in south Florida, owned by Wometco. They dominated the market and were not bashful about saying so. They were cocky but had good reason to be. Many Channel 4 personalities went on to successful careers on the network. I started off doing a daily in-depth stock market report on both the noon and evening news. Drexel Burnham was clearly identified audibly and visually during my segment. The exposure cost the firm nothing. The TV station paid me a talent fee.

> "If 50 million people say a foolish thing, it's still a foolish thing."
> —*Anatole France*

No Teleprompter, No Makeup The logistics involved in doing the noon report were bizarre. I was told to arrive at the station about an hour and a half before airtime. That would mean that my noon report would be current only up to 10:30 A.M., which was unacceptable to me. They wanted the hour and a half to type my handwritten script for the teleprompter (and apply makeup). I actually ended up getting to the station one to three minutes before it was my turn; sometimes it was less than a minute. I never had time to use makeup, no less the teleprompter. But I was never late and I never missed a broadcast.

My goal was to make my noon report as up-to-the minute as I could. It took 11 to 12 minutes for me to walk from my downtown Miami office to Channel 4. I went on the air at 12:15. Subtracting 12 minutes from 12:15 meant I left the office at 12:03. I would leave one minute earlier if it was raining. Waiting till 12:03 enabled me to get the noon averages off the Dow Jones newswires. Most television news was typed on a teleprompter in the studio well before airtime. Instead, I handwrote commentary, with information from the business newswires and the moving ticker tape, right up until the last minute.

The quirky part of my Channel 4 days was my daily jog from the office to the studio. My guess is that it was a routine unique among television newsmen. With my yellow legal pad in hand, I would rush out of the office and then walk as fast as I could, or jog or run, depending on whether I had an extra minute or two. My pace also varied depending on the weather, the traffic, and which cops were on duty (some knew me and held up traffic if I was really running late).

When I arrived at the station, I would go directly on the set, sometimes within a minute of being introduced. I read from my scribbled script rather than from the teleprompter, so I was doing a lot of looking down rather than looking straight ahead at the camera. Because there was no time to prepare visuals to complement my script, the viewer, in effect, was looking at a talking head. It was not slick television but I got away with it because the material was good (my eye-camera contact improved over time). No other TV station could come close to Channel 4's stock market coverage. We developed a large and loyal TV following.

In national competition, *The Dick Davis Stock Market Report* won the Janus Award for the best financial reporting on television in the country. I went to Washington, D.C., and received a trophy from Art Buchwald.

"That's My Son" I took pride in my reports because they were the very best I could do. There was no slack. I left nothing on the table. My days were long and stressful but I never thought about it. My game plan had been simple: Think of a different way to fill a need, make sure it's good, and then do whatever it takes to make it happen. It was an approach that I used over and over again, both in the years before and the ones that followed.

What was missing in my work was enjoyment. Working in front of the public on radio and television is supposed to be glamorous and exciting. I found it cut-and-dried and mostly unfulfilling. When I did something for the first time, I got a rush for maybe a week or two. Then it quickly settled into a routine. It was a means of earning a paycheck to support my family. I guess that's one reason why I was always looking to break the sameness with something new. Whenever I heard about someone who loved his work I was jealous. Being constantly driven to do your best and then doing it may be a source of satisfaction, but it's not fun. Also, there are no surprises. Once I'm committed, there's no uncertainty about it being done. We are all prisoners of our nature and mine is too serious and intense. I wish I were more like my brother and sister who are both skilled at "lightening-up," enjoying life, and having fun.

The popularity of my TV reports on Channel 4 enabled me to air another idea in which I *did* lighten up. I called it *Off-Beat Wall Street*. It was only five minutes but it had the highest TV ratings in the market because it was the lead-in to *60 Minutes* every Sunday evening. I covered a wide range of topics including popular personalities and how they spent their money (something like what *Lifestyles of the Rich and Famous* did later) and new products about to be introduced that looked especially interesting. I requested and received samples which, since the show was taped, I could use as visuals.

Off-beat Wall Street was the only thing I did on television that my kids watched because they knew I'd be coming home with the free product samples. My mother was more supportive. She was a pink lady in the hospital and at noontime she would walk into the patients' rooms on her floor, switch the channel to 4, and announce, "That's my son."

> "No one can achieve real and lasting success or get rich in business by being a conformist."
> —*Unknown*

Then I would get a critique from my mom, not about the report, but about my tie: "Why can't you wear a nice tie like Walter Cronkite?"

Career: Newspaper

I was on radio and television but not in the newspaper. The *Miami Herald* dominated the south Florida market but they were even more uppity and independent than Channel 4. My strategy was the same that I used to get on Channel 4, namely, get exposure in smaller outlets first and acquire experience. I got published in Paul Bruun's *Miami Beach Sun,* then Lee Ruwitch's *Miami Review,* and then I went to the *Miami Herald.* They knew of my work, and business editor James Russell was a fan of my radio and TV reports. They agreed to try me out for six months. I ended up doing a three-times-a-week column for 10 years.

The column was syndicated nationally by Knight Ridder, which owned the Herald. It was the paper's first stock market–oriented column. The format was similar to the popular "Professional Opinion Corner" featured on my broadcasts. I excerpted the opinions and recommendations of the nation's leading newsletters. It was a winning formula; the information that was available only to paid subscribers was available to my readers free. (It was a formula I would use one more time, later on in my newsletter, with enough success to let me retire.) The column was simply titled "Dick Davis," even though I offered no opinions. The fact that I was responsible for conveying to my readers the best thinking on Wall Street, information that they would not otherwise be exposed to, made me feel good.

Now I was working on the leading radio station, TV station, and newspaper in south Florida. It was difficult for anyone following the stock market to avoid me. I did my best to turn out a high-quality product every day. As our following grew, so did the number of happy sponsors on radio and TV and so did the number of leads generated for the salesmen.

I was making money for others. I began to think about doing something on my own.

Career: Newsletter

A digest-format investment newsletter was an idea that naturally evolved from the popularity of the "Professional Opinion Corner" segment of my broadcasts. I enjoyed finding and exposing unusual bits of wisdom and clarity, and sharing well-thought-out stock recommendations. I had a good feel for finding them and for knowing just what to excerpt. The key was the willingness to spend the time necessary to get the okay from the newsletters and come up with consistently good material;

I knew the time commitment was no problem. (As I think back on it, I realize that all my life I have been sending articles to family and friends. I have this compulsion to share information that I think will be helpful. To prepare my kids, I write on the back of the envelope, "Ugh! Not another article!")

So the digest was a format that fit my temperament. Most of all, it permitted me to dispense advice without having to be the adviser. I knew, of course, that interest in stock market advice was limited in bear markets. But I also knew that the market spends more time going up or sideways than going down, that in bull markets the investor wants to be part of the action, and that what he wants most are winning stocks. A cross section of outstanding stock ideas from the best-known market letters, all in one publication, seemed like a good idea. (Besides, I was blessed with a name that made for a great title for a digest-format news-letter, alliteration and all.)

I worked on the digest evenings and weekends so as not to interfere with my Drexel job. I already had relationships with a number of writers, including Zweig, Prechter, Granville, Weinstein, and others. I sent out a letter to about 200 of the leading investment advisory services, promising I would identify their publication in detail, including address, phone, and subscription cost, if they would send me a complimentary subscription and a letter authorizing me to publish excerpts. There was some initial resistance to making available free what their subscribers paid for. But I was just asking for an excerpt, and the advantages of exposure in a widely read, quality publication soon overcame the objections.

Investment newsletters get new subscribers mostly by buying mail-ing lists of prospects and sending them promotional literature. I dispensed with the promotional hype and simply enclosed the latest 12-page issue, the sales pitch being, "If you like it, subscribe." This is seldom done because it is expensive and because clever use of words can make some-thing sound better than it is ("sell the sizzle, not the steak"). I did it my way because I was extremely confident in the quality and appeal of the *Digest* and because it was a more honest approach.

We lucked out with our timing. We launched the *Digest* in June 1982, the very month that marked the beginning of an historic bull market. My brother and sister both helped with our initial mailings by stuffing envelopes. Steve Halpern was my assistant and Carla Neufeld was my secretary/office manager. I could not have hired two more capable, loyal, hardworking employees. I knew little about computer technology and customer fulfillment; they knew everything. Many of the executive decisions that outsiders thought I made, I delegated to Steve and Carla because they were both smarter and faster than me.

It didn't take long for the *Digest* to take off. It was profitable almost from the beginning and I recovered my initial investment quickly. (The newsletter business, if successful, is a beautiful thing because the cash comes in up-front, one, two, or three years in advance.) When it became apparent that the *Digest* was a winner, Drexel Burnham advised me that they expected to be made a 50 percent partner without any investment. Their rationale was that I launched the *Digest* on their watch. I had worked on the *Digest* evenings and weekends using my own money but, technically, I did it while still employed by the firm. They did promise to put the firm's marketing muscle behind the *Digest* and spend money on future promotion. (As it turned out, they never spent a dime on the *Digest*.)

I could have turned Drexel down and gone off on my own. I thought about it, but with two kids entering college, I wasn't willing to risk a sure paycheck for one that was uncertain. It was a good deal for Drexel—they got something for nothing. But even at the reduced 50 percent, I had no complaints when I sold out years later. In the meantime, the business prospered and I drew a nice salary. I gave up my radio and TV broadcasting, turned over the newspaper column to Steve, and devoted myself full-time to writing and growing the *Digest*. I moved from my Drexel Burnham office in Miami to brand new space on Arthur Godfrey Road, Miami Beach, with "Dick Davis Digest" printed on the front door.

> "What's the use of happiness? It can't buy you money."
> —Henny Youngman

Putting the *Digest* Together In the early years, the routine I went through preparing each issue of the Digest (every two weeks) bordered on the bizarre, but it got the job done. Because I had to meet a deadline and because I worked so slowly and had so much to do, I simply had to block out time and work nonstop till I was finished. On alternate

Friday afternoons, I left the office with a carton filled with 200 to 300 newsletters from around the country. I didn't return until the following Tuesday afternoon. For those four days I holed up in my apartment and did not leave. I was isolated and focused with a clear mission. My job was to write the 12-page *Digest* in longhand and bring it into the office completed and ready to be typed.

I left the reviewing of the newsletters to the last. My biggest challenge was coming up with a dynamite idea for the page one "Personal Note" column that I wrote for each issue of the *Digest*. It was the first read of most subscribers and imparted a distinct flavor and personality to the publication. Sometimes it was Sunday before I came up with a topic that I thought was right. I mostly wrote about current happenings in the stock market and how they illustrated important but seldom-discussed universal truths of investing. The focus was often on behavioral or psychological influences. I made no market forecasts or stock recommendations. It took me typically two to two and a half days before, with a big sigh of relief, I finished writing the one-and-a-half-page "Personal Note."

The remaining one and a half to two days, I went through the pile of investment newsletters. I excerpted the 25 to 35 commentaries and stock recommendations that I thought were especially well written, provocative, timely, and insightful. Since there was no way of knowing which of the recommended stocks would go up, the bottom line was which would be the most interesting to the reader. I used a small fraction of the material I read. Over the next years, I went through 157 Friday-to-Tuesday lockup writing sessions. It was a self-indulgence that was made possible because I was not married at the time. My single status also allowed me to leave the office at the crazy hours I did: 1 to 2 A.M. during *Digest* preparation week and 10 to 11 P.M. otherwise.

Exposure in *Forbes* and *Money* Magazines The *Digest* continued to grow, reaching a circulation of some 35,000 (that's a lot for a mom-and-pop operation) with subscribers in every state and 58 foreign countries. The refusal of some newsletters, early on, to give authorization changed to complaints about not being quoted more often. Our list of cooperating newsletters grew to over 400, including expensive ones like the *Bank Credit Analyst* and the *Wall Street Transcript*.

The only source I used regularly that was not a paid-for publication was Robert Farrell, the head strategist for Merrill Lynch and a perennial all-star analyst. Farrell had a rare feel for the market and a gift for writing about it. I thought his analysis was the best on the Street. He always set the stage, giving the big picture and the most likely scenario based on history, fundamentals, and technicals. I made sure to include his comments in each issue (in the "Where's the Market Going?" section of the *Digest*) so that subscribers could benefit from his insight.

The circulation of the *Digest* benefited from some unexpected sources. Many stockbrokers were subscribers. They passed the *Digest* on to their customers who would then call us and subscribe. The exposure the *Digest* received in the national media also gave a boost to circulation. *Forbes* did a feature story and *Money* sent down a crew to take pictures and do a major piece. The *Digest* also benefited from appearances I made as a featured speaker at large investment seminars (10,000 and up) across the country sponsored by Investment Seminars, Inc. (ISI), the nation's largest producer of money shows.

> "It's not your salary that makes you rich; it's your spending habits."
> —*Charles A. Jaffe*

Selling the *Digest* In my partnership contract with Drexel, my attorney had astutely included a buyout formula which Drexel was obligated to follow if I wanted out. I decided to exercise that option. After living and breathing the *Digest* for seven years, I took advantage of what was then a robust but cyclical business and sold my 50 percent back to the firm.

Drexel disputed some of the figures so I went to New York to make sure I received my due. The firm had ignored the *Digest* from day one and left everything to me. Now that the issue was about protecting their financial interest, I had the firm's complete attention. In fact, I ended up dealing with James Balog, who was vice chairman of Drexel. I was surprised not only by the sudden interest of senior management but also by their concern over a relatively small amount of money. This was the same firm that was reaping hundreds of millions of dollars from the high-powered junk-bond operation of Michael Milken.

I sat outside Balog's office for two days, but when he finally saw me he was gracious, we signed an agreement, and I flew home to Miami, check in hand. The proceeds of the sale enabled me to retire at age 62. (Drexel later decided they didn't belong in the newsletter business and sold the *Digest* to a New York publishing firm. I had signed a noncompete clause; the new owners retained the name *Dick Davis Digest,* which is now in its 26th year.) A year after I received my cash payout, Drexel filed for bankruptcy and Milken went to jail. Talk about lucky timing!

On my living room table I keep a pile of all the *Dick Davis Digest* issues that I published—numbers 1 through 157. The pages are faded and discolored and the stack measures only three inches high. I keep it there because it reminds me every day of my good fortune and how one good idea backed up by hard work can change your life.

Post–Wall Street

I was retired from the *Digest,* but my mind kept working.

My first idea was to write a health digest newsletter better than what was out there. The idea for an investment digest worked; why not do the same thing with health? It took me a year to put together a sample. It was a comprehensive 40-page newsletter with lots of original features. I printed 200 and showed it to a few people but nothing came of it. Once I got it out of my system, I lost interest. Anyone can come up with an idea. The hard part is to implement it.

I also failed to follow through on an idea I had nursed for a long time for a radio/TV program. I called it *What Would You Have Done?* A conversation between a broker and a customer is featured on radio, TV, or a web site. The broker lists all the reasons why he's recommending a particular stock and then asks the customer for the order. Would you have bought the stock? The conversation is based on actual past written recommendations from brokers, magazines, newsletters, and the like, quoted in their entirety or excerpted. The broker would first set the stage by describing the big picture—where the market and the economy were at the time and what had led up to the conditions at the time of the recommendation. Also included would be short- and long-term charts of the stock and the market. It would be a re-creation of an actual sales pitch, except this time the customer would likely have more complete information.

On the internet, a click would reveal exactly what happened to the stock in the months and years following the recommendation. The source of the sales pitch would not have to be identified ("a major brokerage firm"). There are thousands of past write-ups to choose from. They all sounded like sure winners at the time. Some of the stocks selected would prove winners, others losers. The purpose would be both to entertain and to educate. On radio and TV there would be a commercial time-out following the question "What would you have done?" I made a demo tape for the Mutual radio network back in the 1970s but never mailed it.

> "My uncle used to have a corner on the market. Now he has a market on the corner."
> —*Alan King*

CNBC, Bloomberg, and Merrill Lynch

I knew I had good ideas for improving the programming at CNBC. I submitted a lengthy report to management and followed it up with many phone calls. I never heard back. I have never been able to understand why people think that being in business gives them an excuse for ignoring the most basic common courtesies that are observed in other human relationships. Everybody has a right to be disinterested. But not to take a few seconds to have your assistant/secretary acknowledge a detailed report or repeated phone calls by simply saying you're busy and will or will not call later, is not only insensitive, thoughtless, and rude, but borders on being mean-spirited. (I can't tell you how much satisfaction I got just from writing that sentence!)

I next came up with an idea for an investment web site that I thought was dynamite. And it passed the crucial overnight test: It sounded as good the next morning as it did the day before. I thought it would be a natural for any of the major investment sites like a Yahoo! or Bloomberg. I called Michael Bloomberg cold turkey (one of his secretaries, tired of my constant calls, gave me his personal number). I left messages till one day he called me back (before he was mayor). He invited me to New York, where I found out that neither Bloomberg nor Yahoo! is a user of original content.

I then peddled the idea to Merrill Lynch for use on their web site, hounding David Komansky, Stan O'Neil, and others in top management. I finally got a letter back from retail marketing saying the idea was "thoughtful and innovative but not something Merrill would be willing to undertake at this time." Today, a decade later, no one has used this idea which I still think is a blockbuster. If it's so good, why isn't it being used? I don't know. Another long-held idea I worked on during this semi-retirement, prebook period had to do with the NYSE ticker tape. Why not broadcast an uninterrupted *verbal* reading of what comes across the tape on a small portable receiver? I took the idea to Sirius and XM but both were focused on music programming in their early years. When I learned that approval by the NYSE was a complicated legal matter, I lost interest.

In the years immediately preceding this book project, I spent most of my time writing articles (including one for *Barron's*), speaking, and teaching. My golf and tennis were cut short by a spinal cord injury so I made up the slack by volunteering to start a stock market class open to the public at the local Jewish Community Center. I prepared diligently for each class and it caught on quickly. The classroom gave me a platform to espouse the deeply held beliefs about stocks and investing that are in this book. Because so many of the students are snowbirds (seasonal visitors to south Florida), I get to interact with investors from all over the country.

Modesty Adds Credibility

So much for my background. It's already more than you want to know. I'll conclude on an introspective note that may explain why some of the core beliefs found in this book ended up here.

It has always surprised me that so many really smart people don't understand that, in most cases, saying "I don't know" or "I was wrong" makes them look *good,* not bad. Or maybe they do understand, but ego makes it impossible. For me, admitting I'm wrong or don't know has always come easy, probably because I've had so much practice. In fact, there are times when I'm falsely modest, proudly declaring that I don't know, only because I believe it sets me apart and makes my other opinions more credible.

The ability to acknowledge one's limitations is especially important in the investment advice business where being wrong is commonplace. The full disclosure found in all security prospectuses should serve as a model of candor. In addition to all the good stuff, the prospectus contains all the negatives and all the risks. The adviser, in my view, should aspire to this same level of disclosure; he should be as close to a walking, breathing prospectus as possible. Recognition of fallibility should be a routine part of his presentation, as in "I don't know," "I was or may be wrong," or "This may or may not work out." I hear this from some advisers, but not many. If I had a problem saying these words, the contents of this book would be very different.

When someone teaches a class or writes a book, the inference is that he's an expert on the subject. In the market advice field, we all know there is no such thing and that, in fact, the term *stock market expert* is an oxymoron. There are literally thousands and thousands of people in all areas of the investment business, including the financial media, that have a depth of fundamental and technical knowledge far superior to mine. Trust me, this is not false modesty. These super-sharp people are in a completely different league. And when they expound on program trading, option strategies, arbitrage, derivatives, currencies, stochastics, quantitative analysis, and so on, they leave me far behind. I make a point of this because I want you to know what you're getting and, more important, what you're not getting. (I am neither a certified analyst nor a financial planner).

However, I have learned that the mastery of complex financial subjects does not necessarily equate to sound judgment, common sense, or an understanding of human nature. I have had no formal training in psychology. But I *have* had some 40 years of interaction with the investment public. Many of my core convictions result from observing the behavior of investors over this long period. For any commentary on investing to be taken seriously, it must be a voice of experience. Lengthy exposure to the vagaries of the market, up, down, and sideways, is essential.

But an author attempting to give meaningful information to investors needs more than experience. After all, everyone at the end of their careers has experience. What's also needed is the ability to gain insight and a measure of wisdom from that experience. Brilliant scholarship is not uncommon but wisdom, insight, and judgment are hard to come by.

The cliché is that we get wiser as we get older. The truth is that the relationship between the two is tenuous at best.

I'm hoping, of course, that you will find some degree of wisdom in these pages. I'm emboldened to think you will because of the encouragement and support I received from students and colleagues in the investment media business. Their endorsement has reinforced my desire to undertake this project. I hope that what you read in the following pages merits the time you've just taken to learn something about the person who wrote them.

> "Money isn't everything, but it sure keeps you in touch with your kids."
>
> —*Milton Berle*
>
> "It's pretty hard to tell what does bring happiness; poverty and wealth have both failed."
>
> —*Kim Hubbard*

Part One

DEEPEST CONVICTIONS ABOUT SUCCESSFUL INVESTING AFTER 40 YEARS ON WALL STREET

Chapter 2

The Three Best Things to Have before Starting to Invest

I f each of us left our money invested for one hundred years, we'd get the full benefit of the market's long-term upward bias. But we invest for only a fraction of that time, and the market's upward bias is beset with numerous interruptions. So it helps to have some other things going for us. The three at the top of my list would be luck, longevity, and deep pockets, all of which have little to do with the stock market per se. While luck, longevity, and deep pockets are not absolute requisites for successful investing, there's no denying that having any one of these attributes gives the investor a distinct advantage.

Luck

Obviously it helps to be lucky in every field of endeavor. What's not appreciated is just how large a role luck, both good and bad, plays in the stock market. Investors are advised to do their homework, to diversify, to allocate, to be patient, to be disciplined—but the *best* thing is to be lucky. You can be successful without luck, but there are times when you can do all the right things and it won't matter much unless you're also lucky.

For example, Mr. Jones's retirement date was January 1, 2000, so he sold his long-held growth stocks a few weeks before that. Ms. Smith's retirement date was October 1, 2002, so she sold her stocks a few weeks before that. Mr. Jones's target date coincided with the peak of the bull market, Ms. Smith's with the bottom of a steep bear market. There was a sharp difference in payout for only one reason—luck, pure luck. Where the market happens to be when, for example, your kids reach college age and you have to sell at least some stock, is strictly a matter of chance. Much of the gain that has accumulated slowly over the years can dissipate if you are unlucky and forced to sell when the market is depressed.

In the bubble years of the late 1990s, the tech stocks soared. Some of the players during that feverish climb weren't old enough to be restrained by memories of brutal down markets. Their rationale for paying astronomical prices for companies with no earnings was, "This time it's different; it's a new paradigm." It was like taking candy from a baby; stocks just kept going up. Buy high, sell higher. It was easy money; it was fast money; it was dumb money. To the uninitiated, having never experienced a punishing bear market, ignorance was truly bliss. Yes, the tech-heavy NASDAQ did plummet (78 percent over 31 months) but before the bubble burst, it lasted long enough for big money to be made.

Did those profits have anything to do with the exercise of patience, discipline, research, or savvy? No. What happened was that the market went to once-in-a-lifetime extremes and young, less experienced players who wanted in on the action saw it as a no-lose opportunity. Those who bought at astronomical prices and sold at even crazier prices were able to do so because of dumb luck.

The biggest money was probably made within the industry. Partners, traders, money managers, and star analysts of Wall Street firms bought mansions in the Hamptons and million dollar paintings. When the bubble burst, these players at least were able to retain their material winnings, but not so the investor. When I think of the steep losses suffered by the public after the bubble burst, I'm reminded of the classic 1940 book by Fred Schwed, Jr., *Where Are the Customers' Yachts?* (New York: Wiley & Sons, reissued 2006).

It's No Mystery; It's Luck—Or Lack of It

The stock market is replete with examples of investors being affected positively or negatively by completely unexpected events. It's *surprise* that moves stocks. If the unexpected makes the stock go up, it's good luck; if it triggers a decline, it's bad luck.

For example, a company you own receives a generous buyout offer out of the blue, or is added to or dropped from a major index. Perhaps a successful CEO resigns, the charismatic CEO of a small company dies, or the majority stockholder of a small company sells all his stock to pay for his divorce. Maybe a company is named the target of an SEC investigation or has to recall its major product, or a pharmaceutical giant is forced to withdraw a popular drug from the shelves. Then there's the company spokesman—a star athlete or celebrity who is injured or disgraced or a company that receives a court decision. Perhaps Warren Buffett buys or sells a stock you own. On a broader scale, there can be stock-depressing shocks like war, assassinations, and plane crashes; or natural disasters like hurricanes and tsunamis. In all these cases your stock is subject to the vagaries of pure chance.

Sometimes the market will focus on the positive aspects of a story and other times it will react to the negative. Let's say you buy a stock in anticipation of a good earnings report. The profits prove to be even better than expected, but sales are down. The fickle market decides to focus on the slowdown in revenues and the stock drops. Bad luck. On another day, for any of a hundred different reasons, the focus would have been on profits and the stock would have gone up. When dealing with the unknowable, luck is a powerful ally.

There are situations when you're able to stack the odds so heavily in your favor, it's hard to imagine a bad outcome. Let's say you hear about a star money manager who has outperformed his benchmark 15 years in a row. You confidently buy his fund and he promptly breaks his streak. Your buy proves to be the kiss of death. Bad luck. On the other hand, benefiting from a broad upsurge, you may buy a stock and see it go up for reasons completely different than those you bought it for. A rising tide lifts all boats. You were lucky. The old maxim is that bull markets make geniuses of us all.

The line where good judgment ends and luck begins is often fuzzy. It's a gray area with crosscurrents and overlapping. Insurance mogul Robert Rosenkranz has run Acorn Partners, a fund of hedge funds since 1982. His job is to find the best hedge fund managers to include in his fund, those with the greatest investment prowess. In a *Barron's* interview (October 4, 2004), he says, "It's a very subtle, difficult thing to distinguish luck from skill in this business."

> "It's human nature to find patterns where there are none and to find skill where luck is a more likely explanation."
>
> —*William Bernstein*

Nassim Nicholas Taleb is a professional trader and mathematics professor who wrote *The Black Swan* (Random House, 2007) and *Fooled by Randomness: The Hidden Role of Chance in Life and in the Markets* (Texere, 2004; Random House, 2005). The latter book deals with the question of why human beings are so prone to mistaking dumb luck for consummate skill. Taleb concludes that by nature we are designed to take our beliefs and knowledge a little too seriously. We tend to view the world as far more explainable than it actually is. We have a compulsion to look for meaning in random events. Taleb labels the typical guru as "the lucky fool in the right place at the right time. The guru attracts devoted followers who believe in his insights but he is unable to replicate what was obtained by chance" (from *Fooled By Randomness,* front cover flap).

If luck is such an integral part of the investment process on a professional level, what does that say about its role for the rest of us?

Dart Throwers Beat Stock Pickers

Since 1988, the *Wall Street Journal* has held an investment dartboard contest. Here there is no fuzzy line between judgment and luck. The outcome clearly depends on the latter. Readers pick stocks they think will go up in the next six months. They compete against stocks chosen by simply tossing darts at the listings in the newspaper. Overall, readers have gained an average 6 percent compared with 9 percent for the darts. In the contest covering the first six months of 2005, for example, readers averaged a 9 percent loss while the randomly picked dartboard portfolio ended up 15 percent. Over a period of time, darts will lose their share of contests (9 of the past 23 contests), but the complete elimination of judgment probably gives darts the edge in all but sweeping bull markets.

If indeed being lucky is so important, how does one explain the track records of those money managers who outperform their peers on a fairly regular basis? First, there aren't many of them. Managers who achieve outstanding results year after year are a special and limited breed (the best are highlighted in Chapter 8). Second, even *they* would likely acknowledge luck as a factor, albeit one they have been able to minimize with their particular approach. And third, the small group of fairly consistent outperformers would be even smaller if they were judged by absolute rather than relative returns. The portfolio manager whose fund is down 25 percent for the year is said to have a winning year if his benchmark index is down 30 percent. I think such a statistic says less about the manager's ability to outperform than it does about the inherent difficulty of avoiding losses in a down market. The investor who is down 25 percent doesn't feel like a winner.

Luck is often invisible. You were lucky, but you didn't know it. You genuinely believed it was your investment prowess whereas, as Taleb explains, it was simply serendipity. This is not to say you can't help the process along. The more homework you do (see my definition of *homework* in Chapter 10), the luckier you're likely to get. Then it's not dumb luck; it's *smart* luck.

The fact that it helps to be lucky is not an earth-shattering concept. It's just that it's never really given its due by Wall Street. Perhaps understandably, the adviser is not going to diminish the value of his advice by adding, "if you're lucky." Luck is rarely acknowledged as more than a peripheral influence. However, it doesn't hurt to be aware that sometimes, luck is more than just icing on the cake. Without it, there may not be any cake at all.

I am not suggesting you avoid investing in the stock market because too much depends on chance. On the contrary, this book is written to

> "Nine-tenths of successful investing is luck. The other 10 percent is being prepared to capitalize on that luck."
>
> —*Jim Cramer*

help you create your own luck. It will help put the odds in your favor, a far more dependable strategy than hoping to be lucky. The best way to take luck out of the equation or at least sharply reduce its importance is to invest long-term. The longer the time frame, the less luck is likely to be a factor.

Longevity

By longevity, I mean good health leading to long life. It behooves the long-term investor to be here long-term. Almost everything good that happens in Wall Street requires the passage of time. Even luck takes time to surface. The longer you hold your securities, the better the odds that nonperformers will perform. Whatever your strategy, what counts is having enough time for it to work. That's why staying healthy is near the top of my list of the most important attributes for investment success. By doing your best to stay stress-free, by giving time a chance to smooth out the wrinkles, by taking lots of vacations away from your stock, by eating well and getting plenty of exercise, you'll be increasing the odds of being here when the time comes to collect your rewards. (Of course, having the right genes doesn't hurt.)

Ralph Waldo Emerson put it more succinctly: "The first wealth is health."

Equally important is staying *mentally* healthy, keeping things in perspective. The pursuit of financial gain can be challenging, exciting, and gratifying. Building a nest egg for retirement or for your kids' and grandkids' education is an important long-term goal. But taken to extremes, the quest for profit can cause you to lose your balance and distort your priorities. Ross Perot, who at one time was the third richest man in the world, says, "There is no worse way in the world to judge a human being than by what he is

> "Time is the single most valuable asset you can ever have in your investment arsenal. The problem is that none of us have enough of it."
>
> —*Richard Russell*

worth financially." So take good care of yourself. Staying physically and mentally healthy is key for growing your money and your soul.

Deep Pockets

If I could ask a genie to grant me one more investment wish, after luck and longevity, it would be—*surprise!*—money to spare. As Woody Allen says, "I never knew a situation where having money made it worse." For those whose pockets are less than deep, let this book be your guide to just how "smart money" got that way. Wealthy investors rarely started off in that condition.

Some of the advantages of having money to spare are obvious; others are more subtle. It's not just being able to buy more. Sometimes, more money means bigger losses (albeit more affordable ones). What deep pockets do is open up opportunities routinely denied to the less affluent. It helps to know what those opportunities are, not as a tease, but as an incentive. If you are not already enjoying some of the following advantages, my plans call for you to do so.

For one thing, investors with cash reserves can afford to wait. If, indeed, patience is key, it's a lot easier to be patient if you can afford to tie up your money for long periods of time. Most of us need to have our money working, generating income or capital gains. The luxury of being able to own low- or non-dividend-paying stocks and holding them for three to five years belongs mostly to those with other sources of income.

Having money available also means you don't have to sell to buy. When funds are limited and you can only afford to buy something if you sell something else, it means having to be right on both sides of the trade. That's tough to do. There are always positives and negatives on a stock. When you focus on the negatives of one stock and the positives of another, a switch can sound eminently plausible, even compelling. More often than not, as sensible as it may sound at the time, it just doesn't work out. What you buy goes up, but so does the stock you sold (and you're out the commissions). Or what you sold goes down but so does the stock you buy. And, worst-case scenario, your sold stock goes up and your bought stock goes down after the trade. The switch may look good for a while but usually not for long. It is much easier if you can buy what you want without disturbing your holdings. Having to be right only once gives you a distinct advantage.

The periodic replacement of stocks in the major averages illustrates the point. Stocks are dropped while others are added for the purpose, among others, of improving the performance of the index. In early April 2004, three stocks were deleted from the Dow Jones Industrial Average: AT&T, Eastman Kodak, and International Paper. Replacing them were three stocks considered to be better growth prospects: AIG, Pfizer, and Verizon. A year later, the three Dow newcomers had fallen an average 21 percent while the three removed were up an average 2 percent. According to Bill Hester, an analyst with Hussman Funds, stocks removed from the S&P 500 since 1998 have regularly outpaced those added to the index.

In another study Terry Odean, professor of finance at the Haas School of Business at the University of California, Berkeley, looked at the results of buy and sell replacement trades of 10,000 investors at a large discount trading firm. "On average, the stocks that these investors bought went on to underperform the stocks that they sold by about 3 percent over the next year." (Robert Julian, *Your Retirement* newsletter, March 2006.) Bottom line: When you're advised to replace one stock with another, it may work out, but the odds are against you.

The investor with deep pockets can buy more shares when his $50 stock drops suddenly to $30 due to problems that the investor believes are temporary. The waiting time before breaking even at $40 can be years shorter than having to hold the stock till it climbs back to $50.

The only way the investor can attempt to duplicate the outstanding performance of an adviser, a financial columnist, a newsletter, and the like, is to buy *all* the securities recommended, even if they're odd lots. That takes money. Most of us can't buy, say, all nine mutual funds in *Morningstar's* monitored "Aggressive Wealth Maker" portfolio. We're forced to pick and choose. When I wrote the *Dick Davis Digest,* each issue included many recommendations. They all sounded good but only some worked out. The deeper the investor's pockets, the more choices are available.

> "The safest way to double your money is to fold it over and put it in your pocket."
>
> —*Unknown*

The Smartest Work for the Richest

Speaking of choices, it's not surprising that, rather than stocks, wealthy investors often favor alternative types of investments—the kind that usually require big minimums and charge large fees. A study conducted by the Institute for Private Investors in New York, found that wealthy families ($10 to $200 million in assets) allocated about 42 percent of their portfolios in 2004 to alternative investments such as hedge funds, private equity, venture capital, and real estate. Only some 37 percent went into equities. Are these more sophisticated investments apt to perform better than traditional portfolios? Since private pools of money don't generally release their results, it's hard to say. Exclusivity certainly doesn't guarantee superior performance. However, in the investment world, what only the rich have access to usually attracts the top management talent, and thus the best moneymaking opportunities. In a money game, having more of it can only help.

Each year, *Trader Monthly* magazine releases its list of the top hedge fund managers ranked by how much money each made personally. In 2006, none of the top five made less than $1 billion for the year. It's unlikely that you or I will be able to avail ourselves of the talents of John Arnold (Centaurus Energy), Jim Simons (Renaissance Technologies), Eddie Lampert (ESL Investments), T. Boone Pickens (BP Capital), or Steven Cohen (SAC Capital). But those with the wealth and connections to be an owner of any of these hedge funds were undoubtedly delighted to see their portfolio managers rewarded so lavishly. It meant there were still huge profits left over to be divided by the fund owners. Privileged indeed.

Then there are the ways that Wall Street, itself, unashamedly favors the affluent customer. The hot initial public offering goes to the biggest or most active accounts. Smaller accounts pay a bigger percentage of their assets as a management fee. Affluent investors who buy and sell bonds in round lots (one hundred bonds or $100,000 at par) are likely to get a better deal than those who trade in smaller, odd-lots. Access to the elite advisers on Wall Street, the private bankers and the hedge funds, is mostly limited to big-money clients who pay substantial management fees. (Does more expensive advice mean better advice? Sometimes.)

The media features glowing reports on successful hedge funds and the sophisticated techniques they use. Invariably, buried in the copy is the multimillion-dollar minimum investment required. Hedge funds used to be exclusively for the wealthy but with their proliferation to over 8,000 funds, some with spotty performances, investment minimums are likely to drop. However, my guess is that as long as hedge funds attract the best money managers (because running hedge funds is where managers can make the most money), it will take big bucks to access that talent.

Competing with hedge funds for big-money investors are the private equity firms, which grabbed most of the buyout headlines in 2005–2006. Using money raised from cash-rich pension funds and the super rich, private equity firms buy publicly owned companies and take them private. They then work to build up the value of the acquired company and hope to cash in at a profit by selling it back to the public via an IPO, or as an outright sale to another company. The deals have come fast and furious, culminating in the planned $45 billion takeover of TXU, the Texas utility, by Kohlberg Kravis Roberts, Texas Pacific Group, and others, the largest leveraged buyout in history. Many private equity firms have generated massive returns for themselves and their investors. Like hedge funds, they hide from the limelight and are accessible only to high net worth investors ($2.5 million minimum net worth is a typical requirement).

I know little about merger arbitrage, but John Paulson (Paulson Partners, New York City) knows everything about it. He's so good at finding hidden values in bankruptcies, restructurings, buyouts, and buybacks that his $4 billion group of hedge funds has decisively outperformed the S&P 500 Index (13 percent compound annual return versus −2.3 percent in the years 2000–2004). According to *Barron's* (May 30, 2005), Paulson has most of his own money in his funds. I would gladly pay him his fee of 1.5 percent of assets and 20 percent of profits to be a partner, but I'd have to invest a minimum of $5 million to do so. Bottom line: In the investment field, only the very, very rich can utilize the moneymaking genius of the very, very smart.

Wall Street Focuses on the Rich

Every firm on Wall Street has its elite stockbrokers. These are the super brokers, the big producers, the heavy hitters—some of whom have billions, not millions, under management. Most of these brokers handle both corporations and wealthy individuals with a net worth of well over a million dollars. These high-powered brokers often have teams of other brokers and even research people working under them. If their success is due to their superior ability to make money for their clients, then the average investor's lack of access to their services can be called a disadvantage. If, on the other hand, the super broker's success is due to connections or to aggressive self-promotion, then lack of access by the average investor may not be a disadvantage.

Perhaps the ultimate in investment concierge services is that offered by a growing breed of advisers unconnected to a broker or bank, who cater to the super rich, that is, people with more than $50 million of total assets. These high-end boutiques help their clients deal with private banks, hedge funds, and venture capital partnerships. They earn big six-figure annual fees by shielding clients from Wall Street's marketing pitches and by providing objective counseling. Apparently, what the most affluent investors want more than anything else is advice that's independent and not tainted by conflict of interest.

Sixty years ago, Merrill Lynch pioneered efforts to bring Wall Street to Main Street. Legions of small investors signed up to buy stocks in programs like the monthly investment plan (MIP). Today the focus has shifted from stocks to the broader concept of financial planning, covering all assets of the customer. The broker's target is the affluent investor and the goal is wealth management. There is lots of wealth to manage—some nine million American households with a net worth of $1 million or more, excluding their principal residence.

Wall Street's focus on the high-net-worth customer doesn't preclude success for the average investor. Financial muscle will open doors, but more money doesn't guarantee more success. The vast majority of investors in the United States, over 90 percent of the 95 million investors, are well below the millionaire level. Yet many are able to outperform the wealthy on a relative basis, and as a result, over time, become wealthy themselves. If you're not a deep-pocket investor, take careful note of the investment truths in the pages to come and you'll be on your way.

How about other factors widely credited for investment success like patience, persistence, proper asset allocation, and proper entry level (buying low)? The difference is this: Luck, longevity, and loot are not directly related to the stock market or a specific market strategy. They

"I'm living so far beyond my income that we may almost be said to be living apart."

—*E. E. Cummings*

are the best things to have going for you *before* you invest. They often impact results, but they are luxuries, not absolute necessities. The other factors, like patience and asset allocation, apply once you begin the investment process, not before. And they are more than peripheral; they are essential ingredients for successful long-term investing. Everything in these pages is aimed at achieving success in the market *without* relying on luck. Reading this book, in my less than humble opinion, may be all the luck you need.

Chapter 3

Six Absolutes

The dictionary defines an *absolute* as that which is universally valid, certain, and unequivocal. The random nature of the stock market does not lend itself to many absolutes. Because there are so few, it is incumbent upon investors to know what they are and to take full advantage of their dependability. The following are six carved in stone, irrefutable market truths never to be forgotten.

1. Nobody Knows the Answers

If you ask the question, "Will the stock market go up or down tomorrow?" the bum on the park bench probably has as good a chance of being right as the savvy professional. There is no such thing as an expert on the market. Because it is perverse, contrary, illogical, random, enigmatic, and unfathomable, the market defies unerring analysis. It is impossible to know the unknowable or to predict the unpredictable. The most brilliant minds often make market projections that are dazzlingly erudite and dramatically wrong. There are two kinds of investment advisors—those who don't know, and those who don't know that they don't know. The latter are scary and all too common. Anyone who gives advice about the stock market without crossing his fingers just doesn't understand.

The color of the market is gray, not black or white. We can't even discuss the stock market without using words like *nevertheless, although, however, on the other hand, for the most part, generally speaking, more often than not, unless of course,* and so on. For every conclusion there is a qualification, for every rule an exception. In fact, a case can be made for doing the exact opposite of almost any rule as long as it's done consistently.

That no one has the answers would appear to be self-evident. Everybody knows that no one *really* knows. Then why discuss it here? First of all, there are some investors who, as they see sharp gains in individual stocks every day, say to themselves, "It can't be that hard. I just have to learn how to do it." Second, as the fever builds up in a rising market, we forget what went before. During and immediately after a severe decline, when we're still feeling the sting of losses and the anger from bad advice, we are painfully aware of the fallibility of the pros. But let the market mount a sustained up move with easy money being made once again, and all is forgotten. Despair and hopelessness fade and greed once again takes over. "Nobody knows" is replaced by a reenergized, emphatic, "I want my share." The steadily rising market makes everybody a genius and Wall Street regains its credibility.

The Eternal Quest for Performance

The investor's desire to make money leads him on an eternal quest for performance. He is forever seeking the best strategy, the best adviser, the best fund, the best stock. He longs to find an unbeatable strategy or an adviser who, for certain, will make his money grow. He is attracted to strong, confident, unhedged opinions. Humility is not what he is looking for. "I don't know" is not a confidence builder.

The investment community knows this and gives the investor what he wants, in spades. So, although it is absolute that no one is consistently right, the adviser (perceived as a skilled professional) offers opinions that sound so knowledgeable, so convincing, and so compelling that the investor has little reason to think they could also be wrong. The irony is that there are few areas of human endeavor where understatement is more apropos and less visible than the stock market.

If, instead of short memories, we all had perfect recall and previous bad calls were seared into our consciousness, few advisers could survive. Past mistakes would be too numerous, too blatant, and too confidence-shattering. But the analyst is not required to reveal the accuracy of his past calls. Instead, he only tells us if he owns the stock he is recommending (to reveal possible conflict of interest—but, to me, ownership is more a plus than a minus).

We have all been the victims of bad advice. It would seem unnecessary to cite specific examples. Every day for decades, thousands of learned, passionate, unequivocal opinions have been expressed that have been proven totally wrong. Giving just a few illustrations would be like revealing the tip of the tip of the iceberg. Yet because this is such a basic truth and because it must always be in the forefront of investor awareness, I feel compelled to cite a few glaring examples. There are enough others to fill up this book and the pages of most every book that's ever been printed. These are but four drops in an ocean of error.

Everyone Agrees—But Everyone Is Wrong

In the devastating bear market of 2000–2002, the NASDAQ Composite Index plummeted a gut-wrenching 78 percent. Many high-tech stocks, long on promise and short on earnings, fell from $100 and $200 a share to under $5. The investment public suffered huge losses which led to widespread disenchantment, distrust, and despair.

After such a crippling blow, Wall Street predicted, almost to a man, that it would take a long, long time for the deep wounds to heal and confidence in the speculative high-tech area to be restored. The financial media, including savvy veterans who had lived through many bear markets, agreed that it would take years to purge the excesses of the recent bubble.

The bear market bottomed in October 2002. Five months later, after testing its lows, a spirited rally began in the very same high-tech flyers that had been universally declared dead. In just seven months, the NASDAQ composite climbed over 50 percent. Many of the trading favorites that had dropped almost perpendicularly and been abandoned in droves came roaring back to score sharp gains. With almost no exceptions, the best minds in Wall Street proved dramatically wrong.

Another giant blunder was Wall Street's near-unanimous forecast for rising interest rates in 2004. Federal Reserve Board Chairman Alan Greenspan stated publicly he intended to raise short-term rates (at a "measured" pace), and then kept his promise with a series of 0.25 percent increases in the federal funds rate (the interest rate that banks charge each other for overnight loans). The Street's advice to sell bonds appeared well founded. Against a background of an expanding economy, with rising commodity prices, especially crude oil, triggering fears of inflation, plus a Federal Reserve Board that was actually on record to raise interest rates (as interest rates go up, bond prices go down), it was a no-brainer that the bond market was not the place to be.

Wrong! After an initial scare, the interest rate on the 10-year Treasury bond fell from 4.9 percent to 3.9 percent (the Fed has direct control over short-term rates only). In just three months, those who had taken Wall Street's advice and sold, saw their bonds go up, not down. The bond market chose to focus on the positive aspects of rising oil prices (that is, positive for the bond market because higher gas prices slow the economy and reduce pressure on the Federal Reserve to raise interest rates). There were other reasons bonds did well (including subdued inflation and foreign buying) but the point was that almost all of Wall Street was dead wrong and investors were ill-advised. (Note: Many wrong opinions eventually end up being right if enough time is allowed to pass).

Another glaring example of a giant goof was the completely unexpected performance of the stock market in 2006. For a host of reasons, Wall Street braced itself for a rocky year. The most optimistic forecast was for a single-digit gain. Perhaps the most formidable obstacle was historical precedent. One of the more dependable historical patterns is the four-year presidential cycle in which the second year,

> "What counts for most people in investing is not how much they know, but rather how realistically they define what they don't know."
> —*Warren Buffett*

the mid-term election year (2006), is usually the worst. For decades, like clockwork, the stock market has made a major low every fourth October (the exception was 1986 when it waited till the next year).

Mr. Market Refuses to Act His Age

There were other ominous seasonal patterns that reinforced a bearish second half scenario. Based on historical performance, the period May through October is the six months to be out of the market ("sell in May and go away"), and September and October are typically the two worst months of the year. What's more, the bull market was aging, completing its fourth year without as much as a 9 percent pullback, which, according to Ned Davis Research of Venice, Florida, had never happened before. And then there were the worrisome fundamentals including rising gas prices, a collapsing housing market, prospects for a drop in consumer spending, and a falling dollar.

But the stock market defied history and refused to act its age. Instead, it climbed steadily higher in the second half of the year, including a robust September and October. The Dow Jones Industrial Average ended 2006 at an all-time high, up an impressive 16 percent for the year. Dramatic evidence, once again, that "nobody knows."

A final glaring example of the ineptness of even the most experienced professionals in Wall Street occurred in late February 2007. The stock market's surprise strength in the second half of 2006 spilled over into 2007. The consensus view was that stocks were overdue for a substantial correction. After all, the market had gone almost straight up for seven straight months and an aging four-year-old bull market was seriously overextended. But stocks continued to climb.

Then, on February 27, the bottom fell out, all in one session. The Dow plummeted 416 points to 12,216, the steepest percentage decline in nearly four years. The frantic rush to sell resulted in the heaviest volume ever. The long-anticipated sell-off had finally started with a vengeance. It was followed quickly by one-day losses of 120 points on March 2 and 242 points on March 13. After going up seven months in a row, the rubber band had been stretched too far in one direction. Now, everyone agreed, the market would correct its excesses. Fundamentally, technically, logically, and emotionally, everything was pointed in one direction. The only question was whether the oncoming period of weakness would represent a badly needed correction or the beginning of a bear market.

Unbelievably, just 35 trading days after its 416 point collapse, the Dow had not only erased its loss but soared to a new all-time high. On April 25, 2007, the Dow moved decisively above 13,000 for the first time. The upside burst occurred despite news that day of weakness in housing and autos and a spike in the price of oil. By April 27, the Dow had put together a remarkable streak of 19 up days out of 21 sessions, the first time that had happened since the late 1920s. You would have been hard-pressed to find a living human being on this planet who would have dared to forecast an almost 900-point climb to a record high less than two months after the apparent panic selling of February 27.

And that's not all. A record short interest reflected the wide perception that after its sharp run-up to 13,000, the market was clearly over extended. What's more, the news background was unsettling. Investors fretted over a crisis in the sub prime mortgage market, continued weakness in housing, rising interest rates, the Fed's anxiety over inflation, near record high oil prices, a beleaguered dollar and the deepening quagmire in Iraq.

So what happened?

The Dow surged *another* 1,000 points in less than three months, closing above 14,000 on July 19, 2007. It was a dramatic illustration of two tried and true maxims: "markets go to extremes" and "markets climb a wall of worry." It also demonstrated the irrelevance of news to the market plus the one thing that will prevent the death of a bull market—even an aging five-year-old bull—widespread skepticism. (P.S. In just 19 trading days after topping 14,000, the Dow fell back below 13,000.)

So don't get upset with yourself because you can't figure out the market. Nobody can—including those who have studied it for a lifetime. Nobody knows. Absolutely, irrefutably, and unequivocally, nobody knows.

If you're wondering what was the news that triggered a one-day plunge of 416 points, there wasn't any. Commentators blamed it on a drop in the Chinese market, news that proved to be meaningless (the Chinese market recovered quickly and went on to new highs).

In his new book, *The Black Swan* (New York: Random House, 2007), Nassim Nicholas Taleb writes about the occurrence of the improbable, the profound influence of chance, the worthlessness of market projections, and our perpetual surprise when the not-predicted happens. "After prices unexpectedly rise or fall, experts impose specious retroactive narratives to divert attention from their ignorance." I say a lot more on the irrelevance of so-called news later in this chapter.

Wall Street Creates False Impressions

Let me repeat: An integral part of the process of buying and selling stocks is being wrong. It can't be avoided. It's endemic to the business. The only prediction that everyone can make with 100 percent accuracy is that no one has the answers. It's a basic, fundamental truth that's too often forgotten, and that's why I keep hammering it home. But the adviser is not going to focus on his own limitations, so it's up to the investor to always keep them in mind despite the power, passion, and persuasiveness of the rhetoric.

If Wall Street is to be faulted, it's not because it doesn't have the answers; it's everything that's done to create the impression that it does. Cigarette companies continue to make millions despite warnings that smoking causes cancer. The other day I saw a Phillip Morris TV commercial that strongly recommended that smokers quit. I remember it because it was the same day that the stock hit an all-time high. The company is able to successfully sell its health-threatening product despite its candid self-criticism. It knows there will always be a large, dependable core of smokers. I believe the securities industry can successfully sell a financial health-threatening product by being equally forthright. Until someone figures out how to put money under the pillow and make it grow, there will always be a need to invest. Creating honest, realistic expectations can only serve the industry well.

When I am asked for my opinion on what the market or a particular stock will do, I respond with the same two-part answer: (1) I don't know, and (2) here are some of the reasons it may go down, and some of the reasons it may go up. What I try to do is give the whole picture, the good and the bad, the pros and the cons, the positives and the negatives.

Often in class a frustrated, confused student will respond, "Okay, so now I know both sides of the story. But what do *you* think? After 40 years in the business, your guess is a lot better than mine." At that point, with my back to the wall, I'll reluctantly respond, but only after a reminder that it's just one man's opinion, that it could be dead wrong, and that many people smarter than me will have the exact opposite opinion.

This is not false modesty. It's simply the way it is. Would I be as honest if I was selling securities for a living? I would like to think so. As I've said, I think a completely candid approach would help, not hurt, the salesman and his firm. The problem is that some advisers, especially those less experienced, are so filled with themselves and feel so strongly that they're right, they're unable to explain the other side, no less say they don't know.

> "In the stock market (as in much of life), the beginning of wisdom is admitting your ignorance."
> —*James K. Glassman*

Investor Gullibility

For years on south Florida radio (long before Jim Cramer), we have had stock market call-in shows. They provide a platform for the dispensing of quick-fix advice. They are programs fostered by ignorance, arrogance, and gullibility. A listener calls in to a stockbroker radio host for an opinion on a stock. The broker quickly checks his information source (usually a chart) and within seconds, tells the caller in no uncertain terms that he should buy, sell, or hold. (Yes, Jim Cramer does this but he's one of a kind and makes his share of mistakes. See Chapter 5, Cramer vs. Kirk.) The listener then gratefully thanks the host for his guidance and makes way for the next caller waiting to be equally enlightened. In my view, the irresponsibility of the radio station and the stockbroker is exceeded only by the naiveté of the caller. The perception that the investor is fully aware that nobody knows is disproved every day on south Florida radio.

Analyst Performance Leaves Something to be Desired

Not only can the pros be wrong, but they can be very wrong for a long period of time. Following are the results of a 2003 study co-authored by

Brad Barber, professor of finance at the University of California, Davis. The findings were reported by Zacks Investment Research out of Chicago and the financial newspaper *Investor's Business Daily* in September 2003.

Specifically, the performance of companies receiving the worst ratings by the Street's best research analysts has topped the performance of highly rated stocks in each of the first four years of this decade. In light of this type of performance, it's not surprising that Wall Street research has received less than enthusiastic reviews. Legendary fund manager Peter Lynch in his book *One Up on Wall Street,* (New York: Simon & Schuster, 2000), writes, "Twenty years in this business convinces me that any normal person using the customary three percent of the brain can pick stocks just as well, if not better, than the average Wall Street expert."

Widely read Jonathan Clements, who has been writing for the *Wall Street Journal* for 18 years, says, "I think the whole business of buying investment advice stinks. . . . You can get great advice or end up losing your life's savings. . . . The level of financial knowledge among brokers and investment advisors is extremely low" (June 13, 2004). *Forbes* columnist Laszlo Birinyi is more succinct. He says, "Much of what so called experts say is pure bilge" (August 16, 2004). Burton Malkiel, Princeton economist (*A Random Walk Down Wall Street,* W.W. Norton), popularized the belief that a "blindfolded chimpanzee throwing darts could pick stocks as surely as the experts." Eighty-five-year-old veteran money manager Peter Bernstein, of whom *Fortune* writes, "he may know more about investing than anyone alive," is gentler: "You have to keep learning that you don't know and that not knowing is part of the process. There's always somebody around who looks very smart. They find models that work and ways to make money. Then they blow sky high. I've learned that the ones who are the most smart aren't going to make it" (interview on PBS.org; Frontline: *Betting on the Market*).

In a February 20, 2006 *Barron's* interview, 40-year market veteran, Walter Deemer, cited the results of an ISI Group hedge fund survey: "The driving force in the market these days, hedge funds, are still most bullish at tops and most bearish at bottoms." In other words, the highly paid, highly sophisticated, cream of the Wall Street crop of money managers are wrong at tops and bottoms just like most everybody else.

Yearnings as Well as Earnings

When analysts do their forecasting, they focus on two areas: fundamentals and technicals. But there's an important third area that's largely neglected. I'm talking about psychological or behavioral influences— that is, investor emotions and perceptions. Sentiment indexes that attempt to gauge investor skepticism, complacency, and optimism have long been used as contrary indicators, but mostly by technicians. There is a growing body of work in the field of investor behavior. Studies show that emotions play a key role in influencing stock prices and often explain what otherwise may be inexplicable. However, analysts and investment advisers are not trained in psychology. Emotions are difficult to measure. But the adviser has to know that deeply embedded feelings like hope, despair, and greed can impact the securities markets as much or more than cash flow and return on equity. An analyst's analysis is not complete without factoring in yearnings as well as earnings.

For example, let's say an analyst recommends a $50 pharmaceutical stock based mostly on pending approval of its drug to treat cancer. The analyst sets a one-year target of $60. As the meeting date for FDA approval draws near, the media is filled with glowing reports of the drug's potential benefits. The stock moves up sharply in anticipation, and moves up still more after FDA approval. Instead of $60 in a year, the stock reaches $70 in two weeks. The analyst failed to take into account the emotional premium triggered by all the powerful feelings that come into play when dealing with the subject of cancer. If the drug had been rejected, the move would likely have been equally exaggerated on the downside.

A case in point was what happened to Dendreon (DNDN), a small Seattle-based drug maker. The company announced that an FDA advisory panel had recommended that the FDA approve its new drug, Provenge, for the treatment of prostate cancer. Not always, but most of the time, the FDA follows the recommendation of its advisory panel. The negatives in the story were that the drug may not kill tumors, that it only treats advanced cases, that only a small number of patients were involved in the trial, and that there was no guarantee of approval. The positives were that the trial suggested that the drug does extend life and that it is safe.

More than one million men in the United States have prostate cancer, with 27,000 to 30,000 deaths each year. The PR release from the company quoted the CEO as saying, "If approved, Provenge could become a breakthrough treatment for patients with advanced prostate who currently have few treatment options."

On the day the news was released, March 29, 2007, no trading was permitted in the stock. The day before, it had closed at 5.22. The next day, March 30, 2007, the stock opened at 17.92, more than tripling overnight. Ten days later, on April 10, it reached 25.25, up almost fivefold. Here was a dramatic illustration of the overpowering role that unbridled emotion (hope, optimism, greed) can play in the marketplace. Every stock price has two components. On its 10-day climb from 5 to 25, the price of Dendreon was probably 1 percent based on fundamentals and 99 percent based on emotion. On May 10, one month after it peaked at 25, it was back to 5.

Why Stocks If No One Knows?

The 18-year bull market (1982–2000) culminated in explosive 20 percent-plus gains in all the major indexes in each of the five years 1995 through 1999. However, many of today's gurus are forecasting mostly sideways or trading-range markets with an average of single-digit annual gains for the foreseeable future. (Of course, an *average* single-digit annual gain means some years could record a lot more and some a lot less.) If we are not going to see a sustained uptrend for some years, does that eliminate the stock market as a vehicle for making money? And if, as we have been pounding the table, it is indeed a universal truth that no one knows the answers, is that a reason to shun the market?

For older investors with limited means, a fixed income, and an unfixed (undisciplined) temperament, perhaps. But for most of us, the prevalence of wrong advice and the prospect of limited appreciation for a while are obstacles we can work around. Like an injury that is not life threatening, we learn to live with it. In the pages ahead I discuss how to minimize the bad and capitalize on the good. For the long-term investor, having time to accumulate good companies at value prices is not a bad thing. In years to come, despite rough markets along the way, patient investors who stick to a well-conceived game plan will prosper because, over time, the market will prosper.

What's more important is that we know what we're up against ahead of time so there'll be no surprises. Once we're aware of the downside as well as the up, we can make the proper adjustments. By focusing on the long term; limiting losses; buying at reasonable prices; using index funds, asset allocation, and rebalancing; and by trying as best we can to stay physically and emotionally healthy, we can position ourselves to make the most of whatever the market gives us. It all comes under the heading of putting the odds in our favor. More on this, coming up.

> "The truth is that there aren't really any answers in investing, at least none that last very long. The world is just too dynamic for that. There are only questions. And the only way you're going to make money in investing is by asking them."
>
> —*Donald Luskin*

2. There's Always an Exact Opposite Opinion

For every professional opinion about a stock, the market, the economy, interest rates, inflation, and so on, there is an exact opposite opinion by someone equally knowledgeable. Think about it: Every trade that crosses the ticker represents a buyer who thinks the stock is going up and a seller who thinks it's going down. What's more, since institutions represent a high percentage of the daily trading volume (via mutual funds, hedge funds, program trading, etc.), there's a good chance that when you buy or sell, a professional with a directly opposite opinion is on the other side of your trade.

Since more than 7 out of every 10 recommendations from Wall Street analysts are buys (down from 9 out of 10 in the prebubble years), it may take some digging beyond the typically upbeat brokerage firm research to find an opposite view, but it's always there. When one firm adds a stock to its "buy" list, the same stock is being removed by another firm. Salespersons of the two firms are giving their customers directly opposite advice. They genuinely want to make money for their clients, but half will be wrong. When a stock is being upgraded, it's being downgraded someplace else. For every bullish article in a magazine, newspaper, newsletter, or web site, there is a directly contrary write-up somewhere else—sometimes in the same publication. In recent years, some brokerage houses have permitted dissenting views within their own ranks. In late 2004, for example, Merrill Lynch's Research Investment Committee forecast higher interest rates in 2005 while the firm's Interest Rate Committee was calling for lower rates.

The adviser does little to make his or her client aware that there are other smart people who disagree with him. For example, in the fall of 2006, Steven Roach (Morgan Stanley) was advising clients that he thought commodity prices could fall another third from current levels. It's unlikely he was also telling them that commodity guru Jim Rogers was investing his own money in commodities because he felt prices were headed higher well into the next decade with many expected to double in price.

There's always a column A (the pluses) and a column B (the minuses). By focusing on the factors in just one column, the adviser can easily convince, indeed overwhelm the customer with compelling reasons to act. Making the sales pitch even more effective is the genuine conviction of the broker. In most cases, salespeople honestly believe they are right and express their opinions with hard-to-refute enthusiasm. Intellectually, the investor may be aware that there are always contrary opinions. Emotionally, however, a forceful presentation can hit all the sensitive greed and fear buttons. The last thing on the investor's mind is that the professional in the office across the street is giving the exact opposite advice.

It's important to note that sometimes opposite opinions are not really opposite. The headline may read, "ABC Forecasts Higher Interest Rates; Adds Merck to Its Buy List." At the same time, another headline reports, "XYZ Forecasts Lower Interest Rates; Recommends Sale of Merck." Read the articles carefully and it turns out both firms are in agreement. The forecast of XYZ Company is strictly for the short term but both firms feel the same way about prospects for the long term. The confusion arises over the failure of the headline to designate the different time frames involved.

Although there are always opposite views, they're harder to come by at market tops and bottoms when euphoria and gloom reach their peaks. It is at these market extremes that it is most difficult and most profitable to be a contrarian and go against a seemingly universal consensus. More on contrarians in a bit. Suffice it to say here that, regardless of how wonderful the news is, there is always a seller at a price. And no matter how devastating the news, there is always a buyer at a price.

The Valuable Role of the Perpetual Bear

We cannot talk about opposite opinions without mentioning the key role played by Wall Street's perennial bears. (Because we tend by nature to be optimistic, and because markets go up more often than they go down, there are a lot more perennial bulls). The professional who can be depended upon to always provide the bearish side serves a valuable balancing function, especially in times of rampant bullishness. Observers like Jonathan Grantham, Michael Metz, Alan Abelson, John Mauldin, Robert Prechter, Bernie Schaeffer, David Tice, Steven Roach, Fred Hickey, Doug Kass, and Gary Schilling are there to remind us that Wall Street is not a one-way street. In fairness, they are not bears 100 percent of the time, but they can always be relied on for independent thinking and sensible skepticism. And because they have a pessimistic bias and because bear markets always follow bull markets, we know that at some point they will be right.

Knowing that there's always someone smarter who thinks you're dead wrong can make it tough for the informed investor to act with confidence. What adds to the dilemma is that every news event can be interpreted both bullishly and bearishly. The same news can help some and hurt others. Recession causes interest rates to fall and helps quality bonds but it hurts junk bonds on fears of default. The price of oil goes up and Exxon stockholders are happy because it means higher profits, but higher gas prices can slow the economy and add to inflation—both negatives for the general market. Stock buybacks mean fewer shares outstanding and higher earnings per share, but they can also mean a drain on the company's cash and a reduction in its bond ratings. Students complain that the daily torrent of conflicting opinions and corporate spin makes them confused. I tell them that's because the market *is* confusing—not to mention baffling, bewildering, and perplexing. If they're not confused, they simply don't understand.

In class, I explain to students as best I can both the pros and cons of the issue being discussed. I outline reasons why the market or a particular stock should go up (column A) and then why it should go down (column B). I end the session with, "If you're not confused, I haven't done my job." It may take some sorting out, but in the end, an awareness of both sides of the story is what produces informed opinion, reasonable expectations, and less surprise. Using an adviser or mutual fund makes it someone else's job to be aware. But for you, there still remains the sticky question of which adviser, mutual fund, or index fund to use and when.

There are always opposite views about that. The one ameliorating factor is this: The longer you hold your stock, the less likely you'll be unsettled by opposite views.

> "The way to get rich from investment advice is to sell it, not to take it."
>
> —*Malcolm Forbes*

3. We're Predisposed to Fail, But Not Predestined

To summarize, to this point: We've said the three best things the investor can have going for him are luck, a long life, and deep pockets. We've also recognized that investors operate in a world where absolutely no one knows the answers consistently and where there is always a directly opposite, compelling opinion.

There is another obstacle the investor has to deal with. By temperament, most of us are predisposed to making the wrong moves in the market. If that were not true, we'd all be rich.

Powerful, deep-seated emotions like fear and greed motivate many of our decisions. Such feelings work against us because, for the most part, investment success requires our being fearful when we feel greedy, and greedy when we feel fearful. Acting contrary to human nature takes practice and great discipline. It can be done and, in fact, is done all the time, but not by many. The herd instinct is overpowering. We all take psychological comfort in knowing that what we do, everybody else is doing. But what everybody is doing is usually (not always) wrong. So, motivated by greed, we end up buying near tops and, triggered by fear, selling near bottoms. Hardly the formula for success.

Legendary investor Benjamin Graham felt that not only are investors *emotionally* ill-equipped but they also face *mental* challenges. In his classic *The Intelligent Investor* (Harper Business, Paperback revised 2003), he cautioned that the aggressive investor should approach his security dealings the same as he would operating a business enterprise. "The majority of security owners do not have the time, or the determination, or the mental equipment to embark upon investing as a quasi-business," he said. He therefore recommended a defensive, long-term portfolio of "bargain issues."

The detached Wall Street professional is also human and therefore not immune to emotionally based decisions, but he makes them less often. Because he is more experienced and more disciplined, he is more likely to be motivated by reason than emotion. His reasoning, of course, can be wrong, especially if it is influenced by his desire to keep his job. One way he does this is by *window-dressing* at the end of the quarter— that is, buying stocks that have already gone up sharply. Since the cost price is not revealed in his portfolio when it's published each quarter, inclusion of the big winners make him look good.

There's another reason why even the most disciplined, dispassionate professional can be wrong. When fear or greed take over and fever is in the air (mostly near bottoms and tops), the market (or a stock) always goes lower or higher than the fundamentals justify. This excess move is triggered strictly by emotions (hope, despair, etc.), and there's absolutely no way to know how far it will carry. On December 5, 1996, Federal Reserve Board Chairman Alan Greenspan, concerned about high valuations, warned of the market's "irrational exuberance." In the four years following his warning, the Dow Jones Industrial Average almost doubled and the NASDAQ quadrupled. Stock analysts routinely underestimate the emotional component of stock prices.

The Ability to Zig When Others Are Zagging

It's not that we don't have calming influences in times of market fever. In this day of information overload, there are plenty of commentators in the financial media urging caution and restraint. Their words make sense intellectually. But common sense is easily trumped by emotion. Fear in a free-falling market and desire for easy money in an up-surging market drown out the voices of reason and usually lead to bad decisions.

If the gurus' single-digit forecasts in the years ahead prove correct and we have range-bound markets and fewer sustained moves in either direction, it could prove a blessing. There will be less provocation for the emotional excesses that play havoc with our investment results. However, the single-digit gain that is forecast is an *average*, which still leaves room for soaring and swooning markets.

Some investors are able to control their emotions and zig when everyone else is zagging. Perhaps they have a more cerebral or stoic nature or maybe they more easily learn from their mistakes. Whatever the reason, it should work to their advantage if it's true that the consensus is wrong more times than right. That would make a contrarian approach, by definition, a successful strategy more times than not.

As I have stated, unless you're a skeptic or a loner by nature, taking the contrarian view is easier said than done. First of all, the consensus view is often difficult to identify. It is murky more times than it is clear. Second, the consensus view is sometimes right (except at tops and bottoms when it is always wrong). And third, when the majority view *is* clear and sentiment is overwhelming in one direction, human nature makes it exceedingly hard to swim against the tide. The ability to resist euphoria and gloom with unwavering conviction requires iron discipline and unshakable self-confidence. It's one thing to think everyone is wrong; it's quite another to back up your conviction with money. Which is why those few who do so and subsequently prove right deserve every penny of their profit.

Temperament Trumps IQ

In acknowledging the crucial role human nature plays in investing, we should be careful to differentiate between *predisposed* and *predestined*. We are *not* predestined to fail in the market—in other words, it has not been decisively determined beforehand. But because of human nature, we are inclined to make the wrong move. We have a natural, human tendency to be extremely irrational when it comes to money. Says legendary investor Warren Buffett, "Investing is not a game where the guy with the 160 IQ beats the guy with the 130 IQ. . . . Once you have ordinary intelligence, what you need is the temperament to control the urges that get other people into trouble" (*Warren Buffett Speaks,* Janet Lowe, John Wiley, 1997, page 101).

Henry Blodget, president of Cherry Hill Research, believes chances for developing such a temperament are slim. If the name Blodget sounds familiar, there's good reason. A major contributor to the late 1990s bubble mentality, Blodget had a huge following as a star internet analyst for Merrill Lynch. He was charged with securities fraud, fined, and barred from the industry after e-mails revealed his private views were inconsistent with his published pie-in-the sky forecasts. He later recognized the error of his ways, describing his actions as "idiocy" and confessing, "in hindsight, I was a moron." I quote him because working with the investment public and with his fellow professional analysts at Merrill gave him a unique vantage point. I believe his insights on investor behavior are meaningful (you can read him on his blog, internetoutsider.com; he also contributes to *Slate* and *Forbes*).

In a column in the December 14, 2004, Internet magazine *Slate*, titled "Born Suckers," Blodget writes, "Human beings are wired to make dumb investing mistakes. What's more, we are wired not to learn from them, but to make them again and again. It's not our fault. We have innate tendencies that doom most of us to investing mediocrity. . . . The biggest lie of the 1990s—the biggest lie of every bull market is that investing is so easy that anyone can do it, that all you have to do to win is play. The reality, of course, is that only a tiny handful of people are dedicated and talented enough to overcome their DNA, confront the long odds, and come out ahead of the market average, and they are as rare as world-class athletes. As for the rest of us, we may have fun trying (and this, in and of itself, is enough reason to play), but alas, we are almost sure to lose."

I'm not as pessimistic as Blodget. I believe more than a "tiny handful of people" can succeed. But because most of us do not have the emotional control needed, we end up underperforming the overall market. That's why selected professional money managers and mutual funds with good track records make sense, and why index funds make even more sense. More on this later.

> "I'm the master of brilliant investment decisions I almost made."
>
> —*Harry Newton*

4. There Is Symmetry in the Market

There is a certain symmetry to the market, an ebb and flow, a giving and taking away that gives it balance over time. Sometimes the pattern is traced over a long period of years, other times over a much shorter period. Sometimes the up and down waves are sharp, other times gradual. The more extreme the move, the greater the reaction is likely to be—the higher the platform, the deeper the dive. NASDAQ climbed four-fold to 5,100 in four years, then gave it all back in two years. The Dow Jones Industrial Average lost over one-third of its value in a two-month period in 1987, dropping over 500 points in one day. Two years later it had fully recovered and then some. Rallies are followed by sell-offs, which are followed by rallies. But sharp V-shaped bottoms and tops are uncommon after a sustained run, because intense emotion lingers and rarely changes on a dime.

Reversion to the mean is another expression used to describe the market's symmetry. James O'Shaughnessy (*Predicting the Markets of Tomorrow*, Portfolio Hardcover, 2006) calls reversion to the long-term mean "one of the ironclad rules of financial markets." Mean reversion simply denotes that what goes up eventually comes down and what goes down eventually bounces back. It reverts back to the mean or historical average but the timing is unknowable.

Symmetrical patterns are far from perfect. (History never repeats itself exactly, but it usually comes close.) A 500 point move up in the averages is not followed by a 500 point decline. And a 42-month uptrend is not followed by a 42-month downtrend. That would be too predictable. There are always variations, anomalies, aberrations, exceptions, and surprises. But when we talk about symmetry there *is* one central point that remains a constant.

Bull markets are always followed by bear markets, and bear markets are always followed by bull markets. There are few absolutes in the market; this is one of them. It's a certainty that's easy to forget, however, amid bear market gloom and bull market euphoria. There will never be a time when markets keep going up or just keep going down, even though that's exactly how it feels at market tops and bottoms. The inevitable change in the market's major trend is more a source of comfort in bear markets since investors know that at some point in time, things will get better. It may provide little consolation at the time, but the truth is that market weakness is what makes market strength possible. The bad sets the stage for the good (and the good for the bad).

What's a Definition of a Bull Market?

There is no one, concise, widely accepted definition of what qualifies as a bull or bear market. Probably the one most commonly used is a move of at least 20 percent in a major index. What complicates the issue is that there are three major indexes. The Dow Jones Industrial Average with 30 stocks and the Standard & Poor's Index with 500 stocks are usually in general sync but often do not parallel each other. The NASDAQ Composite Index with over 3,000 stocks is more volatile and more independent. For example, its bull market lasted two months longer than the Dow in early 2000. Although the bear market in all three indexes bottomed on the same climactic day (October 9, 2002), the steepness of the slide and the extent of the loss varied greatly. The bear market in the Dow measured 37 percent, the S&P went down 49 percent, and the hi-tech NASDAQ collapsed 78 percent, more than twice the damage in the Dow. Not surprisingly, both the Dow and the S&P 500 have more than recovered their losses, albeit slowly. The NASDAQ is still well underwater.

Also adding confusion is the fact that bull and bear market trends can be short-term (cyclical) or long-term (secular). And we can have a cyclical bear market within a secular bull market. The exact beginning of a bull market is often open to interpretation, depending on whether a secular or cyclical time frame is used. Most technicians mark the beginning of the historic bull market that bubbled in early 2000 as 1982, but some say it started in 1974 and others 1990.

So, despite it being part of every investor's vocabulary, there is no clear understanding of what a bull or bear market is or precisely when it starts and ends. The post-bubble bear market reached a low on October 9, 2002, but some analysts measure the ensuing bull market from March 3, 2003, when the October 9 low was successfully tested. It's an academic point, meaningful only to technicians and historians. As investors, we *know* when things are good and when they're bad. The term *bull market* is irrelevant if our stocks are going down and so is the term *bear market* if we own securities that are going up.

An individual sector may be in its own bull market while the overall market is going down. There is a constant rotation of industry groups into and out of favor. This means there are always individual stocks and industry groups that are moving counter to the major trend. When we talk about "the market" we usually mean the Dow, the S&P, or the NASDAQ indexes. The market usually is in one of three stages:

1. A sustained uptrend, (with corrections along the way).
2. A sustained downtrend (with rallies along the way).
3. A sideways or trading range trend (which takes place before, after, or during stages 1 and 2).

Most of the time stocks move indecisively within a trading range. Studies have shown that the big upside moves in the market take place on less than 20 days during the year. In fact, in bull markets, much of the profit is made on the five biggest up days. That means that most of the market is treading water most of the time. It may be called a bull market but it doesn't feel like one when your stocks aren't moving. Nevertheless, money managers like Fidelity's Peter Lynch believe in staying fully invested at all times because you never know when those explosive up days are going to come.

As I have indicated, there is a predictable though imperfect symmetry to the market's major moves. The longer the time period, the more visible the symmetry. The ebb and flow gets lost when focusing on shorter-term phenomena like rallies, corrections, and trading ranges. But step back and look at the big picture and the market's counterbalancing action falls into place. What

> "If you don't have a clear picture, it's much better to do nothing. Remember, you make money by not losing it."
> —*Richard Russell*

goes down eventually comes back up and then goes back down again (the bull phase typically lasts longer than the bear phase).

There Are Many Examples of Symmetry

This predictable wave-like pattern is not limited to just the overall market indexes. It applies to other market-related phenomena such as group favoritism and volatility. Periods of low volatility in the market are invariably followed by periods of high volatility.

For example, by early 2007, the Dow had not suffered a one-day drop of more than 2 percent in almost four years. It was a period of unusually low volatility which had to end, but nobody knew when. Then, on February 27, 2007, after going almost straight up for seven months in a row, the Dow plummeted 3.3 percent or 416 points in just one day. Two weeks later it fell another 242 points or 2 percent. Succeeding sessions saw wide intraday price swings. Wall Street said it marked a new era of volatility.

Individual industry groups enjoy periods of popularity and rising prices followed by periods of unpopularity and declining prices, and then the cycle repeats itself. For example, the hated telecom stocks that no one wants become the loved telecoms that everyone wants. If a group has been out of favor for a long time, the odds are that its return to favor will also be lasting.

The same shift of sentiment occurs with equal dependability with investment styles and asset classes. Growth stocks are all the rage until they falter and value stocks move to the front. Small stocks lead the pack until they fade and are replaced by large capitalization stocks. The change in popularity from loved to unloved is predictable but the shift can take a long time, which often blurs the transition. Because it can be gradual, because there can be false moves, and because it can be a long time in coming, the new trend is often difficult to identify except in retrospect. Like so many other things in the market, it's only the passage of time that puts things into clear focus.

There are other activities related to the securities industry that follow a symmetrical pattern. The number of companies going public goes from almost zero to a flood and then recedes. Company mergers and acquisitions can be dormant for a long spell, gradually increase to a fever pitch, and then subside. Cash flowing into mutual funds rises to record levels and then dries up. Security firms go on a hiring binge, greatly expand their staffs, and then initiate widespread layoffs. These opposites may take years to play out but their repetition is predictable.

Other key aspects of the economy move symmetrically. Recessions are always followed by expansions. A declining trend in interest rates, in inflation, the dollar, and taxes is always eventually followed by a rising trend. The time frame, however, is usually long. The decline in interest rates and inflation, for example, covered the last two decades of the twentieth century. (Of course, both major trends were interrupted by minor countertrends along the way.)

The Cycle of Corporate Corruption

Perhaps the most visible example of a business activity that fades in and out of the headlines with regularity is corporate corruption. It is a recurring phenomenon because greed is a constant in human nature. Acts of corporate immorality are happening every day but mostly behind the scenes. Periodically and predictably, however, they come center stage, dominate the headlines, and trigger corporate reform. The catalyst for these recurring waves of corporate scandal is the action of the stock market—specifically, severe market declines.

When stocks are rising, the public tends not to worry about compliance, and politicians are reluctant to rock the boat. But rising markets create a ripe environment for management shenanigans. The misdeeds come to light in the ensuing bear market, which puts an already unhappy public in an investigative, unforgiving mood. Politicians hastily package regulations to defuse the anger of their constituents and the storm slowly subsides. Stuart Banner, in his book *Anglo-American Securities Regulation* (Cambridge University Press, 2002), says market declines have been triggering governmental regulation of the securities markets for 300 years. At the beginning of the last century we had the Sherman Antitrust Act. At the beginning of this century we had the Sarbanes-Oxley Act. In between we've had robber barons, corporate raiders, accounting fraud, and scandals galore.

When the scandal headlines fade and a few of the guilty are punished, the perception is that such blatant abuse of the public trust is not likely to happen again. The day that money no longer becomes an object of human desire is the day that such expectations will be realized. In the meantime, don't hold your breath. The cycle of corporate thievery, public outrage, and reform legislation will continue to occur as predictably as the bull and bear markets that spawn them.

After a rash of corporate scandals, it's widely perceived that investors will come back into the market only after Wall Street takes decisive measures to restore trust and confidence. However, it's the action of the market itself and not government reform that's key to the return of the public. When the market is good, the investor will be there for his share. I'm not minimizing righteous public outrage nor the importance of reform. But the lure of making money in a fast-rising market is a far more powerful restorer of confidence than punishment of the guilty or legislative reform. All of the protest and indignation fades in the wake of the profits waiting to be made in a hot-story stock that keeps going up day after day.

The Most Important Observation in This Book

If there's one thing you take away from this discussion of symmetry in business, let it be that bull markets always follow bear markets. This truism has two corollaries that I've touched on but bear repeating. First, markets always go to extremes and so do most individual stocks. They go higher or lower than they should based on fundamentals because human emotions are not bound by reason. You might think otherwise, but extreme tops and bottoms are difficult to identify at the time. Greed makes us think they'll go still higher and fear makes us think they'll go lower. How far extremes will go and how long they'll last is unknowable.

The second corollary to the inevitability of bull markets following bear markets, and what may be the most important observation in the book, is this: *Over the past century, the underlying bias of the stock market is up.* Just as our economy grows over time, stock prices rise more often than they fall. Bull markets (on average) last longer than bear markets. In the past 60 years the S&P 500 has ended up 42 times, down 17 times, and unchanged once. Trace the path of the Dow Jones Industrial Average on a long-term chart with a ruler. It's immediately apparent you have to slant the ruler upward because every new high is eventually followed by a higher high. That beautiful sustained uptrend reflects dependable long-term performance. It's the reason I'm writing this book and it's the reason you're reading it.

Ibbotson Associates, a leading Chicago-based research firm owned by Morningstar, says that for the past 80 years (1926–2005), large company stocks, as embodied in the S&P 500 Index, have compiled an average annual return of 10.4 percent including dividends. Small-company stocks (the 20 percent of NYSE-traded stocks with the smallest capitalization) have done better, up an average 12.6 percent.

Former hedge fund manager and TV personality Jim Cramer makes the case for stocks with more flair. In an online interview back in the 1990s (PBS.org), he said, "If you had bought the ten most active stocks on the New York Stock Exchange, on the Friday before the October 1987 crash, arguably the dumbest day in history to ever buy stocks, you would have been up huge three years later. Doesn't that say that here's an asset class, common stocks, that works over the long term if you can buy it on the dumbest day in history and make a bundle?"

In the securities markets, there are few things you can forecast with certainty. One is that the buyer of all but the most speculative bonds knows that even if things go bad, he'll get his money back when the bond matures. (Moody's Investors Service projects a default rate in junk bonds of only 1.4 percent in 2007, increasing to 4.5% in 2008. But even a 4.5 percent default rate means 95.5 percent of even the most speculative bonds pay off. Admittedly, the default rate will be higher during recessions.)

The long-term buyer of stocks should do better than get his money back. If he buys a broad-based market index, for example, he knows that in time he'll make a profit (assuming you believe, as I do, that what's happened in the stock market and the economy the past 100 years will continue to happen). All that's required is that he hang around long enough, which is why my mantra for the past 25 years has been that the real key to successful investing is eating right, exercising, and reducing stress. Sometimes the wait for a new high in the market can be a long one (1973 to 1982 in the Dow). But money is being made in cyclical uptrends along the way. Awareness of this eventual happy ending should provide at least some comfort during depressed markets.

A Strong Argument for Investing Long-Term

Not all stocks are certain to make new highs—not even close. Nor am I suggesting that a buy-and-hold approach is necessarily the way to go (more on this and other strategies later). What's certain is that, in time, the overall market will make a higher high, which is a strong argument for investing at least some money long-term in the broad market indexes. (Because the NASDAQ soared to such extreme heights in early 2000, the waiting period for new highs could be a very long one.) It's also reasonable to assume that when the market makes a new high, so will most of the better-quality larger companies, since they *are* the indexes.

The word *always* is seldom used in writing about the market. That's why the certainty of the bull market, bear market, bull market sequence is a big deal. It means that periods of below-average return or even losses will be followed by periods of above-average returns. Sometimes we get so immersed in the minutia of daily news that we fail to see the market's symmetry. The investor needs a sense of the ebb and flow of events over time to have a realistic perspective. He needs to be able to avoid the tunnel vision that comes from preoccupation with the ultra short-term focus of CNBC-type news coverage. By stepping back and looking at the big picture he can draw confidence that strength will follow weakness. And he will be better able to take in stride the emotionally draining peaks and valleys that the market visits during its inevitable climb upward.

> "Rather than think everyone should be their own investment advisor, I think we should accept the idea that (1) some people will be clueless to the grave and (2) we'd have a more productive society if people could do what they do best—which probably isn't money management."
> —*Scott Burns*

5. The Market Is King—News Is Mostly Irrelevant

The investor is faced with a daily barrage of business news. There's keen competition over who can break the story first. The clear inference is that the news matters—that keeping abreast of the news, especially as it relates to one's holdings, is one of the keys to investment success.

I disagree. I believe one of the worst things that can happen to a long-term investor is to be instantly and totally informed about his stock. In most cases, spot news fades into irrelevance over time. What's relevant is what *the market* decides to do. The news follows the market, not the other way around.

The Market Is King

If nothing else, the stock market is perverse, irrational, and illogical. Yet, both investors and the financial media are forever trying to explain the moves in the market with logical reasons (the words *market* and *individual stocks* can be interchanged throughout this discussion). If the news is bad and the market goes down, there's a logical connection. The problem is when the news is bad and the market goes up. Where's the logic?

The answer, of course, is that the market has its own agenda. It will do what it has to do to fill its own needs. It takes an independent path that may or may not be in harmony with the news. Technical analyst for *Barron's Online* Michael Kahn says, "If the market does not want to go down, no amount of bad news is going to drive it lower. To put it in economic terms, demand will overcome supply, so leave your logic at the door." *Barron's* columnist Michael Santoli puts it this way: "Like a referee, the market doesn't have to give an explanation for decisions; its verdict is all that counts."

A word about Wall Street's favorite fictional character, Mr. Market. There is constant reference to the market, or "Mr. Market," as the reason for whatever happens in the stock market that's otherwise inexplicable. It's a confusing concept. Mr. Market is ascribed human qualities. He acts independently, irrationally, and unpredictably. When the market makes a big move on a particular day and there's no surprise blockbuster news to pin it on, Mr. Market is cited as the catalyst. Why it chose to move on that particular day rather than the day or week before, or the day or week after, is a mystery.

When we use Mr. Market as the reason behind the move it sounds astute. I use it all the time, but the real translation is, "I don't know how else to explain it." My students call it a cop-out. After all, we *are* the market. Why shouldn't we be able to forecast what we will do and when? The media uses whatever the news background was that day as the catalyst, but invariably that news has been around or is less than earth-shaking.

My best guess is that emotions, triggered by fear and greed, play a key role. It's a herd mentality that builds as emotions feed off of each other. When Wall Street has been calling for a correction for weeks in a way overextended market, why it finally comes at 2 P.M. on Thursday afternoon defies explanation, at least to me. So, I'll continue to defer to Mr. Market.

Perhaps the most striking example of the primacy of the market's own agenda is evidenced in times of worldwide crisis. When news is reported of war, assassination, international financial crisis, terrorist attacks, and so on, the shock predictably triggers heavy initial selling. The record shows, however, that it is not too long before the market resumes the course it was on prior to the crisis.

Ned Davis Research out of Venice, Florida, examined the impact on the Dow of 28 major crises over the past 60 years. Most of the crises occurred during bull markets. The results followed a similar pattern. The Dow lost ground initially, but typically regained its loss within three months and was well ahead in six months. In the 1990s, for example, the market forged ahead in a powerful advance, and neither the 1991 Gulf War ultimatum, nor the 1993 World Trade Center bombing, nor the 1998 U.S. embassy bombing in Africa could put a damper on its primary uptrend. Although unsettling initially, the news proved of little consequence to the long-term investor.

Crisis News During Bear Markets How about the impact of crisis news in a bear market? Doesn't the bad news make an already down market worse? When the terrorists attacked us on September 11, 2001, the market was in the middle of a severe downtrend. In the week that followed the attack, the Dow plummeted 1,370 points and the NAS-DAQ fell a much more moderate 272 points. (The Dow got hit the hardest because prior to the attack it had declined much less than the free-falling NASDAQ and so was more vulnerable.) The market bounced back from its initial shock but not for long. The relentless downtrend resumed and didn't hit bottom until October 10, 2002. That's what it took—declines of 38 percent in the Dow, 49 percent in the Standard & Poor's 500, and 78 percent in NASDAQ—for the market to correct the excesses of the prior bull market. It did what it had to do to purge itself of the exorbitant valuations reached when the bubble burst in early 2000.

Obviously, we don't know how the bear market would have played out if there had not been a 9/11. Yes, 9/11 created more uncertainty and fear, more volatility, and perhaps a more perpendicular decline. But the market was on a mission; the fulfillment of its internal needs was not to be denied. External events were secondary. It's my guess that if we did not have a 9/11, there would have been no lack of other bearish news cited to justify the market's slide. In 1987, there was no trigger news event to explain the market's 22 percent collapse in one day (October 19) —none. Yet there was no shortage of negative stories cited after the fact. The news follows the market. Yes, surprise blockbuster news temporarily impacts markets, but in time the market takes over and resumes its underlying trend.

News plays a role in triggering the fear that causes market bottoms. But the ultimate bottom only becomes a bottom (the same goes for tops) when the market decides the rubber band has been stretched far enough and prices have dropped enough to satisfy its need to purge prior excesses. It will not change its underlying course until it is ready. History tells us that if the news is in conflict with the market's primary trend, it will cause a temporary detour at most. When it comes to major long-term trends, the market is always the final arbiter. This is how columnist Ben Stein at Yahoo! Finance (http://finance .yahoo.com) puts it: "The stock market is an immense entity made up of trillions of dollars and billions of people. I float on the market like a cork on the ocean. I don't control it, I merely navigate it as best as I can to get to my port without drowning" (*When Investing, Profit From Serenity*, December 25, 2005).

> "One hundred percent of the information you have about a company represents the past, and 100 percent of the value depends on the future."
>
> —*Bill Miller*

The News Is Mostly Irrelevant

When discussing the impact of news on the market, it's important to differentiate between short-term impact and long-term impact. Up to now, I've focused on the long term because that's the time frame that puts the odds in the investor's favor. News is mostly irrelevant on a long-term basis. I use the word *mostly* because there *are* times when a particular news story *does* have long-term significance. These are the few instances when the news represents basic, fundamental change, when the news profoundly alters future prospects, either for good or for bad. In the vast majority of instances, this proves not to be the case. However, at the time the news is released, it is almost impossible to make a definitive judgment. We learn the answer only with the passage of time. What we can say for sure is that rarely is news as good or as bad as it sounds when first reported.

In retrospect, we can cite examples of news that did prove pivotal. In some cases, the story developed over a period of time, making it even more difficult to evaluate. The emergence of digital photography proved a crippler for Eastman Kodak and its traditional cameras. In 2003, when the market surged ahead, Kodak fell from a high of 41 to 20 and the next year was deleted as a longstanding component of the Dow Jones Industrial Average. (Its gradual transition into digital products has helped it to partially recover.) Krispy Kreme was a spectacular market performer, climbing more than ninefold from its initial public offering in April 2000 to a peak of 49 in mid 2003. Then Wall Street's speculative darling turned into an ugly duckling. The stock plunged 90 percent to 3.35 in 2005 as it bucked up against the nation's low-carb diet craze and accounting investigations. It slowly recovered to 13, and then fell back to 7, a long way from 49. The bad news proved to be more fundamental than temporary.

A Charismatic Leader Occasionally, a key change in management can have long-term implications. The hiring of a charismatic chief executive with a big reputation by a company in trouble can have a strong impact on the stock. In February 2005 the embattled CEO of Hewlett Packard, Carla Fiorina, was replaced by the highly regarded Mark Hurd. In two years, the stock climbed from 20 to 49.

In the 1980s and 1990s, Al Dunlop enjoyed the reputation of being highly effective at reversing the fortunes of problem companies. His impressive rescue record included American Can, Lily Tulip, Crown Zellerbach, and Scott Paper. News of his hiring triggered big up-moves in those stocks. In Scott Paper, for example, the stock rose 225 percent in 18 months, increasing the company's market value by $63 billion. The press labeled him "Chainsaw Al, turn around artist and downsize champion." Humility was not his strong suit. He called himself "the best chief executive in America." (His ruthless policy of widespread layoffs made his name synonymous with the words "You're fired" long before Donald Trump.)

The day after it was announced that the troubled appliance maker Sunbeam had hired Dunlop for its new CEO, the stock rose nearly 10 percent to 18.63. It subsequently reached a high of 53 during his tenure. But Sunbeam was Dunlop's Waterloo. Vast payroll cuts and plant closings and elimination of most of its product line produced chaos within the company instead of profits. When the deterioration in its balance sheet, the departure of several top executives, and the expected loss from operations all became public, the stock plummeted to 6. This time it was Dunlop who was fired. So, like everything else in the field of investing, a strategy works (in this case, betting on a proven winner) until it doesn't.

A Blockbuster Product Companies are always introducing new merchandise. It's what provides the fuel for their growth, but there are few real, stand-alone, blockbuster products. When you think of the 3M Company you probably think of Scotch Tape and Post-Its. The company also happens to sell 55,000 other products. From time to time new products *do* come along that burst on the scene with such widespread, explosive appeal that they reenergize and sometimes transform a company. It's the type of news that can represent basic, fundamental change.

A good example is the iPod digital music player from Apple Computer. It took a year and a half before sales took off. Anyone who recognized early on that this was a product with huge potential that would likely boost sales of Apple's other products as well, made themselves a fortune. In the two-year period 2003–2004, Apple sold 10 million iPods, and doubled the sale of its desktop personal computers due to the increased iPod traffic. By July 2007, 70 million Americans owned iPods and the stock climbed over 148, up from 13 three years earlier.

> "At least 95 percent of what you read or hear (about the stock market) will be worthless. Watch the cooking or gardening channels on television if you want useful advice. Heed the words of comedienne Lily Tomlin, 'No matter how cynical you become, it's never enough to keep up.'"
>
> —*Burton Malkiel*

(The excitement surrounding the introduction of another new potential blockbuster product, the iPhone, didn't hurt the stock either.) Apple had become the undisputed king of the digital music mountain. It's clear the company will never be the same. Nor will the net worth of those who tuned in early.

The Surprise Element It's the surprise element in a news story that causes sudden sharp moves in a stock. If the surprise is a real shocker, the reaction can be dramatic, up or down. When the emotions subside and the dust settles, the gnawing question remains: Will this unexpected news have a fundamental, lasting impact on the company's future or is the effect likely to be temporary? That can be a very tough call. It may be years before the answer becomes clear.

In the devastating bear market of 2000–2002, Sirius Satellite Radio plummeted from 69 to under 0.40. Then, fueled by hype and a huge day trader following, the speculative favorite made a giant percentage recovery. It rose to 2.0 by mid-2004, doubled to 4.0 a few months later, and then doubled again, reaching 9.43 by early December. All this despite the fact the company was reporting widening losses with no profits expected until 2008 at the earliest. What the company did have was promise.

The bombshell news that raised expectations was the announcement that Sirius had lured popular shock jock Howard Stern away from AM radio with a $500 million, five-year contract starting in 2006. The company said it was confident that enough of Stern's loyal listeners would pay to listen to him on satellite radio to make the contract profitable. The hiring of a personality of the stature of Stern by the fledgling Sirius was considered a coup and a big step toward its goal of compelling programming. The Stern move was quickly followed by the signing of former Viacom president Mel Karmazin as the new CEO for Sirius and the announcement that SIRI had been added to the widely traded NASDAQ 100 index. The surprise back-to-back-to-back announcements gave Sirius a major infusion of credibility.

A Sirius Situation The news on Sirius illustrates an everyday dilemma for investors. How do you evaluate the long-term significance of headline news? Is the impact likely to be temporary or permanent? Is the news fundamental enough in nature to importantly affect future prospects for the company? Obviously, there's no way to know for sure.

However, there *are* a few things we *do* know: (1) The news is rarely as good or as bad as it sounds on release. (2) In the vast majority of cases, headline news is replaced by a succession of other related headlines, each one gradually fading in importance, each one hardly perceptible on a long-term chart of the stock's performance. (3) Seasoned, quality, large cap companies are, for the most part, less sensitive to news, both good and bad, than speculative companies. (4) It usually pays to wait till things quiet down before making a decision. Buyers of Sirius at the peak of the fever generated by the news saw the stock back off from 9.5 to 6.5 in a few weeks and then down below 3 in 2007. (5) No one stock has to be bought. There's always another stock and there's always another compelling story. (6) Whatever your decision, you will never be without those experts who think you're dead wrong.

Two years after the Stern-Karmazin news, speculators had to deal with another big question mark. In February of 2007, a merger was proposed by the only two satellite radio companies, Sirius and XM. The number of paid subscribers to both services continued to grow but heavy talent and marketing costs kept the red ink flowing. It was hoped a merger would reduce costs and give the subscriber a better product. Approval of the FCC and the Justice Department was needed but considered uncertain because of monopoly concerns. What *is* certain is that however the story unfolds, there will always be new questions in the future. It's a never-ending process, which is why they're called *speculations*.

Quality at Bargain Prices With the Sirius illustration, we are talking about the impact of seemingly good news. How do we assess the significance of bad news? For the investor, the dilemma is the same. On September 30, 2004, Merck announced it would voluntarily stop selling its blockbuster arthritis pain drug, Vioxx, because new data showed that it doubled the risk of heart attack and stroke in patients taking it longer than 18 months. The company also reduced its earnings forecast for the year. Less than three months later, on December 17, 2004, Pfizer dropped a similar bombshell when it reported a government-sponsored cancer study found higher risk of heart attack and stroke from high dosages of its arthritis pain killer, Celebrex. Both are high-quality, seasoned companies and leaders in their field. Both announcements were completely unexpected and, because of the surprise element, both stocks were clobbered.

Merck lost 28 percent of its value in one day, free-falling from 45.07 to 32.46 on the news. A month later it was lower still at 25.60, a five-year low (an example of where it paid for the bargain buyer to wait for the after-shocks). In the ensuing two and a half years, however, helped by some favorable court decisions, management changes, new drugs, and improved earnings prospects, Merck recovered to 55. It had doubled in price from its bad-news low, and by May of 2007 was selling well above where it was *before* the bombshell Vioxx news.

Pfizer lost 24 percent of its value the day the bad news came out on Celebrex. It plunged from 29.10 (it had been 38 earlier in the year) to a seven-year low of 21.99, but rallied to close the hectic session at 25.75. A year later it recovered to 29 but then settled back in the 24 to 27 range, not doing nearly as well as Merck. Apparently, Wall Street regarded Pfizer's problems as more long lasting. Yet in 2007, Pfizer declared its 40th consecutive dividend increase, yielding over 4 percent, sending a message that it may be down but it was far from out.

In the months following the sudden collapse of both Merck and Pfizer, there was a heated debate on Wall Street on whether to buy, sell, or hold the stocks. Bears argued that consumer distrust, lost revenue, sagging earnings, and potential heavy litigation exposure would severely limit the companies' growth for years to come. Bulls claimed that historically low price/earnings multiples represented outstanding value in blue-chip companies with strong balance sheets, high levels of free cash flow, good dividends, and other new products in the pipeline. Besides, doesn't "buy low" mean taking advantage of situations just like this? Unsettling news created an opportunity to buy quality merchandise at bargain prices.

The Same Nagging Questions At the end of the day, the investor is left with the same nagging question: Does the news represent a basic, fundamental change in the growth potential of the company? Or is the problem just a temporary bump in the road? Or is it somewhere in between, namely, an interruption in growth that will keep money tied up in a range-bound, stagnant stock for longer than you wish while other, better opportunities pass you by?

As always, there's no way to come up with a definitive answer at the time. However, the investor's decision has to be based, in part, on knowledge of his own temperament. How much patience is he able or willing to exercise, knowing there will likely be more unsettling headlines in the future? And another basic question: How much of that headline risk is already built into the depressed price of the stock?

One thing we do know is that the solidity and pedigree of the two companies greatly reduces the risk of any doomsday, bankruptcy, or break-up scenario. There is an essential difference between an unseasoned speculation like Sirius and a quality investment like Merck or Pfizer. The A-rated blue-chip stock (MRK and PFE), over time, will almost always come back from a bear market or from bad news; the short-on-earnings, long-on-promise speculation (SIRI) may recover and it may not. This is the basic distinction between investing and speculating: A depressed investment-grade stock will almost always recover in time; a speculation may climb back or it may not. In terms of comfort level, that's a big difference.

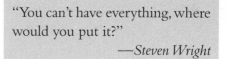
"You can't have everything, where would you put it?"
—*Steven Wright*

Non-News News The examples we've used in our discussion of the impact of news have involved sharp and sudden stock reactions to blockbuster news stories. However, most of the never-ending flood of daily news is routine, insignificant, and meaningless in terms of durable impact. It is important to PR firms, journalists, TV reporters, and traders because it gives them a means of making a living. To the long-term investor it is little more than filler and noise.

I'm talking about news of a penny increase in quarterly earnings, most acquisitions, litigation, layoffs, product recalls, strikes, management changes, broker buy and sell recommendations and up and downgrades, short interest, insider selling, and so on. Then there's the nonstop stream of statistics on the economy, including retail sales, car sales, home sales, durable goods orders, construction spending, industrial production, commodity prices, wholesale prices, inventories, jobless claims, consumer confidence, and so on.

All of these items serve to fill up airtime and newspaper space. Some may reach headline status and cause immediate moves in stocks or the market. But in and by themselves, they are mostly irrelevant in the big picture. Any sharp moves are usually blunted over time and look like no more than a blip on a long-term chart. Most of the time the stock or market will resume the course it was on before the news was released. Seldom is any one news story consequential enough to reverse a firmly entrenched trend.

I may be stretching my credibility by asking you to believe that earnings, sales, management, and the like are meaningless. Indulge me in just a bit more explanation; if I'm repeating myself it's because I want to avoid any possible misunderstanding of such an important subject.

Totality of the News The news topics I've mentioned—earnings, sales, cash flow, the economy, interest rates, inflation, government policy, and so on—are all important. They all matter. They matter a lot. They are what shape the underlying direction of a stock and the overall market. But there are few news stories that, standing alone, have long-term significance. What's important is repetition or the lack of it. The long term is made up of a lot of short terms. When one news story, let's say a report of higher earnings or a decline in the trade deficit, is confirmed or negated by the next news release and then the one after that, we begin to get a trend with some possible long-term consequence. Sometimes it takes years for such a trend to develop. Looking back we can say it is the *totality* of the news, the *continuity* of the news, the *cumulative effect* of the news as it is released from many sources over time that is meaningful.

Of course, every day there are investors and speculators who choose not to wait for a trend to develop or for news to be confirmed. They're acting on the assumption that the initial news is indicative of the future. Even more daring, others make their move *before* any news is released, in anticipation of it coming. The earlier the decision, the greater the risk and the greater the reward if proven right. It is only with the passage of time that we can know if the news is part of a significant ongoing pattern. However, in my opinion, few news stories, by themselves, require immediate action by the long-term investor.

The tendency of investors to hurt their performance by overreacting to news has been well documented. In a March 12, 2007, article in the *New Yorker* magazine titled "Reasonable Panic," James Surowiecki cites a famous experiment by psychologist Paul Andreassen: "Investors who selected a portfolio of stocks and then saw nothing but the stocks' changing prices managed their portfolios significantly better than investors who were also given a stream of news about the companies they'd invested in. The reason, Andreassen suggested, was that the media's tendency to overplay stories led investors to place too much weight on news that turned out to be of only transient importance."

What we have said about the irrelevance of most news does not apply to the short-term trader. Since the odds are against making money on a short-term basis, it is necessary for the trader to have everything he can going for him. One of those things is an up-to-the-minute awareness of what's going on. News is important to the trader, not because of its eventual significance, but because of its immediate impact. Whether the trader buys in anticipation of the news, on the news, or after the news (or for technical or chart reasons), it behooves him to stay informed.

Column A and Column B Every day there is always good and bad news on the market and on a stock. Let's call it column A and column B. We'll put all the bullish or positive news in column A, all the bearish or negative news in column B. The columns are never empty. Seven days a week, 24 hours a day, there's news in both columns ready to be referenced.

Sometimes the news is of an immediate nature such as an acquisition or the release of sales or earnings figures. That type of news goes at the top of the column. Sometimes the news is not as directly related to the company, such as weakness in a peer group or a sharp move in the overall market that day. That news is placed in the middle of the column. The items toward the bottom of the column are more general and long-term in nature: the popularity of the group with investors, a company's stock buyback program, a price/earnings ratio that's historically low, a friendly interest rate environment, a slowing economy, and so on.

And then there's the always-reliable profit taking on the news, and the news was already reflected in the price.

Because there is always a long list of items in both columns, investors and commentators, looking for logical reasons to explain what happened to a stock or to the market, are never at a loss for material. Whether the news is late-breaking and specific or ongoing and general, there are always items from column A and column B ready to be used by the evening news programs to make an irrational market sound rational.

It makes it easy for the commentator when there's a natural fit between the news on a stock and the performance of a stock. The connection is clear: New home sales are reported higher, home building stocks go up. The causal relationship is so obvious and so logical that none of the other items in column A have to be cited (even though they may be equally if not more pertinent).

However, when home sales soar and the home building stocks go down, the explanation shifts to column B and the negative items. Maybe it's fear of higher interest rates, or a disappointing unemployment report, or the decline in the overall market—or the old standby, profit taking in a stock whose price already reflects the news. Every day a myriad of stocks behave exactly the opposite of what you'd expect based on the news. The same day that a terrorist plot to blow up a commercial jet flying from England to the United States is reported, the airline stocks rally. Ford Motor reports a record $12.7 billion loss for 2006 and the stock closes higher. Henry Paulson, a favorite of Wall Street, called "the perfect fit" to lead the U.S. Treasury by *BusinessWeek,* is appointed to that key position and the market sells off sharply. The ever-present column A and column B enable reporters to come up with a reason to explain what would otherwise be inexplicable.

> "You're fortunate if 25 percent of what you know is true. And if you're right, the playing field is not level. The game is fixed and the house (Wall Street) always wins."
> —*Paul Farrell*

Same Story, Different Spin What makes the impact of news even more nebulous is this: Not only is there always good and bad news on a stock, but the news story itself almost always has both a positive and negative aspect. So the same news item can be placed in both columns at the same time—it depends on what spin you put on the story.

Let's say the price of oil goes down. That means lower inflation, which would usually mean a boost for bond prices. But let's say bonds go down, so we use the explanation in column B, which is that lower oil prices could spur growth in the economy, making it more likely the Fed will raise interest rates. Suppose oil prices go up. That's good news for the petroleum companies because it boosts profits. But it's bad news for the airlines because rising fuel costs squeeze earnings.

Let's say a company reports another in a string of quarterly losses. If the stock goes down, it's due to disappointment that the company still hasn't been able to climb into the black. If the stock goes up, it's because the loss was less than the previous quarter. Or say a company pays a big extra dividend. The stock goes up and the news is a slam-dunk candidate for column A. But suppose the stock goes down? Then we put a different spin on the news and put it in column B, where it's listed as disappointment that the funds weren't used more aggressively to help grow the company. Or perhaps traders had run up the stock in anticipation of the special dividend and sold on the news.

So the action in the stock comes first. Then the news on the stock is tailored to fit the move by accentuating either the positive or negative aspect of the story.

We Never Know for Sure   The truth is that, except in cases of obvious causality (when the news triggers an immediate and decisive reaction), we never know for sure why the market or a stock does what it does. Since a stock is bought and sold by thousands of individuals every day, it's reasonable to assume there is more than one reason causing its behavior. In fact, there can be a myriad of reasons, some knowable, others not knowable. The longer the list of possible explanations, the more likely it'll include at least one that's right.

What makes a precise explanation so difficult is that stocks often move for reasons that have nothing to do with the news. Buy and sell decisions are often motivated by a host of non-news-related, silent triggers that are rarely cited by the media. These include, but are not limited to, psychological factors such as the mood and confidence level of investors; the ongoing process of unwinding previous valuation excesses; the focus and direction of the overall market that day; a personal need to raise money or invest money by a deadline; the amount of cash reserves institutions have available for investment; the execution of investment strategies like rebalancing, dollar-cost averaging, hedging and arbitrage, stock buyback programs, secondary offerings, sympathy moves, tax considerations, short covering, chart breakouts, and other technical signals; and so on. These are all factors that can influence the daily movement of a stock as much or more than an earnings report, but you'll rarely find them in the headlines.

The influence of human emotion on the investment decision process cannot be overstated. The media may report, for example, that a 15 percent drop in profit margins triggered selling in XYZ Corp. However, it's likely that many of the sellers had no knowledge of the news. The reason they sold was the alarming action of the stock itself. The precipitous decline caused fear that the loss they already had would get a lot bigger. The heavy selling in the stock that day obviously meant a lot of people decided to throw in the towel before things got worse. That type of fear is highly contagious.

So is the desire to make easy money. There can be all kinds of fundamental reasons given to explain the rise in a stock, but the most important one may simply be the emotion triggered by the upside action of the stock itself. Almost every stock price has an emotional component. The motivation of investors who buy near tops and sell near bottoms has almost everything to do with emotions provoked by the action of the market itself and almost nothing to do with the news. It's likely that the irrelevance of news reaches its zenith at market tops and bottoms.

The Herd Mentality among Professionals Even the cool, detached, disciplined professional can be guilty of letting emotion influence his investment decisions. He, too, can display a herd mentality.

Robin Carpenter runs a firm called Carpenter Analytics that tracks hedge funds. The money managers that run hedge funds are perceived to be among the brainiest, most sophisticated on Wall Street. The typical wealthy hedge fund client is willing to give the manager 20 percent of the profits and a 2 percent fee to access his expertise. Mr. Carpenter said in the January 17, 2005 *Barron's* that tactical hedge funds have shown a tendency to rush to catch up with the market. When the funds have high relative stock exposure, the market tends to be near a short-term peak (i.e., they've bought near the top). Their action in the bond market can also be late. Carpenter says extreme bullishness in bonds by these super-savvy managers is even more predictive of short-term declines in the bond market than is their equity exposure. So sophistication does not preclude the influence of basic emotion.

Despite the dominant role of emotions in our decision making, the media cites only the news to explain what happens in the market. In the same way that doctors will often ignore diet in their diagnosis of an illness, writers and analysts pay little heed to the role of feelings in their commentary on the market. In their defense, we can say that doctors are not trained nutritionists nor are analysts trained psychologists. What's more, emotions are impossible to quantify.

Interestingly, there *are* psychologists who have focused on investor behavior. There is a growing body of literature in the field, which has come to be known as *behavioral finance* or *behavioral economics*. One of the most widely quoted on the subject is economist Richard Thaler. He has studied the different ways in which people behave with their money and how their actions fall into predictable patterns. (See Roger Lowenstein's *New York Times Magazine* article, "Exuberance Is Rational," January 11, 2001.) Psychologists Amos Tversky and Daniel Kahneman are also pioneers in the behavioral finance field, best known for their finding that people experience more pain from losses than pleasure from gains. Specifically, their research showed that investors feel the anguish of taking losses two to two and a half times as strongly as they feel the joy of taking profits.

The psychology of investing is a relatively new field with limited exposure beyond professional journals. If "know thyself" is one of the keys to investment success, then those who seek out this behavioral information will be much the better for it.

> "The only reason to invest in the market is because you think you know something others don't."
> —*R. Foster Williams*

The Human Need to Find Causes Over the years we have been conditioned by Wall Street and the financial media to believe that stocks move up and down for identifiable reasons. The perception is that somewhere out there is news to explain what happened. When it's reported that the market declined on news of a slowdown in the housing market, what's not mentioned is that the day before, equally bad news on housing was the big story of the day and the market went up.

Using news to explain stock moves is often flawed reasoning but it permeates the news industry and, by extension, the investment public. *Barron's* columnist Michael Santoli says, "Drawing straight causal relationships between news and market action is usually folly, a product of an errant human need to conjure patterns where they don't exist."

As we have suggested, the truth is that we often don't know the whys, and that on a long-term basis most breaking news stories, in and by themselves, simply don't matter. In theory, if all reporters aimed for accuracy and they had no time or space constraints, every time they talked about a stock or the overall market, they would say something like this: "The Dow or XYZ Corp. went up 1¾ points. Some of the factors which may or may not have contributed to the rise include . . ." Then, at least, the listener/reader would have some sense that explanations of why the market or stocks do what they do are educated guesses at best.

This, of course, is not going to happen. The media is not going to know all the possible reasons and if they did, the report would be endless and tedious. The only way a summary of what happened in the market can be honest and accurate is to report prices and news without trying to establish causal links between them. "The Dow went up today . . . Biggest point movers were . . . In the news background . . ." Or, if the news about a company and its stock price are reported together, the reporter could say, "GM went down a point; it reported higher earnings," or "GM went down a point; it reported higher earnings and a rise in insider selling," and he could add, still further, "The stock has been up 3 points the past week." Baseball purists long for the facts-only, understated commentary of legendary sportscasters like Curt Gowdy and Vin Scully, who simply related to the listener what was happening on the field without hype, analysis, or speculation.

What's scary is that so many writers and TV reporters don't have a clue. They actually believe what they're saying and that what they're saying matters. As the French novelist Anatole France said, "If 50 million people say (believe) a foolish thing, it's still foolish." This is not a conscious effort by the media to be deceptive. It simply knows no better. Its members are trained as professional writers and broadcasters, not as students of the market. How can we expect a more enlightened media when so many in the securities industry itself, especially brokers, believe the news of the day is important to their customers?

Actually, It's the Divorce Settlement The media and, by extension, the public it serves are satisfied that if a news event provides a logical explanation for what's happened, then it must be so. When it's reported that XYZ Corp. went down due to a Merrill Lynch forecast of lower earnings, there's little awareness that there could be 20 other possible reasons, maybe more. (I say this after 25 years of reporting on the stock market via radio, TV, and newspapers.) In the case of XYZ Corp., the actual major depressant on the stock was the sale of a large block of thinly traded stock by a corporate officer who needed the money to pay off his irate wife's divorce settlement. But weakness in the stock caused by a lower earnings forecast sounds perfectly logical. There is no reason for the reporter or the listener to question its accuracy.

The result: Every day what is unknowable (why the market or a stock does what it does) is presented to the investor as knowable. The myth has been perpetuated for so long that it's simply taken for granted. It is so routine, so pervasive, and so believable, there is no reason for the investing public—senators, doctors, teachers, businessmen, factory workers, and so on—to suspect that much of what is presented as fact is more likely fiction, or at best, speculation. Hopefully in the future, as the media becomes more market savvy, its reporting will reflect what's so sadly missing today: an awareness and respect for the primacy and mystery of the stock market.

In the meantime, what it boils down to is that we don't know what we don't know. And how can we? The concept that the market sets its own agenda and the news follows doesn't fit in a world of 24/7 news overkill. How can the long-term investor believe that most news doesn't matter when there's an army of people in the media who think it's so important to keep him instantly informed? Venerable *Barron's* wordsmith

Alan Abelson describes the dilemma this way: "There is an infernal bombardment of billions of bits and pieces of unrequested information that rain down on us each and every day—a witless welter of facts and figures, words and piffle . . ." (*Give 'Em Shelter*, June 20, 2005).

However, once we are able to keep the noise from the media in proper perspective, we have a big leg up. Famed portfolio manager Peter Lynch, who made Fidelity's Magellan Fund a household word, makes this observation about tuning out the static (I call it his "snore and ignore" rule): "When it comes to predicting the market, the important skill is not listening but snoring. The trick is not to learn to trust your gut feelings, but rather to discipline yourself to ignore them" (Morningstar.com, Course 507, *Ignoring Mr. Market*). If we can accept the market for the illogical cnigma that it is, we can more easily stop looking for short-term answers and focus, instead, on the long term. By letting the passage of time work in our favor, we can be successful without having to know the answers. And we can put the news in proper perspective, using it to satisfy our intellectual and social need to be informed and entertained but not as a basis for understanding the day-to-day action in the market.

Technicians, incidentally, make it easy. They ignore the news. When a stock goes up, it's simply because there were more buyers than sellers; if it goes down, there were more sellers than buyers. But the terminology is misleading. If there are more buyers, where do they get the sellers to buy from? The answer, of course, is that as a stock goes up in price, more sellers emerge. There's always a seller if the price goes high enough and there's always a buyer if it goes low enough. So, for purposes of clarity, the expression should not be "more buyers than sellers" but rather something like "more upward pressure than downward pressure." I only mention this in case there are readers as confused as I was when I first heard this expression and took it literally.

Extra Ammunition I've written more about the impact of news than any other topic so far. It's partly because the news surrounds us; investors have to deal with it every day. But it's mostly because there are deeply ingrained perceptions about the influence of the news that I believe are wrong. Because these perceptions are so pervasive and entrenched, I need extra ammunition to make my case. The next paragraph is my summation and final shot.

Every day there are countless news stories and every day stocks go up and down. Most of the time, the relationship between the two happenings is less than certain; oftentimes it is nil. Frequently, however, there is an immediate and direct impact, especially when the news involves surprise. There are examples of this happening every day. On Tuesday, January 3, 2006, the minutes of the latest Federal Reserve Board meeting hit the newswires at 2 P.M. They indicated the Fed would soon stop raising interest rates. The flat market went vertical, the Dow soared 130 points by the 4 P.M. close. Because these moves in stocks and the overall market are dramatic and because they can be explained logically by the news, they make the headlines. They are what we hear and read about.

This collection of short-term reactions to the news constitutes the market's story for that day. Every headline has its 15 minutes of fame. Like a meteor racing across the heavens, it shines brightly before it withers and then disappears, replaced by tomorrow's headline. There is an ever-growing graveyard for forgotten headlines and it is rarely visited. Of course, most news stories do not reach headline status; they fade into irrelevance even faster.

However, before they fade, they leave a dot. Over a period of time, those dots may or may not form a pattern or a trend. Alone, they are barely discernable; together they form a glow that gradually increases in intensity. When and if the path of dots becomes clear and unmistakable in direction, we can look back and say the news was, indeed, relevant. The great majority of the time, the dots are meaningless.

No discussion on the subject of business news would be complete without commenting on the role of CNBC. I'll save that for later (see Chapter 4, conviction number 5.).

> "No one ever got rich fighting the fed or the tape."
> —*Unknown*

6. The Durability of Major Trends Is Underestimated

A tough part of an investment analyst's job is forecasting change, especially trying to predict when that change will occur. What makes it difficult is that at any given time, the odds favor a trend in force remaining in force. In its early stages, it's unclear whether a developing trend will last. But once it takes hold, once it gets its sea legs and gets used to its surroundings, it's usually reluctant to go away. The more it hangs around, the stronger, the more confident, and the more anchored it becomes.

This type of stability is often viewed with skepticism by an investment world that is in constant flux. It's a world where stocks, groups, and styles continually move into and then out of favor. It's a world of shifting currents with a myopic focus on the short term. It's the kind of world that looks mostly for endings, not lastings. And it's the kind of world that typically forecasts the demise of any trend that perseveres to multiyear status.

The truth is that well-entrenched trends, whether they apply to the overall market, stocks, interest rates, inflation, or the economy, are exceedingly difficult to reverse. They usually last longer and go further than most everybody expects. The stock market went from Dow 769 in 1982 to Dow 11,722 in early 2000, an *18-year* bull market. During that time period, thousands of stocks mirrored the Dow, each one in its own long-lasting bull market. Interest rates on the 10-year U.S. Treasury bond declined from almost 16 percent in 1981 to 3.07 percent in June 2003. That's a *22-year* bull market in bonds (as yields go down, bond prices go up). Inflation dropped from 13.5 percent in 1980 to 1.9 percent in 1998. That's an *18-year* downtrend in inflation. The economic expansion that started in 1991 ended *10 years* later in 2001 (after a brief recession, another expansion started in early 2002). The price of gold dropped from $870 an ounce in January 1980 to $250 in 2001, a *22-year* bear market in gold (it has since recovered to a high of over $700).

Perhaps the persistent domination of value, small cap, and real estate investment trust (REIT) stocks is the most impressive example of major trend durability. All three defied a loud and growing consensus of naysayers. Each of the past few years has started with forecasts of "this year large caps will be the place to be." In the meantime, by mid-2006, small stocks were entering their eighth straight year of outperforming big caps by a wide margin (1975 to 1983 was also an eight-year winning streak for small caps). And by year-end 2006, despite widespread predictions of their demise, value stocks extended their supremacy over growth stocks and REITs surpassed the S&P 500 Index, both for seven straight years. This meant, of course, equally long losing streaks for large caps and growth stocks. The longer the streak, the more numerous and certain are the forecasts that it will end.

Of course, none of these were straight-line trends. There are always corrections or countertrends, some quite long, along the way. But in all of these instances (and the list of examples is far from complete), the primary, underlying trend prevailed. Once grooved in, major trends often show amazing durability. Their staying power is consistently underestimated by Wall Street (which may or may not have something to do with the fact that forecasting change is likely to generate more business than the status quo).

Like everything else in the investment world, there are always exceptions. By definition, a major trend is major because it has achieved a certain maturity, but not all major trends last beyond expectations. What we can say is that the longer it endures, the more likely the principal of the durability of major trends will apply. It's similar to the reasoning behind projected life expectancy. The 60-year-old male with a life expectancy of 80, once he turns 80, is expected to live another eight years and then another five after that.

This is Gonna Last

Over the years that I've followed established trends in the market, I've often said to myself, "This is gonna last a lot longer." Sometimes I'm wrong, but more often than not, widespread expectations of the demise of an aging trend prove premature. Part of investing is dealing with extremes. Extended markets typically become more extended, and extended trends in individual stocks tend to do the same. Forecasts of a revival in the lagging large cap growth stocks will, indeed, prove correct. Other poorly performing asset classes and investment styles will also emerge. But that doesn't erase the fact that over a long period of years poor investment decisions have been made based on false expectations.

I believe an awareness of this concept of major trend durability can be a big help to investors. It can prevent buying and/or selling too soon. Still, it is seldom discussed. Its neglect probably has something to do with the obsession of Wall Street and the financial media on news of the here and now. The short-term focus is so intense and all-pervasive that it blots out what really matters—the long-term trend.

One caveat: In terms of the stock market's overall direction, downtrends typically don't last as long as uptrends, so the durability principle is less likely to apply. The shorter life of market declines means they have less time to dig in (the great crashes of 1929–1932 and 2000–2002 both lasted less than three years). A sideways or range-bound market, however, *can* last and last. It took the Dow 17 years, from 1965 to 1982, before it broke out of the 600 to 1,000 range.

Most gurus are forecasting modest single-digit gains in the major indexes on average in the foreseeable future. If they're right, the dura-bility principle will apply to a sideways, trading-range trend, not a sus-tained move up or down. But there are always deeply entrenched trends outside the market indexes themselves. They might include asset classes, market sectors, styles, groups, interest rates, inflation, gold, the dollar, and so on. There's always something going on that's going to last longer than everyone thinks.

If you can develop the patience and discipline to stay with the major trend, and are not faked out by the false countermoves along the way, the odds favor your being pleased and surprised at just how far it will take you. A quiet but confident awareness of this recurring phenomenon in mar-ket history will give you an edge. It will prevent you from disturbing solid positions and help keep you on the right side of the market. And it will make it easier to put into proper perspective the daily onslaught of short-term oriented news and opinion.

> "It is one of the great paradoxes of the stock market that what seems too high usually goes higher and what seems too low, usually goes lower."
>
> —*William O'Neil*

Chapter 4

Seven Core Convictions

A lifetime on Wall Street has left me with strong feelings on what to do and what not to do to succeed as an investor. A clear understanding of the core convictions discussed in this chapter will help put the investment odds in your favor. Along with the "absolutes" from the proceeding chapter, these six principles should be seared into the consciousness of all investors.

1. Asset Allocation Is Key to Managing Risk

There have been volumes written on the subject of asset allocation. It is the mantra of financial planners. If you type "asset allocation" into the Yahoo! search box, you'll come up with over seven million references. I can't add anything here that hasn't been said better elsewhere. Instead, I'll briefly cover the bare essentials, make some observations about risk, and explain why I think the concept of asset allocation is so important for investors to understand.

Investing is a *risky* business. Some investors prefer to maximize risk in exchange for the prospect of maximum returns. Others want to keep risk to an absolute minimum and are willing to settle for minimum gains in return for greater safety of principal. Most of us are somewhere in between. It all depends on where we're coming from—our age, our goals, our finances, and our temperament. One way or another, though, we have to deal with risk. There's probably nothing more important that we do as investors than control risk. As the saying goes, "Return *of* capital ranks right up there with return *on* capital."

Probably the most effective way of limiting big losses in a portfolio is through asset allocation. The consensus view is that spreading money over different asset classes is the single most important factor in determining investment results over time. That's why so much is said and written about proper asset allocation and why I put it on the top of my list of core convictions.

The concept is uncomplicated. If all your eggs are in one basket and you've got the right basket, you're a big winner. If your eggs are in the wrong basket, you can lose everything. Spread them around and gains are likely to more than offset losses over time because of the market's historic upward bias. Different asset classes have different degrees of risk—the greater the risk, the greater the potential return. Stocks are riskier than bonds, which are riskier than cash.

Roger Ibbotson is chairman and founder of the Chicago research firm Ibbotson Associates, which is owned by Morningstar, and a professor of finance at the Yale School of Management. He says, "For the average investor, the asset allocation mix that's chosen—what percentage of stocks, bonds, cash, and other asset classes they include in their portfolio—accounts for 100 percent of their return level . . . asset allocation is the first and most important step in building a diversified portfolio" (PathToInvesting.com, *Allocate Your Assets,* 2006).

Those investors who owned stocks but not bonds or cash during the crippling bear market of 2000–2002 suffered severe losses. Those who owned bonds as well as stocks took much less of a hit because bonds went up as stocks went down. These two major classes of assets don't always move in opposite directions but they often do (a declining economy is friendly to bonds, unfriendly to stocks; an expanding economy is bullish for stocks but bearish for bonds). So, in general, owning bonds or other fixed-income securities moderates the risk of owning only stocks. When stocks are rising, bonds can be a drag on performance, but less so because of the income they generate and because, over time, stocks tend to gain more than bonds lose.

The Ultimate Simple Portfolio

Probably the purest way to apply the principle of asset allocation is to buy a total stock market index fund and a total bond market index fund. This would be the ultimate in portfolio simplicity; it would provide exposure to thousands of stocks and bonds with just two securities. You would probably want to adjust the ratios gradually over the years, let's say moving from 60 percent stocks—the riskier class—and 40 percent bonds to just the opposite as you approach retirement. (Life cycle or target funds are mutual funds that will do this for you. See the section in Chapter 8 titled "Life Cycle/Target Retirement Funds.")

Could such a no-frills, two-index fund approach compete favorably with more sophisticated portfolios containing many asset classes? It's certainly possible, especially if you're like me and assign a money value to keeping it simple. The consensus view, however, is that the magic simplicity number is three, not two, with international exposure the third ingredient.

In addition to stocks and bonds, other asset classes often interact with each other in a broadly predictable manner. When the dollar goes down, gold often goes up; when value stocks are in vogue, growth stocks are apt to languish; commodity prices rise and bonds, worried about inflation, decline; or when the Dow drops sharply, unhedged foreign currency bonds are likely to rise. The key word is *correlation*. One asset class is said to have a low correlation with another, meaning they are unlikely to move in unison, usually for logical, fundamental reasons. Asset allocation is all about taking advantage of these correlations to reduce risk and to capture strength wherever and whenever it exists.

Like other investment principles, this one works most of the time, but not all the time. If nothing else, the market is perverse and unpredictable, which means individual asset classes at any given time may not act in their traditional role. The many asset classes cover a wide range of risk, everything from high-risk classes like commodities, small cap stocks, high yield bonds, and real estate investment trusts to low-risk classes like U.S. Treasuries, bank CDs, high-grade preferreds, or cash.

For even greater diversification, we can add classes such as emerging markets, international funds, precious metals, developed countries, and foreign bonds. And for the wealthiest, most sophisticated investors there are such esoteric, hard-to-research areas as Australian agriculture, Thailand stocks, and Istanbul real estate. By picking and choosing different categories and deciding how much to invest in each, we can influence, if not fine-tune, our risk exposure. And because we can access an entire asset class with just one security, we can do all this without ever having to pick a stock.

During his tenure as longtime head of Harvard University's $29 billion endowment fund, Jack Meyer compiled an outstanding performance record. He was labeled "the Mickey Mantle of the investing world." His core strategy was diversification with 11 different asset classes in his fund. He put as much money into foreign and emerging stocks combined as he did into U.S. stocks. He owned commodities, especially timber. And his bond portfolio covered not only conventional U.S. bonds but also foreign bonds, high-yield bonds, treasury inflation-protected securities (TIPS), and emerging-market debt. When asked by *BusinessWeek* (*How to Invest Like Harvard,* December 27, 2004) how individuals might learn from Harvard's experience, he said, "Get diversified. Come up with a portfolio that looks a little like ours and covers a lot of asset classes." (His other three recommendations: keep your fees low, pay attention to taxes, and invest for the long term.)

> "There's nothing wrong with cash. It gives you time to think."
> —*Robert Prechter*
>
> "It's easy to make a buck. It's a lot tougher to make a difference."
> —*Tom Brokaw*

Making Lots of Bets

Peter Bernstein, 85-year-old investment guru, talked about risk and diversification in a February 6, 2005, interview on MarketWatch.com:

There's a tendency among individual investors either to take too much risk or not enough. . . . In every decision we make, it's worth saying how much does the outcome of this decision matter to me, and if it doesn't turn out the way I want, what are the consequences. . . . An investor should have enough different kinds of bets so that no matter what happens, he's not going to be wiped out and so that he'll benefit if one turns out to be a real hot hit. . . . Diversification does not mean holding 100 stocks instead of 20. They're all going to go up more or less together. You want to be sure that you have all kinds of outcomes covered. You don't know what the next big winner is but you want to be exposed to that possibility. Somebody once said to me that you're not diversified unless you're uncomfortable with what you own. If everything is what you're familiar with, it's probably going to go up and down together.

Few investment subjects trigger more heated debate than that of diversification. If you believe in the vital importance of asset allocation, then, by definition, you're an advocate of diversification. If you recommend model index fund portfolios, which I do in this book, then by definition you believe in diversification. In fact, for decades, the virtues of diversification have been promoted as the cornerstone of successful investing. Nevertheless, some of the world's greatest investors are adamantly opposed to diversification.

Warren Buffett and George Soros, both born in 1930 and both among the world's most renowned investors, do not diversify. Over 50 percent of Buffett's Berkshire Hathaway portfolio is in just four stocks (see Chapter 9, the section titled "Piggybacking the Masters"). Buffett believes diversification makes little sense for those who know what they're doing. Charlie Munger, 83, Buffett's partner for over 45 years, says, "The academics have done a terrible disservice to intelligent investors by glorifying the idea of diversification" (Kiplinger.com, December 2005). The same sentiment is voiced by 93-year-old money manager Seth Glickenhaus: "The greatest error made in Wall Street is diversification. Diversification inevitably leads to mediocrity and average performance" (*Barron's,* September 11, 2006).

Whether you diversify or not depends a lot on your temperament, your tolerance for risk, and mostly your skill as a stockpicker. The less you have of the latter, the more you're going to need luck. The odds of being successful without diversifying are astronomically better if you're working with the same brains as Buffett and Soros. If you're not, I'd stay with diversification.

A discussion of asset allocation often includes categories that, strictly speaking, may not be defined as asset classes but nevertheless are lumped under that umbrella heading. Categories such as *investment style* (value, blend, growth), *investment sectors* (e.g., drugs, utilities, Internet), and geographic regions (e.g., Europe, Asia, Latin America) are used interchangeably with traditional asset classes. The overlapping can be confusing. The thing to remember is that all of these categories are legitimate options for achieving diversification and risk control in a portfolio.

Rebalancing

Even a cursory discussion of asset allocation such as this would be incomplete without touching on the subject of rebalancing. The two concepts go hand in hand. Like asset allocation, rebalancing is an important means of managing risk and increasing long-term return potential.

Over time, your actual asset allocation will stray from your desired percentages because different asset classes will experience different rates of return. As one asset increases in value, another loses value. Periodic rebalancing (usually annually)—that is, moving money from the asset that's appreciated to the one that's declined—restores the portfolio to its proper alignment. As a practical matter, maintaining the exact alignment of each asset class, whether it be 29 percent, 35 percent, or 41 percent, is probably not that crucial. What counts is that you have exposure to the asset class you want and that you stay with it.

Rebalancing is not an easy exercise because we are often reluctant to let go of stocks that are working for those that are not. In fact, committing to a program of selling winners to buy laggards can seem unnatural. "It's always going to feel bad," says financial planner Harold Evensky of Coral Gables, Florida. But it's a practice that forces us to buy low and sell high, not a bad discipline to get used to when it comes to investing. Keep in mind, rebalancing does not involve big changes. After trimming, you still own most of your winning positions. It's a procedure that will not always produce the desired result but, if you stick with it, most of the time it will. Anything that works in the market more often than not is worth doing.

Gut Feeling Is Not Good Enough

If we don't pay attention to managing risk, if we just go with our gut feeling and if we guess wrong, the game can be over. Asset allocation and rebalancing keeps us in the game. It increases the chances of our participating in the good things that always happen in the market sometime and somewhere. Here's how Peter Bernstein puts it in the MarketWatch.com interview cited earlier: "It's more important to think about risk and make sure that you survive than to try to be right. To be able to survive is really the key to riches in the long run—to know that you're sufficiently diversified and have enough ability to recoup at the end of bad times to take advantage of the good times."

In Chapter 6, rebalancing is discussed further, and in Chapter 7 you'll find 28 model portfolios that illustrate the use of asset allocation. Each portfolio is recommended by a well-known expert in the field and includes specific securities and their weightings.

A final note on the topic of risk control: There are times in market history when there is little defense against high risk. These are times when valuations go to extremely high levels. At such intervals, it's not *if* but *when* will the market fall? Everyone knows a substantial drop is coming but after a while, because it doesn't come, the "this time it's different" mentality takes over. The scary part is that when it does come, there's no place to hide. If it's really nasty, the promised protection from uncorrelated asset classes disappears. Everything gets dragged down (with exceptions being bonds, option strategies, and short-selling).

In the market's recent uninterrupted eight-month advance (July 2006 to February 2007), valuations became excessive, especially in fields like emerging markets and commodities. Junk bonds didn't yield that much more than

> "In looking at a portfolio as a whole . . . you need securities which don't go up and down together."
> —*Harry Markowitz, Nobel Laureate in Economics*

U.S. Treasuries. Speculators, caught up in the fever, bought risky assets, without being paid for the risk. Then suddenly, on February 27, 2007, the Dow plummeted 416 points and the S&P lost $452 billion of its market value in one day. It is probably fair to say that the greatest danger investors face is navigating those markets, or sectors or stocks that are priced as if they held no risk.

2. Proper Entry Level Is Crucial

Buy low, sell high—hardly a bulletin. Self-evident, deceptively simple advice that is as difficult to implement as it is obvious—especially the first half. There is no "sell high" unless first there's a "buy low."

Next to the proper allocation of your assets, the most important thing you can do as an investor is to acquire those assets at a reasonable cost. Walter McCormick, portfolio manager for Evergreen Investments, says, "Finding the optimal entry point is key to any investment strategy. The only protection you get as an investor is by buying it right." (*Barron's,* May 15, 2006). Legendary investor Warren Buffett says, "At Berkshire Hathaway we buy businesses only when purchases can be made at prices that offer us the prospect of a reasonable return on our investment" (2004 Annual Report to shareholders).

Benjamin Graham, in his 1949 classic *The Intelligent Investor,* set forth his margin of safety concept. He believed that buying stocks on the cheap offers significant protection against any potential bad news. I prefer the word *reasonable* to *low* or *cheap* because it is more inclusive. If I can buy something at a reasonable price or within a reasonable buying range, it may be somewhat higher than at a *low* price, but it still should leave ample room for profit. As a buyer, *reasonable* gives me more flexibility than *low* and makes a trade more doable. (We'll tackle the question, "What is reasonable?" shortly.)

If it's simply common sense that buying stocks at a reasonable price is important, why go on about it? The reason is because it's more than important, it's crucial. But because it is so obvious, it doesn't get hammered home the way it should. In my view, more than any one factor except asset allocation, a reasonable entry level is key to investment success. Here's why.

You can buy the highest quality stock, the bluest of the blue chips, but if you buy it high, you can sit forever before you get your money back.

Investors who bought IBM at 175 in 1987 (pre-split) had to wait *10 years* before they saw that price again. 3M sold at 91 in 1973 and didn't reach that level again until 1985, *12 years* later. (Interestingly, both stocks did recover and go on to new highs, whereas a speculative stock may or may not have done so. Thus the essential difference between quality and speculation.)

Buying a stock at a reasonable price, then, makes all the difference in terms of the length of time you may have to hold it. Value stock guru Robert Olstein (of Olstein Financial Alert Fund) says, "The only thing that counts is paying the right price. If you pay the wrong price for a good company, you may have a bad stock" (Barron's, *The Price of Victory,* February 20, 2006). Buying at the right price can avoid the interminable years of stressful waiting that comes from buying high, riding the stock all the way down, and then (hopefully) all the way back up again. The same thing applies to bonds. Dan Fuss, manager of the top-performing Loomis Sayles Bond Fund, says, "Ninety percent of your focus has to be on buying the bonds at the right price point, the right time. If you do that, the sell side will take care of itself. The right price is the key" (Barron's, *A Global Quest For Yield,* January 9, 2006).

Buying low has to top the list of things that are easier said than done. The allocation of assets requires minimum judgment because there are many models to guide you. Buying at a reasonable price, on the other hand, requires an ability and discipline that most of us don't have. In fact, investors generally put the most money in stocks at the highest prices and the least at the lowest prices. Instead of buying during quiet times in a reasonable buying range, most investors buy amid the fever and excitement of rising prices. As a result, they can go through an entire bull market and lose money.

Investors who do wait for weakness to buy may not wait long enough. Yale professor and author Robert Shiller says, "Just because prices are more reasonable than they were, doesn't mean they're reasonable" (Money.CNN.com, *Fortune,* "We're Still Too Exuberant," December 17, 2005). And if the market is in a confirmed downtrend, it may not be the best time to buy. Reportedly, three out of four stocks follow the market's overall trend.

What's Reasonable?

What is a reasonable price? There are probably as many answers as there are analysts. As we have discussed at length, different advisers can look at the same security and come to directly opposite conclusions. In doing so, each uses his favorite set of criteria. The whole subject of valuation is a murky area with few absolutes. Probably the best we can do, if we're doing it ourselves, is to make an informed guess. *Informed* means consideration of the traditional statistical yardsticks as well as factors that go beyond the stock itself. In deciding what is a reasonable price, we tend to rely on statistical guidelines but, in the end, it's more of a subjective decision that has to do with a lot more than numbers.

But numbers is where we usually begin. The most widely used valuation tool is the price earnings ratio. If a stock's price/earnings (P/E) multiple has ranged between 8 and 22 and it's now selling at 12 times its expected annual earnings per share, we can reasonably conclude, based on this statistic alone, that it is reasonably priced. Obviously, it's not that simple. There may be a myriad of other factors to consider that make this number meaningless, if not misleading. For example, the explosive rise of China as a key market for American products may justify a higher P/E than in the past for a Starbucks or a Yahoo!.

Comparing the price of a stock with the price it sold for in the past is another popular but flawed valuation tool. If the historic range is, let's say, 18 to 70, and it's now 24, we can conclude, based on this one statistic, that it's a good value. That may or may not be a valid conclusion, depending on what else is going on. The common wisdom is that it's not where a stock has been but where it's going that counts. It's unlikely that the reasons why the stock sold at 70 some years ago prevail today. As prospects change, along with the market climate, valuations change. That's why a stock may be cheaper at 30 than at 24.

Besides the relative price of a stock and its earnings multiple, there are a host of other statistics that are commonly used to help measure value. Each analyst has his favorite. Some of them include return on equity, price to cash flow, price to free cash flow, price to book value, price to sales ratio, price to earnings growth (PEG) ratio, price to debt ratio, market capitalization to total revenues ratio, price to cash and debt ratio, dividend yield (dividend divided by price), dividend payout ratio, inventory to sales ratio, debt to equity ratio, current ratio, and so on. These figures can be compared with what they were in the past, with what they are today for other companies in the field, and with what they may be in the future under certain assumptions.

This is the stuff that helps analysts and accountants earn their salaries. Their interpretation of the data may vary widely and their findings may or may not help in actually determining value. (The use of screens available on financial web sites is a common measurement tool, with some stock screens allowing searches based on more than 100 criteria. More on screens in Chapter 9.) As a practical matter, most of us have neither the training nor the inclination to dig into long pages of financial data and draw meaningful conclusions.

> "No stock is overvalued if it's going up."
>
> —*Jim Cramer*

Beyond the Numbers

And even if we did, we'd just be scratching the surface. In deciding whether a stock is reasonably priced, we should expand our scope beyond the company's statistics. There's a long list of market-related, economic, and psychological factors that must also be considered.

Some, but by no means all, of the factors on that list might include the current market climate (bullish, bearish, neutral), the consensus outlook for the market, the current condition and consensus forecast for the economy, the level of interest rates current and anticipated, the level of inflation current and anticipated, investor sentiment (fearful, turned off, cautious, complacent, hopeful, confident, optimistic, exuberant), the current administration's agenda including fiscal policy (taxes), geopolitical risks, strength or weakness of the dollar, status of the industry the stock is in (in or out of favor), size of the short interest, insider activity and stock buybacks, and so on. Additional factors to consider relative to the company itself, over and above the internal statistics, might include the visibility of future earnings, the consistency of past earnings, the quality and reputation of management including dependability of earnings forecasts, the amount of stock owned by management, the position of the company within its industry, how the company is regarded by its competitors, new products and services coming on line, litigation problems, ease of entry into the business, and the technical condition of the stock.

This is not to imply that all or even some of these factors have to be considered before buying a stock—only that there are times when any one or any combination might be key to judging price levels. For example, investors are usually willing to pay higher multiples for a stock when interest rates and inflation are expected to be low. Favorable tax treatment of dividends makes an income stock worth more. Prospects of a company being bought out might make you more willing to pay up for its stock, whereas you'd likely want a discount for a company facing ongoing litigation.

No matter how thoroughly you research, it still comes down to an informed guess. Even if you know everything there is to know, there's no way you can predict how the market will react to what you know. This is why some investors simply satisfy themselves that a stock is selling at the low end of its historic price/earnings multiple range, and let it go at that. Others want to make the guess as informed as possible and do more digging, while still others will just watch a stock for a long time, get to know it well, and develop a feel for the way it acts.

Wait for It to Come to You

Whatever the approach, whatever efforts are made, it's a worthwhile endeavor because proper entry level is so crucial. There's an old Wall Street maxim: "A stock well bought is half sold." You must buy a stock in a reasonable buying range to avoid being an involuntarily locked-in, long, long-term investor. If the stock doesn't come to you, if it doesn't enter your buying range, turn away. There's always another stock.

Once you've bought, you'll need lots of patience. Stocks purchased at depressed or semidepressed levels are, by definition, unloved and out of favor. Unpopular stocks can stay unpopular for a long time. The wait can be tedious and frustrating. There will be times when it seems like everything is going up but your stock. But through it all, you've got one big thing going for you: You bought the stock at the right price. If you're lucky, you may not have to wait that long.

Because of their broad appeal, you'll likely be dealing with index funds. It's just as important with index funds as it is with stocks that you buy without reaching. Let's say you've accumulated a portfolio of index funds for retirement. Let's say further that when that long-awaited retirement day comes, you find yourself having to sell in a bear market (your luck!). If you exercised discipline on the buy side, chances are you're still going to be okay. Of course, if you take a dollar-cost-averaging approach and invest a fixed sum at regular intervals, a lot of the guesswork is eliminated from the "when to buy" conundrum. I say more about dollar cost averaging and a lot more about indexing in the pages ahead.

For every market approach, there's an opposite approach that can also work. Instead of buying low and selling high, there are those who look to buy high and sell higher. They're called momentum buyers and instead of looking for bargains, they typically find their buy candidates on the new high list. These are stocks that are often traders' favorites, the hot stocks that often dot the most active list and capture the headlines.

The momentum buyer, more speculator than investor, relies on two basic principles. First, a high-profile stock that's barreling ahead to new highs or that breaks out on big volume, is more likely to extend its uptrend than to peak with his buy order. Second, there are always likely to be others who are greedy and willing to buy from him at even higher prices (the "greater fool" theory). Obviously, there comes a time when the momentum dies. At that point the greatest fool becomes an involuntary long-term holder.

Admittedly, much of what's really important to know about investing is common sense and/or common knowledge. Basic tenets I've discussed up to now like "nobody knows," "there are no experts," "there are always opposite opinions," "the market is the final arbiter," "diversification is key," "buy low," and so on, are not exactly thunderbolts of insight. But my 40 years of experience with investors has convinced me that these truisms get lost in the shuffle. They are buried in the subconscious and stay there. Investor attention is diverted by the media's relentless focus on the immediate and the persuasive sales pitch by the broker. We are motivated by what's happening around us, not by worn-out "buy low, sell high" platitudes.

We need a wake-up call. We need to be reminded that these are not just abstract ideas but essentials for success. They should be forcefully and frequently verbalized. It is critical that they be permanently embedded in the forefront of our thinking, always at the ready in our decision-making process.

> "Success is going from failure to failure without loss of enthusiasm."
> —*Winston Churchill*

3. Be Aware of the Negatives: There's Always a Column A and a Column B

Bad news may sell newspapers but it doesn't sell stocks. Most recommendations from Wall Street advisers tread lightly, if at all, on the negatives. Understandably, all salesmen focus on benefits. If you want to know the downside, it usually takes research and some probing questions.

When investing, it's especially important to be aware of what can go wrong. Knowing what the risks are ahead of time is the only way to avoid surprises. As I've said before, there's always bad news on the market and on a stock. It may not be as widely known because it is less publicized, but it's always there. If the adviser recommends purchase, he believes the positives outweigh the negatives (assuming he knows the negatives). If he includes column B (all the negatives) as well as column A, the recommendation is more convincing. By exposing both sides of the story, the adviser comes off as more informed and more credible. At times, a particular negative may turn off an investor, but in the long run, complete honesty is more likely to capture the loyalty and business of the investor. (Of course, the same full disclosure applies to sell recommendations which should include all the column A positives.)

Think about this. If you're buying a stock, someone is selling it to you. Since well over half the volume today is institutional (hedge funds, mutual funds, pension funds, etc.), that "someone" is likely to be a professional. Before you buy, doesn't it make sense for you to know why someone, who likely knows more than you do, is selling? The seller thinks the negatives are not yet fully reflected in the price. Obviously, as the buyer, you disagree, but you really can't make that judgment unless you know what the negatives are. Only then can you make a fully informed decision.

There's only one place that you get a detailed explanation of all the bad stuff. That's in the prospectus that accompanies a new offering; all the risks are described because full disclosure is required by the SEC. Very few people read prospectuses. If they did, if they knew all the scary things that could happen, it's likely they'd never buy the stock.

If an adviser is less than knowledgeable about the negatives, I would ask him to check with his research department and get back to me (analysts cover a limited number of securities and know most of them like the back of their hand). Specifically, I would want to know from the analyst recommending the stock all the major negatives in the overall picture, about how far down he thinks the stock could go if he's wrong, what has to happen for him to change his mind, and how the stock is positioned technically. I would also want to be clear on the adviser's (or his firm's) outlook for the overall market. It's more difficult for a stock to go up in a market that's expected to go down. Just another factor to consider.

Of course, sell recommendations focus on the negatives. Presenting a gloom-and-doom outlook can be unsettling to the investor and difficult to ignore. Opinions sound wiser and more authoritative when they detail the bad things that can occur. The perception is created that the observer is more thoughtful and better informed. When veteran columnist Alan Abelson writes, "... any investor who blithely assumes we've borne anything near the full impact of the great housing bust is dangerously kidding himself" (*Barron's,* January 8, 2007), it just sounds like he knows things that others don't. It's a subtle but distinct advantage for the bearish viewpoint (but one that fades if it's wrong too often).

Awareness of possible negatives not only limits downside surprises, it also allows for contingency exit plans. A selling strategy decided on ahead of time is likely to be more effective than one reached under the stress of unexpected bad news. In the always difficult process of trying to decide whether to buy, sell, or hold, prepared is better than unprepared, informed better than uninformed, eyes wide open better than eyes wide shut.

> "The ecstasy of getting investment performance right is always eclipsed by the agony of getting it wrong."
>
> —*Doug Kass*

4. The Best You Can Do Is Put the Odds in Your Favor

There are few absolutes in stock market investing. Almost nothing works all the time, but some things work most of the time. The very best we can do is to put the odds in our favor. We want to have going for us as much as we possibly can. In the previous three core convictions, I've said that proper asset allocation, a reasonable purchase price, and an awareness of the negatives are no guarantee of success, but they do tilt the investment odds in our direction.

Another way we can tip the scales is by being in harmony with history. Because the market has been around for over 100 years, some of its behavior has had a chance to repeat itself often enough that it can be identified as a likely outcome in a given set of circumstances. For example, if the Federal Reserve Board raises interest rates at more than a gradual pace over a sustained period of time, history tells us that such action will likely put a stop to a major uptrend.

Fred Hickey *(The High-Tech Strategist)* is quoted in Whitney Tilson's column ("A Cautious 2005 Outlook,"Fool.com, January 28, 2005): "Most bear markets begin with the Fed raising rates. The Fed initiated a series of rate hikes in 1973, 1977, 1980, 1987, 1994, and 1999. Significant market declines followed each of these hikes." Says James Stack of Inves-Tech Research,"Nothing has killed more bull markets than rising interest rates. Nothing!" (thebullandbear.com, "Stack's Stocks," March 2005).This is a rare clue that an unpredictable market gives to aware investors. There are so many things in the investment arena over which we have no control, it makes sense to take full advantage of any edge the market gives us. If something has worked in the past over and over again, it behooves us to at least know about it, even if we choose not to act on it.

It's not written in stone that history must repeat itself exactly, but the point is that it comes close enough to warrant serious consideration. *Barron's* editor Ed Finn says, "History doesn't always repeat, but it often rhymes, so you have to pay attention." The dangers of ignoring history have been well documented. As one anonymous economist put it,"Every time history repeats itself, the price goes up." In the investment field, the mantra of "this time it's different," especially amid market euphoria, has proven to be wishful thinking. Paying attention to the lessons of history has proven a far more productive approach. It will likely continue to be so until we see a change in human nature.What merits special consideration are those recurring behavior patterns that can be explained logically rather than just coincidentally. Following are some examples of both.

The Election Cycle

The four-year presidential election cycle is among the most widely cited historical indicators. It's popular because of its impressive track record and because its performance can be explained logically. Years 3 and 4 of the election cycle are usually the strongest because administrations tend to give a boost to the economy in the years closest to election time. The rationale is that measures such as tax cuts and increased spending will help win votes for the incumbent or his party. Then, when the election is over, the winner has to correct some of the excesses of the previous two years by exercising a measure of fiscal restraint. Years 1 and 2, therefore, are the housecleaning years during which the President is most likely to take on tough, unpopular issues. So the bad stuff happens in the first half of the cycle, the good stuff during the second half.

As you would expect, the market's performance during the first year of the four-year cycle is traditionally the weakest of the four years. With the exception of Ronald Reagan and Bill Clinton, the first year of a presidential second term has always been negative, going all the way back to Abraham Lincoln's second term. (2005 barely made it—the Dow was down a tiny fraction, the S&P up slightly.) Since 1929, 9 of the 13 recessions the country has experienced have come in the first year of a presidency. The second year is second-weakest and the third year is clearly the best, there having been only one down year since 1931. Since 1950, the Dow has gained 18 percent on average in the third year—the one preceding the presidential election (per Ned Davis Research, Venice, Florida). The fourth year in the cycle is also good, but not as robust as the pre-election year.

Because of the unusual consistency of the data, well-known portfolio managers like Jeremy Grantham (Grantham, Mayo, Van Otterloo, Boston) and Sheldon Jacobs (editor of the *No Load Fund Investor* newsletter) pay close attention to the election cycle in formulating their strategy. Investors should do the same, mindful that there will be exceptions to the rule.

Most recently, 2006, the second year in the presidential cycle, proved to be a glaring exception. In fact, the market did not suffer a serious correction in either 2005 or 2006. Instead of the usual major low seen in the second half of the second year, the market did just the opposite. Starting in July 2006, it went up in almost a straight line for seven months in a row. Instead of entering the third year of the cycle oversold, setting the stage for the usual big gains in the third and fourth years, the market entered 2007 overbought and overextended. Not surprisingly, the consensus on Wall Street looked for a long overdue correction.

The 416-point drop in the Dow on February 27, 2007, appeared to confirm that prognosis but, as I have detailed, that proved to be a bear trap.

Why discuss historical patterns when they are unreliable? Because when something happens in the market *most of the time,* that's about as reliable as you can get. Besides, when a high-percentage, fundamentally based historical pattern is ignored, it's unlikely that it will be ignored twice in a row.

Finally, there's this to consider regarding the dependability of historical patterns: While failing to repeat one precedent, the market may keep alive a different one. In 2006, the second year in the presidential cycle, the market failed to record a usually reliable major low. But it dutifully extended another streak. According to Milwaukee-based Sadoff Investments, years ending in "6" have produced average gains of 6 percent since the 1880s. The gains since the 1970s have been especially robust, all showing strong double-digit gains. So 2006 kept the string alive, with the S&P 500 and the Dow up 13 percent and 16 percent respectively. If you dig deep enough, you can find evidence to support almost anything.

"Sell In May"

"Sell in May and go away" is an old Wall Street saw and another popular seasonal indicator. It sounds too simplistic to work, but it mostly does.

The idea is that if you're in the market the right six months of the year (November 1 through April 30) and out of the market the other six months (May 1 thru October 31), you'll do far better than if you stayed put. Since 1950, for example, 98 percent of the gain in the Dow has come between November and April (*New York Daily News,* June 1, 2004). Put another way, a $10,000 investment in the bad months from May to October since 1950 would have resulted in a *loss* of $1,625, according to the Hirsch Organization's *Stock Trader's Almanac* (published annually by John Wiley & Sons). The same investment since 1950 in the good months of November through April would have resulted in a *gain* of $461,774. As I have mentioned, the year 2006 stubbornly refused to follow precedent. A steady advance the second half of the year made a decision to "sell in May and go away" a bad one.

Why November through April is so much better than May through October is unclear. Explanations range from a stronger period of retail sales (November through April, buoyed by most of the major holidays), a technical bounce following an often weak September–October, a traditional buildup of optimism for the new year, and new money coming into the market in the first quarter from corporate bonuses, pension plans, and IRA contributions. Poor performance in May through October is said to reflect a lack of investor interest due to vacation and outdoor activities, a slowdown in corporate mergers and in business news in general, and uncertainty regarding the upcoming election. Some of these reasons sound like a stretch. The results of investing only during the best six months are more impressive than the reasons used to explain them.

As January Goes, So Goes the Year

At the beginning of each year, followers of the January barometer pay homage to its predictive powers while others express skepticism. Its biggest fan is Yale Hirsch, who popularized this seasonal indicator in his *Stock Trader's Almanac* (New York: John Wiley & Sons, annually). He claims that since 1950, the S&P 500 over the course of the year has followed January's performance 91 percent of the time. January 2007 was an up month, and bulls were quick to point out that the stock market has followed January's lead an impressive 13 of the last 14 pre-election years.

Widely respected portfolio manager Jeremy Grantham says, "How January goes matters quite a lot, with a bad January a good predictor of a probable poor year" (*Barron's,* January 3, 2005). But former *Bloomberg* columnist John Dorfman claims that "January has no special predictive effect." In the middle of the debate is prolific columnist and newsletter writer Mark Hulbert. He says (at MarketWatch.com, January 11, 2005), "Though January's direction may be something worth looking at, it is no more worth paying attention to than the direction of almost any other month," and he gives supporting statistics. Confused? If nothing else, the market is confusing.

In bull markets, the biggest gains usually come in the beginning, when it's still not clear that it is, indeed, a bull market. As the uptrend

> "A bargain that remains a bargain is no bargain."
> —*Marty Whitman*

gains maturity, the advance typically loses momentum and often tapers off toward the end. On average, since World War II, the first-year gain of a bull market has been 36 percent, second year 11 percent, and third year only 3 percent (according to Bob Doll, Global Chief Investment Officer, Black Rock). The age of a bull market, then, is another indicator to take into consideration in the decision-making process. (In 2007, an unusually extended bull market entered its fifth year with few signs of fatigue.)

18-Year Cycles

Take a look at a long-term chart of the Dow Jones Industrial Average, going back to at least World War II. Your first overall impression is that of a prolonged, steadily rising trend. A closer look reveals that the decades-long, uneven uptrend can be divided roughly into four parts: 1942 to 1962, upward; 1963 to 1982, sideways; 1982 to 2000, upward; 2000 on, sideways. Of course, these broad characterizations are gross oversimplifications since they mask many briefer countermoves, not to mention violent bear market interruptions (1987). Neither up nor flat markets move in straight lines. Nevertheless, the division of market history since World War II into roughly four stages is what's behind the often-cited and loosely labeled 18-year cycle.

It's a popular indicator today because it can be used to support the current consensus view on the market outlook. According to advocates, we started a new 18-year flat or range-bound cycle in early 2000 after the bull market peaked. This projection fits in nicely with the near-unanimous opinion of market gurus that unlike the 20 percent-plus annual gains of 1995 through 1999, the average annual return in the decade ahead will be in the single digits.

From Warren Buffett on down, the view is that we are unlikely to see the spectacular gains or the extreme excesses of the 1990s repeated for a long time to come, and that the pendulum has now swung in the other direction. Annual gains averaging just single digits sounds modest but it's very close to the market's overall return since the 1920s of just over 10 percent. Also, a single-digit average can mask lots of double-digit results, both plus and minus. For example, the average annual gain in the S&P 500 Index in the five-year period 2002–2006 was about 6 percent, which conforms to the single-digit scenario. But individual year results were −22 percent, +20 percent, +9 percent, +3 percent, and +13 percent.

Followers of the 18-year cycle point out that the sweeping uptrend of 1942 to 1962 was followed by a sideways market for over 18 years. In similar manner, it is their contention that the powerful, sustained uptrend from 1982 to 2000 will be followed by another long period of range-bound action on the Dow. Range-bound means that down cycles will be offset by up cycles with little net progress for the index (the Dow traded at 767 in 1963, and 19 years later in 1982 it traded at 777). A sideways scenario would be consistent with consensus expectations for modest returns, although we had surprisingly robust gains in both 2003 and 2006 and an all-time high in 2007.

Technical analyst Michael Kahn takes note of the 18-year cycle in his twice weekly "Getting Technical" column on *Barron's Online* (April 4, 2007): "When the entire history of the Dow Jones Industrial Average, starting when it was first published on May 26, 1896, is plotted on a single graph, a cycle of approximately 18 years of rally followed by about 18 years of giant consolidation comes to light." Citing the mature aspect of the 2002 to 2007 cyclical bull market, Kahn says the 18-year cycle suggests there will be an important decline coming.

To ride out the bad times and prosper in the good, Kahn offers this advice: "A shift from a strategy of 'buy and hold forever' to one that encompasses market timing on its most macro level can be the best plan for even conservative investors." Of course, timing the market, even in the most general sense, is not easy. Perhaps the best defense against an expected market drop, other than selling ahead of time, is the type of asset allocation suggested in the model portfolios presented in Part Two of this book. You'll still get hit, but proper diversification can greatly soften the blow. Kahn adds a comforting note: "When discussing cycles, remember that rallies always follow declines."

Buffett, Bogle, and Cohen All Agree

Repeated forecasts of modest future returns in the market by leading gurus adds credibility to prospects for an 18-year cycle. Warren Buffett says, "I don't expect any enormous returns at all for the market. Overall,

6 percent to 8 percent is what I think people can expect" (*USA Today,* March 20, 2006). Vanguard's founder, John Bogle, is on record with a similar forecast made in early 2007. Even hedge fund king Steven Cohen told the *Wall Street Journal* (September 15, 2006) that he expects lower returns. His SAC Capital hedge fund generated returns of over 40 percent for most of the 1990s and around 18 percent since then. But Cohen has reportedly told his investors he's now aiming to return between 10 percent and 15 percent a year.

Another possible long-term drag on the market is the psychological residue from the devastating 2000–2002 bear market. This was no ordinary decline. Asset manager Dr. Robert Arnott (Research Affiliates) calls it "the bursting of the largest bubble in U.S. capital markets history" (*New York Times,* October 1, 2006). The NASDAQ index is still only 50 percent recovered. Investors poured into the market in the 1980s and 1990s, causing a mutual fund explosion. They got burned so badly in the crash that an entire generation started to reassess stocks as a suitable investment. Many still have wounds that are not fully healed. Others are permanently turned off. Usually, in time, greed takes over but sometimes the wounds are too deep to heal. Suffice it to say that lingering disenchantment by investors may or may not add validity to the 18-year cycle.

Most of the indicators we've discussed have been long-term in nature. Now we go from decades to days. The no-longer-published VTOReport.com tells us that in the 33-year period 1971 thru 2004, the day before major holidays has been mostly a good day in the market. The day before New Year's Day, Martin Luther King Jr. Day, Good Friday, Memorial Day, Independence Day, Labor Day, Thanksgiving, and Christmas has been an up day between 57 percent and 87 percent of the time. The reason for buoyancy may be that the positive feelings of hope and optimism associated with holidays create a bullish bias. The typical slow trading before a holiday permits stocks to rise on light volume. Honors for the three best performance days go to the day before New Year's Day (the last trading day of the year) and the day after Thanksgiving, both up 87 percent of the time, and the day before Thanksgiving, up 81 percent of the time. Good numbers to have on your side.

> "All I ask is the chance to prove that money can't make me happy."
> —*Unknown*

Coincidental Patterns

So far, I've summarized five different patterns of market behavior that I believe are noteworthy and have some basis in reason. There are other indicators that have excellent track records but are based on nothing more than coincidence.

The National Football League is divided into two conferences. Each year in January the winner in the National Football Conference plays the winner of the American Football Conference in the Super Bowl. According to the widely referenced Super Bowl indicator, if the NFC team wins, the stock market is destined to go up that year. If the AFC team wins, the stock market is headed lower. This indicator has been right 30 out of 38 years. Most Wall Street strategists would do cartwheels to be right 79 percent of the time.

The decennial pattern or year 5 phenomenon has even a better record. Going all the way back to 1885, there have been 13 years ending in "5." During that 120-year span of market history, there have been no losing "5" years. The average annual gain of the middle years of the decade was close to a robust 30 percent according to the *No Load Fund Investor* newsletter. However, editor Sheldon Jacobs is quick to add, "This is simply a random pattern. It's no different than a coin coming up heads thirteen times in a row."

We have to conclude then, that although the Super Bowl and decennial indicators make sexy copy, the absence of any plausible explanation means the next time around they have no better than a 50-50 chance of working. It also means that stretched out over the next 100 years, results from both indicators should revert back to 50-50.

Of course, the best position to be in at the beginning of the year is to have not one but many favorable indicators working at the same time—the more the better. It's like the New York Yankees signing a slew of star baseball players before the season starts. As we saw in 2006, it doesn't guarantee a championship but it certainly makes it more likely.

In January 2003, for example, there were six historical indicators all converging at the same time and all pointing to an up year:

1. It was the third year of the election cycle, historically the best, with only one down year since 1931.

2. It was the good six months to be in the market—November thru April.
3. The market had been down three years in a row (2000–2002). For it to go down again in 2003, it would have to do what it had done only once in the past 100 years (1929–1932).
4. The market had hit its low point in October 2002. Five of the previous 10 bear markets had bottomed in October.
5. The four-year cycle saw the market hit major lows in 1962, 1966, 1970, 1974, 1978, 1982, 1986, 1990, 1994, and 1998. So the low set in October 2002 would fit the pattern.
6. The bond market had outperformed stocks three years in a row (2000–2002) for the first time in 60 years. It was unlikely to happen again.

In Harmony with History

As it turned out, 2003 *was* the best year in the four-year presidential cycle (the Dow rose 25 percent); the October 22, 2002, low *did* prove to be the bottom; and stocks *did* outperform bonds. My guess is that most investors in 2003 were unaware of all they had going for them. I'm suggesting that you (or your adviser) be aware. Knowledge of the convergence of a host of seasonal patterns all pointing in the same direction may give you that extra bit of confidence you need to make a move.

Perhaps the most important historical pattern of all is one we just take for granted—the market goes up more than it goes down. Over the past 60 years, the S&P 500 Index has been up 42 times, down 17 times, and unchanged once. That's a 70 percent track record. Even more impressive, according to Roger Ibbotson (Yale University finance professor, Zebra Capital Management), the Standard & Poor's 500 stock index has never declined in any rolling 10-year period since 1940. Let's face it, if the market over the years didn't have a strong, underlying upward bias, you wouldn't be reading this book and I wouldn't be writing it.

To sum up, I'd say that it's better to be in harmony with something that has worked over and over again in similar situations than to be aligned against it. It's just one arrow in your quiver. There'll be others, probably more important, to factor into your market judgments. But having history on your side can be a source of great psychological comfort.

Keep in mind that indicators are just that, indicators. They are seasonal/cyclical tendencies or inclinations, not absolute rules. Utilizing something that's worked 8 out of 10 times in the past means the odds are with you, but it doesn't mean that "this time" can't be one of the two times it doesn't work. That's why historical indicators are usually just one of many factors in the judgment process.

Another limitation to consider is the frequent unreliability of the statistics upon which these indicators are based. I can't tell you how many times I see different researchers reporting results of the exact same study (using the same time frame, the same guidelines, the same sources, the same methods, etc.) and coming up with totally different numbers. With this in mind, it's best that we treat history as a guide, not as gospel. Nevertheless, the impressive track record of so many of these indicators makes Damon Runyon's observation relevant: "The race doesn't always go to the swift, but that's the way to bet."

Technicians and Their Charts

Finally, any discussion of reliable historical indicators must include the role of the technical analyst and his charts. A chart represents history, a picture of the past price action of a stock. The formation and patterns formed by the lines on a chart can be interpreted differently by different technicians. However, there are certain easy-to-identify, textbook patterns that mean the same thing to everybody.

For example, if the price of stock has moved within a trading range for a long time and then finally breaks through overhead resistance, the stock will usually attract big upside volume. Chart followers pile on because such breakouts in the past have proven good buy signals. Sometimes they turn out to be false moves. More often than not, however, if for no other reason than so many take notice, a long-awaited breakthrough or breakdown is an indicator worth knowing about.

There are two basic approaches to the market—fundamental (analyzing the economy, inflation, interest rates, competition, management, sales, earnings, profit margins, etc.) and technical (using the story told by the past price action of a stock as depicted on a chart to find clues as to what may happen in the future). One of the best ways to put the investment odds in your favor is to have *both* the fundamentals and the technicals on your side. You can do that without having to be a technical analyst. With very few hours of research, you'll be able to look at a chart and determine whether your stock, fund, market index, or other investment is bound within a long- or short-term trading range or is in a long- or short-term uptrend or downtrend. Also, a glance will tell you if your stock is near any long- or short-term support or resistance levels.

Two Positives Are Better than One

If you buy when the fundamentals look good and, at the same time, when your stock is just above a strong support level or has just broken above a longtime resistance level on big volume, you're bettering your odds of success. Two positives are better than one. Yes, this is oversimplification, and yes, sometimes the action on a chart proves to be misleading. But more often than not, what has worked in the past does so again. And the beauty of it is that investors can benefit from most of the helpful information that charts have to offer without having to master the methodology. The intricacies of point and figure and candlestick charting, stochastics, triangle and head and shoulder formations, Fibonacci arcs, Bollinger bands, Elliot Wave, and Dow Theory can all remain a mystery.

Investors are often told to investigate corporate financial statements, which is unrealistic since few have the expertise. But looking at a long-term chart (six months, or 1, 3, 5, 10, or more years) requires no more than a click of your mouse on any of a thousand different web sites. Also easily available on the Internet are brief tutorials on how to recognize and use support and resistance levels, breakouts and breakdowns, volume patterns, trend lines, moving averages, and the like. Easiest of all are the many chart sites that do the work for you and label each stock technically bullish or bearish for both near term and long term.

Of course you can go as far as you want with this, but to me it just doesn't make sense not to at least know whether your stock, fund, or index is near support or resistance before making a buy, sell, or hold decision. The information is widely accessible, it's free, and it works well enough to attract an army of loyal chart followers. Most techies could care less about

> "There are only two rules for achieving anything: (1) get started and (2) keep going."
> —*Unknown*

fundamentals (which they say are already reflected in the charts). But one approach is not exclusive of the other. Making the right investment move is difficult enough. Why throw away something that can help?

5. The Worst You Can Do Is Be Totally and Instantly Informed (A Critique of CNBC)

The worst thing that can happen to a long-term investor is to be instantly and totally informed about his stocks. Somewhere along the way the information onslaught causes emotional decisions, one or more of which are likely to be wrong. Your adviser, your broker, and your favorite TV reporter all mean well by wanting to keep you informed. More often than not, however, they are misguided. There is *always* negative news on a stock. News is rarely as bad or as good as it first sounds. On occasion, the news may require an investment move, but most of the time the news is simply not crucial; it doesn't represent basic, fundamental change, and it doesn't alter the long-term outlook. Like yesterday's headlines, it fades and is soon forgotten. At most, it shows up as a tiny squiggle on a long-term chart.

Nevertheless, a sudden, sharp price move triggered by surprise news and reported by an animated broker or newscaster can create a sense of urgency, a call for immediate action. The result is a buy/sell decision often based strictly on emotion. The truth is that it is only the passage of time that puts news in perspective. Such knee-jerk reactions are better avoided and decisions made when emotions have had a chance to subside and reason a chance to prevail. Unless you're a trader, it's simply not healthy to be too close to your stock. Just like your spouse needs space, your stock needs room to perform. Being totally and instantly informed can lead to premature separation. If you're holding long-term positions that were bought at reasonable prices and are properly diversified, ignorance of the news can, indeed, be bliss.

If overexposure to the news can be harmful, how do we deal with the torrent of financial news spewed forth on the all-day financial news channels? The obvious answer is to tune it out. In bear markets we do that anyway. Who wants to listen to someone on TV explaining why we're poorer today than we were yesterday? For the same reason, monthly brokerage statements go unopened in down markets.

Of course, with effective programming, cable TV has a unique opportunity to help investors put bear markets in proper perspective. Shopping malls put "You Are Here" signs throughout their arcades to help customers find their way. Cable TV rarely tells its viewers where they are in the big picture. It's too preoccupied with what's happening that hour, that minute, that second.

CNBC—Good and Bad

CNBC is the dominant player in the field. During the historic 1995–2000 bull market when dot-com fever swept the country, watching stock symbols move across the bottom of the CNBC TV screen became a national pastime. But as investors' net worth eroded in the ensuing bear market, so did investor interest. Guest analysts who had been heroes during the market's upsurge were paid little heed amid the carnage of a collapsed NASDAQ. CNBC's credibility was seriously compromised, and it was derisively labeled "bubble vision" and "tout-TV." In the post-bubble years of 2000–2004, daytime viewership of CNBC dropped 60 percent from its peak (*Barron's Online,* January 12, 2005).

A sweeping, sustained bull market will always bring the public back. Investors have short memories and bull markets make TV gurus look good. But until CNBC presents programming that will help its viewers become better *long-term* investors, it will fall far short of its potential. What CNBC *does* do well is provide news, education, and entertainment. That's all to the good (although much of the news is meaningless except to traders, the securities industry, and corporate management), but it's not good enough. For most investors, the potential damage from the distorted short-term emphasis exceeds the potential benefits. The incessant message to its viewers is that the nonstop news minutia that it reports matters and requires action, when in fact it does not (not to long-term investors).

The basic problem is one of focus—CNBC's obsession with dissecting the mostly vacuous statistical trivia of the day (personal income up 0.1 percent, followed by four interviews on what it means!). Its emphasis on immediacy, on the breaking story, is incompatible with the broad perspective and patience needed by the long-term investor. Following is one of a multitude of examples that could be cited to illustrate CNBC's preoccupation with minutia.

At 10 A.M. on the morning of April 26, 2007, it was announced that in a half hour, the natural gas inventory number would be released. A visual appeared on the TV screen labeled "Energy Investing Data" along with an ongoing countdown of the number of minutes and seconds left until the release was due. During the ensuing half hour, co-anchors Mark Haines and Liz Claman kept reminding viewers they were only a few minutes away from the release of the energy number. Finally, at 10:30 A.M. the news was announced: "The natural gas inventory number is 18 billion cubic feet." At the same time in bold letters on the lower screen were the words, "Breaking News: 18 billion cubic feet." Then a natural gas analyst was interviewed on the significance of the weekly number.

In my view, this sick focus on trivia shows just how out of touch CNBC programmers are with America's 95 million investors. Their answer, of course, is that they're reaching the niche audience they're after, which is not all American investors. The shame of it is that they could be helping so many people with all that valuable airtime.

On CNBC, the viewer faces a relentless barrage of business news, as well as interviews with less than forthcoming CEOs and stock pickers who try to predict the unpredictable (unfazed by past error). These on-air personalities are all engaging and articulate. It's a nonstop, fast paced, play-by-play format pumped up with energizing music and slick graphics. This results in an entertaining financial variety show but does not make for good investing. Nobel prize–winning economist Paul Samuelson says, "Investing should be like watching paint dry. . . . If you want excitement, take $800 and go to Las Vegas" (*Bloomberg,* August 23, 1999).

Sound Investing Is Boring

There are other critics. Bill Mann wrote in *The Motley Fool* (February 14, 2005): "CNBC needs to matter. . . . Who cares what analyst on Wall Street raised or lowered guidance. . . . Viewers are doing nothing but chasing the thing that has just happened. . . . CNBC is at its best when it's an honest broker. . . . Having a network that serves as a spirit squad for Wall Street isn't terribly useful." And writing in *Slate* (December 22, 2004), former securities analyst Henry Blodget had this to say: "The way to give yourself the best chance of success in the markets is to diversify, buy low-cost funds and hold them forever. . . . The sad truth is that sound investment policy is boring. . . . To the media, the long term is death. How often will you . . . tune in to be told that you shouldn't do anything, that nothing has changed? Answer: Never. So the media must find other ways to keep you entertained."

In my opinion, there *are* ways to make CNBC more relevant to long-term investors. Ongoing exposure to many of the ideas in this book would be a good place to start. As for being boring, there is one thing I've learned from being a talking head on TV for some 20 years. The viewer will be remarkably forgiving if he sees you as a reliable source of information that's consistently honest, insightful, balanced, and devoid of hype.

One excellent technique is to point out things that are happening in the market *that day* that illustrate *basic* market truisms that the long-term investor can learn from (I do this in my classes). The introduction of a "What Would You Have Done" feature (see Chapter 1) would be innovative, educational, and entertaining. Also, more attention to such subjects as the importance of buying at reasonable prices, asset allocation, indexing, seasonal patterns, durability of major trends, contrary opinion, behavioral psychology, fallibility, humility, and other long-term investment influences would all add relevance and credibility to CNBC programming.

In the meantime, when and if you do watch financial television (including not only CNBC, but Bloomberg TV and Rupert Murdock's new Fox Business Channel), you can learn a lot about the market and keep abreast of what's happening to your money—but be aware of the limitations of those who are talking to you. I get a sense that some of the more experienced, market-savvy anchors realize they're part of a show and don't take themselves too seriously. But there are others who honestly think that what they're saying really matters (the penny increase in earnings, the 1 percent drop in the consumer confidence index, the 2 percent rise in factory orders) and that's sad and scary.

Perhaps competition from FOX will be a blessing in disguise for CNBC. It will be forced to reassess its programming, especially when it loses its valuable affiliation with the *Wall Street Journal*. If FOX approaches business news with its signature tabloid style, it will give CNBC an opportunity to provide contrast. More thoughtful *investing* rather than business-news–oriented programming, focused—at least in part—on the concerns of the educated, long-term investor comes to mind. CNBC is a valuable franchise despite its modest ratings because sponsors want to reach its high-income trading-type viewers. The much larger number of well-to-do, long-term–oriented investors attracted to less titillating, more genuinely helpful programming, may also represent an attractive market for sponsors.

There are times when watching financial TV can be an emotional minefield. Try and put it in perspective. Little of what you hear will have any significance tomorrow. Work on listening with detachment and steeling your emotions against unsettling news. Increase your filtering skills. Extract the good stuff—the insightful interview, the lucid commentary of old-timer guests like Art Cashen and Bill Seidman. What's important is that you not be diverted from your long-term goals.

> "Always put emotion aside and keep your relationship with your portfolio platonic."
> —*Stephen Jarislowsky*

6. Many Strategies Can Work—The Key Is Consistency

There are hundreds, probably thousands of strategies that can be used by investors. If any one of them was right all the time, there would only be one. Each has its followers, its strengths and weaknesses, its successes and failures. What they all have in common is that they require unwavering stick-to-it-iveness. Probably more important than the strategy itself is the steadfastness of the investor. In fact, because perversity, randomness, and unpredictability play such a big role in the market, you can take almost any market approach, do the exact opposite, and, if you stay with it, accomplish the same result.

Examples abound. Bargain hunters will scour the new low list for ideas; momentum buyers will do just the opposite and feed off the new high list. Some professionals buy last year's top-performing stock funds and do well (according to the *No-Load Fund Investor*) while others zero in on the prior year's worst performers and achieve equally good results (Oppenheimer Funds). Most investors seek diversification in their holdings, but Warren Buffett's Berkshire Hathaway has achieved outstanding results by making a few big bets, where it felt it had a strong edge, and staying with them. Neil Hennessy has compiled an enviable track record in his Cornerstone Growth Fund by ignoring the conventional long-term approach to growth investing. Instead, he religiously sells each stock after holding it for a year.

However you approach the market, the essential point is not to deviate. This is much easier said than done. There are always compelling reasons to change course, not the least of which is seeing other stocks surge ahead while yours remain dead money. The temptation to switch can be overwhelming. It's like standing in the checkout line at the supermarket. You spot what looks like a shorter or faster line so you quickly move over. Invariably, it turns out you would have been better off if you had stayed put. History teaches us that every stock group, at some point, returns to favor, so that perseverance will be rewarded in time (rewards are highest when you're doing your waiting with securities bought at reasonable prices). Being wishy-washy, jumping ship, and going in all directions is the killer.

Mark Hulbert, editor of the *Hulbert Financial Digest* which has ranked the performance of investment advisory newsletters for 25 years, comments on one quality common to all of the top performers. Writing in the September 2005 *AAII Journal,* he says, "What counts is the patience and discipline to follow a strategy through periods in which it is out of sync with the market. Without this patience and discipline, advisers are tempted to second-guess their strategies at the first signs of market-lagging performance. . . . Ulysses had his men tie him to the mast so that he would be able to resist the Sirens' songs. Investors—tie yourself to your chosen approach—whether it be through mechanical rules or dogged will power—and don't let the Siren song of the market-of-the-moment lure your portfolio underwater."

When Your Turn Comes, Be There

This, then, is the sixth of my seven core convictions: The most important aspect of any market approach is consistency. The investor needs the emotional discipline to rise above distraction, temptations, and frustration and remain resolute.

The market is rotational. What works today will continue to work until it doesn't. Then it will fade and languish until, once again, it takes center stage. Nobody knows how long it will take for a group to come back. What we do know is that whenever your turn comes, it won't mean much unless you're still there.

Perhaps the hardest thing to do is to put money into stocks, bonds, CDs, and so on every month, or every three months or every year, regardless of the existing market climate. Strategies such as dollar cost averaging, dogs of the Dow, and laddering CDs require this type of iron discipline. Wally Weitz (the Weitz Value Fund) says, "It's just a matter of having the courage of your convictions." It's extremely difficult to stick to a formula that insists you invest when it doesn't seem right, when it seems you're out of step, especially during periods of gloom and doom. Once again, the key to the success of the strategy is consistency, not comfort. If you feel frustrated and left out, you're probably on the right track.

There's a difference between consistency and rigidity. It's an important distinction. Almost nothing about the market is fixed in stone. Being consistent does not rule out a degree of flexibility. Extenuating circumstances such as a change in your personal financial picture may justify some deviation. Also, it makes little sense to stick with an approach that was ill conceived to start with. Maverick Charlie Munger, Warren Buffett's older partner and adviser, believes investors should be quick to admit failure. In an article titled "Munger's Wisdoms" (Bankstocks.com, February 14, 2005), Eric Miller writes, "Munger believes success comes from curiosity, concentration, perseverance and self criticism. These traits improve a person's ability to change his mind and allow one to destroy one's best-loved ideas. Munger tends to regard any year in which you don't destroy one of your own ideas as a wasted year."

The record shows that although Munger and Buffett may have changed their minds, once they acted, there was no wavering. In fact, in his stewardship of Berkshire Hathaway, Buffett's approach has been to buy what he labels "great companies" at the right price and never sell. If that isn't consistency, it'll do. In the decision-making process, there's certainly room for changing positions. There's no virtue in being pig-headed or close-minded. But once implemented, investment strategies need time to play out, and that requires patience and steadfastness of purpose.

Some of the subjects I've already addressed, like asset allocation, proper entry level, and seasonal indicators, can be included under the umbrella heading of "investment strategies." What follows are observations about other popular market approaches, some of them broad in concept, others more specific, but all requiring consistency in their execution. None are described in detail. My purpose in writing this book is not to repeat what is better written elsewhere, in thousands of tutorials and textbooks. I simply want to make you aware of how many different ways there are to approach the market (I'll just scratch the surface), and to offer some overall perspective.

> "If you can find a good active manager who can beat the market consistently, invest with her, and please introduce me to her."
> —*Jim Rogers*

A. Do It Yourself The first decision that has to be made is, should I invest on my own or have someone else do it for me? Investors' situations vary, so the answer will vary.

Ideally, I favor using both approaches with a nod toward the pro. What's difficult for the professional is much more so for the rest of us. Emotional discipline, knowledge of the markets, accounting expertise, and years of experience don't guarantee success but they *do* better the odds. The professional is more likely to have these attributes and, to the extent he does, he has an edge. How do you harness the best professional advice? I address that question in the second half of the book.

There are situations that clearly call for a do-it-yourself approach. Psychological and social benefits may trump other considerations. Rather than dealing with mutual funds or index funds, buying individual stocks is more fun and more challenging. Buying a stock based strictly on your own research and seeing it do exactly what you expected (even though the stock's rise may have little to do with the reason you bought it) can be extremely satisfying. Competing with the big boys in the world of high finance, especially if done with some success, can be a source of pride, confidence, and self-esteem.

There are also social benefits. Few topics are more popular than money and how to make it. Those who share stock ideas and investment experiences are likely to be welcomed to the conversation. Whether it be at the office, the gym, the golf course, the bar, or other social settings, the subject of the stock market is likely to create an area of common interest with peers.

Investing is a subject of special interest to retirees. A common interest in the stock market can be the catalyst for forming and sustaining friendships. It can also provide those who are elderly, alone, or infirm something else to do with their time, an interest that may add to their quality of life. And it's not a frivolous activity. It involves money so it is important, useful, and self-image building.

They're All Great and They're All Lousy An often-used compromise on investment decision making is having a professional handle some of your money while you handle the balance. Who knows? You may find out that you're one of the very few who has a special gift. (One way to do that is to join the online stock picking community of marketocracy.com, manage a virtual $1 million portfolio, and see how you do competing with some 65,000 other portfolios. See Chapter 9, "Virtual Investing.")

As for working with stock brokers, they're all great and they're all lousy. Given the same level of experience, there's probably little difference in talent. At the end of the year, some of their accounts will be up and some will be down. If you're lucky, you'll be in the up group. Where there *is* a difference in brokers is in personality, sincerity, humility, caring, and personal service, especially in bad markets. That's what I'd be looking for. (Both my father and my brother enjoyed talking to their broker. It was the social highlight of their day.)

An active interest in the stock market can add a whole new dimension to a person's lifestyle, one that can be enjoyed for a lifetime. The longer one stays in the game, the better one is likely to become. Even if profits are elusive, the social rewards can be invaluable. In most cases, I think setting aside a portion of your funds for fun investing, for challenging the system, makes sense, especially if you go in with a realistic attitude that "the odds may not be strong in my favor but if I buy low, limit my loss, diversify, and be patient, I can do well." I say more on do-it-yourself investing in Chapters 8 and 9.

B. Long-Term Investing If you *do* get involved in managing your own money, there are three other basic choices to be made before getting down to specific strategies—long term versus short term, fundamental versus technical (previously discussed), and active versus passive management (a subject of Part Two).

Choosing a long-term market approach over the short-term is a no-brainer. Benjamin Graham's advice in his classic *The Intelligent Investor* (Harper Business, paperback revised 2003) is as timely today as it was when it was written almost 60 years ago: "The real money in investing will have to be made . . . not out of buying and selling, but out of owning and holding securities, receiving interest and dividends and benefiting from their long-term increase in value." Christopher Browne in his *The Little Book of Value Investing* (New York: Wiley & Sons, 2006) points out that between 80 and 90 percent of the investment returns in stocks occur during only 2 percent to 7 percent of the time. But we never know when that 2 to 7 percent will take place. That's why Magellan's hall of famer Peter Lynch was always fully invested. Says Browne, "It's a marathon, not a sprint."

It's not that short-term traders don't make money. Some, who study long and hard and develop special technical skills, do well. Most do not. Those who do make money invariably give it back, and then some, over time. (The most successful short-term trader I know is Charles Kirk [TheKirkReport.com].) A combination of sweat and talent has produced an uncanny track record (as outlined in Chapter 7). What is irrefutable is that when it comes to picking stocks or forecasting the market, the longer the time frame, the better the chances for success. There are many mutual funds and individual money managers that, with some losing years along the way, have compiled excellent long-term track records.

The long-term approach works better because it is in harmony with the essential nature of the market—namely, completely unpredictable short term but with a dependable upward bias over the past century. (The inexorable, underlying bias is up but sometimes it's a long wait till the uptrend resumes. Since its launch in 1896, there have been six periods of six years or longer between record highs in the Dow, the longest being the 25 years from 1929 to 1954. The latest was the six year eight month wait between

> "There are two times in a man's life when he should not speculate: when he can't afford it, and when he can."
>
> —*Mark Twain*

the Dow's high on January 14, 2000, and the final topping of that high on October 3, 2006.)

Time Takes Time Financial columnist and astute observer Ben Stein says, "Unless you are trading on inside information or having a lucky streak, you will need a long time to get rich in the market. But if you stay in the market, getting average or slightly-better-than-average returns year after year and avoiding horrendous losses you will eventually make some major bucks. You can't hurry the stock market. The market just flows, like the mighty Mississippi. Flow with it, and you will reach the ocean of comfort sooner or later. Time takes time" (finance .yahoo.com, December 26, 2005).

Examples abound of successful portfolio managers who are strong advocates of the long-term approach and who practice it with unwavering discipline. Warren Buffett (Berkshire Hathaway), when asked about his favorite holding period, replied, "Forever" and added the best time to sell is "never!" Martin Whitman of the top-performing Third Avenue Value Fund says the exact same thing. Once he determines a stock is vastly underpriced relative to its value, he says he's "willing to hold it forever." His patience is reflected in his fund's annual turnover rate of less than 10 percent.

The investment newsletter that's ranked number one in performance over the 10- and 15-year periods ending January 31, 2005, according to the *Hulbert Financial Digest,* is the *Prudent Speculator.* Founded by Al Frank in 1977, it's now managed by John Buckingham, who says, "The key to successful investing is to buy a broad basket of undervalued stocks. . . . When a stock is trading at less than half of what we think it's worth, we buy it. . . . Our philosophy is based on patience, we hold our average stock for six and a half years. Why? Because it reduces risk and because no one can predict the market." (*Barron's,* "Searching From Sea to Sea for Value," April 9, 2007.)

Portfolio manager Ron Baron has excelled at picking growth stocks for his family of Baron Funds. In a January 10, 2005, *Barron's* interview he said, "While the market is focused on next quarter's earnings, we're looking ahead years and years and years. When I say long term, I mean long term. We own stocks on average four or five years. Some we've owned for 10, 12, even 15 years."

Highly regarded money manager Bill Nygren (Oakmark Funds) has an outstanding track record. In a speech before the Thirteenth Annual Louis Rukeyser Investment Conference ("The Hunt For Intrinsic Value," March 31, 2005, oakmark.com), he said his success is based on exploiting the frailties of human nature, ignoring the daily news, and letting a very long-term perspective make it all work. "Taking advantage of the values created by emotional investors is the cornerstone of the Oakmark Fund's approach to investing. We try to buy from fearful or bored investors and sell to greedy investors who want excitement. We invest some $30 billion in six different funds which utilize a long-term value approach. It requires patience. We believe that thinking about an investment time frame of at least five years creates our biggest competitive advantage. In a world where many base their investment decisions on a steady diet of financial news, we focus on what a business might be worth five years from now."

How to Make the Unknowable Knowable We could quote hundreds, probably thousands of other money managers on the merits of the long-term approach. That's how most money managers manage money. To them, the market's perverse, capricious nature precludes any short-term strategy. In fact, there are some funds, like those that look for problem companies selling at deep discounts but with prospects of recovery, that depend completely on the willingness to ride out turbulence over long periods of time. The basic, underlying premise embraced by all long-term investors is that there is only one way to make the unknowable knowable and that's the passage of time.

However, even long-term investing has its detractors. Opposition is based mostly on the belief that a "buy and hold" philosophy is ineffective in range-bound or sideways markets. The thinking goes this way: If we are not going to have long, sweeping, sustained uptrends (1982–2000 was the last one), then every stock bought is a potential sale. Investors need a game plan that fits shorter time horizons. They should monitor their holdings more closely and be willing to accept smaller gains. Why ride a stock up and then watch as it slides back down? Chico's, one of Wall Street's favorite growth retailers, rose from 16 to 49 over a three-year period. But three years of gains were eased in three months, mostly in one day, when the company lowered its earnings guidance and fell to 17 in the summer of 2006.

Don't Fall in Love Ralph Bloch, former chief market technician for Raymond James & Associates, is passionate in his opposition to buy and hold: "When the average investor says I'm in this stock for the long term, what they do, in effect, is turn their back on the stock. What you're supposed to do with every investment you ever make is to constantly play devil's advocate. People too often fail to recognize their errors. You buy a stock and it drops a few points. You remain confident. It drops a few more points. Your palms get sweaty. It drops a few more points. Now, you're a long-term investor! If you buy for the long term have a plan in place to recognize when you've made a mistake. I feel for the guy who bought Sun Microsystems at $60. I hope he was two or three months old at the time because he'll have to wait for it to rise 15-fold to break even. So please have a plan. Don't fall in love with stocks. They are inanimate objects. Don't play ostrich. Remember what part of your anatomy is left exposed when you stick your head in the sand" (Moneyshow.com, *Why Buy-and-Hold Investing No Longer Works* video, recorded San Francisco Money Show, October 2006).

It pays to listen to someone like Mr. Bloch, who has survived Wall Street's battles for close to 50 years. You can always learn from the savvy veteran. But there's *always* an opposing view. Mr. Bloch is, by his own description, an "aggressive, short-term oriented" technical analyst. I believe the long-term investor who buys at the right price with stop-loss protection, a profit target, and patience is better served by turning his back on the stock and tuning out the noise. The whole key is buying at a low, reasonable price. That's what avoids horror stories like Sun Microsystems, or at least limits the damage. It's best to own long term by design. Unfortunately, most long-term positions are probably stocks bought for a shorter term that didn't work out, mostly because they were bought too high.

> "Investors would do well to learn from deer hunters and fishermen who know the importance of being there and using patient persistence—so they are there when opportunity knocks."
> —*Charles Ellis*

C. Contrarian Investing We've discussed the long-term and technical approaches to the market. Another widely used strategy is the contrarian approach. It is often difficult to implement but its track record makes it worth the effort.

If, by nature, most of us are emotionally programmed to do the wrong thing in the market (buy at tops, sell at bottoms, etc.), then it's logical to assume that we can do the right thing by going against the majority. Sounds good in theory but it's a lot easier said than done. The problem is trying to identify just what *is* the consensus view. Information overload and instant communication have caused a blurring of popular and contrary opinion. Today, information travels at the speed of a mouse click. The entire world is instantaneously and simultaneously informed about everything. If there is a view that's clearly in the minority, that fact alone is enough to attract an army of other contrarians, quickly removing it from the out-of-favor category. The result is that on most of the widely discussed investment issues, opinion is divided pretty evenly. If there is a tilt (usually at the onset of an issue), the tilt soon flattens out and, in fact, over time, the minority view often becomes the majority view.

There are times, however, when a clear consensus does emerge. There is no blurring of crowd fear and despair at market bottoms or of euphoria and greed at market tops. It is at these junctures, when it is most difficult emotionally to execute, that acting as a contrarian pays off the most. These extreme, black-and-white situations don't happen often, however, and, if the pundits are right, they're apt to occur even less in the future. Most gurus look for range-bound markets in the years ahead, which precludes steep, long-term trends. It's a consensus view that could be wrong, but if right, we'll still have cyclical uptrends and downtrends within the trading range. There's always a bull and bear market somewhere so there are always opportunities to swim against the tide.

The contrarian looks for two essential ingredients in a stock. First, it must be out of favor, depressed, and unloved. Second, it must have the distinct prospect of going up. Simply because you're acting as a contrarian doesn't mean you're right. Benjamin Graham says, "You are neither right nor wrong because the crowd disagrees with you. You are right because your

> "I owe my success to having listened respectfully to the very best advice and then going away and doing the exact opposite."
> —G. K. Chesterton

data and reasoning are right" (*Intelligent Investor*, Harper Business, paperback revised 2003). As the buyer of an unloved stock, you must determine whether its problems are temporary. Few of us have the training to make that judgment. So we make an educated guess or seek the advice of a professional.

The Herd Instinct of the Pros   The contrarian approach requires another essential ingredient—patience. A stock out of favor can stay out of favor. A recovery that's expected "sooner or later" is likely to come later.

In most discussions of contrary opinion, the investment public is described with derisive words like the *herd* or the *crowd*. That's a bad rap. Most opinions expressed by individual investors reflect what they're told by their advisers and what they hear and see in the media. The consensus view of the herd is, in effect, a mirror of the same consensus view voiced by brokers, commentators on TV, and writers in print. The oft-quoted truism is that the small investor (the herd, the crowd) is usually wrong in the stock market. If indeed this is true, then it follows that most of the supposedly more knowledgeable professionals, who shape the opinion of the public, are responsible for its misdirection. In theory, the pro acts in a cool, detached manor. As a practical matter, he is a human being and often succumbs to the same herd instincts as the rest of us.

Sometimes the contrarian is wrong and the consensus is right, usually during the middle stages of an extended bull or bear market. The longer a trend exists, the more time there is to build a consensus. After the market's dramatic rebound in 2003, the widespread view was that we would see a cooling-off in 2004 and record single-digit gains at best. That's exactly what happened, the major indexes advancing 3 to 9 percent for the year.

No strategy works in every situation, but the contrarian approach has stood the test of time. Indeed, most successful investors have a contrarian bent. The more experienced they are, the more likely they are to be a contrarian. There are few savvy old-timers who are not members of the fold.

Top-performing veteran portfolio manager Bill Miller (Legg Mason Value Trust) says he gets his edge by fighting Wall Street's mob mentality. He is not afraid to buy a good stock caught up in a scandal. In his 2006 letter to stockholders, he attributed his success to "investing long term in a short term world, being contrarian when conformity is more comfortable and being willing to court controversy and be wrong." The old saw is that "the market will do what it has to, to make the majority of people wrong." That would make the minority a good place to be. The more difficult it is to take a contrary position, the more likely it is to be right.

The most reliable contrary indicator may be right under your nose. Some investors, by virtue of a complete lack of discipline, are born losers. Everything they buy goes down; everything they sell goes up. If you know someone who is consistently wrong, you can do the exact opposite of what he does, and be consistently right. (If that someone is you, think about shifting into reverse.)

D. Dollar Cost Averaging Dollar cost averaging is the investment of a fixed dollar amount at fixed intervals of time (usually monthly or quarterly) without regard to the share price. It's a popular approach because it solves the dilemma of when to buy in a market that's unpredictable. The removal of both emotion and decision making from the investment process makes it less stressful and more doable. And it makes a stock that's going down a positive instead of a negative because more shares can be bought for the same amount of money. Says financial columnist Andrew Tobias, "If you're young, get into the habit of investing $500 a month, or whatever you can afford—and be thrilled if the market drops. That just means you can buy new shares 'on sale'" (AndrewTobias .com, February 17, 2005).

There are two essentials for making dollar cost averaging work. The first is the discipline to regularly add to your position during rough times when disenchantment is causing others to sell or when you have a lot of other uses for the money. The second is a stock (or mutual or index fund) that goes back up, preferably not too quickly so you can accumulate cheap shares.

The big knock on dollar cost averaging is that if you go back and plug in the numbers during certain stretches of years, investing at fixed intervals produces weaker results than a lump sum investment or even random investing (meaning whenever you have the money). The explanation given is that the market goes up more than it goes down and the underlying upward bias makes the chances for extended accumulation at low prices less likely. Ed Elfenbein (*Crossing Wall Street,* July 10, 2007) says, "There is absolutely no inherent advantage in dollar-cost-averaging over lump sum investing. Don't diversify by time, diversify by assets." Adds columnist Timothy Middleton, "What dollar cost averaging has become is a salesman's tool to prize away in small increments the larger sum he couldn't talk you out of in the first place" (Moneycentral.msn. com, "The Costly Myth of Dollar-Cost-Averaging," January 4, 2005).

Essentials for Success In my view, a successful dollar-cost-averaging program requires four basic steps, with luck being a key component. First, initiate the program with the stock or mutual fund or index fund at a reasonably low price. (If it collapses after you start and stays collapsed for a long time before it recovers, that's okay.) Second, accumulate stock at the low price—the longer the stock is down, the better. Third, pick a stock that will eventually rise to a high price. And fourth, sell your shares, not when your time table calls for it but when the price is high. Granted, this sounds like an unrealistic Will Rogers scenario ("Find a good stock and when it goes up, sell it. If it doesn't go up, don't buy it!"). One thing you can do to help make it happen is to focus on quality stocks that are depressed, selling near strong support, and with problems that are likely to keep them under pressure for a while. The "quality" aspect sharply increases the prospect of eventual recovery.

The bottom line is that even if you're not lucky enough to pick the right time frame, if you stay with it long enough, you'll likely do fine. Let's say you end up with an 8 percent average annual return versus 11 percent with some other approach. It's still 8 percent you might not have had otherwise. Even critic Middleton says, "If dollar cost averaging is what it takes to get you to invest, so be it. Investing is better than not investing."

> "Wide diversification is only required when investors do not understand what they are doing."
> —*Warren Buffett*

E. Dogs of the Dow Another well-known investment approach requiring continuous discipline is labeled "Dogs of the Dow." It's a classic value strategy popularized in the early 1990s. Its founder, Michael O'Higgins, advocates the purchase of equal dollar amounts of the

10 highest-yielding stocks in the 30-stock Dow Jones Industrial Average on December 31 of each year. Each year-end, you keep the stocks that are still on the top 10 list and replace the others with the new qualifiers. The high yield usually means the stock is depressed, and if it's depressed, it usually means it has problems.

Since the 30 stocks in the Dow are seasoned issues, the "Dogs of the Dow" is an approach that forces the investor to buy quality stocks at depressed levels, sell them when they're up, and get paid a nice dividend in the interim. Of course, some on the list may continue to languish or go lower but, on balance, this simple strategy has outperformed both the Dow and the S&P 500 Indexes. For the 15-year period ending December 31, 2006, the average annual total return was 13.3 percent including reinvested dividends (dogsofthedow.com). In bear markets it will likely show low returns or losses, more than offset by good returns in up-markets, especially markets that favor large cap and/or dividend-paying stocks. It's an approach that needs stick-to-it-iveness and time to work out (see Michael O'Higgins' *Beating the Dow,* Harper Collins, 2000, and dogsofthedow.com).

As with all successful formulas, there are always variations that report-edly produce even better results. One is the European version of the Dogs of the Dow (*Barron's,* January 29, 2007). Charles Carlson, editor of the *Drip Investor,* focuses on the worst-performing stocks in the Dow rather than the highest yielding. On the January 20, 2004, MarketWatch.com web site he said his research of the Dow Jones Industrial Average revealed one theme that stuck out: The worst-performing of the 30 stocks in the Dow over a one-year period "tended to do quite well" the following year. He exam-ined the returns of Dow stocks going back to 1930 and found that simply buying a basket of the Dow's 5 or 10 worst-performing stocks each year "would have far surpassed the return of the Dow Jones Industrial Average, especially in recent years." Carlson outlines his "worst to first" strategy in his book *Winning with the Dow's Losers* (New York: HarperCollins, 2004). Finally, there's the "Small Dogs of the Dow," which focuses on the five lowest-priced of the 10 highest yielders in the Dow.

F. Laddering CDs Next to buying U.S. Treasury bonds and holding them to maturity, probably the safest investment strategy is laddering certificates of deposit (CDs). Bank CDs are federally insured up to

$100,000 per depositor. For those who cannot assume stock market risk, it's an obvious choice. What it lacks in excitement, it makes up in dependability and predictability. You collect a steady flow of interest because there's always a CD maturing soon.

The dilemma is that in a period of low interest rates, you may not be able to generate the income you need. So the temptation is to reach for riskier income vehicles that offer greater returns. Invariably, those that can least afford to lose, do so. Most times the investor interested primarily in income and safety will be better off not reaching and staying with risk-free CDs, Treasuries, and short-term bonds. Joe Rosenberg, chief investment strategist for Loews Corp., says, "More money has been lost reaching for yield than at the point of a gun" (*Barron's*, "Loews' Trusted Adviser," May 22, 2006).

Laddering is particularly suited to a time of rising interest rates. It prevents being locked into a low yield while rates are rising. To structure a ladder, you buy equal dollar amounts of CDs of varying maturities, let's say six month, one year, two year, and five year. When the six-month CD matures, you shift the money into a five-year CD; as each CD comes due you put the proceeds into the longest-term (highest-yielding) CD. By using this strategy, you end up with a higher average yield than if you had put everything into the five-year CD, providing interest rates go up. If they don't, or if they go down, your return will be less. In either case your money has the full protection of the government. Those who can afford to can maximize their return by reinvesting their interest.

CDs can be bought through stock brokerage firms as well as banks. However, broker CDs are more like bonds since they fluctuate in price (depending on interest rates), they can be bought and sold anytime, and they may be callable before maturity. But they, too, are FDIC insured.

The ladder approach can also be used with varying maturities of U.S. Treasuries, corporate bonds, and municipal bonds. Fidelity, Schwab, and others offer online bond laddering services featuring low bond commissions for small investors. A mutual fund that uses the laddering technique is another option. Thornburg Limited Term Income Fund, for example, is a low risk fund that ladders mostly floating-rate corporate bonds of 1- to 10-year maturities (*Barron's*, June 12, 2006).

Personal finance columnist Humberto Cruz has a "significant chunk" of his personal portfolio in low-cost, broadly diversified stock mutual

> "One of the biggest mistakes individual investors make is the notion of 'I'll hold it until I get back to even.'"
>
> —*Duncan Richardson*

funds but Cruz is also a big fan of laddering. He owns fixed-income investments coming due every year from 2008 through 2012. Those CDs maturing in 2007 he will replace with other CDs and/ or investment-grade bonds with staggering maturities from 2013 through 2017. In his syndicated column "The Savings Game" (*South Florida Sun Sentinel,* April 2, 2007), Cruz says, "It's hard to beat 'laddering' to smooth out the overall volatility of a portfolio and create a stable and dependable source of cash flow."

G. Other Strategies These are just a few of the ways to approach the market (or, in the case of laddering CDs, to avoid the market). There are countless others. Each has its own following.

Some investors look for companies with wide economic "moats." These are firms that enjoy strong competitive advantages due to things like an entrenched brand (Tiffany's), cost and distribution superiority (Wal-Mart), and massive customer base (eBay). The high barriers to entry allow such companies to generate a high return on capital. Other investors concentrate on companies that report earnings surprises. The one element that can be depended on to move stocks is surprise. Some studies have shown that gains in a stock triggered by unexpected higher earnings tend to be repeated. There are "earnings surprise" screens that list stocks in order of how much their reported earnings were above or below the consensus estimate (Zacks Investment Research).

Some investors concentrate on particular asset classes or investment styles. For example, they might favor low-multiple or value stocks and funds; others focus on high-multiple or growth stocks and funds. The boundaries separating value and growth, however, are fuzzy and the two investment styles often overlap. Growth managers will claim their hold-ings represent good value, and value managers argue their stocks have growth characteristics as well. The term *blend* is an umbrella term that encompasses both styles. To complicate matters further, value, growth, and blend funds are dividend into large capitalization (cap), small cap, and medium cap funds, depending on the total market value of the shares outstanding.

All investment styles rotate in popularity. Their day in the sun can last a long time. For example, a table of the top-performing asset classes each year (Merrill Lynch, September 2003) shows large cap growth topped the list in each of the five years 1995 through 1999. In the following three years, 2000 to 2002, the same asset class was at the bottom of the list, with bonds, both government and corporate, the clear winners. During the years 2000–2006, small caps were on a hot streak and so were real estate investment trusts (REITs). In the same seven-year period, value stocks had a strong run while growth struggled. Out-of-favor categories will always return to favor but the "when" and the "for how long" are unknowable.

When holding unpopular groups, it's well to keep in mind these two basics: First, as I pointed out in Chapter 3, trends, once entrenched, usually last longer and go further than most everybody expects. Second, the only way to benefit from the knowledge that all out-of-favor groups will return to favor sometime is to hold on. Patience and stick-to-it-iveness are the key.

On a Magazine Cover? Sell It Short Finally, there are those who build their strategy around special situations. Some investors, for example, may focus on turnaround candidates or companies coming out of bankruptcy. Others may target takeover prospects or stocks that are the object of heavy institutional accumulations or insider buying. There are investors who zero in on companies that have revised their earnings upward or increased their dividends. Others focus on cheap stocks with strong momentum or on stocks that have seen their first analyst upgrade because more upgrades are likely to follow. And still others copycat the purchases of legendary investors like Buffett, Soros, Icahn, and others, or sell short the subject of a bullish magazine cover story (by the time it's on the cover, it's old news, the easy money has been made, and it can only go downhill, or so the theory goes).

Whatever the strategy or strategies employed, the odds favor the investor with the intestinal fortitude to stick to his game plan, buoyed by the knowledge that what has worked before will, in time, work again. The obvious question: Instead of being stubborn, why not stay with a particular approach or asset class only as long as it's popular and then when it fades, simply switch into the new favorite? There may be a few talented or lucky managers who can do this, but knowing when to buy and sell a trend is very, very tricky and is usually a loser's game. Staying the course removes the guesswork.

Consistency, then, is my sixth core conviction. It's central to all investment strategies. More important than the particular approach is the degree of commitment. Whatever the tactic used, it is perseverance, steadfastness, and stick-to-it-tiveness that make it work. It's worth remembering, however, that no strategy is more important than the two discussed earlier, namely, the proper allocation of assets and the buying of those assets at the right price. Nothing you do as an investor can help more to control risk and generate profit.

> "However beautiful the strategy, you should occasionally look at the results."
> —*Winston Churchill*

7. Index Funds: The Answer for Most, But Not the Whole Answer

In discussing various market strategies and the vital role that consistency plays in their execution, there are two basic approaches to the market that I purposely left out. One is based on the knowledge that most investors underperform the overall market. Therefore, buying the market itself via an index fund is an approach that ensures a performance better than most. In the process, the investor gives up any attempt to do better than whatever benchmark index is being cloned.

The other approach is more aggressive and, because it entails more risk, has the potential for greater rewards. It's based on the assumption that an actively managed portfolio has the ability to outperform one that simply mirrors a static market index. Most active investors know the market is tough to beat but they welcome the challenge. It may be a minority, but they know that some *do* outperform the indexes; why not them?

There is a perennial battle between the advocates of active and passive investing. My guess is that the more experienced the investor, the longer he's been exposed to the market's pitfalls, the more likely he is to favor index investing for most if not all of his money. Being in the game a long time generates an increasing sensitivity to the extreme difficulty of besting the market with any sort of consistency. After 40 years exposure, I come down strongly on the side of indexing for most investors. It's my seventh and final core conviction. Investing is all about putting the odds in our favor, and this is the best way to do it. The word *guarantee* can seldom be used in discussing the stock market. This is one of the few times it applies. Investors who decide to index are guaranteed whatever return the market gives.

I do believe, however, that some of your money should be actively managed. Part Two of this book, discusses passive versus active investing. The focus is on 28 diversified, low-cost, model index fund portfolios from 28 authorities on index funds. Each buy-and-hold portfolio includes percentage allocations and recommended index funds within each asset class. The first five or six are so-called "lazy man" portfolios, the ultimate in simplicity. Each portfolio, because of the uncorrelated nature of its components, has the potential of outperforming the broad general market.

For active investors not interested in indexing, I highlight a select group of elite money managers, mutual funds, and monitored portfolios. These are names that stand above the rest in results achieved over a long period of years. There are a myriad of choices for the creative investor. I discuss those that have worked the best. I also examine the best sources for getting the best stock ideas.

> "Beat the market? The idea is ludicrous. Very few investors manage to beat the market. But in an astonishing triumph of hope over experience, millions of investors keep trying."
>
> —*Jonathan Clements*

Chapter 5

Thirty-Five Nuggets

The following nuggets are not as basic as the absolute maxims and core convictions outlined in Chapters 3 and 4, but they are almost as valuable. They are insights that provide an edge in dealing with challenges that face the investor every day. They will help reduce the confusion and frustration that is a part of the investment process. These "truisms to trust" complete everything I know about the market that you should know.

1. After You Buy, It'll Always Go Lower

Forget about buying a stock, a fund, or an index at the bottom or selling at the top. Yes, somebody does, but that elusive somebody will never be you. The truth is that after you buy a stock it will go lower—not sometimes but always. And when you sell a stock, it will always go higher. It's not bad luck or bad timing. It's simply unrealistic to expect that, competing with thousands of other players, you're going to be smart or lucky enough to get the very top or bottom tick.

If you know ahead of time that it's going to go lower after you buy it, why not wait? The reason is because if you do and the stock goes lower, you'll want to wait some more. But then, at some point, it'll turn around and you'll be left on the sidelines. The best you can do is to buy in a reasonable buying range, know that it's going to tick lower after you buy it, but also know that you have a position in the stock and will benefit when it goes up. Don't be disappointed when this happens. It happens to everybody. It's part of the game.

Also worth remembering: In more cases than not, stocks go down faster than they go up. The likely reason for this, at least in part, is that the emotions that trigger selling are felt more intensely than those that motivate buying. It's usually more urgent to get off the train than to get on.

2. CEOs on Their Own Stock

There is an important distinction between prospects for a company and prospects for the stock of that company. One can be good and the other can be bad. All the good things management says about the company may already be reflected in the high price of the stock which may, in fact, be due for a fall.

The head of a company is often the worst source of advice regarding his own stock. His focus, understandably and rightfully, is on the operations of the company, and his appraisal is based on an intimate knowledge of the company and the industry, not the stock market. If asked about the stock, the CEO will typically respond, "I'll leave that to Wall Street."

It's not that the CEO is not interested in the stock. Getting the price up and keeping it going up is a top priority. Not only will a rising price keep stockholders happy but his own compensation is often tied contractually to the performance of the stock via the exercise of options. The CEO will often express frustration and puzzlement over the disconnect between what he sees as rosy fundamentals and the depressed levels of his stock. Most CEOs have less than a sophisticated grasp of the myriad of factors that can influence a stock over and above the fundamentals.

In dealing with management interviews, the investor has two problems. First, much of what is said is predictable. Things are either good or about to improve. The executive *has* to believe that (at least publicly) to please stockholders and keep his job. The CEO has an agenda—to make good news sound even better and to put other news in the most favorable light. Everything he says may be perfectly true but you rarely get the whole story. The focus will be on the items in column A (bullish news and the rewards that will follow) rather than the items in column B (bearish news and the risks involved). Instead of a balanced, even-handed presentation, the interview turns out to be little more than a PR release with the usual corporate spin. Some reporters are better than others at asking the tough questions. But all media has the same two restrictions: Like politicians, CEOs are adept at dancing around hard questions, and reporters don't have enough airtime to press. Also, reporters usually don't want to risk offending guests for fear of closing the door to future interviews.

CEOs are not in the business of directly recommending their company's stock. Invariably, however, the clear implication of their favorable remarks is that the stock should be bought *without regard to its present price*. If, indeed, there has been a sharp run-up, there is no tempering of enthusiasm. This constitutes the second major problem for investors in evaluating CEO remarks. Corporate executives are likely to be equally bullish about their stock whether it's at 20 or at 80. There is never acknowledgment that all the great things they are saying may already be reflected in the price of the stock. As much as the CEO knows about his company and industry,

> "We do not talk to management. We know management is lying when their lips are moving. They are by definition cheerleaders. I don't fault them for it, but I don't care to hear it."
>
> —*Ted Aronson*

that's how little he knows or wants to know about the stock market (there are always exceptions, of course). It behooves investors to be aware of this and to remember that the stock of even the best company with the best prospects should be bought only if it's reasonably priced.

3. Conventional Wisdom Is More Conventional than Wisdom

The term *market truism* can be misleading because truth is thought of as absolute but market truisms are often less than 100 percent true. The only time a market maxim can be relied on as unwavering, unquestionable truth is when it is rooted 100 percent in human nature. If the truism stems from basic emotions like fear and despair or hope and greed, you can take it to the bank. Otherwise, there is always room for divergence, as in the following less than 100 percent truisms.

To "buy low," for example, is a key investment principle, but sometimes a stock at $40 is a better buy (following an upside breakout from a long base) than at $20 (in a free-fall slide). "Bulls and bears make money, pigs get slaughtered" has been bandied about forever. It's a maxim well worth listening to—but not always. Markets and individual stocks always go to extremes and not everybody holds on and gets slaughtered when the bubble bursts. In the meteoric NASDAQ run-up to 5,000 in years 1999–2000, hundreds of thousands of speculators bought dot-com stocks at ridiculously high price/earnings multiples and then sold them at even more ludicrous prices. Many of the trades that crossed the tape during that dazzling climb represented a seller cashing in. Greed paid off big-time.

The same applied during the 1980s when income buyers ignored the age-old investment principle "The higher the yield, the greater the risk" and loaded up on juicy 10 to 15 percent yielding junk bonds and Nuveen-type closed-end bond funds. Not only did buyers enjoy extraordinarily high yields but they also saw the value of their bonds go up as yields gradually receded. It was a case where investors paid little heed to the usually dependable advice, "Don't reach for yield," and profited handsomely from their greed, luck, and/or ignorance.

There is no market rule that doesn't have exceptions. "Stocks climb a wall of worry" is the old saw, but there *are* times when stocks climb with few worries, as, for example, in the middle of a sustained uptrend. After the market peaks and starts to decline, the worry starts to build and reaches its maximum at the market bottom. That's where it provides the right climate for a market turnaround but it gradually fades as the market recovers. In the mid and later stages of the market's climb, the dominant emotional fuel is hope, then optimism, and then euphoria, not worry.

Advice That's Paid For or Free—Which Is Better?

Most of the time, "Don't fight the Fed" is sound advice, meaning don't buy stocks aggressively when the Federal Reserve Board is tightening money. A Fed that's committed to raising interest rates aggressively will invariably kill a bull market. The rising cost of money usually squeezes corporate profits, slows the economy, and triggers a down market.

It didn't work that way in 2004–2006. Starting in June 2004 and finishing in mid-2006, the Fed raised short-term interest rates by ¼ percent (25 basis points) at each of 17 consecutive Fed meetings. Instead of turning lower, stocks continued to post gains in all three years. Why did the steady rate climb fail to deter the market? Likely because this time the interest rate increases started from a historically low 1 percent level, they were small and gradual, and the steady buying of U.S. Treasuries by foreign governments kept long-term rates low.

We should treat so-called market truisms with respect but not as gospel. These sayings have stood the test of time for good reason—most of the time they work. "Let your winners ride and cut your losses" is solid investment strategy, but so is rebalancing, which requires you to trim back on your winners. "You get what you pay for" is a truth we can all attest to in our daily lives, but when applied to the field of investment advice, its value is less than certain. Advice you pay for may or may not be better than what's free. If it costs money it probably has an edge because it usually (but not always) reflects more experience and a better track record.

"This time it's different" is rightly ridiculed when used to explain what appears to be a first-time occurrence in the market. Most often it turns out to be just a variation of what's happened before. But sometimes this time *is* different. The Dow Jones Industrial Average went up sharply in every year ending in "5" since 1895, without exception. In 2005, the Dow ended the year flat. It was different.

A World of Misinformation

"Sell on the news" is a popular trading strategy that works for a good reason. A stock will often move up in anticipation of news and then sell off when the news is released. Traders take profits figuring the news is already reflected in the stock price. But it doesn't always work that way. Biopharmaceutical company Celgene moved from 24 to 57 in 2005, triggered in part by expectations for its new drug Revlimid for transfusion-dependent anemia. On December 29, 2005, two days *after* the company announced FDA approval, it traded at 65, up another 14 percent.

Hewlett Packard provides another example of premature selling on the news. At the time CEO Carly Fiorina was ousted, the stock was selling around 18. It started moving up in anticipation of a new leader and hit 22 on the day that news of the appointment of Mark Hurd was released. But it continued to climb steadily, reaching 30 nine months later, and over 40 a year after that.

"There's always a bull market somewhere" is a market maxim that's generally true. But it applies more to dull, sideways markets than it does to broad, sweeping, downtrends. The odds are against being able to pick a stock or sector that can swim against an onrushing tide. In that situation it's better to heed another maxim that'll put the odds in your favor, "don't fight the tape." (See item 34 for more.)

Along with market truisms that may not be true, the investor has to deal with financial reporting that may not be true. Regardless of how authentic-sounding the source, there is precious little investment information that you can depend on being unequivocally accurate. But we accept it as truth for good reasons: Usually there are enough half truths to make the whole sound credible; the source's impeccable, long-standing reputation precludes questioning; the findings have been repeated so often for so long, they are too ingrained to be doubted; or the information is so overwhelmingly logical, it leaves no room for skepticism.

Why is there so much misinformation in the media? Some writers simply don't care enough about the quality of their research. With obvious exceptions and to various degrees, researchers can be lazy. Checking facts for accuracy can be tedious and time-consuming. It's far easier to repeat what's been said before, especially when there's a deadline. (I have been guilty of this, hopefully not often.) I have written about this before but it cannot be overemphasized. Lack of pride in the quality of product and the acceptance of mediocrity means it behooves investors to be skeptical about information no matter how reputable the source. It may be true, it may be partially true, or it may be untrue. Everyone is entitled to their opinion but sometimes conclusions are presented as facts, and that's where it can get sticky.

Doing the research for this book and finding different sets of facts from different sources on the exact same subject has been frustrating. A growing skepticism has developed into a nasty habit that I find difficult

to control. When I'm told a supposed fact by friend or family, I
have a reflex reaction—I blurt
out a number, say, "4." (I try and
say it under my breath). This is
my less-than-subtle way of saying

> "I measure what's going on and I adapt to it. I try to get my ego out of the way. The market is smarter than I am, so I bend."
> —*Martin Zweig*

that I attach a 40 percent chance of the information being true. My
family puts up with it because they're family; friends are less tolerant.

4. Humility Is Sadly Lacking on Wall Street

There is no area of human endeavor where understatement is more
appropriate and less visible than in the stock market. Despite the fact
that no one has the right answers all the time, there are some who
imply that they do, with never a hint that they may be wrong. The old
saying is that there are only two types of people on Wall Street—those
who don't know and those who don't know they don't know.

In my opinion, investment advisers who don't disclose their advice-
giving limitations are doing a disservice to their customers, who often
come to them with unrealistic expectations. The adviser may think it's
obvious that he can be wrong and that there are opposite opinions, so
there's no need to verbalize it. But that's simply not true. In no uncertain
terms, the customer should be reminded that the fees and commissions
he's paying do not insure a favorable result. Yes, most customers may know
that, but some do not, and even those who do may need reminding.

If ego or the prospect of killing the sale get in the way of an admission of fallibility, the adviser should at least be able to present both sides
of the story. If there's always a column A (positives) and a column B
(negatives), which there always is, why aren't they both revealed as a
matter of routine?

There are probably two reasons. First, the adviser is not fully
informed and honestly believes he's presenting the whole story or, at
least, everything the investor needs to know. He has little motivation to
dig up the negatives because, based on what he knows, he strongly
believes his recommendation will make money for the customer.
Second, undiluted enthusiasm is an effective sales tool whereas full

disclosure and restraint are not. The adviser gives the customer what he wants, namely assertive, unhedged opinion. Presenting negatives creates doubt and confusion, not confidence. Discussing risks as well as rewards creates the impression that the adviser may have doubts. However, in my view, those who do not indicate in some way that they can be wrong and make some attempt to present the negatives are acting irresponsibly.

In Wall Street, it's the savvy old-timer, the one who has had a long and successful career, who is most likely to show humility. Being wrong often over a long period of time has a way of deflating ego. Also, the crusty veteran has the least to lose by admitting his fallibility. He's already made his mark. He's also wise enough to know that open admission of limitations enhances rather than detracts from his credibility. Most investors, on the other hand, blame poor results on bad luck or bad advice while attributing good results to their own skills.

Buffett: "I Made a Big Mistake"

The self-effacing comments of Wall Street legends Warren Buffett (chairman, Berkshire Hathaway) and Peter Lynch (former manager of the Fidelity Magellan Fund) have been widely quoted throughout the years. Their brilliant track records have earned them universal acclaim. Yet, when commenting on their own performance, it's their mistakes in judgment that they often talk about the most.

Lynch claims even the top managers are wrong almost as often as they're right. "In this business, if you're good, you're right six times out of ten" (interview on PBS.org). Buffett admits bad judgment on both the sell side and the buy side. "I made a big mistake in not selling several of our larger holdings during the Great Bubble" (2003 Annual Letter). "I set out to buy $100 million worth of Wal-Mart shares at a pre split price of $23. We bought a little and it moved up a little and I thought maybe it will come back a bit. That thumb sucking has cost us in the current area of $10 billion" (annual meeting, May 2004).

Bill Miller, portfolio manager for Legg Mason's Value Trust mutual fund, is described in the *Wall Street Journal* (November 5, 2004) as "one of the most widely respected stock pickers in Wall Street." His record of outperforming the S&P 500 Index for 15 straight years (1991 to 2005) is unmatched by any other mutual fund. In his third-quarter report to shareholders (September 2004), he said, "I have no idea what the market is going to do. I thought things looked pretty good fundamentally at the end of the second quarter and the market went right down. . . . By early December of 2003 I was prepared to initiate a position in the energy group. The shares then started to advance and hating to pay up for anything, I waited. That was a mistake. . . . Is it a mistake not to own them now? I don't know."

When Miller was asked whether he was relieved when his 15-year winning streak ended in 2006, he replied, "We are paid to do a job and we didn't do it in 06. . . . I'm not at all happy or relieved about that."

Finally, Pimco's Bill Gross, the nation's best-known and most widely followed bond expert, said in his November 2004 *Investment Outlook,* "The one investment certainty is that we are all frequently wrong."

This type of humility, often displayed by star performers at the top levels of management, is seldom repeated lower down in the pecking order. We don't often hear the words "I was wrong" or "It was a mistake" or "I don't know," not to mention the factors in both column A *and* column B, from the advisers most investors deal with. But we should. Such admissions show sensitivity and respect for the enigma that is the stock market. It's a case where "I don't know" conveys knowledge, not the lack of it. Humility in an adviser gives me more confidence, not less. It sets him apart. And when candor is backed by performance, that adviser has my attention.

> "Stay humble or the market will do it for you."
> —*Unknown*

5. A Sure Thing If You Have the Patience

Buy a quality, best of breed, blue chip stock at a depressed price and hold on. That's probably as close as you can get to a sure thing in the stock market. The "hold" part is what's tough. Staying committed to dead money while the world passes you by can exhaust the patience of even the most disciplined. The redeeming feature is the near certainty (I use that word advisedly) that, at some point in the future, the patience will pay off. As I've noted, the major difference between a speculative and quality stock is that the latter almost always comes back in time.

There are many examples of seasoned stocks, leaders in their industry, that have gone nowhere, seemingly forever. What they have in common, in addition to being bogged down, is a relatively low price/earnings multiple, a large capitalization, a much higher price in years past, and the general recognition that they represent good value. What they also have in common is that they are all members of an asset class—big cap growth—that has been out of favor since the beginning of this century. After six years, the large cap Dow Jones Industrial Average broke out into new all-time highs in late 2006 and early 2007. That may or may not signal a return to respectability for the group.

Microsoft reached a high of 60 in 1999 but later traded mostly between 24 and 30 for some six years through mid-2007. Pfizer, after falling from a high of 50, has spent recent years trading mostly in the narrow 24 to 28 range. With more than its share of problems, Pfizer nevertheless is an A rated, 4 percent-plus yielding stock that has raised its dividend 40 years in a row. General Electric, after a high of 60, has traded mostly between 30 and 38 for years. Wal-Mart touched 70 late in 1999 but got mired mostly in the 45 to 49 range. Citigroup peaked at 59 in the fall of 2000 and subsequently spent years stuck mostly in the 44 to 50 range. There are many other examples of industry-dominant companies that have gone unloved for long stretches, like Cisco, Time Warner, and Home Depot.

The long-term investor can derive comfort from owning a quality, dividend-paying stock with minimum downside risk and maximum prospects for an eventual payoff. Does this comfort level offset the frustration of having to wait what may seem interminably before seeing a return on his money? Each investor's temperament and tolerance is different. But in all cases, if the stock throws off a good dividend the frustration will be less.

Earnings Double But Stock Goes Nowhere

What's puzzling is that many depressed blue chips often sell at the same price they did 5 or 10 years ago despite having doubled their earnings.

How can that happen? In mid-2006, Microsoft was at 22, the same price it sold for in 1998 when its earnings were half of what they were in 2006. In 2007, Wal-Mart traded at 47, almost where it stood six years earlier, even though its profits had more than doubled. In July 2006, GE (an A+ rated stock with a 3 percent dividend yield) sold at 32, the same level as 1998 despite a substantial rise in earnings.

How can strong earnings growth be accompanied by little or no gain in price? Why is there such a sharp contraction in the price/earnings multiple investors are willing to pay? There are a number of reasons cited, none of them very compelling. They include, for the 2000–2006 period under review, a climate of mostly rising interest rates, concern over prospects for accelerating inflation, fears of a slowdown in earnings domestically and of a peak in economic growth globally, an erosion of U.S. influence and power in the world, and the ever-present threat of terrorism. The rationale is that investors are not willing to pay as much for stocks in a time of war (on terrorism) as in times of peace.

Whatever the reason, it behooves investors to be aware that when steady earnings growth is not reflected in the price of a stock, especially a high-quality stock, the resulting buildup of value represents opportunity—providing you have the necessary staying power. Joe Rosenberg has worked on Wall Street for 45 years as the chief investment strategist for Loews and the Tisch family. *Barron's* writer Andrew Bary labels him "one of the most knowledgeable investors around." In a May 22, 2006, *Barron's* interview, Rosenberg said, "We now have a situation where some of the largest companies, that were overvalued six years ago but have continued to grow earnings at 10 percent to 15 percent a year, are completely unloved on Wall Street. These companies are all household names. I never in a million years thought that I would be recommending stocks like Microsoft, Pfizer, Johnson & Johnson or Wal-Mart. These are some of the best values anywhere in the world."

They say on Wall Street, a bell doesn't ring at the bottom. But if you listen closely, you'll probably hear a muffled sound when bargain situations like these occur. At some point, price/earnings multiples return to their long-term averages and patience is rewarded. In the meantime, what you know for sure is that the stock will go lower after you buy it, and that it may take a long, long time for your ship to come in.

6. No Single Stock Has to Be Bought

Sometimes a stock recommendation is so enticing, the reasons for buying so convincing, and the pitch so passionate, that it is almost impossible to resist. In the time it takes to read a provocative article or to hear compelling advice on "tout TV" or from an animated broker, what may have been an unknown stock suddenly becomes a must-have. Flamboyant prose and/or liberal use of superlatives quickly activate the greed button. If it's a compelling recommendation on TV, heard by thousands all at the same time, the invariable result is a pop in the stock. The fast-rising price makes the stock even more wanted (before it "gets away").

Waiting for the initial excitement to subside makes sense. Doing so provides a calmer time for decision making and probably a cheaper price. It's usually best to let the stock come to you. If it doesn't, so be it. It's a big ocean and there are lots of fish. When I published the *Dick Davis Digest,* the following appeared in every issue: "If a stock has risen above its recommended price, we suggest waiting for the pullback that usually comes with patience. If it doesn't, this *Digest* is filled with alternative ideas. No one stock has to be bought. There is always another stock and there is always another day."

> "The best way to make a million dollars in the stock market? Start with $2 million."
> —*Henny Youngman*

7. The Sticky Question of When to Sell

Perhaps the most difficult of market skills is knowing when to sell. There is no one definitive answer, no formula that applies in all situations. To sell within a reasonable distance of the high is probably the best we can hope for, and even that is easier said than done. Since we already know that, invariably, stocks go higher after we sell, it makes sense not to sell all our shares at once. It doesn't always work and it takes longer, but the odds favor a higher average price if sales are spread out. The most common mistake is selling winners too soon and holding on to losers too long.

Investors sell stocks for many different reasons. Here are some that make good sense.

- The stock has reached your price objective, adjusted as company fundamentals evolve.
- The stock is selling at the high end of its historic price/earnings multiple—or its price/book, price/sales, or other pertinent statistical ratio.
- You need the money.
- The long-term fundamental outlook for the company has changed due to deterioration in its basic, underlying business (the change usually not knowable except in retrospect).
- The original reason for purchase (an expected buyout or anticipated new product, for example) no longer applies. Peter Lynch, famed ex-manager of the Fidelity Magellan Fund, says, "Before you make a purchase, you should be able to explain why you are buying it in terms that an 11-year-old can understand—three sentences at most. Remember this reason and sell the holding when the reason no longer continues to hold" (gurufocus.com, "The Wit and Wisdom of Peter Lynch," January 4, 2006).
- The time you were willing to wait for performance expires (a good dividend is likely to make you more patient while waiting).
- The technical or chart position of the stock suggests a sale (primary uptrend line or support level broken, for example).
- A guru like Warren Buffett or an adviser with a great track record sells the stock you're holding (although his reasons may have little to do with your situation).
- Management's integrity is under investigation by authorities (where there's smoke, there's usually fire).
- Selling (rebalancing) is required to keep your portfolio properly aligned.
- You want to nail down profits or protect partial profits (especially when a stock goes up too much, too quickly in response to news that may prove untrue).
- You want to limit loss when a stock drops to a predetermined price.
- There exists a threat of major, new competition.

- The departure or death of a dominant corporate leader has occurred, especially in smaller companies.
- The stock you own is near its target price and you find a better relative value elsewhere.
- The company reports a sharp unexpected drop in earnings and a weak forecast.
- You want to take some money off the table. Securing a partial profit reduces risk of loss.

Other reasons come into play in determining when to sell mutual funds. Some fund owners will sell if their fund is underperforming its peers for two straight years. Other red flags include a new manager (especially in a fund long run by a single successful manager) and a large influx of money invested in a small, successful fund (forcing it to work in an arena it's not used to). In both cases, however, the passage of time may be needed to make a fair evaluation.

Aside from needing the money, none of these reasons to sell stocks or funds are carved in stone. In every case there may be extenuating circumstances that fully justify holding on. If nothing else, however, they should give rise to a rethinking of your position.

Stop-Loss Orders: How Much Room?

When to take losses is as thorny and controversial a question as when to take profits. How do we determine the price when entering a stop-loss order? The purpose is to limit our loss, but how do we know when we're giving the stock either too much room to fall or not enough?

Professionals differ widely on the subject. Veteran market observer William O'Neil, founder of the national daily newspaper *Investor's Business Daily,* makes it simple: "My primary rule is to sell any stock that falls 8 percent below your purchase price." (*How to Make Money in Stocks,* McGraw Hill, 2002). Lou Dobbs, host of CNN's long-running *Lou Dobbs Tonight,* in an interview in *AARP Magazine* (November/December 2002) was equally precise: "If you lose 10 percent, get out of your investment." Eaton Vance portfolio manager Duncan Richardson uses the same 10 percent guideline.

At the other extreme is long-term oriented fund manager Jim O'Shaughnessy (Dreyfus Premier Alpha Growth Fund). A September 19,

2005, *Barron's* profile gave the reasons why O'Shaughnessy may sell. One of them was the loss of 50 percent of market value from the date of purchase. Finally, successful stock trader Charles Kirk (TheKirkReport.com) says, "When setting stop-loss targets, it is important to understand the stock's normal trading pattern. I try to set my stop-loss order at a price level I don't think the stock should hit unless something really has gone wrong."

Wherever you place your stop-loss, you should be fully prepared to see it go off. That means it should be a loss you can live with. If it's a quality, wide-moving stock that you own for the long-term, I believe a close 8 percent to 10 percent stop makes it too easy to get whipsawed. Your stock needs more room. How much more is tough to pinpoint (a chart may be helpful) but it can't be so wide that, if executed, you will be too.

There are two ways of eliminating completely the question of when to sell. As discussed later in this chapter, one is to give someone else full discretion to handle your portfolio. This is only a good idea if you have the right adviser and the right "let go" temperament. The other way is to adopt a strictly buy-and-hold strategy—in other words, "never" sell.

When Buy-and-Hold Was King

The prevailing view during much of the past century was that the safest and surest way to succeed in the market was to buy good-quality stocks, hold them indefinitely, and, if desired, pass them on to heirs. "Buy and hold" was considered the least stressful, most efficient, logical way to deal with a market whose underlying long-term bias was up but whose daily behavior was unpredictable. It was an approach nurtured by mostly steadily rising markets led by big cap, blue-chip growth stocks. Bouts of weakness were dependably followed by new highs, vindicating the investor's patience.

It was a strategy championed by the premier investor of the era, Warren Buffett. The "sage of Omaha" made no secret of his intention to hold on to his core holdings "forever." He described the cornerstone of his investment style as "lethargy bordering on sloth." And he advised stock buyers to visualize themselves as partners of a business that "they expect to stay with indefinitely."

Famed fund manager Marty Whitman (Third Avenue Value Fund) told Jim Grant (*Interest Rate Observer*), "I've been in this business 50 years. I've had a lot of experience holding stocks for three years during which time they doubled. Then I sold it to somebody else for whom it tripled in six months. You make more money sitting on your ass" (Eric Fry, "The Thrill of Boredom," June 28, 2005).

Charles Ellis, Greenwich Associates founder and author of the classic *Winning the Loser's Game,* (McGraw Hill, 4th edition, 2002), says, "If you're not willing to hold on for 10 years, you shouldn't start." Daniel Kahneman, psychology professor at Princeton University received the 2002 Nobel Prize in Economics for his contributions to behavioral finance. Advocating a buy and hold approach, he says, "All of us would be better investors if we just made fewer decisions" (turtletrader.com).

There's another good reason to buy and hold—it often achieves better results than buying and selling. Read what newsletter tracker Mark Hulbert writes in a MarketWatch.com column titled "The Value of Doing Nothing" (January 19, 2007): "You don't always have to be doing something in your portfolio in order to make money. Consider the results of an exercise I periodically conduct for the several hundred newsletters I track. I compare their calendar year result with how they would have performed had they undertaken no transactions—sticking with whatever they were recommending at the beginning of that year. Believe it or not, in every year I've done this, the average newsletter would have been better off doing nothing. . . . Unless the arguments for making a change in your holdings are compelling, you probably should simply do nothing."

> "Only buy something that you'd be perfectly happy to hold if the market shut down for 10 years."
> —*Warren Buffett*

Every Stock Is a Sale

There will always be support for a buy-and-hold strategy because it's so ingrained in our investment psyche, because making one decision is easier than making two, and because with unwavering patience and the passage of enough time, it's likely to work. But the widespread perception that market movements and investor returns will be modest in the foreseeable future, has fostered a growing disenchantment with the "never sell" mentality.

Forty-five years ago the average share of NYSE-listed stock was held for more than eight years. Today (influenced by program trading), turnover data from the Big Board reveals that the average holding period is less than a year. Investors who favor taking profits over a shorter time frame point to the sharp declines of 50 to 60 percent suffered by a broad range of blue chips in the 2000–2002 bear market. They also cite the steep sell-offs in the housing, commodity, and emerging market sectors during 2006. Also, the sudden 416-point slide in the Dow in late February 2007 that erased months of gains in one day certainly didn't help the case for buying and holding.

Even today, stocks like General Electric, Microsoft, IBM, and Coca-Cola are still far below their pre–bear market highs that were made years ago. Opponents of buy-and-hold maintain that every stock, including those of the highest quality, is a sale at some point in time. Jonah Kent, writing in *Investors Business Daily* (August 10, 2005), said, "Selling market blue-bloods can be a tough task but there's a time when every great stock must be sold." You'd have an equally tough task selling that argument to the investor who bought 100 shares of Phillip Morris (Altria) at 44 in 1957 and now has stock worth over $20 million, including reinvested dividends. Of course, the toughest task of all might be finding someone around today who has actually done that.

The shift away from a buy-and-hold strategy is justified, according to those who have shifted, because markets today act differently than they used to. It was okay to hold on to stocks when we had sweeping, all-inclusive, sustained uptrends. Today, however, markets are characterized mostly by sideways trading ranges. Instead of three steps forward and one step back, it's more likely to be three steps forward and three steps back. Until we see a resumption of sustained follow-throughs on the upside, a convincing case can be made for taking profits or at least taking some money off the table opportunistically. Even Warren Buffett conceded as much. In his 2003 annual letter to Berkshire Hathaway stockholders he said, "I made a big mistake in not selling several of our larger holdings during the Great Bubble."

In his book *The New Laws of the Stock Market Jungle* (Financial Times Press, 2004), Michael J. Panzner says today's markets are characterized by information overload, increased speculation, less reliable economic indicators, and less dependable seasonal patterns. His conclusion: Buy-and-hold investors may be fighting the last war. He's joined by George Kleinman, editor of the newsletter *Commodities Trends,* who opines, "When you're fortunate enough to have paper profits significant enough to make a measurable improvement in your net worth, then turn them into cash" (FinancialSense.com, February 21, 2006).

Investment personality Jim Cramer (TheStreet.com) has some personal long-term holdings but his primary focus is on the short term. He says, "Buy and hold means sticking around for a train crash. Sell is a curse word on Wall Street. The most typical advice is to sell when the train has already left the station" (*Oakland Tribune,* October 1, 2005). The numbers support the contention that Wall Street is reluctant to suggest selling. In the late 1990s, 9 out of every 10 analyst recommendations were buys. That number has dropped substantially, but buys still outnumber sells by a good margin.

"Don't Hold It Against Me"

Stock market adviser Dan Ferris, in an article about selling stocks (in "The Blast" e-mail service, July 21, 2005), reaches this conclusion: "So when do you sell? I don't know, I've been wrong about how to do it about half the time. Please try not to hold it against me because no one else seems to know either."

The 17 reasons to sell listed earlier are meant as guidelines but they are far from inviolate. The very best time to sell can only be known in retrospect. But the best time for *you* to sell has a lot to do with your temperament. That's a quality that *is* knowable ahead of time, but only by you. This would be a good question to ask yourself: "Which situation can I handle better—a repeated cycle of seeing a stock rise, seeing the gain erased, and then waiting, perhaps for a long time, before it rises to new heights again? Or am I better able emotionally to cope with selling a stock at a profit and then seeing it continue to go up, perhaps substantially, after I sell it?"

You can buy a stock at 40 and sell it at 48, comforted by the old saying, "you never go wrong taking a profit." But for most of us, the comfort quickly disappears when the stock proceeds to climb to 100.

Some, by disposition, can have closure and not look back; others hang on emotionally. "Know thyself" is the key, but you may have to go through the actual experience before "knowing thyself" for sure.

So, like most everything else that has to do with investing, we have a question with no definitive answer. The only honest response to the dilemma of when to sell is, "I don't know." It's a cloudy, complex, confusing subject with different investors and different situations calling for different responses. The best we can do is make an educated guess, keep our fingers crossed, and move on.

No one sells at the perfect time. If you end up selling within 20 percent or less of the high, you're doing well. Keep your expectations realistic. Try and keep greed out of the equation. When I was breaking into the securities business in Miami in the 1960s, my biggest and wisest customer was philanthropist Maurice Gusman. I mentioned this in Chapter 1, but I think it bears repeating: When Mr. Gusman sold a stock, he would say, "I hope the person who bought it from me does as well as I did."

8. Mergers Are Good for Everyone Except Stockholders

Mergers, especially between large companies, generate lots of excitement and often energize the stock market, but on a long-term basis, few work out well. It's often likely that shareholders would have been better served if their companies had never gotten together.

Of course, this truth emerges only after the passage of time. It's a reality that stands in stark contrast to the early self-congratulatory hype and glowing forecasts of greater profits for the combined companies. Like all public relation releases, the merger's "wedding" announcement focuses exclusively on Column A (all the positives like cost savings) and completely ignores Column B (the negatives like employee layoffs, outlandish executive payouts and investment banking fees, conflicting corporate cultures, a buyout price that's too high or too low, etc.).

Big mergers are often complex and difficult to understand. So investors take the word of management, especially if the CEO's enthusiasm and optimism is accompanied by a nice rise in the stock price (usually the acquired stock goes up, the acquiring stock goes down). If the stockholder objects and uses his proxy to vote against the merger, it means little. The large institutional and individual stockholders control the outcome. In most cases, the big stockholders will support management (unfriendly takeovers grab the headlines but are the exception). This may change in time as stockholder advocacy groups gain muscle and institutional holders align their interest more with that of the individual stockholder.

Commenting on the efficacy of corporate unions, Robin Goldwyn Blumenthal, writing in the August 22, 2005, *Barron's*, said, "The history of big corporate mergers is hardly a study in glory. Most deals have failed to produce the promised benefits, and many have caused lasting damage. In the 20 years through 2000, one study found mergers destroyed a total of $221 billion of shareholder value. And that was before AOL–Time Warner and Hewlett Packard–Compaq came along."

> "When two men in business always agree, one of them is unnecessary."
>
> —*Unknown*
>
> "People will buy anything that's 'one to a customer.'"
>
> —*Sinclair Lewis*

The Mother of All Merger Debacles

In his book *Deals from Hell* (John Wiley & Sons, 2005), Robert F. Bruner, professor of business administration at the University of Virginia, presents a list of dramatic merger failures. High up on the list are the mergers of Sony and Columbia Pictures, AT&T and National Cash Register, Quaker Oats and Snapple Beverage, and the mother of all merger debacles, Time Warner and AOL. Each of these unions resulted in substantial losses to the acquiring company—a whopping $54 billion write-down in the case of Time Warner.

Gretchen Morgenson, writing in the June 25, 2005, *New York Times,* cited research that suggests "few mergers add up to significantly more prosperous or successful companies." She addressed some of the less noble motives behind corporate mergers: "There's a disturbing trend among some of the most aggressive corporate acquirers to use deals (mergers) to mask deteriorating financial results at their companies and to reap outsize executive pay. The complexity of folding companies into one another makes it more difficult, whether by accident or design, for investors to fathom what's really going on. . . . Perhaps the biggest downside to mergers is their human toll . . . lavish benefits and perquisites are paid to executives as lower level employees lose their jobs."

The takeover of Gillette by Procter & Gamble represented an enormous $165 million payday for Gillette CEO James Kilts at the same time thousands of his employees were receiving pink slips. Morgenson's conclusion: "The bigger the company, the more the CEO gets (never mind how the company's doing)." Columnist Michael Santoli concurs that "most deals destroy shareholder value over time, as study after study has documented." (*Barron's,* June 14, 2004).

So if you get the happy news that your stock is up 10 points on the surprise announcement of a buyout offer, congratulate yourself on a short-term bonus. But if you choose to hold on to the surviving company stock, the benefits may prove short-lived. Keep this in mind when you're watching the two grinning CEOs shaking hands and praising each other in front of the TV cameras. They have good reason to be excited. In most cases, you don't.

9. Get Children Started Early

The stock market is really a young person's game because young people have so much more time to get it right. Youth is a huge advantage and it's a message we should be getting across to our kids. Syndicated financial columnist James Glassman (TCSDaily.com) says, "After 30 years of studying finance, I have found few eternal verities, but the most important—the Golden Rule of Accumulation—is this: Start early! Time is the most powerful weapon in an investor's arsenal" (Kiplinger .com, "From Piggy Bank to Pension," February, 2006).

At the 2005 Berkshire Hathaway annual meeting, Warren Buffett said that the age at which one begins investing is the best determinant of success, not IQ. Only youth can afford the luxury of making mistakes with enough time left over for losers to become winners. Ideally, all our investing should be done before the age of 20, with our mature years spent reaping the rewards. Instead, it's done in reverse. We usually have neither the money nor the smarts until we're well past our youth, and that's a fact of life unlikely to change.

If *you* didn't start early, your kids can, with your guidance. It's one way to help put your children on the path to a better life, and it doesn't take that much doing. There are all kinds of ways you can interest kids in investing. Since the youngest years are the most impressionable, starting them off in their pre-teens or teens can trigger a lifelong interest. They can buy as little as one share of stock directly from a long list of companies that offer dividend reinvestment plans (DRIPs—see dripinvestor.com). For example, the minimum investment for the purchase of Wm. Wrigley stock is $50 and you get 20 free packs of gum mailed to you every year around holiday time. Whatever you decide to buy should be a quality stock likely to go up over time and one that the child can relate to, like Nike, Pepsi, Disney, Google, Apple Computer, McDonald's, and so on.

What's important is to just get started, not on paper, but for real. With his own money at stake, the child can begin to experience the up and down emotions that, hopefully, he'll learn to deal with in time. Checking out the stock price will expose the child to other financial information on the Internet or in the business section of the newspaper.

The sequence of exposure is important. Buying shares comes first, the homework comes second. The other way around risks a quick turnoff from confusion or boredom. Web sites like buyandhold.com, sharebuilder.com, and firsttrade.com make it easy to get started. It's the excitement that comes from the child/teenager seeing his own money become more money without doing anything that's the big energizer. It's a turn-on that can spark a lifelong interest in investing.

The Sooner the Better

As soon as your child has some money of his own, whether it be from an allowance, gifts, babysitting, or a first-time job, he's ready to get his feet wet. It's up to you to get him started since kids under 18 can't buy stocks on their own. The sooner he begins, the sooner he can make mistakes to learn from, and the longer his money has to work.

Rather than dollar cost average in one stock, it probably makes sense initially to invest in one or two shares each of five or six familiar names.

Then, as the money becomes available, start dollar cost averaging in each of the stocks. Exposure to the magic of dollar cost averaging, acquiring the discipline to execute it, and seeing the benefits of diversification are all viable lessons learnable at an early age. The fees are usually high when buying just a few shares. At this stage, they're meaningless. Being in the game and learning is what counts.

At some point in their investment lives, your children will likely be dealing with index funds. Familiarizing teenagers with the concept by investing some of their money in the "Second-Grader Starter Portfolio" (see Table 7.1) might be a good way to go, along with a clearly written primer on index funds.

Once you get your kids started and they have something to follow daily, there's a good chance they'll want to know more. There are a number of web sites designed especially to teach kids about money, about savings, and about stocks. They include orangekids.com, younginvestor .com, investingforkids.com, kidsbank.com, teenanalyst.com, stockmar-ketgame.com, and kidstock.com. Go to Kiplinger.com and click on "Starting Out" for an excellent resource for beginning investors. Many other major investment web sites have sections devoted to educating the beginner (Yahoo!, MSN Money, Morningstar, Motley Fool, etc.).

Make-believe investing can be fun and instructive. According to Kathy Yakal, "Some of the best tools for teaching kids the nuts and bolts of invest-ing are the many stock market simulation games on the Web, where players are given virtual money and allowed to test their trading skills. *Young Money* magazine sponsors a site (youngmoney.com) with a new game and a fantasy allotment of $10,000 starting every month." (*Barron's,* April 23, 2007).

> "The easiest way for your chil-dren to learn about money is for you not to have any."
> —*Katherine Whitehorn*

You don't want to overwhelm kids with information, but when you think they're ready, I would augment their newspaper and web site exposure with one or two outstanding, easy to read books. Andrew Tobias' *The Only Investment Guide You'll Ever Need* (Harcourt, updated 2005) and Joel Greenblatt's *The Little Book That Beats the Market* (John Wiley & Sons, 2005) come to mind. Books written specifically for kids include *The Motley Fool Investment Guide for Teens* (Fireside, 2002), by

David and Tom Gardner; *Growing Money: A Complete Investing Guide for Kids* (Tandem Library, 2001), by Gail Karlitz; *Street Wise: A Guide for Teen Investors* (Bloomberg, 2000), by Janet Bamford; and *When I Grow Up I'm Going To Be A Millionaire* (Trafford, 2006), by Ted and Lora Lea. A book for guiding parents on the subject, such as Janet Bodnar's *Raising Money Smart Kids* (Kaplan Business, 2005), would also be helpful. Others written for parents include *Wow the Dow!* (Fireside, 2000), by Pat Smith and Lynn Roney; *Kids and Money* (Bloomberg, 1999), by Jayne Pearl; and *The First National Bank of Dad,* by David Owen (Diane Publishing Co, 2004).

Every Kid Can Learn to Save

Not every kid is going to respond to your efforts but you're missing a big opportunity if you don't give it a shot. In terms of potential rewards versus your time invested, it's a no-brainer. You can add a rich, lasting dimension to the lives of your children by giving them the smallest push in the right direction. We would probably be amazed if we could actually measure the profound impact a few early experiences have in shaping our adult lives, for better or worse. The downside here is almost zero. The upside is financial security, emotional fulfillment, and an avocation that could last a lifetime.

While on the subject of kids and investing, I would be remiss if I didn't make the point that developing the habit of saving money early in life may be the most important rule of all. Not every kid is going to invest—far from it—but every kid can learn to save. "Live below your means" is the mantra of the personal finance community. In surveys of baby boomers preparing for retirement, the most common complaint is that they didn't start saving and investing early enough.

Princeton economist and author Burton Malkiel says, "The secret of getting rich slowly but surely is the miracle of compound interest. It may sound complicated, but it simply involves earning a return not only on your original investment but also on the accumulated interest that you reinvest. The amount of capital you start with is not nearly as important as getting started early" (*The Random Walk Guide to Investing,* W.W. Norton, 2007). Columnist Jonathan Clements adds, "As soon as you enter the work force, start saving and investing. Initially your financial progress will seem agonizingly slow and the sacrifice involved will hardly seem worth it. But if you sock away 10 percent or 15 percent of your salary every year for 10 to 15 years, you should hit critical mass—and suddenly your portfolio will start growing by leaps and bounds." (*Wall Street Journal,* December 10, 2006).

If a bank is paying an attractive interest rate on savings and you decide to deposit funds and let them compound, the rule of 72 can be a handy tool. Divide whatever interest rate you're earning into 72 and you'll know how long it will take to double your money (8 percent compounded will double in nine years: $72 \div 8 = 9$).

If this was a personal finance book instead of one on investing, a good portion of it would likely be devoted to the subject of saving. That's how crucial it is. Don't let its brief treatment here lead you to think otherwise.

"Even with only $100 a month—$50 into, say, T. Rowe Price Total Equity Market Index Fund (POMIX) and $50 into T. Rowe Price International Equity Index Fund (PIEQX)—you would have investment in over 3,000 different companies spread around the globe. So don't tell me you don't have enough money to diversify."
— *Less Antman*

10. Don't Rebuke Yourself

When it comes to buying and selling securities, most investors don't appreciate just how incredibly difficult it is to make the right moves, and then to make them again and again. It's likely that many would not be involved in the market if the magnitude of what they were up against was truly understood. Or at least those who were involved would limit their participation to passive (index) investing and, for active investing, over only the longest time frame.

The market's intractability makes wrong decisions a given. Some missteps are minor and easily recoverable; others lead to heavy losses. When a stock makes a huge move on the upside we typically berate ourselves for not being in it. "I knew Google was going to be a winner. Why didn't I buy it?" When he managed Magellan Fund, star stock-picker Peter Lynch says he almost never owned one of the 10 best-performing stocks in a given year. It's likely that neither you nor I will either.

The most financially painful mistakes are usually made as a result of selling near bear market bottoms and not selling near bull market highs. During the bloody bear market retreat in 2000–2002, fear and despair gripped investors. Many sold out their holdings, trying to preserve what they had left. They simply reached a point where they felt they could not afford to lose any more. Then, when the market turned around in 2003 and staged an unexpectedly robust recovery, sellers reproached themselves for having panicked. Retiree friends and students told me their sad stories, berating themselves for not holding on.

The Right Thing at the Time

There are legitimate grounds for feeling bad about ourselves, such as if we lie or cheat or steal, but not if we sell stocks prematurely because of deep-seated worry over a steadily eroding net worth. Before blaming yourself, remember three facts:

1. At the time you decided to sell, *nobody* knew what was going to happen, including the most erudite market veterans. Forecasts at the time were all made with fingers crossed.
2. What you were fearful of could very well have happened. The market could have gone a lot lower and then stayed in the cellar for a long time. The stock(s) you owned may or may not have recovered. For whatever the reason (maintenance of your lifestyle, protection of your college or retirement nest egg, etc.), you made a judgment that it was a risk you were unwilling to take. The fact that the market turned around and you would have avoided heavy losses if you had not sold does not change the fact that *at the time* the risk was very real. Often investor fears are well founded. For example, in 2004, some stockholders in Delta Airlines, not willing to risk a company collapse and wanting to salvage something (the stock had been at 72 years earlier), sold shares in the low teens. Their worries proved prescient. One year later the company was in bankruptcy and the stock was 65¢.
3. You are not alone. Your so-called bad call was repeated by many others. Half of the trading volume that takes place in a sliding market before it turns around represents fearful sellers who could have been right but weren't, just like you.

The mind-set of top athletes in handling poor performance serves as an excellent model. I remember how impressed I was watching Miami Dolphin quarterback Dan Marino fielding questions after a loss. Regardless of how many incompletions or interceptions he threw on a rare off day, he was never rattled or down on himself. His attitude was always supremely positive. He'd shrug off his mistakes as simply being part of the game. He exhibited an inner, quiet confidence that appeared unshakeable and in the next game he'd set new records. The same calm self-assurance is seen in the demeanor of superstars like Tiger Woods and Shaquille O'Neal, who make questioners feel like idiots when they're asked about a lapse in their performance.

In the securities industry, professional trader Charles Kirk exhibits the same type of quiet confidence in the face of error. During the market's surge to new highs the first four months of 2007, Kirk failed to adopt a bullish posture. On April 25, the day the Dow burst through 13,000, Kirk wrote (at TheKirkReport.com), "It would have been nice to be positioned right a few weeks ago and to be able to ring the cash register now. Instead, those of us who were too careful or cautious look like royal idiots which, frankly, I'm used to by now. I don't like being wrong, but given the facts we had just a few short weeks ago, I still think I would have played it the same way. This is a game of mistakes and emotions."

Kirk is talking to traders but what he says applies to all investors. "Given the facts, I would have played it the same way." No regrets, no self-censure. (I should mention that despite his overly cautious approach, Kirk did make 36 trades in the first four months of 2007, of which 30 were profitable. That's an 83 percent winning record, a ratio he's maintained for the past eight years. Extraordinary. More on Kirk later in this chapter and in Chapter 7.)

The Mother of All Conundrums

So don't beat up on yourself. For you, at the time and under the circumstances, you did the right thing. Legions of investors smarter and more experienced than you make moves that in retrospect seem dumb. But they could have been brilliant. What we know for sure is that few of us are born with the ability to overcome powerful emotions like fear and greed. Some of us can learn to control them, but even if we are cool and deliberate in our decisions, we can still be wrong.

Former Treasury Secretary Robert Rubin has argued that decisions should not be judged solely on the outcome. "Somebody could do a perfectly good job of weighing the relevant risks, make a call that maximizes the chances of success and still not succeed, because the world is a messy, unpredictable place" (*New York Times,* November 1, 2006). Savvy investor Harry Newton (technologyinvestor.com) says, "I'm the master of brilliant investment decisions I almost made. I'm learning to stop rebuking myself for my dumbness but it's hard." The one constant, irrefutable fact is that the market is the final arbiter, not you or I, and stock market behavior is the mother of all conundrums. If you truly understand this, you will not blame yourself for a universal human flaw. And you will reinforce your focus on the best means of diminishing those flaws—indexing and strictly long-term investing.

> "From time to time it is the duty of the serious investor to accept the depreciation of his holdings with equanimity and without reproaching himself. He should be judged solely by long-term results."
>
> —*John Maynard Keynes*

11. Face It, It's History; Put It Behind You

Probably, the question most frequently asked an adviser goes something like this: "I bought 100 shares of XYZ stock at 60 and it's now at 3. Do you think I should sell it?" The investor has held on during the long slide, hoping it would come back. By not selling, he avoids having to take an actual loss and finalizing his mistake. He hopes the adviser will validate his procrastination and tell him to hold on.

If I were asked the question, my response would be this: It's academic whether you sell or not. You've already taken your loss. The odds are against a stock collapsing and then coming back. Whatever money you can salvage would likely be better used in a different situation with brighter prospects. But whether you hold on or sell doesn't really matter. What's important is that you understand that it is not a question of whether or not you take the loss. The loss is already history. Write it off mentally, if not actually, and go on from there. If you hold and the stock beats the odds and comes back, that's gravy—but don't count on it.

Of course, there's another option. If the stock in question has formed a solid base around 3, and if the investor has money to throw away and figures to live a long life, he may want to gamble and buy more shares. The stock only has to get back to 9 instead of 60 for him to break even if he buys 1,000 additional shares at 3. Of course, for that to happen, a beaten-down stock has to make a huge 200 percent move. Anything's possible, but waiting around to get even in a decimated speculation is likely to prove a poor use of both time and resources.

12. Investigate, Then Invest—Hogwash

I make this same point in other sections of this book because it is a controversial, contrary opinion that I feel strongly about. Hopefully, expressing it in different ways helps me make my case and helps you to remember it. Some of the following comes from a speech I made 20 years ago. My experience since then has only deepened my convictions.

A popular slogan on Wall Street has been "Investigate, then invest." We're advised by the gurus to do our homework, to study the report, and "see what you think." That's okay for some, but in my opinion it's nonsense for most of us. We have neither the time, the inclination, nor, most of all, the training to read and truly understand financial statements, cash flow analysis, accounting principles, currency translations, corporate governance regulation, book-to-bill rates, and so on. No less an authority than the top accountant for the SEC, Walter P. Schuetze (SEC chief accountant 1992–1995 and 1997–2000), says, "Today's financial statements and reports are so complex and arcane as to be incomprehensible. . . . Financial statements are not fit for their intended use" (*Barron's*, May 31, 2005). Even CPAs can look at the same statistics and come up with different interpretations—not to mention the fact that the final arbiter, the market itself, may not assign the data any significance at all.

In addition to the financials, there is endless other information to be investigated. Let's assume we checked out all the data, did nothing but study 24 hours a day, and learned everything there was to know about a company and its stock. We learned about the company's product line, its pricing, its markets, its workforce, its management, its culture, its history, its competition, its industry, and so on. Would all of this knowledge help us make the right investment decision? Only if the information that we think matters, also matters to the market. Not only do we have to know, but we also have to know how the market will perceive what we know. None of this is spelled out when we're glibly told to do our homework if we want to be successful investors.

Harry Newton's technologyinvestor.com featured a letter from an anonymous hedge fund manager to his limited partners (November 3, 2006). In it, the manager described his frustration at reporting a poor month's performance despite a prodigious amount of homework. "Traditional fundamental drivers of stock prices have been largely ignored by the market. . . . At times, I've felt our team has been penalized rather than rewarded for doing deep fundamental research on the names in our universe." He went on to explain how the fund took positions based on expected earnings catalysts. The earnings forecasts proved correct but the market moved in the exact opposite direction of what was anticipated. Reflecting despair and confusion, the fund manager expressed the hope that other funds will start to care about fundamentals.

There are a few mathematically gifted investors whose reading and studying financials may actually increase their odds of success. If you find yourself in this group, if you have acquired the expertise that most of us don't have to understand the complexities of financial statements and their significance, and if you are prescient enough to know how the market will react to what you know, your homework may pay off. Others who may benefit from doing their own research include retirees who welcome the challenge because it gives them something else interesting to do with their time. There are also those who simply are reluctant to rely on the research of others, especially regarding their own money. They want to be a part of the information-gathering process. And then there are those who, by nature, are aware people. They want to stay as informed as they can in *everything* they do.

Best Use of Homework Time

Unless you're in one of those groups, it's likely you'll end up spinning your wheels when advised to study company-specific statistics like inventory turnover, gross margins, or cash flow ratios. You may be able to dig out the numbers but the market's likely response, if any, will remain an enigma. Homework of this type *will* make you more informed and may help marginally but, as a practical matter, the direct benefits are limited.

Company-specific research may help the most when it uncovers negatives. As I have stated, when recommending stocks, Wall Street is stingy about sharing the potential downside. Awareness of the bearish scenario fosters more informed decisions and avoids surprises.

I feel that the time used to research a company or stock would be far better spent in other ways. First would be reading the best books on overall investment/stock market strategy. Over the years there have been outstanding thinkers who have said some very wise things that have stood the test of time. It behooves all investors to seek out that wisdom. Everyone has their favorite all-time list but certain classics appear on almost all of them. See Chapter 10 for a comprehensive list of the most widely acclaimed, must-read investment books.

A second way to spend homework time is checking out the track records of index and mutual funds and professional advisers. Once chosen, let them do the research for you. It's true that you may have just as good a chance of being right as the pro when it comes to one or a few decisions. But over the long term, the professional with a proven track record is likely to do better. A number of such outstanding money managers are highlighted in the pages ahead.

Another way to spend homework time productively is to check out the negatives (column B) if you're buying and the positives (column A) if you're selling. You want to know the reasons motivating the other side of your trade. One way to do this is to ask your adviser, "What are the things that could happen that would make this a bad move for me?" and "What would have to happen to make you (the adviser) change your mind?" If your contact doesn't know the answers, ask him to check with someone who does and get back to you. The most important part of acquiring good information is asking good questions. The whole idea is to avoid future surprises.

My bottom line is that using a combination of index funds for most of your money plus elite mutual fund managers and, sparingly, individual stocks is the way to go for most investors. It's a theme developed in detail in Part Two.

I recognize that "Do your homework" is a universally embraced doctrine. Jim Cramer may be criticized, but never for strongly advocating that his viewers do their homework. David Winters, Wintergreen Fund portfolio manager, sums up the broad consensus view: "Do the homework. You really increase your odds of success as an investor if you're willing to dig at things, poke at them and kick the tires. For me it's exciting to read the next footnote." (Barrons.com, "Old Hand Has A New Fund," Lawrence Strauss, October 24, 2005). Sounds like unassailable logic—until you break it down.

> "You shouldn't spend time on your investments. That will just tempt you to pull up your plants and see how the roots are doing, and that's very bad for the roots. It's also very bad for your sleep."
> —*Paul Samuelson*

> "If you spend 15 minutes a year studying the economy, that's 10 minutes too many."
> —*Peter Lynch*

13. Cramer versus Kirk

Jim Cramer, 52, is unique. Stock picker and showman, he provokes reaction, both pro and con, that is as passionate as his own opinions. Independent organizations that monitor his stock picks give him grades that range from excellent to poor, depending on how and what they measure. Saturation exposure and some half a million viewers every night make him a market-influencing force to be reckoned with.

Cramer is a groundbreaker in a number of areas. No analyst/adviser/money manager has had so much television time (formerly three and now two hours every night) with a one-man show. No one has come close to that kind of exposure. No one has had the ability to give instant, on-demand, informed analysis on some 2,000 stocks. No one comes close. No one has ever attempted to approach the traditionally serious subject of money in what is sometimes a circus atmosphere. No one has had his impact on stocks. His ability to move markets is awesome. It's a power far greater than Walter Winchell, Joe Granville, Robert Prechter, Henry Kaufman, Louis Rukeyser, and anyone else you can think of, combined, because it's a force that's evident in the market every trading day as long as he's on the air.

But perhaps what's most unique about Cramer is that for the first time, the individual investor has daily access to an explanation of how the market really works from an insider—a wealthy, former top-ranked hedge fund manager. A magna cum laude graduate from Harvard and Harvard Law, Cramer is a numbers addict who is passionate about the stock market and about helping his viewers. Prior to Cramer, the closest we got to elite hedge fund managers was reading about the outrageous amounts of money they made and the million-dollar minimums required to invest in their funds. Now, every night, Cramer shares the same stock-picking expertise that allegedly made him millions—for free.

My issues with Cramer have mostly to do with his focus, his assertiveness, and his on-set persona. Even though he teaches some valuable long-term lessons (diversify, buy in small amounts, favor the best of the group, etc.), his orientation is mostly short-term. His message is that you can do better than the professionals and beat the market if you do your homework (one hour per week for each stock owned). Buying and selling stocks will make you mad money if you follow his advice. As he says, "I've done it and if you do your homework, you can do it, too."

The fallacy in the advice seems obvious. Most investors simply don't have the ability to do the type of homework—the statistical analysis and interpretation—that Cramer is talking about. They don't have the training (see the previous section and also Chapter 10 for more on homework). It seems totally unrealistic for Cramer to believe that if they do their homework, viewers can do what he can do. Cramer says viewers may not have the time or inclination to do homework but he never mentions ability. He would probably say he has a higher opinion of his viewers than I do—witness the popularity of his books and college tours. I would reply that 40 years in the trenches, including teaching stock market to the public one on one, has made me especially sensitive to the makeup of the average investor. I hope a lot of people read and learn from this book, which hopefully is easy to understand. But reading this book is not the type of statistical homework Cramer is talking about.

Creating a False Impression

I spend considerable time talking about homework here and elsewhere in the book because it is the cornerstone of Cramer's whole approach and is widely advocated by others. But a more important criticism of Cramer is that his short-term, mad-money approach obscures one of the basic truths about investing: The best way to put the odds in your favor is to invest long-term. Instead, he creates the strong impression that investing is all about beating the market over a period of months, not years. While steadfastness and persistence are keys to successful investing, Cramer creates unrealistic expectations of immediate gratification. Mad money may only apply to the speculative portion of a portfolio, but once hooked on Cramer's exciting "watch TV, get rich" mind-set, the patience required to hold stocks or index funds for years through dull markets may be hard to come by.

Cramer's assertiveness, his unwavering conviction, and his black-and-white opinions give off another false message. The impression is created that, just as in other professions like law and engineering, investing is about definitive answers—and that Cramer is the source of those answers, instantaneously. The fact is that the market is unforeseeable, but the many novice investors who watch him are led to believe that if they follow a certain regimen the market is, indeed, knowable. Confidence breeds confidence, and Cramer's unequivocal forecasts can be both mesmerizing and misleading.

As for Cramer's onstage histrionics, although they may trigger wide media attention (*BusinessWeek* cover story, "The Mad Man of Wall Street," October 31, 2005), I believe in the long run they turn off more than they turn on. His antics demean his wisdom and prevent many from taking him seriously. Cramer has the talent to be entertaining without playing the clown. When the bells and whistles are turned off and he is low-key and soft-spoken, he is very effective. In the meantime the circus buffoonery and strident voice may appeal to college kids but others find them irritating to unwatchable. I'm sure his once a week feature, "I was wrong" is sincere, but it's his overall cockiness that the viewer is left with.

Would a more sober approach with greater focus on the long term boost audiences to the much higher levels of cable TV shows like Bill

O'Reilly and Lou Dobbs? Obviously, CNBC doesn't think so. Over time, I think it would, but of course, I can't prove it. My opinion is based on the large and loyal following I developed over the years in south Florida (WTVJ-CBS) doing colorless market commentary. I was a talking head with no visuals. My viewers watched every day for only one reason—the information was helpful and so they wanted to hear what I had to say. Cramer is far more talented than me, not only as a showman but as a source of insight on the inner workings of the market. In my opinion, he would gain more viewers than he'd lose with more long-term oriented features and less theatrics. His adoring college fans might be less boisterous but they would be far better served.

> "Carpe per diem—seize the check."
>
> —*Robin Williams*
>
> "If you have to forecast, forecast often."
>
> —*Edgar Fiedler*

What's Behind the Cramer Phenomenon?

In the world of stocks, where it's common knowledge that no one has the answers on a consistent basis, how can you explain the Cramer phenomenon?

There are many reasons. His one-of-a-kindness draws attention. He is willing to do things in the name of entertainment that other very smart people are not. There is always a hunger for easy profits and Cramer makes it sound easy. He leaves no doubt that he can make you money, and his confidence is contagious. He is very bright and his wide-ranging intellect projects through the TV screen. He knows how to turn on his fans. He adds credibility to his TV persona with wide exposure in other media. He has a daily radio show, columns on TheStreet .com and in *The New Yorker* magazine, he's authored three books, and he shows up as a guest on many nonfinancial shows. His opinions are right often enough to keep viewers coming back. His screens of viewer phone calls weed out complainers. So far, he has not had to contend with a sustained bear market. At times he is disarmingly candid in admitting his mistakes. A large segment of his audience is less experienced and thus more impressionable. And his abundance of ego, energy, and ambition enable him to perform some of the shtick that modesty would preclude.

In fairness to Cramer, his in-depth self-analysis in the *New York* magazine cover story (June 4, 2007) shows he can be brutally introspective. In the same way that others either love or hate him, he loves and hates himself. He takes credit for a talent at picking stocks and for filling the need for spontaneity and madness craved by his average 28-year-old audience. But he also calls himself "painfully insecure," a "loudmouth, cocky, obnoxious idiot" who is even repulsive to himself.

Cramer says he's tired of making money for wealthy people (which he did in his hedge fund) and wants now to help the "little guy." I don't question his sincerity. I admire his motives and his passion. I just think it's misdirected. In 2006, less than 20 percent of U.S. fund managers running diversified stock funds were able to top the S&P 500, according to Lipper Fund Research in New York. And these managers are experienced professionals. Cramer has proven he can outperform the market. And so can some 20 percent of other professionals. But to think that Cramer can enable his viewers to be in that elite 20 percent group with any consistency is a fantasy.

The best way he can accomplish his goal of helping the small investor, and all other investors, is by putting on the type of prerecorded shows that are aired on holidays when he's away. Devoid of rapid-fire stock tips, these are programs that feature valuable guidance for the long-term investor. He acts as a serious teacher, not (as he's been described) "a Louis Rukeyser on steroids." Since there are far more long-term investors in this country than there are short-term traders, and because he has the talent to make such informational shows entertaining as well, I believe programs of this type would expand his viewership, in time.

Cramer has enormous untapped potential to really help the investor. But until he can shed the "watch TV, get rich" hype as exemplified in his latest book (*Jim Cramer's Mad Money: Watch TV, Get Rich,* Simon & Schuster, 2006), I believe that as the years pass, he will have done more harm than good. By subscribing to a mad-money world of unrealistic expectations, Cramer fans will be ill equipped to succeed long-term. In the meantime, if you can survive the grating sound effects and general foolery, there is much to be learned from Cramer. Filter out the noise and there are gems of wisdom that have little to do with making mad money.

Kirk—The Anti-Cramer

Because he is so directly opposite to Cramer, I have to mention Charles Kirk. The contrast is striking. As bombastic and full of himself as Cramer is, that's how laid-back and self-effacing Kirk is—which is why you've probably heard of Cramer and not Kirk.

Yet, in terms of performance, Kirk has achieved remarkable results. He is a glaring exception to the general futility of short-term trading. During the seven-year period 2000–2006, he posted an average annual gain of 35.56 percent, including a gain of 36.7 percent in the crushing bear market year of 2000. In 2003–2004 his average annual gain was over 75 percent. Even more impressive is his success ratio of 79.02 percent, which he has maintained consistently (in 2006, 82 percent; 2005, 78 percent; 2004, 77.5 percent). In other words, four of every five trades have been winners. Though he more than maintained that success ratio in 2006, his cautious approach caused him to miss some of the second-half advance. It resulted in a gain of 10.4 percent, which Kirk describes as "my dismal performance." His fully documented seven-year track record is so unique that *Barron's* saw fit to do a profile on Kirk (April 3, 2006). They called his record "amazing."

Most of the information on Kirk's web site, TheKirkReport.com, is free. On the "for members only" portion ($50 per year), members can follow every trade he makes, but only after he makes them. He often tells readers the stocks he's following and the techniques he uses, including his favorite screens. He earns his living as a full-time trader. He's up at 5 A.M. and devotes some 10 hours a day to weeding out buy or short sale candidates, sometimes waiting weeks for the right conditions or setup. Each morning he gives readers the premarket movers, upcoming news expected to influence the market, and a feel for the mood of the market. On the day he buys for his own account, he gives members all the details, but only after the purchase. On the day he sells he reveals the details, but after the sale. Every trade is with his own money for his personal account. His average holding period in 2006 was around five days. He has never had a down year in his eight years of full-time trading.

Low-Key But with a Passion to Help Others

It's unusual for someone in the stock market world with that kind of talent to be modest and soft-spoken. In stark contrast to Cramer, Kirk is most comfortable out of the spotlight. Rather than exposure, he seeks the anonymity that enables him to ply his trade without diversion. As for his high-powered performance, he brushes it aside, saying, "You're only as good as your next trade." On his web site, he writes more about his losers and the lessons that can be learned from them than he does about his four out of five winners.

Like Cramer, his passion is to help others become better traders. Cramer, incidentally, also has a real-time personal portfolio. The Action Alerts Plus portfolio is set up as Cramer's charitable trust in which he buys and sells stocks with a 6- to 12-month time horizon. Profits are donated to charity. For a $400 annual fee, Cramer will e-mail subscribers just before he buys and sells. The trust earned 6.38 percent in 2006 and had a *total* return, not an average annual return, of 27.68 percent for the five-year period January 1, 2002, to January 1, 2007.

I have no interest in trading but I visit TheKirkReport.com regularly, as do many other nontraders. Long-term investors can learn much from Kirk's insightful commentary, profuse links to other sites, and monthly Q&A sessions. His work ethic, his discipline, and his patience, all reflected in his daily postings, give readers a good idea of what it takes to be a winner, long- or short-term. Unfortunately, the feel that he has for the market is something that cannot be learned.

Kirk currently trades with about half his money and invests long-term with the other half, but that ratio is subject to change. In Chapter 7 I have more to say about Kirk, including his personal retirement portfolio and what he thinks of index funds.

> "Don't invest all your money in just one or two stocks. I know a man who put all his money in just two stocks—a paper towel company and a revolving door company. He was wiped out before he could turn around."
>
> —*Dave Astor*

(In the interest of full disclosure, I am an e-mail friend of Kirk. I have never met or spoken to him but he has helped me, as he does many others. And I remain an admirer of his character and commitment.)

14. How to Answer Questions about the Market

I have touched on this subject in previous pages. It is important so I expand on it here.

Ideally, there should be a four-part answer to every question about investing. Part 1 is "I don't know." The unpredictability of the market precludes any definitive answer. No one knows for sure what will happen in the future. Saying "I don't know" clarifies for the questioner that any attempt at an answer is simply an educated guess.

Part 2 is, "This is column A—all the *positives* that I'm aware of." Part 3 is "This is column B—all the *negatives* that I'm aware of." The phrase "that I'm aware of" is significant since it keeps the answer completely truthful. If those words are omitted, the inference is that you are presenting *all* the positives and *all* the negatives, which is highly unlikely. Research reports rarely if ever include *all* the good and *all* the bad. The longer the list of items in each column, the more informed the investor, the more likely you'll include the right answer(s), and the greater the chance of avoiding surprise.

Finally, part 4 of the answer goes something like this: "Based on an awareness of the positives and negatives I've just outlined, I believe the odds favor . . ." followed by an opinion. Whatever that opinion is, it should end with this qualification: "This is just one person's opinion. There are others equally if not more knowledgeable who hold the exact opposite view."

Professional advisers are expected to advise and, understandably, will include part 4, especially if they have strong convictions. Personally, I prefer to eliminate part 4, content to give investors both sides of the story and then leave it to them to form a conclusion. It's my sense that once the investor has the big picture, his guess is as good as most others.

In my 40 years in Wall Street I cannot remember recommending a stock; I'm too aware of the other side of the story and that I can be wrong. I've been humbled by the accumulation of countless experiences where the market did exactly the opposite of what I and everybody else thought was a gimme. I am more than willing to bury my ego and resist the pleasure of pontificating in exchange for not having to feel guilty for giving bad advice. Over the years it has become easy for me to do this as I grow increasingly aware of the market's randomness and my own fallibility.

Thanks for Nothing

"A little knowledge can be a dangerous thing," but *too much* awareness can also be a disadvantage. Knowing what's in one column but not the other makes it easier to come to a definitive conclusion. The mind is not cluttered, there are no impediments. Knowing both sides, however, can cause uncertainty and confusion. I recently received a phone call from a friend who wanted to know whether he should hold or sell a stock that had just spiked higher on rumors of a buyout offer. I gave him my routine part 1, part 2, and part 3 answer with fairly detailed columns A and B. When he hung up, he was probably more confused than ever. I could just hear him muttering under his breath, "Thanks for nothing."

Here we have the very essence of the enigma facing all investors. As stock market commentator Jim Cramer says, "People want advice and they want you to stick your neck out. They don't want even-handedness. The last thing they want to see is a bull-bear debate with no conclusion" (*Pittsburgh Post-Gazette* interview; March 5, 2006). He is absolutely right. Human nature steers us in the wrong direction; we are attracted to assertive, no-hedge opinions. Just as we succumb to greed at market tops and fear at market bottoms, we give in to the irresistible lure of easy money. Words like "Follow me and I'll make you money. I want you to buy XYZ Corp. but sell, sell, sell, ABC Company," said with authority and passion by a savvy insider, are tough to ignore.

Answering questions about the market in the four-part manner I suggest—either by yourself or by your adviser—is completely unrealistic. It is behavior inconsistent with human nature. It's not going to happen. If Jim Cramer were to follow my approach and include a detailed column A and column B for every stock he recommended on TV, his ratings would plummet. Full disclosure and blunt honesty lead to uncertainty and confusion. But the essential, eternal, impossible-to-get-around truth is that the market *is* confusing. Its random nature precludes certainty.

So how do we overcome the dilemma? Should we avoid indecision by settling for a convincing one-column-only story and hope it's the right column?

We don't have to. There *is* a way to avoid falling prey to Wall Street's one sided, short-term orientation. First, own a diversified list of low-expense index funds bought at the right price for the long term. This would represent the major portion of your portfolio. Second, a smaller portion of your holdings would consist of individual stocks and elite mutual funds—the fun part of the portfolio. I have a lot more to say about index and elite funds, including model portfolios, in Part Two.

Yes, the market is frustrating and confusing, but underlying all the uncertainty is a century-long bias to the upside. Trading-range markets may interrupt the primary advance. But history teaches us that recessions and bear markets are finite. A look at a long-term chart of the Dow Jones Industrial Average clearly illustrates that sooner or later, the upward climb resumes. No more than we can hold back the tides or the seasons can we stop the inevitable rise of the markets over time, fueled by our flourishing capitalistic system and American ingenuity.

15. Giving Advice to Relatives—Tread Lightly

There are few things that give us more pleasure than helping those who mean the most to us. There may be times when you are so convinced that the stock or fund you are buying or own is a surefire winner, that you have an uncontrollable urge to let your loved ones in on it. It's an act of genuine caring that will make them money and, in the process, make you look good. Everyone benefits.

Nothing could be further from the truth. Use all the restraint you can muster to control your beneficence. Invariably and sadly, the family and friends you want to help the most are the ones you most often cause to lose money. Why? Perhaps the decisions we feel strongest about are based more on emotion than detached reason. In our eagerness to do good for family, we may lose some of our objectivity. Whatever the reason, heartfelt advice given with only the best intentions can result in some awkward, unpleasant situations. Resist trying to be a hero and avoid having to be a bum.

A slightly different situation occurs when a friend or family member comes to you and asks for advice. Maybe they want to know how you feel about their buying or selling a particular stock or fund. If you have no knowledge or opinions on the matter, there's no problem. But it's extremely difficult, when someone (especially someone close) thinks enough of your judgment to ask for advice, to resist the opportunity to pontificate.

Let's say your daughter has gotten a tip on a hot stock but wants to check with you before she buys it. You feel strongly it's too speculative. This is what I would say to her: "Ellen, my answer is I don't know. Nobody knows. But this is what I think . . . Remember, this is just an educated guess. I could be dead wrong. There are others smarter than me who have the exact opposite opinion." If, indeed, you do prove wrong, it's not as if you didn't clearly allow for that possibility.

> "No matter how rich you become, how famous or powerful, when you die the size of your funeral will still pretty much depend on the weather."
> —*Michael Pritchard*

16. When Greed Paid Off

The market is not only unpredictable; it can also be unfair and sometimes cruel. A good example is the market's treatment of mostly older, conservative investors during the late 1990s. Most of us have been taught in Investing 101 that the market punishes the greedy, and that when stocks with little or no earnings sell at extremely high prices, it's time to sell, not to buy. But amid the fever of the late 1990s, stocks that were unreasonably high went higher and then higher still. Avarice was rewarded with easy money. Disbelieving, frustrated old-timers, restrained by caution and memories of past debacles, watched a surging market pass them by. Younger investors with short memories had no such constraints.

It's true that when the bubble burst, many gave back their winnings and then some. But there were fortunes made and kept by others who had little idea they were violating any long-standing rule of valuation. They simply didn't know any better. Ignorance was bliss and greed paid off—at least until the bubble burst. Those who made quick profits justified them by saying they were in harmony with the new paradigm and that those left behind were simply out of touch.

A similar situation occurred in the early 2000s in the bond market. Conservative income buyers, taught to believe that high yields mean high risk, shied away from the juicy yields offered by high-leverage bond funds and especially by below investment-grade or junk bonds. How could 12 percent and 16 percent yielding bonds spell anything but trouble when prevailing yields were so much less than that?

But a recovering economy enabled marginal companies to meet their payments, and defaults were few. In the four years 2002–2006, speculative-grade corporate bonds enjoyed a spectacular run with default rates dropping to a record low of 1 percent (default is the failure of a bond to pay its interest or principal when due; its frequency increases sharply during economic downturns). During these four years, yield hungry bond buyers willingly accepted less and less yield for their high risk. Those who had reached for the fattest yields early on saw their greed pay off big-time. Not only did they pocket exceptional returns, but they also saw the value of their bonds appreciate.

Whether it be stocks or bonds, excesses are eventually corrected, but until they are, the market can be heartless as it rewards greed and punishes restraint.

17. Losses Are Inevitable—A Big Loss Unacceptable

Taking losses in the stock market isn't a probability, it's a certainty. William Bernstein in his book *The Intelligent Asset Allocator* (McGraw-Hill, 2000) says, "No investor, no matter how skilled, ever avoids bone crushing losses at times, even when undertaking the most prudent market risks."

Suffering reverses is a routine part of the investment process. What's not routine is taking *big* losses. In his 1992 letter to Berkshire Hathaway stockholders, Warren Buffett says, "An investor needs to do very few things right as long as he or she avoids big mistakes." A sharp reduction in the value of your holdings can be a crippler, both emotionally and financially. There are few things in investing that are more important than preservation of capital. You can't play the game if you lose your chips. Show me a disenchanted investor who has thrown in the towel and I'll show you at least one big loss on his Schedule D tax return.

Unless you've been through it, it's hard to appreciate just how difficult it is for a truly beaten-down stock to come back. And if it does, it can take forever. T. Rowe Price portfolio manager Brian Berghuis said in a May 16, 2005, *Barron's* interview, "You make money [in the stock market] by not losing money. Most investors realize too late the harsh arithmetic of missteps, that a 50 percent loss requires a 100 percent gain just to break even." In his book *The Winning Investment Habits of Warren Buffett and George Soros* (St. Martin's Griffin, 2006) Australian business-man Mark Tier writes, "When Buffett and Soros invest, they're not focused on the profits they expect to make. Both are far more focused on not losing money."

The best way to avoid major losses is to buy at a reasonable price and then use stop-loss orders for protection. If and when the price falls to a specified level, the stock is sold and the loss taken. Opinions vary as to just how to determine the stop-loss level. As we mentioned before, some will settle on a percentage number, let's say 10 percent below cost, as the maximum loss they're willing to take. Others may check out the stock's technical position, hoping the chart will indicate an obvious spot to place a stop (just below a nearby support level, for example). For further discussion on how, when, and where to place stop-loss orders, see the earlier section in this chapter titled "The Sticky Question of When to Sell."

Waiting Forever to Get Even

Whatever the approach, once entered, a stop-loss order provides an effective defense against the erosion of capital. There's always the possi-bility of being whipsawed—the stock going back up after being sold. But more times than not, the stop will do its job. You may be down, but you're not out. If you keep your losses moderate, you can actually be wrong more times than right and still come out a winner. It's much like a baseball batter who is a loser 7 out of 10 times at the plate, but as a 300 hitter is considered a star and is paid millions.

Few investors use stops. At the time you're buying a stock or a fund, you're thinking about the money you're going to make, not lose. It's true that if you're a patient, long-term investor and buy quality merchandise like a General Electric or a Johnson & Johnson, the need for stop-loss protection is less compelling. But even with blue chips, especially when bought at less than bargain prices, if you've guessed wrong and the stock goes down, you can find yourself waiting forever to get even. With speculative securities, loss protection takes on a special urgency. The time for getting even may never come.

Even though setbacks are completely predictable, some investors find taking losses tough to handle emotionally. As long as there's no sale, there's always the hope of a comeback. Hope is a lot easier to live with than capitulation and admission of error. The findings of psychologists who study investor behavior confirm this. Research has shown that investors feel the pain of loss twice as intensely as the pleasure of gain. Being out of a stock and wishing you were in it produces much less emotional strain than being in a stock and wishing you were out of it. (Loss aversion is one of the central discoveries of behavioral economists Daniel Kahneman and Amos Tversky. See "Prospect Theory: An Analysis of Decision Under Risk," *Econometrica XVLII,* 1979, pages 263–291.)

What most successful investors have in common is their ability to take losses in stride. They feel no more pain than the ball player does when he strikes out on the way to his next home run.

> "The entire essence of America is the hope to first make money, then make money with money, and then make lots of money with lots of money."
>
> —*Paul Erdman*

18. ETFs Are a Beautiful Thing

There's probably no investment product more widely discussed than exchange-traded funds (ETFs). A daily deluge of information, analysis, and advice is heaped on investors. From all corners of the media we are inundated with articles on the advantages of ETFs, the disadvantages of ETFs, how to use ETFs, the best and worst performing ETFs, are there too many new ETFs, the risks in niche ETFs, and so on ad infinitum. Anything I add here is like a spit in the ocean. I'm only echoing what's been said often and better elsewhere.

Nevertheless, ETFs are central to our investment approach. Most of the components of the model portfolios featured in upcoming pages are ETFs. So I'll add my two cents here, and another dime or so in Part Two.

With all the pitfalls that face investors, anything that simplifies the process has to be a good thing. I've discussed the importance of asset allocation and diversification. Exchange-traded funds make it easy to do both. It's a relatively new resource that has caught on because it fills a basic need. (The American Stock Exchange introduced ETFs in 1993 with the listing of "Spiders" which track the S&P 500 stock index with the symbol SPY.)

Exchange-traded funds drastically narrow the number of choices that have to be made to achieve diversification. Instead of having to select individual stocks, bonds, or commodities, the investor can buy the entire U.S. stock market, or international stock market or U.S. bond market or foreign bond market, or a basket of commodities, or a particular sector of the market, or any of the major market indexes—all in one security. Most of this was doable via a mutual fund but the new twist is that, unlike mutual funds, ETFs are listed. That means that not only can you buy all 100 stocks in the NASDAQ 100 Index (mostly technology companies), or all 3,000 stocks in the iShares Russell 3,000 Index (a proxy for the entire U.S. stock market), or all the drug stocks or all the major stocks in the energy group, and so on, in one security, but you can trade that security at any time during market hours, just like any other stock.

Exchange-traded funds then, are more flexible than mutual funds, which can be bought and sold only at net asset value at the end of each trading day. They are convenient, liquid, transparent, and offer instant diversification. Since they are passive investments (no active management is required since they all follow a benchmark index), expenses and tax consequences are minimum. You pay a commission to buy and sell an ETF just like other stocks, but that's a negative only if you trade frequently.

The amount of money in mutual funds dwarfs the assets in ETFs—roughly $11 trillion versus almost $500 billion—but the gap will likely be smaller in future years as the introduction of new exchange-traded funds continues to accelerate. One of the reasons for the big discrepancy in the size of the two industries (aside from the fact that ETFs are relatively new on the scene) is the difference in the way they are promoted. Mutual funds, especially load funds, represent an important profit center to the brokerage firm and so they are pushed by an army of salespeople. Exchange-traded funds are not.

The Wave of the Future

As previously discussed, I disagree with those whose mantra is "Do your homework" as it is usually meant. For most investors, poring over annual reports, financial statements, statistical ratios, Form 10-Ks, and SEC filings is not a productive use of time. However, studying Warren Buffett's annual letter to Berkshire Hathaway stockholders or reading some great investment book is eminently worthwhile. And so is learning about index funds and ETFs.

Unlike trying to understand cash flow growth or the ratio of turnover to receivables, whatever you learn about indexing could have an immediate impact in securing your financial future, especially if you decide to implement the suggestions found later on in this book. Almost every major investment web site includes voluminous information on ETFs and many, like www.ETFconnection.com, are devoted exclusively to the subject. If you type "ETF" in the Yahoo! search box, you'll come up with over 18 million ETF-related web sites! (I list 30 of the best ones, along with some outstanding books on ETFs, in Chapter 6.).

Indexing is here to stay because it gives investors a viable option for dealing with unpredictable markets. A testament to its widespread appeal is the dramatic success of Vanguard, the pioneer and dominant player in the index field (in the ETF arena, Barclay's and State Street are the powers). You can index only in two ways—via mutual funds and via exchange-traded funds. Mutual funds have been around for many decades and constitute a huge industry. Exchange-traded funds are less than 15 years old and represent only 4 percent of total mutual fund assets, but that percentage will surely rise.

The investment advice business has embraced ETFs with a passion. Charles Schwab Institutional conducted a survey of almost 1,400 independent investment advisers in January, 2007 and found that 76 percent of them currently use ETFs in client portfolios. No other instrument was as popular. Concludes Michael Santoli (*Barron's,* July 2, 2007), "Clearly, ETFs have come of age and more than ever comprise the core investments of advised retail portfolios." However, usage by do-it-yourself investors is not as prevalent.

If ETFs are not the wave of the future, they're certainly a big ripple. At some point in the not too distant future, there will likely be thousands of ETFs, not hundreds. And when they figure out how to remove some of the obstacles (the commission involved in buying an ETF, for example), the large numbers of Americans currently accumulating index funds in their retirement plans will accelerate.

Professional trader Charles Kirk believes in the years to come we may see a trend away from owning individual stocks and toward using ETF-based strategies to accomplish financial objectives. He even suggests the possibility of buying a diversified ETF portfolio all in one security, in the same way that you can buy a cross section of mutual funds in just one fund—a fund of funds. I have a lot more to say about ETFs, including suggested model portfolios, in Chapters 6 and 7.

> "The market, like the Lord, helps those who help themselves. But, unlike the Lord, the market does not forgive those who know not what they do."
>
> —*Warren Buffett*

19. Rising Dividends Are More Important than Big Dividends

Investors interested in safety and income have traditionally focused on stocks with the highest yields. In the 1960s and 1970s, when dividends were in vogue, there were hundreds of solid companies yielding over 8 percent. Of the 1,700 stocks covered by the Value Line Investment Survey (April 6, 2007), there were only 10 listed with yields over 8 percent and they were mostly speculative Canadian Energy Trusts. In recent years we have been in a low interest rate environment with the dividend return on the S&P 500 around 2 percent. Asset classes traditionally bought for income—utilities, preferreds, REITs, bonds, and so on—still enjoy a yield advantage over the S&P 500, but that margin is dwindling.

If you come across a stock that's yielding 8 percent when the other stocks in the group are returning 4 percent, it's unlikely you've found a hidden gem. Publicly traded stocks are just that—public. Everybody knows about your find, and what they know is that it has an unusually high return for a reason and that reason is not good. In most cases, the higher the return, the greater the risk. If you depend on the income from your investments to maintain your lifestyle, you may be forced to reach. Just do so with your eyes wide open.

If you have more flexibility, you'll do much better, in most cases, by focusing on stocks that increase their dividend every year and then reinvesting those dividends. Lower-yielding stocks that boost their payout regularly, a sign of financial health, are much more likely to appreciate over the years than high dividend payers. The income buyer benefits not only from a rising income flow but also from a rising stock price.

Annual dividend increases can grow a skimpy yield into a fat one. If you buy General Electric today your yield will be around 3 percent. But if you bought it 10 years ago, your effective annual yield today would be close to 10 percent based on your original investment and subsequent reinvested dividend increases. PepsiCo is yielding under 2 percent today but shares bought 20 years ago are throwing off an effective yield of 37 percent based on original cost and rising dividends.

Every year, Standard & Poor's publishes a list of what it calls "Dividend Aristocrats," companies that have enhanced their payouts for at least 25 consecutive years. Their most recent tally listed 85 such companies, including Procter & Gamble and 3M Company—both of which are nearing 50 years of annual disbursement sweeteners—and Johnson & Johnson, Coca-Cola, and Kellogg, with a record of 40 years plus. Shirley Lazo's weekly dividend column in *Barron's* is an excellent source of information on companies that keep raising their payouts.

The Power of Reinvesting a Rising Dividend

What really gooses returns over time is the reinvestment of dividends, a systematic method of accumulating shares of a stock that pays a dividend. After you purchase a stock, simply enroll in the company's dividend reinvestment plan (over 1,000 companies offer DRIPs) and your dividends will automatically be used to purchase additional shares without charge. In effect, you're silently but regularly increasing your position, benefiting from both dollar cost averaging and compounding. (Checkout Charles Carlson's *DRIP Investor* newsletter for more information, at dripinvestor.com.)

The reinvestment of dividends, especially a dividend that keeps rising, can have a dramatic effect on the growth of your investment.

Two of the earliest and strongest proponents of the reinvestment of dividends strategy were Benjamin Graham (*The Intelligent Investor,* Harper Business, 1949) and his best-known student, Warren Buffett.

The performance of Altria Group, formerly Philip Morris, is perhaps the most striking example of what can happen by methodically reinvesting steadily rising dividends. Philip Morris is a rarity because it is a high-yielding stock (to compensate investors for tobacco litigation risks) that also regularly raises its dividend. Wharton professor Jeremy Siegel points out in his book *The Future For Investors* (Crown Business, 2005) that $1,000 invested in Philip Morris in 1957 would have been worth $4.6 million by 2003 versus just $124,000 for the same investment in the S&P 500 Index.

ETFs That Focus on Rising Dividends

It's not surprising that at a time when market returns are expected to be modest on average for some years to come, there has been a revival of interest in dividends (triggered, in part, by a low 15 percent tax rate). Of the approximate 10.8 percent total return over the history of the S&P 500 Index, some 40 percent has been due to dividends and their reinvestment. If, indeed, the future average annual rate of return on stocks proves to be in the single digits, it is likely that a smaller percentage of that return will come from capital gains and a larger percentage from dividends.

To avoid having to pick individual dividend stocks, there are ETFs that will do it for you. Most popular is Barclays' iShares Dow Jones Select Dividend (DVY). It tracks a basket of 100 of the highest-yielding stocks that have boosted their dividends for at least the past five years but don't pay out more than 60 percent of their profits. It's listed on the NYSE and yields around 3 percent. There are a number of other dividend ETFs including Wisdom Tree Total Dividend (DTD) and Vanguard High Dividend Yield ETF (VYM).

The temptation may be great, but in the long run it pays to resist the lure of a high yield for one that's smaller but rising annually. The latter represent an elite group of stocks that invariably offer both quality and superior performance over time. Eight percent average annual appreciation added to a 2 percent yield more than offsets a static, less than secure

7 percent return. (Remember, to benefit from that appreciation, it's important not to overpay for the stock.) If you're investing strictly for income, there's no harm in taking some of that income, or even most of it, from appreciation. It may be the only way to meet your financial needs. And there's another bonus: Since companies usually raise their dividends by a percent greater than the inflation rate, a stream of constantly increasing dividend income acts as a hedge against inflation.

> "Though I'm grateful for the blessings of wealth, it hasn't changed who I am. My feet are still on the ground. I'm just wearing better shoes."
>
> —*Oprah Winfrey*

20. The Broker and the Case for Discretion

In addition to buying index funds and mutual funds, investors may want to use some of their money to buy securities through a broker. That is, as long as they're around. The traditional stockbroker may be an endangered species. The growing popularity of online accounts may lead to the day when all or most security transactions will be done via the computer, with fulfillment done via a call center overseas. Brokers would function more as financial planners and accumulators of their customers' total assets. That would be sad. Many investors form lasting friendships with their stockbroker advisers and would miss the personal relationship.

There are three ways to utilize the services of a stockbroker. You can use a broker strictly as an order taker and make all your own decisions. This approach makes most sense when the psychological and social benefits of do-it-yourself investing are important or when the investor feels he can do a better job than the broker (most of us tend to have an exaggerated opinion of our own talent). Or we can work with the broker as a team, using both his ideas and our own.

There's also a third choice—the use of discretion. Because of widespread lack of confidence in the judgment of brokerage firms and their sales staff, it may seem irresponsible to suggest that brokers be given discretion in handling accounts. Nevertheless, I believe under certain circumstances, that's the way to go. The primary condition is a thorough background check of the broker, which can take some doing. In every brokerage firm office there are a handful of salespeople, maybe one or two, usually the most experienced, who clearly have the most to offer and consistently do well for their customers. They may or may not be the most personable or the biggest producers, but they're the best at managing risk and achieving results over the years. Your objective is to land one of these top tier brokers. The time you spend in accomplishing this mission is, in my opinion, more productive than your studying balance sheets or cash flows. Following are some suggestions on how to go about it.

Finding the Right Broker

Soliciting referrals from savvy investor friends (who may or may not be totally objective) is a logical place to start. Or you can call the broker's office and ask the operator or any sales assistant for the name of the broker who's been in the business the longest (minimum requirement for me would be 10 years; 20 years would be better). Then I'd ask that broker what's a good time to call back so I can ask some questions preparatory to opening a new account. Some sample questions: "Are you able to document your performance over the years? What are your areas of expertise? What average annual return do you think is reasonable for me to expect from you? Would you be willing to get the okay from some of your customers so I can call them for a reference?" (Obviously, you'll only get names of happy customers, but if you ask the right questions, you can still learn a lot). "Would you be comfortable handling a discretionary account?" and so on.

Even though some answers may be predictable, the discerning questioner can get a good sense of who he'll be dealing with. It's not so much what is said, but how it's said. What would impress me is a demeanor that exudes quiet confidence, experience, and knowledgeability, and a deliberate low-key approach devoid of unrealistic promises. Acknowledgement of the likelihood of making mistakes may be too much to expect from a salesman trying to open a new account, but it would go a long way with me.

In conducting your search, don't overlook the office manager. He has an overview of the track records of all the brokers in his office and, if motivated, can point you in the right direction. The very fact that you are seeking his opinion will set you apart. I would say this to him: "You have some 30 brokers reporting to you. I want to open an account with the top veteran in your office—the man or woman with the most consistent record of growing the assets of their accounts over the years while limiting losses along the way. I'm not greedy, I'm not looking for unrealistic returns, and I'm not looking necessarily for personality or hand-holding. I have lots of investor friends who are looking for the same things I am. Put me in the right hands and we'll all benefit."

What I Expect from My Broker

Once I completed my due diligence and settled on one broker, this is what I would say to him/her: "Look, I'm going to let you do your own thing. You'll have free reign. I'm doing this because I believe the best way to get the best from you is for me to butt out. If your firm frowns on discretionary accounts and you have to call to get my okay, that's fine. I'll go through the motions but I'll ask no questions. I expect to take losses but not big ones. Mine will be a zero hand-holding, aggravation-free account. In return, at the end of a year or two, when you rank all your accounts in order of performance, I expect mine to be near the top of your list. When that happens I'll give you more of my assets to manage and I'll refer some of my wealthy friends."

It's my view that in most cases it doesn't make sense for the typical investor to impose his amateur judgment on that of his adviser. You'll both make errors in judgment, but if you've done your homework and identified the right broker, the odds are he'll make fewer mistakes than you would. He has a leg up for no other reason than that your emotions no longer play a role in the decision-making process.

In the final analysis, your success in using discretion depends on your ability to do five things:

1. Put in at least as much time in selecting a broker as you do in choosing a vacation site, a car, or an insurance policy. If you end up with the right broker, which is key, it should be because you did your homework, not because you were lucky.

2. Communicate to the broker your objectives, risk tolerance, and expectations in crystal-clear language so there's no room for misunderstanding.
3. Allow the broker enough time to perform.
4. Be willing to give up the social, psychological, and fun benefits of investing on your own to focus strictly on making money.
5. Exercise the discipline necessary to keep your word and stay out of it (assuming your temperament permits you to do so).

Backing Off

On that latter point, it's interesting to note that we give discretion routinely in other areas of investing and think nothing of it. When we buy a mutual fund, we give up control to a money manager we've never met. It's an impersonal transaction and we feel no compulsion to get involved. The reason, of course, is that the professional portfolio manager has a track record and a reputation. But so does the broker. It's just more difficult to access.

An interview with the right questions asked (along with feedback from the manager and selected clients) can give you ample basis for making a judgment. If it's a positive one, and you give discretion to your broker, and he understands exactly what you're looking for, all that's left is for you to back off. That's tough because when it comes to a broker handling our money, there's an ego-based compulsion to make our presence felt.

If you have most of your money in index funds but want to invest the balance on your own, obviously discretion is not for you. You cannot experience the fun and excitement of picking a winner or growing any talent you may have as an investor by authorizing someone else to make the decisions. But even if you're content not to get involved, discretion applies only in cases where you're convinced you have an outstanding broker. As in every profession, some are below average, most are mediocre, and a few excel. In the brokerage business, excelling has mostly to do with controlling risk and minimizing losses. If your homework

> "Most people have no business investing in individual stocks on their own."
>
> —*Joel Greenblatt*

has uncovered one of the few excellent brokers, discretion should enable him to perform even better. In good markets you should be among his best-acting accounts and in bad markets your losses should be among the smallest.

21. All Investors Are Not Created Equal

Every year we read about the outstanding returns posted by the top performing advisers. Whatever the overall market did, these money managers did a lot better. In the mutual fund field, you and I can buy the best performers and then hope they continue their winning ways.

But there are funds that you and I can't buy that are managed by an elite group of advisers who make their services available only to the very wealthy. These are lesser-known managers who routinely distance the field with spectacular results. Their eye-popping numbers are mostly the result of investing in the more esoteric areas of the market, the so-called alternative investments.

Yes, you, too, can invest in commodities or real estate or even hedge funds and private equity with lower minimum requirements (Wall Street is always ready to market a me-too product for Main Street), but the pedigree and conditions are not the same. Dazzling returns as high as 60 percent annually by such hedge fund superstars as Steven A Cohen (SAC Capital), Edward Lambert (ESL Investments), and Joe Feshback (Feshback Partners, minimum investment $2 million) are the exclusive province of the well-connected and very rich. The cream of the crop in managerial talent will always gravitate toward the big money (some star hedge fund managers command as much as 44 percent of the profits).

The January 9, 2006, *U.S. News & World Report* quotes Joseph Aaron of Wood, Hat and Silver, a California investment firm: "You're either in with one of the truly great hedge fund mangers of the world or you're not, and if you're not they won't let you in because they don't need your money. What's left is pretty mediocre pickings." Jeffrey Saut, managing director of Raymond James, adds this consoling thought: "There are now more hedge funds than there are stocks and 60 percent of those funds are less than five years old. This trend will end with mediocre performance by most hedge funds" (Investment Strategy by Jeffrey Saut, *Escape from New York Redux,* December 26, 2006).

Return of 34 Percent, But Closed to Investors

Nor will you and I have access to the private equity deals, leveraged buyouts, derivative products, distressed debt, oil and gas, and timberland investments that have produced mouth-watering annual returns for the Yale, Harvard, and Stanford University endowment funds. And perhaps the most stunning and inaccessible performer of all is the Medallion hedge fund, run by mathematical genius, publicity-shy billionaire James Simons, whose team of 60 or so mathematics and physics PhDs work from complex quantitative models to produce returns averaging 34 percent annually since the fund began in 1988. Medallion has been closed to investors for the past 13 years.

Forbes lists Simons with a net worth of $4 billion. Institutional Investor's *Alpha* magazine estimated that in one year, 2005, he took home $1.5 billion. In that same year, the *average* pay of the 26 highest-paid hedge fund managers was a hard-to-believe $363 million. The bottom line is that the average investor (and most not-so-average investors) simply don't have access to the same high level of expertise as the super rich. Money brings honey on Wall Street as it does everywhere else.

Here's another reason why the best and brightest on Wall Street are unapproachable: We don't know who many of them are. They shun publicity and work behind the scenes. Anonymity enables them to operate more flexibly and effectively. Many feel their techniques will instantly stop working if they let others know their methodology. Unlike most, their own quiet success is all the recognition they need.

Charles Kirk, who, as we've reported, makes a profit on four out of every five trades, says he has many friends who do better than he does. For every media darling like Bill Miller or Bill Gross or Jim Cramer, there are probably 10 others who perform equally well if not better but whom we never hear about. Fortunately, you and I do have access to many top money managers who don't work anonymously. I feature those with the best track records in Chapter 8.

22. Low Commissions Make Online Trading Hard to Resist

Buy a stock and as soon as it goes up a little, sell it, hopefully the same day.

That's the seductive challenge that tempts so many investors, especially new ones, because it sounds so simple. Years ago the lure wasn't quite so powerful because commissions were much higher. The stock had to go up almost a full point just to break even on a round-trip transaction.

Today you don't have to be that right or that lucky. With bare-bones commissions (depending on the amount of trading activity and assets under control of the firm), all you need is for the stock to go up as little as ¼ point. For example, with a $16 round-trip commission, it's possible to buy a stock at $30, sell it at $30.25, and, on a 1,000 share trade, pocket a profit of $234. You can do even better with discount brokers like TradeKing.com ($4.95 flat fee) and Just2Trade.com ($2.50 for active traders). Bank of America and Wells Fargo have offered free stock trades to anyone keeping $25,000 on deposit. And you can make up to 10 trades in any one day up to a total of 40 trades a month, absolutely free at Zecco.com.

Making it even more enticing are the huge advances made in technology that allow individuals to trade the markets with the same tools and data that were available only to professional floor traders not too long ago. Just read a few books on trading strategies, attend some trading seminars, buy some trading software programs, set up your computer screens, open an online trading account, and when you're ready to make your move, hit the

> "Listen attentively to the experts. They'll always tell you exactly what can't be done and the reasons why. Then do it."
> —*Robert A. Heinlein*

"execute" button. What a beautiful way to make money! Working at home at your own pace, making trades only when conditions are just the way you want. It's an alluring concept that has proven irresistible to hundreds of thousands of people. The simplicity of the idea, however, belies the difficulty of its execution.

A Special Gift

There are positive things that can be said about short-term trading, but they don't include making money. It's an activity that can provide an interest, a challenge, and, as long as it goes well, fun and excitement. Over a period of time, however, most individual investors lose money on short-term trading. I have only anecdotal evidence to support this conclusion (I know of no large, objective, long-term surveys that have measured results of trading by the public). It's possible to have a streak of good luck, especially in roaring bull markets. It's possible to follow a trading strategy that will work—until it doesn't. If you use close stops and settle for minimum gains, you can stay in the game longer. But, over time, an unpredictable market will do what it has to do to make the majority of traders lose.

Like every market truism, there are exceptions to the rule (see my earlier comments on Charles Kirk) that no one can consistently time the market. The discount brokerage firms and others who have an agenda would have you believe the exceptions are many. Of my own personal knowledge, I know only one, and Kirk is a professional. There are others, of course, but they are relatively few in number and mostly prefer to work under the radar screen. My sense is that the handful who succeed are investors (*speculators* is more accurate) who are sophisticated, committed, and have special gifts not shared by the rest of us.

Of course, if you believe all those who claim they make money trading, then my "relatively few" characterization is off the mark. Perhaps I'm too influenced by my own ineptness and should be less skeptical. I do know this much: Good markets are likely going to yield more successful trades than bad markets; results must be measured over a period of years, not months or days; and those who talk about their exploits are likely to be less successful than those who don't.

23. Understand Your Own Temperament

"Know thyself" is good advice no matter what the situation, but it is especially helpful when it comes to investing. Sometimes it's not until you're tested under fire that you can really come to an accurate self-appraisal. That may require experiencing a severe bear market with your portfolio under water.

Some of us simply lack the objectivity to see ourselves as we really are. To the extent that we can, however, we can make wiser investment choices. If we know how we're likely to react emotionally in given situations, we're better able to pick a strategy that complements our temperament. As the saying goes, "If we don't know ourselves, the market can be a very expensive place to find out."

One thing we can do is draw up a written profile of our emotions. Column A would list what we see as our emotional strengths (patient, skeptical, curious, deliberate, etc.), and column B our weaknesses (impulsive, gullible, disorganized, indecisive, etc.). Input from those who know us well would add objectivity. If column A is a lot longer than column B, we're a candidate for at least some do-it-yourself investing. If column B is crowded, letting someone else make the decisions via a money manager, mutual fund, index fund, or the like probably makes more sense. Experience, if we're able to learn from it, will lengthen column A and shorten column B.

Almost as important as the ability to judge yourself is a talent for anticipating the behavior of others. In the market, correctly forecasting a policy change by the Federal Reserve Board, or the outcome of legislation or a key election, is helpful. But it's a two-step process. What's more important is correctly assessing the market's reaction to what you accurately forecast. These skills are hard to come by. Few investors can consistently anticipate both the news and the market's reaction. But experience will make you better at it.

Feelings Trump Logic

The Martha Stewart saga is a good example of how reality takes a back seat to perception. Investors who correctly gauged public reaction to that news story as it unfolded profited handsomely. Domestic diva Martha Stewart served a five-month jail sentence for obstruction of justice. Her sentence came as a surprise to many and sent the stock of her company, Martha Stewart Living Omnimedia (MSO) to a low for the year of $8.01 in mid-July 2004. While she was in prison (October 18, 2004, to March 6, 2005), the stock skyrocketed despite the fact that the company was awash in red ink. The stock reached a high of 37 just before she was released. Against a background of ever-widening losses, the stock almost quintupled. Wall Street analysts were overwhelmingly bearish on the stock, citing its "astronomical valuations" (TheStreet .com, February 2, 2005).

But the Martha Stewart story triggered strong emotions on the part of the public. The center of a media frenzy, she was an enormously popular celebrity with a loyal following. Many saw her as a victim of an overzealous effort to punish crime in corporate America. The public identified with her as an underdog. The rising price of the stock reflected confidence that with the help of saturation media exposure, Martha Stewart and her advertisers would come back stronger than ever. After release from prison, the stock came back to earth but, during its seven-month climb from 8 to 37, it yielded big profits.

Investors react to events with both reason and emotion, but feelings invariably trump logic. Being able to anticipate the correct emotional response in a given situation is tricky. It's the part of the investment equation that is often ignored by analysts who focus strictly on the fundamentals. Being a good investor means being a good amateur psychologist. An understanding of human behavior, both that of other investors and especially your own, will help make you money.

> "Success comes from smart budgeting, not super-smart investing. Build your nest egg by trimming expenses so you can invest as much as possible in long-term, low-fee index funds that track the overall market."
>
> —*Jeff Brown*

24. The Upside-Down Stock Market

Part of what makes the stock market so baffling is that many basic concepts are completely illogical. What would appear to be perfectly obvious is not. The truth is often the exact opposite of what a rational person would expect. What's good is bad and what's bad is good. A jump in interest rates causes bond prices to go down. It's good news for the income buyer, bad news for the bond owner. A rise in oil prices means more profits for Exxon but lower earnings for American Airlines and Wal-Mart. A sharp sell-off in the market makes investors glum, but short sellers are happy. A buyout at a premium is good news to stockholders of the acquired company but bad news for the bondholders of the acquirer (buyouts are often leveraged and the increased debt can weaken the balance sheet and lower the bond's price and rating).

As we become seasoned investors, it becomes obvious that the market's inconsistencies are part of its fabric. We learn that what's bullish for some can be bearish for others and that what's good today may be bad tomorrow. Here are some commonplace examples of the market's convoluted behavior. None of these examples are true all the time, but all are true most of the time.

- *When investors are optimistic, it's good for stocks.* **Wrong.** It's caution and skepticism that are bullish for the market. "The market climbs a wall of worry."
- *Good companies are generally good stocks; bad companies are generally bad stocks.* **Wrong.** William Bernstein in his book *The Four Pillars of Investing* (McGraw-Hill, 2002) claims that over the long term, the stocks of poorly run, unglamorous companies have higher returns than those of the most glamorous, best-run companies. This thesis is echoed by Jeremy Siegel in his book *The Future for Investors* (Random House, 2005) in which he says that over the past 40 years, the fastest-growing firms showed lower returns than the slow-growing firms, primarily because investors overpay for growth.
- *Hold on to stocks that are down and take profits in those that are up.* **Wrong.** In most cases it makes sense to do what retailers do, namely, get rid of the slowest movers and stay with the best merchandise. Just like the inventory manager in a department store, it's best to add to stocks as they go up, not as they go down. Exceptions to this include the purchase of stocks in a dollar-cost-averaging program (see Chapter 4) and in a periodic rebalancing program (see Chapter 6).
- *A healthy, growing economy is good for the* bond *market.* **Wrong.** The bond market thrives on a weak economy. A slowdown in business lessens the demand for credit. Instead of having to raise interest rates to cool off a heated economy, the Federal Reserve Board can lower interest rates to stimulate business (an easy monetary policy). Lower rates mean higher bond prices. Also, investors often seek the safety and income from bonds during an economic slump.

Surprise Moves Stocks—But Not Always

- *Bad news on a stock (or on the market) means lower prices.* **Wrong.** The key determinant is the surprise element. If the bad news is expected, the stock may very well go higher, not lower, especially if the overall market is strong. Only if the bad news comes as a surprise is it likely to go lower. Even then it may not follow the script. On both the day of the terrorist subway bombing in London (July 7, 2005) and of the near-biblical devastation inflicted on the Gulf coast by Hurricane Katrina (August 29, 2005), the market closed higher.

- *I can lose a lot less money buying a $3 stock than a $100 stock.* **Wrong.** If anything, lower-priced stocks are likely to entail more risk than higher-priced ones, which is why long-term investors will often buy 10 shares of a $100 stock rather than 200 shares of a $5 stock. In terms of value, the $100 issue can be a lot cheaper. Yes, the price of the $5 stock is much lower, and if it's down from a previous high of $200 it can look like a bargain. But, as the cliché goes, it's where a stock is going and not where it's been that counts. You can buy more shares of a cheaper stock and make more money if you're right, but you're also increasing the odds against you.

- *The faster earnings grow for corporate America, the better the stock market performs.* **Wrong.** Although, sooner or later, rising earnings help individual stocks, the stock market performs best when overall earnings are falling. Since 1927, Ned Davis Research of Venice, Florida, says the market has risen at a sharply higher rate during quarters in which the earnings of the S&P 500 were 10 to 25 percent *below* year-earlier levels (Mark Hulbert, MarketWatch.com, May 3, 2005). One apparent reason is that rapidly rising earnings usually lead to Fed tightening and to higher interest rates.

- *Periods of declining markets are periods of declining earnings.* **Wrong.** This is the reverse of the preceding item. There have been lots of bear markets when earnings kept rising. In 1946 and 1962 we had a big crash and a bear market and yet earnings exploded. In the 1973–1974 bear market, earnings rose during the entire period. And in 1987, we had a crash and earnings did very well.

- *When officers are selling shares in their own company and it's a stock I own, I should sell too.* **Wrong.** Disenchantment with their company's prospects is only one of many possible reasons for insider selling, which often has nothing to do with the outlook for the company (other reasons include raising funds to pay for a house, college, taxes, philanthropy, a divorce settlement, etc.). However, there *are* instances when insider selling is meaningful, specifically when it represents a high percentage of shares owned. The heavy insider selling in the housing stocks in 2005 proved prescient. Company officials who buy their own stock with their own money, on the other hand, do so invariably because they like what they see. It's a far more reliable indicator. Says Insider Trend Fund manager Tony Marchese, "Insider buying is important, especially in small cap stocks, because it's the ultimate test of faith. It's not a press release. It's not company money. It's somebody writing a personal check" (*Wall Street Journal*, "Insider Track," February 16, 2005). An exception would be insider buying that's required by the company's employee contract.

Least Recommended Outperform Most Recommended

- *If fifty analysts cover a stock and each and every one recommends purchase, that's reason enough to buy the stock.* **Wrong.** The stock may, indeed, prove to be a winner but universal endorsement is more likely to be a negative than a positive. *Investors Business Daily* (October 3, 2003) reported that for the almost four-year period 2000 through September 2003, the 600 stocks least liked by Wall Street analysts (they were up 45 percent for the period) trounced the 600 most recommended (down 19 percent).
- *A robust economy is always good for the stock market.* **Wrong.** It's *anticipation* of a strong economy that usually triggers an uptrend. The economy itself may still be in a recession but investors are already looking ahead to a recovery. The action of the Federal Reserve Board is often the key. During the two-year period from mid-2004 to mid-2006, the Fed raised interest rates by ¼-point increments 17 times, from 1 percent to 5¼ percent. During much of 2005–2006, the prevailing view was that the market could go up on a sustained basis only if the economy went down because that would allow the Fed to stop raising interest rates. So, for the most

part, the market went up on bad economic news and down on good economic news.

- *"A" rated quality stocks will outperform lower-quality stocks.* **Wrong.** They will sometimes but often they will not, depending on what style of investing is in vogue at the time. In 2006, the 76 stocks ranked B– or less in the S&P 500 gained in excess of 20 percent on average. The 98 issues ranked A and A+ gained roughly half of that, according to Harris Private Bank in Chicago.

- *Stocks that are covered by the most analysts will do better than those with the least coverage.* **Wrong.** Richard Bernstein, chief investment strategist for Merrill Lynch, studied the results of some 40 different investment strategies for the year 2006. The one that performed the best was buying the 50 stocks in the S&P 500 Index that were followed by the fewest Wall Street analysts.

- *Stocks that pay shareholders higher dividends outperform those that pay lower dividends.* **Wrong.** Stocks that pay small dividends, especially those that regularly increase their payouts, generally speaking, do better. A high yield is often the result of a slide in the price of the stock triggered by problems that may threaten the safety of the dividend. Or a generous payout may reflect limited opportunities for the company to put the money to work elsewhere. (Of course there are always exceptions, like an Altria Corp. or Exxon Mobil, that historically have provided both high yield and growth.)

This is a small sampling of the many contradictions in the market's behavior. For beginning investors it can be terribly confusing when what we think something means turns out to mean the exact opposite. But the more exposure we have to the deviant ways of an upside-down market, the better able we are to anticipate and understand them. Through trial

> "I realized that technical analysis didn't work when I turned the chart upside-down and didn't get a different answer."
>
> —*Warren Buffett*

and error, we learn to adjust to how things *are* rather than how we think they should be. During the process, we become keenly aware of perhaps the market's most glaring contradiction: The least experienced think they know, the most experienced know they don't.

25. Every Group Has Its Day

There is little about the market's behavior that is predictable. Here's an exception: Every stock market group that's out of favor will return to favor in time. Not every stock, but every *group*. Some sectors (in this context, *groups, sectors,* and *industries* can be substituted for each other) stay depressed longer than others and patience can be sorely tested. But history shows that sooner or later groups that languish in the wings return to center stage. It's a continuous cycle of being loved, unloved, and then loved again.

If we know for sure that a depressed group will eventually regain its popularity, but not necessarily all the stocks within the group, it makes sense to buy the industry in total. Rather than having to decide which is going to be the better performer in a down-and-out drug group—Schering, Johnson & Johnson, or Eli Lilly—we buy the entire pharmaceutical industry in one security. These sector funds are available via mutual funds or exchange-traded funds (ETFs). Fidelity Investments, for example, offers over 40 "Fidelity Selects" which are mutual funds each representing a different industry. Exchange-traded funds offer several choices within each sector—19, for example, represent the health/biotech industry, with more on the way.

If you prefer to buy unloved individual stocks within the group rather than the depressed group itself, it pays to stick with quality. When the group returns to favor, it's the best-of-the-breed industry leaders that are most likely to participate in the recovery because, in effect, they *are* the group. The more marginal, unseasoned members of the group may recover and they may not.

Different investment styles slide in and out of favor just like stock groups. Growth takes turns with value; large cap with small cap. Regardless of how long a particular investment style is out of favor, it will always eventually regain its popularity. In like manner, all front-running styles lose their status at some point in time. The eventual result is a certainty; the timing is unknowable. Moreover, there are times when groups and styles are in neutral. In sideways, lackluster markets, it may be a while before a favorite group or style emerges. And sometimes, two styles converge. Growth stocks, because of their depressed price, may be considered value plays as well.

The Importance of Picking the Right Group

Two other caveats about group behavior: First, at market tops, stock groups and sectors peak one by one. They don't all make their highs at the same time. At market bottoms, however, usually all groups reach their lows at about the same time. Individual stocks also tend to act more in unison at bottoms than at tops. Paul Desmond is the editor of *Lowry's Reports,* the oldest technical advisory in the country (1938). He reminds clients, mostly institutions and professionals, that in the past 77 years, an average of only 6 percent of all stocks made new highs on the peak day of bull markets. But, on average, over one-fifth were down 20 percent or more on that same top day, meaning the bear market for many stocks had begun months earlier.

Second, stocks seldom act contrary to their group. The odds are against a stock doing well if its group or industry is depressed. Some stocks within a group will lag and others will excel but they will tend to move in the same direction. So picking the right group is at least equally important to picking the right stock. The key, as always, is to buy at the right price. When buying unloved stocks, funds, or styles, the price you pay should fully reflect its out-of-favor status. And if the chart shows you're buying in or just above strong technical support, so much the better.

26. "When" Is More Important than "What"

In most cases, *when* you buy is more important than *what* you buy. You can make money on the most marginal company if you buy it at the right time; you can lose money in the bluest of blue chips if you buy it at the wrong time.

The right time is when a stock is selling reasonably near the low end of its trading range or at an historically low price/earnings multiple, or when any other trustworthy guideline indicates a sharp reduction in risk. This low entry level provides a safety net dangerously missing at higher prices.

The wrong time to buy for the long-term investor is when a stock is selling near the high end of its trading range or at an historically high price/earnings multiple. After Lucent Technologies plummeted from

80 to 1 and Sirius Satellite Radio from 69 to 1, those who bought between 1 and 2 were speculating on low-quality, high-risk situations. But because they bought on the cheap, with both stocks having formed a long, solid base of support, speculators were limiting downside risk in case the stocks didn't bounce back as they hoped. As it turned out, both stocks made impressive percentage recoveries.

By contrast, the buyer of GE at 60 or Microsoft at 59 or Merck at 96, all high-quality blue chips, have spent years waiting to break even, if they haven't already taken their losses. Investors who bought the seasoned industry leader IBM at its high in 1970 or in 1987 waited 10 years to get their money back. And even today, those who bought IBM at 139 back in July 1999 are still waiting to get even. Everything depends on the price you pay, regardless of how gilt-edged the stock.

27. No Place to Hide for the Investor

A never-ending onslaught of conflicting opinion inundates the investor. Compelling arguments both for and against every investment approach imaginable is spewed forth 24/7 from the Internet, broadcasters, and newspapers. An article pounding the table on the benefits of diversification is countered by another one praising the advantages of concentration. *The investor is in the middle.* Countless so-called experts extol the merits of a buy-and-hold approach while others argue that today's trading-range markets call for far more flexibility. *The investor is in the middle.* There are ringing endorsements of active management countered by passionate praise for passive investing. *The investor is in the middle.* Trend followers want to begin a year riding the momentum of the current favorite groups or styles, while other pundits warn of the folly of going with last year's winners. *The investor is in the middle,* often baffled, befuddled, and bewildered.

In a stressful world enveloped by crosscurrents of conflicting opinion there is no place for the investor to take refuge, no island of tranquility. He faces the constant dilemma of knowing whatever decision he makes today will be countered tomorrow by some article telling him he was wrong. In such an environment, being unaware may prove to be a case of "ignorance is bliss." If the investor is aware and thoroughly

> "One thing we know about the stock market is that when everyone is gazing skyward, it's never a bad idea to take a quick peek down."
>
> —*Alan Abelson*

confused, he may very well throw in the towel and exit the market for good. Or he may form his *own* opinion and act accordingly, convinced that no one really knows what they're talking about. Or he may take the easiest, most uncomplicated path to profit he can find. The latter explains the growing popularity of anything on Wall Street that keeps it simple.

Keeping It Simple

For example, among the fastest-growing segments of the mutual fund industry are target maturity or life cycle funds. Why? Because target funds do the work for you. Fidelity Freedom 2010, Vanguard Target Retirement 2015, and T. Rowe Price Retirement 2040, are among many "all in one" funds that will automatically shift to a more conservative position as you approach your retirement date. They do this mostly by gradually trimming stocks and adding bonds. The timing can be tricky and they may or may not execute successfully, but it's a strategy customized to your individual retirement date. That means less decision making for you (see Chapter 8).

Exchange-traded funds have exploded in popularity mostly because they make it simple. With broad exposure to entire markets and sectors via just one listed security, ETFs make many investment goals easier to implement. Another stress-free product is the customized portfolio service offered by a growing number of investment web sites. With knowledge of your goals and risk tolerance, they'll design a tailored portfolio that's allocated across different asset classes. The appeal of the numerous "lazy man" portfolios recommended by some savvy market observers is also rooted in their simplicity and ease of maintenance.

The popularity of the recent best seller, *The Little Book That Beats the Market* by Joel Greenblatt (John Wiley & Sons, 2005) has been fueled by the fact that it offers a magic formula for investing in just 155 pages that can allegedly be understood by a teenager. The same appeal of simplicity, brevity, and insight explains the popularity of the three Little Books that followed Greenblatt: *The Little Book of Value Investing* by Christopher H.

Browne, 2006; *The Little Book of Common Sense Investing* by John C. Bogle, 2007; and *The Little Book That Makes You Rich* by Louis Navellier (all four Little Books published by John Wiley & Sons).

The wild success of stock market adviser and TV personality Jim Cramer is based, in part if not entirely, on the irresistible lure of easy money. A high-paid, top-performing, streetwise hedge fund manager, the kind who typically works exclusively for wealthy individuals and institutions, makes his advice available to the public, in person, every day, free of charge. Making money was never easier; all the hard work and confusion is stripped way. Just listen to him on TV or radio, buy what and when he tells you to buy, and sell what and when you're told to sell. The charismatic Cramer makes the unpredictable predictable, reduces decision making to zero, and adds fun and excitement in the process. I say more on Cramer, *The Little Book That Beats the Market,* and the lazy portfolios later in this book.

All these attempts to make it easier for the "which way do I turn?" investor are commendable, as long as they don't create more problems than they solve. One thing they cannot do is change the inherent per-verse nature of the market itself. One way or another, the investor or someone making the decision for him must deal with the directly oppo-site views about an unknowable market. However, there is one area of broad consensus. Within the past decade there has emerged a near-unanimous opinion about the essentialness of foreign investing. Here the investor does not stand in the middle of conflicting views.

Owning Foreign Stocks Is Now Mainstream

For most of my investment career, investing abroad was not in the main-stream. It was an esoteric approach reserved for the super sophisticated. Today, however, we live in a flat, interdependent world. Stocks and bonds of both developed and emerging foreign countries are recommended as a "must" component in a diversified portfolio. Fueled by the convenient access to foreign markets provided by ETFs and mutual funds and by their stellar performance in recent years, investors have entered overseas markets with a vengeance.

In the two-year period 2005–2006, 85 percent of all inflows into stock mutual funds went into international funds. The huge cash influx reflected typical performance-chasing behavior. International stocks outperformed their U.S. counterparts for five straight years, 2002–2006. And in the three-year period 2004–2006, the rest of the world achieved almost double the return of the S&P 500 Index. All this reflects the dynamic growth in the world's emerging countries, especially China and India.

In his book *The Emerging Markets Century* (Free Press, 2007), author Antoine van Agtmael predicts that in another 50 years, the economies of today's emerging markets will eclipse those of the developed world in size. At Berkshire Hathaway's May 2006 annual meeting, Warren Buffett said that if he were starting his investment partnership over again, he would invest in securities around the world and focus on smaller companies.

To be sure, foreign markets will have their down years and their allure will fade, but probably not for long. Despite geopolitical and currency risks, they have performed comparatively well over the years, often when others didn't. Unlike almost all the other weighty decisions conflicting the investor, in tomorrows "one world," the inclusion of a foreign component in a balanced portfolio seems close to a no-brainer.

28. The Rarity of Inside Information

There's a popular perception that some privileged investors are able to profit from inside or advanced information about a company or stock. In fact, this rarely happens. In my years on Wall Street, I can only recall two times when someone I knew bought a stock on the strength of supposed inside information. In one case, the information proved to be false; in the second case, the news had little impact on the market. And there's the rub. Even if you do have advance news, it's far from a sure thing that it'll make you money.

There are three reasons why inside information may prove worthless. First, the information itself may be partially or totally inaccurate. Second, the information may have been leaked to many others beside yourself, causing the stock to make its move before the release date. And third, the information may not influence the market in the way you anticipate. This third factor is the most frustrating to deal with.

Let's say for the one and only time in your life, for whatever the reason, you come into possession of what you consider important news before anyone else. It could be an upcoming contract or product introduction or acquisition. It sounds bullish so you buy the stock. On the day the news is released, the market simply ignores the story. What you think is a big deal, the market greets with a yawn. Or the stock goes down instead of up because, on the same day, the company releases unexpected lower earnings or because the overall market is broadly lower on unsettling inflation news.

The only type of inside information that is likely to be valuable is that which comes as a complete surprise. But if you know about it, chances are you're not alone. If you are the single beneficiary, you still have to have the aforementioned variables fall into place.

There are many decision-making employees of corporations, unions, mutual funds, publications, enforcement agencies, and so on that have routine access to sensitive information. In the post-Enron era of transparency, the dissemination of such information is controlled by strict rules and regulations. There will always be some who will try to circumvent the rules and invariably some will succeed. But in the overall picture, even if I'm naïve and more people act on inside information than I suspect, the chances of them profiting are not enough to arouse envy. The successful use of inside information is mostly a myth.

> "What is already known and published by others has already been acted upon. Assume you're always the last to know."
> —*Charles Kirk*

29. What's a Reasonable Return?

It's unrealistic to expect investments to yield a positive return year in and year out. That's what hedge funds aim to do—show a gain even when the market is down. They have a better shot at it than most investors because they employ short selling and alternative investments. But in their relatively brief history, hedge funds have had mixed results, doing best in down markets. As for the 6,000+ equity mutual funds, almost none have gone up every year over long periods of time. (A notable exception is the T. Rowe Price Capital Appreciation Fund. Since its inception in 1986, it has not reported a loss; more about PRWCX later.) Even famed portfolio manager Bill Miller, widely credited for being the only mutual fund manager to outperform the S&P 500 Index 15 years in a row (Legg Mason Value Trust), had down years in the bear markets of 2000, 2001, and 2002, albeit smaller declines than the index.

The crème de la crème, the very best-performing mutual funds over long periods of time, suffer down years. When you see a list of the elite performers over the past 10 or 15 years, the usual annual gain is in a range of 15 to 25 percent. But this is an *average* annual gain, meaning some years it is a lot higher and some years a lot lower. For example, the number one performing fund over the past 10 years according to Morningstar, the Wasatch Micro Cap Fund, went from being up 49 percent in 2001 to being down 14 percent in 2002. But its average annual gain during that 10-year stretch was an eye-catching 24 percent.

Funds are bought mostly because of their track record. If an investor buys a consistent winner and then sees it falter, he will often sell, figuring that it was his purchase that jinxed the fund and that its streak is over. He may or may not prove to be right. But it's probably asking a lot to expect a fund that has outperformed thousands of competing funds for 10 years to extend that performance for another long stretch. The multi-talented fund manager may leave and/or its asset class, style, or sector orientation (small cap, for example) may rotate out of favor. As a practical matter there are probably few fund owners who stay with one of these top performers for a full 10- or 15-year up-and-down stretch, just as there are few stockholders who invested $1,000 in Microsoft in 1986 and 13 years later had $532,000 because they held on. There are just too many reasons to get shaken out along the way.

The Target Return Used to Be 15 Percent

What kind of investment return is reasonable to expect in the stock market? If we're content to take no more than what the market gives us, the average annual return of the S&P 500 Index is the standard that's most widely used. Going back to 1925, that return is 10.4 percent including reinvested dividends (according to Roger Ibbotson, Yale University). If you go back to 1957 when the S&P 500 as we know it today made its debut, the average annual return is 10.8 percent (Jeremy Siegel, University of Pennsylvania).

We can say then that, roughly speaking, the market has yielded a 10 percent-plus average annual return for close to a century. The active investor/manager, if his activeness is going to be meaningful, has to do better than that. (It's estimated that over the years, dividends represent some 40 percent of that return, although the yield on the S&P 500 in recent years has been under 2 percent. Also, if you reduce the 10 percent return by inflation, taxes, management fees, and/or trading costs, the net return is considerably less.)

In the years prior to the mid-1990s, with 10 percent as a benchmark, most professional advisers would shoot for an average annual gain of around 15 percent. It was a number that exceeded the market's return by a wide enough margin to validate the time spent by the do-it-yourself investor or the fees charged by his adviser. To reach that 15 percent target, the idea was to nail down substantial profits in good years and preserve capital in bad years.

Broad Consensus: Single-Digit Gains Ahead

Then came the booming second half of the 1990s. The five-year period 1995 thru 1999 spoiled us with successive gains never seen before—the Dow up an average 25 percent annually, NASDAQ up a hard-to-believe average of 42 percent. Some described it as a probable once-in-a-lifetime phenomenon. Investors' performance expectations rose sharply and then dropped just as severely in the crushing 2000–2002 bear market that followed.

Since then, market pundits, almost without exception, have forecast an extended period of low returns. Almost all predictions have been in single digits, ranging from average annual returns of 5 to 9 percent. Warren Buffett's forecast is typical. In 2002 he said he expected returns in the stock market to average 7 to 8 percent over the next 10 years. In 2007, Vanguard founder John Bogle made a similar prediction. He sees a 7 percent average return for the next decade.

There's always reason to be nervous about near-unanimous forecasts. Even if they prove correct, an *average* single-digit return allows for numbers much higher or much lower than that in any given year.

Remember that discussions of market returns refer to the annual returns of the major indexes, mostly the Dow and the S&P. Unless all your money is in index funds that follow these two benchmarks, your returns will be different.

How to make that difference a positive one via specifically recommended portfolios is the thrust of Part Two of this book. Through the careful selection of diversified, independently moving index funds, elite performing mutual funds, and individual stocks, we should be able to restore the traditional 15 percent average annual return as a realistic goal.

30. The Market Is Typically Dull and Indecisive

In a typical baseball game, most of the action takes place in just one or two innings. The rest of the game can be unexciting, even boring. The same can be said of the stock market, which most of the time moves indecisively in a narrow trading range. The bursts are concentrated in just a few sessions. Otherwise, it can be a dull affair. According to Ned Davis Research in Venice, Florida, "If you look back, about 35 percent of the time the market stays in a 8 percent range. There are a lot more periods of sideways action than most people believe" (interview in Barron's).

After waiting six years and eight months, the Dow Jones Industrial Average finally made a new record high on October 3, 2006. Before -making that move, however, it was stuck in an approximate 600-point trading range for almost two years. The inability of the market to mount a sustained move either up or down tested the patience of frustrated investors. But that patience was rewarded. As is often the case when a long sideways move is finally resolved to the upside, all the pent-up energy resulted in a vigorous advance. The Dow started 2006 around 10,700. Seventeen months later, after breaking out of its long 10,100–10,700 lethargy, it was over 3,000 points higher.

Numerous studies have concluded that the profits made in any given year are the result of the action in just a handful of the market's biggest up-days. Anyone out of the market on those days would show substantially lower results than the investor who stayed in the market for the entire year. Mark Hebner in his book *Index Funds* (IFA Publishing, 2005) reports that over a 10-year period, about 88 percent of the market's total gain was concentrated in just 40 days. Eric Kobren, editor of *Fidelity Insight* (December, 2005), says that over the 20-year period through November 30, 2005, "If you missed just the best 10 days (10 days out of over 5,000!) you would have missed 42 percent of the market's return for the whole 20 years."

The same applies to being out of the market during the year's best months. *ING Investment Weekly* reports that "from January 1990 to April 2005, the average annualized return of the S&P 500 Index was 11 percent. If an investor missed the best 5 percent of the months during that time, his return would have been cut in half. And if the investor missed the best 20 percent performing months, his annualized return would have dropped from 11 percent to minus 5 percent."

Since the market's brief explosive moves are unpredictable, the investor must always be in the market to catch them. That's why Magellan's legendary portfolio manager, Peter Lynch, said he was fully invested at all times. Most of the investor's time is spent in tedium, waiting for good things to happen.

> "In this business it is no disgrace to guess wrong. The only disgrace is to stay wrong."
>
> —*Jeffrey Saut*

31. Interest Rates—The Most Difficult of All to Forecast

Predicting accurately the course of the economy and/or inflation is never easy. Forecasting the stock market is next to impossible. But trying to figure out what interest rates are going to do is the most difficult of all. Going back 20 years, the nation's leading economists surveyed twice a year by the *Wall Street Journal* have been wrong on the direction of interest rates a whopping 70 percent of the time (and there are only three ways they can go). And these are professionals who are paid big bucks for their forecasts.

In mid-2004, Fed Chairman Greenspan removed the guesswork. He increased rates and announced to the world, clearly and unmistakably, that the Fed would be raising interest rates repeatedly in the future because they were too low. With the Fed's intentions a matter of public record, Wall Street's job of forecasting interest rates was made easy. Everybody predicted higher rates.

But what seemed like a no-brainer proved dead wrong. Short-term rates went up because the Fed raised them as promised, but to Wall Street's bewilderment, long-term rates (which the Fed cannot control directly) actually went down. Commenting on the bond market's completely unexpected behavior, Michael Roberge, portfolio manager of the top-performing MFS Research Bond Fund, said in the March 7, 2005, *Barron's,* "Contemplating where rates will be in six months, or a year, or even tomorrow, is a futile exercise. Just look at the number of bond fund managers caught flatfooted by last year's persistently low interest rates which defied almost all expectations."

Even the most brilliant minds in the field, those who have compiled outstanding track records and risen to the pinnacle of their profession—people like Henry Kaufman, chief economist for Solomon Brothers and the leading bond market maven of the 1970s and 1980s; Martin Barnes, editor of the prestigious *Bank Credit Analyst;* and James Grant, editor of the influential *Interest Rate Observer*—have made forecasts that proved less than prescient.

Bill Gross, manager of the world's biggest bond fund, Pimco Total Return Fund, probably has the most visible track record because he makes so many public forecasts. The frequency of his widely quoted interviews and writing (monthly "Investment Outlook" commentary on pimco.com) enables him to make ongoing adjustments. So if he's wrong, it's not for long. His overall performance has been exemplary, due partly to his willingness to buck the consensus view. Because of his skill and because of the huge bond portfolio he controls, when Gross speaks, people listen. His words can trigger rallies and sell-offs in the $24 trillion bond market. *Fortune* calls Gross the "bond king" and reports that he earns $40 million a year. You don't get paid that kind of money for being wrong.

Interest Rates Are a Conundrum Even to Greenspan

Yet, with all his credentials, Gross is not immune from error. In May 2005, for example, he predicted the Fed would stop raising rates when the federal funds rate reached 3.5 percent. By year-end it was 4.25 percent and six months after that it was 5.25 percent. (In the world of interest rates a move of 50 basis points, or 0.5 percent, is a big deal). In September 2005, he said the yield on the 10-year Treasury bond would range between 3.8 percent and 4.3 percent through year-end. Just seven weeks later the yield was 4.6 percent. This may sound like nitpicking in light of Gross' overall record of excellence. He's still the go-to guy for getting a handle on the bond market. He makes fewer mistakes than others, but the point is, he still makes them.

Arguably, the man who has had the biggest, most prolonged influence on interest rates in our history (18 years as the forceful head of the Federal Reserve Board), the erudite Alan Greenspan, admitted publicly in February 2005 that he was puzzled about how interest rates were behaving. He called the failure of long-term rates to follow the Fed's repeated increase in short-term rates (they usually move in the same direction) a "conundrum."

The fact that the best and the brightest can be confused and wrong doesn't deter Wall Street from cranking out its predictions. The Street's preoccupation with interest rate forecasting is understandable because the cost of money has such a broad ripple effect. However, it's up to the investor to be aware of just how fragile and fallible all such forecasts are and to treat them with a jumbo-sized grain of salt.

In November 2001, the yield on the 10-year Treasury bond was 5 percent. *Barron's* ran a cover story declaring boldly, "It's time to lighten up on bonds. The 20 year slide in interest rates is just about over." Instead, the slide continued. By mid-2003 the yield touched a low of 3.1 percent and was still under 5 percent in early 2007. Of course, the longer term the prediction, the greater the chance of it being right. Analysts who really go out on the limb and attempt to anticipate *short-term* movements in interest rates are acting less than responsibly if they don't reveal the good chance for error.

(Let me interject here a response to an anticipated criticism. Some will say I'm asking for a dream world. "It's unrealistic to expect professionals to call attention to their fallibility. Nor should they have to. They're just expressing an opinion and everybody knows it's just an opinion. That's what they're paid to do." Maybe so. But people have to be reminded. What's a supposed "given" is often not. It has to be verbalized. Human nature-wise, it may at first be difficult, but with a conscious effort, "I could easily be wrong," can become a routine part of the adviser's everyday vocabulary. It's doable.)

Interest rates are rarely hot topics of conversation at social gatherings even though they affect everybody there (their bank deposits, mortgages, credit cards, car loans, etc.). We discuss them here, not because they're sexy subjects but because whatever is happening in the economy and the stock market, interest rates are playing a major role. Based on history, we know that a bull market cannot survive in a climate of *rapidly* rising interest rates. As the cost of doing business goes up, profits decline and the economy cools off, along with the stock market. Corporate and consumer spending declines and higher yields make alternatives to stocks more attractive.

Rising Interest Rates Are a Bull Market Killer

James Stack, editor of InvesTech Research's *Market Analyst* and *Portfolio Strategy* newsletters, says that virtually every bull market in history has died under the weight of high interest rates. There are exceptions, of course, as when the increase in rates is gradual and from an historically low level (2004–2006). Another exception, as Jim Paulsen, chief investment strategist for Wells Capital Management, points out (*Barron's,* October 17, 2005), there *have* been a few times in history when rates and stock prices have moved up together. But, for the most part, a relentless climb in interest rates creates a hostile environment for stocks.

The reverse also applies—a series of rate cuts, or the prospect of it, is usually well received by the market. During 2005 the conventional wisdom was that in order for the market to have an upside breakout from its long trading range, it needed some assurances that the Fed was near the end of its long string of rate hikes.

So, whatever the situation—a bull, bear, or sideways market, an expanding, receding, or flat economy—the future direction of interest rates will always be a hot topic on Wall Street. What's so frustrating is that this key factor that impacts so many aspects of our lives is so elusive and unpredictable. That's one reason why diversification and asset allocation are essential to sound investing. Owning securities with different levels of interest rate sensitivity provides both risk and profit protection (when interest rates go down in anticipation of a recession, for example, stocks may react negatively but bonds will likely go up). Owning different asset classes, and owning them for the long term, is the best way to neutralize the fickleness of interest rates. A surprise move in rates may cause short-term damage but the passage of time gives the market's symmetry a chance to smooth out the wrinkles.

> "The key to everything financial, and to nearly everything economic, is interest rates."
> —*Andrew Tobias*

32. The Brilliant Market Call

Many of the widely quoted gurus on Wall Street gain their celebrity as a result of one dramatic, contrarian market call that proves to be correct. The publicity surrounding that one defining event can keep the analyst in the limelight for a long time, sometimes a lifetime, despite the fact that there is rarely a repeat performance.

This is partly because reporters only have so much time for original research. Writing their stories on deadline, they often go back to the same names in their files over and over again. It's quick, it's easy, and it's safe. The result is that the same sources are repeatedly quoted on the same subject despite the fact that there may be others equally or better qualified. What's more, the reappearance of the same names feeds on itself. The more they appear, the more their reputation is validated, and the more they are added to the files of other reporters.

I experienced this personally. In articles about newsletters, I was profiled in *Money* (July 1985, page 85) and *Forbes* (May 9, 1983, page 194). Many years later, well after I retired from the *Dick Davis Digest,* I was still getting calls from reporters doing stories on investment newsletters. My name was still in their files as the go-to guy under the heading "Newsletters."

Of course, the desire to attract attention may have motivated some of the more startling market calls over the years. A lesser-known forecaster may feel he has little to lose and everything to gain with a way-out prediction. It may even secure a book deal (*Dow 36,000,* by James K. Glassman & Kevin A. Hassett, Crown Publishing, 1999).

However, most stock market forecasters most of the time are trend followers. They have to be. If they were constantly sticking their neck out, they'd be wrong too often to stay in business. So those who have enough conviction to go public with a bold forecast that comes true deserve credit. And their advice can certainly continue to merit attention. However, because they were dramatically right once does not mean they will be dramatically right again. The market's perversity makes it unlikely.

33. Your Results Will Differ From Your Fund's

When a mutual fund or an index fund or a money manager reports an average annual gain of 15 percent over the past three or five years, you would have had to be in that fund for the entire period, from the first day to the last day, to show the same result. That may seem obvious but it's often forgotten when results are compared. Your purchase and sale dates are unlikely to be January 1 and December 31. More important, you may have bought high and sold low. Reams of statistics support the conclusion that most money comes into funds when they're popular (high) and moves out of funds when they're unpopular (low). That can have a serious negative impact on your return. What's more, unless you reinvest the dividends and thus benefit from compounding, your money will grow less than that of the fund.

We usually buy a mutual fund based on its past performance, hoping it can extend that performance in the future. Whatever record it does compile after you buy it, the likelihood that your results will match, exceed, or lag the results published each year will depend on how good you are at buying low and selling high. As stated previously, entry and exit levels are crucial. Of course, if you buy high and hold on long enough, bad timing will have less and less of an impact.

There are a few other things to remember about forming realistic performance expectations. First, the juicy returns published by individual funds are usually for relatively brief periods of five years or less. They often result from average or below-average years and one spectacular year. Check out the top-performing funds over 5-, 10-, 15-, and 20-year periods. You'll note that very few in the 5-year category also appear in the 10-year list, and fewer still appear in the 15- and 20-year categories. With a handful of exceptions, the stock market is simply too difficult for any one fund to stay on top for a long time, at least not a fund that you and I can buy (I focus on the exceptions in Chapter 8).

Second, when a newsletter boasts that its monitored growth portfolio is "up 143 percent since inception versus the S&P 500 up only 47 percent," it is misleading. You would have had to buy all the stocks in the portfolio and bought them at the same time and at the same price without commissions, to match the touted results. Recommended monitored portfolios often have 25 to 100 stocks and make frequent changes.

Third, to motivate investors, salesmen will cite spectacular gains in certain legendary stocks over the years. You've heard the stories: "$1,000 invested in Phillip Morris (Altria) in 1957 would be worth $6 million today." The reality is no one has experienced that, real-time, unless the stock has been buried in a family trust. The number of individual investors who bought Phillip Morris over 50 years ago and resisted hundreds of different compelling reasons for selling it over the decades and still own their original shares is infinitesimal, if not zero.

It Doesn't Happen in Real Life

The same applies to all the other examples of eye-popping returns achieved over very long periods of time. Somewhere along the way, and it's usually a lot less than a decade, fear or greed or personal need take over. "If you had invested $1,000 back in . . ." makes good copy but in real life, it doesn't happen. If Google is selling at the equivalent of $100,000 per share some 30 years from now (a la Berkshire Hathaway), will any of today's stockholders still own it? Unlikely.

In order to duplicate the average annual gain of your individual adviser or mutual fund, you may have to experience some bad years. You're not being fair to yourself or your adviser unless you give him a stretch of time to show what he can do (at least one complete bull/bear cycle).

> "Management skill has its limitations. Put Bill Gates or Jack Welch in a lousy company and it'll still be a lousy company."
> —*Peter Lynch*

That's how long it may take for his "average annual return" numbers to be reflected in your portfolio.

34. You *Can* Make Money in a Down Market

It's a certainty that markets will go down, sometimes for a long time. Even in up or flat markets, there are always stocks or sectors that are in their own private bear market. It's a two-way street, and if you're nimble or pre-scient or lucky you can make money going in either or both directions. It may be that news or a chart (preferably both) convince you that the market or a stock is headed lower or, if it's already declining, that it's likely to go down farther. If you're willing to back up that conviction with cash, and if you're right, you can profit while everyone else is hurting.

There are a number of ways to exploit the market's downside. The three most common strategies involve the selling short of individual stocks, the selling short of the overall market or individual sectors via ETF index funds, and the purchase of bear mutual funds devoted exclusively to short selling. The buying of put options is still another way to bet against the market, but, to keep it simple, we'll limit this discussion to the process of short selling. (Despite this dismissive treatment of options, it's fair to point out that the buying of puts and calls can provide a valuable tool to the investor wanting to speculate, boost yield, and/or manage risk.)

Let's say you're convinced a particular stock is headed lower. You ask your broker to short the stock at the current price (in June, 2007, the SEC repealed the 70-year-old short sale rule and said an up-tick is no longer required for selling a stock short). The broker will credit your account with the proceeds of the sale. Since you have sold something you don't own, the broker has to borrow the shares. Then, if all goes well, you can buy back or cover your position at a lower price, replace the borrowed shares, and profit by the difference in price.

If you believe the overall market or a particular sector within the market is going down, you can short the ETF that represents the broad market (the S&P 500 ETF, the Dow Jones ETF, or the NASDAQ 100 ETF, for example) or you can short the pharmaceutical or energy sector ETF in the same way you would short an individual stock. The third way you can take advantage of a down market is to buy a mutual fund from Rydex or ProFunds or other fund families that feature funds that go short.

Every month a list of the stocks with the largest short positions is published. This gives the short seller an idea of the extent to which his negative feelings are shared by others. In the upside-down world of the stock market, a large short interest is considered bullish for a stock because it represents a pool of future buyers (at some point they must cover their shorts). Many times when the market or a stock goes up inexplicably, the reason behind the rise is covering by nervous shorts. (If they all panic at the same time, it's called a *short squeeze*.) There are some observers, however, who believe a large short interest is bearish, perhaps because short selling is considered a sophisticated technique practiced by investors that are more in the know. Todd Senick, a broker at WFG Investments in Dallas, has worked with short-selling institutional clients for 15 years. He says, "If short interest exceeds 20 percent of the float, buyer beware" (*Wall Street Journal,* January 21, 2007).

Short Selling Is Difficult and Risky

Traditionally, short selling has been used mostly in the commodity markets and by hedge funds as a hedge against long positions to minimize risk. Selling short for profit only and not as a hedge is not a technique that's popular with individual investors even though declines in stocks are inevitable. The reason is that it is just too risky and too difficult. If you go long a stock at 20, your downside risk is limited to 20, but if you go short a stock at 20, your potential loss is unlimited. The short seller watching a growing loss that he knows has no boundaries is not a happy camper. He is nervous, sweaty, anxious, and fearful. Even if he's right and the stock eventually goes down, it can take a while before that happens. Until it does, a rising price can trigger the fear button. (The short seller is also responsible for any dividends paid on his borrowed stock, interest charged on his margin account, and any margin call for more money.)

There are other forces working against the short seller, principally the market's clear directional bias. For over 100 years the underlying trend of corporate earnings, the gross national product, and the stock market has been up. Bull markets last longer on average than bear markets and there are more up days than down days. So the short seller, if he is to take advantage of the periodic declines within that long-term uptrend, must exercise impeccable timing.

He must also overcome another fundamental bias. Most of us, by temperament, are inclined toward a hopeful, if not optimistic, glass-half-full mentality. Making money because things go well seems in the natural order of things. Profiting from misfortune is less instinctive. For all these reasons the practice of short selling is mostly the province of professionals, many of whom find it equally difficult.

Less challenging than short selling is profiting if you think interest rates are going up and bond prices down. A number of mutual fund families such as Rydex and ProFunds sell inverse bond funds. They go up when the bond market goes down. Another option is to sell short a bond ETF. For example, you could sell short the most popular fixed income ETF, the Lehman 20+ Treasury Fund (TLT). It tracks the performance of the long-term sector of the U.S. Treasury market. If treasury bonds go down, you're a winner.

Attempting to buy stocks in a declining market may be even trickier than going short. The odds are against a stock going up in a down market. An ebbing tide lowers all boats. Regardless of how positive or hopeful the fundamentals, the negative mood generated by the market's downside momentum can be all-encompassing. The more pervasive the downtrend, the less likely the chances of swimming against the tide.

As obvious as this may sound, there is a steady stream of Wall Street buy recommendations regardless of the state of the market. It's as if stocks traded in a vacuum, unaffected by the underlying trend of the market itself. The bottom line is not to expect to be smart or lucky enough to pick a stock that's going to go up when most everything else is going down. The whole process of buying stocks is difficult enough without trying to do it in a hostile environment. On Wall Street the old maxim is, "Don't fight the tape." On Main Street they say, "It's much easier to ride the horse in the direction he's going."

35. No One Has a Monopoly
on the Right Answers

There are myriad sources of information and opinion on the stock market. No single one of them has a monopoly on being right. It would be arrogant for any adviser to imply otherwise. Dealing with imponderables makes the conscientious adviser receptive to all the help he can get.

For example, stockbrokers should be familiar with research outside their own firm. A cross section of the best investment thinking from sources with the best track records serves the interest of the customer better than the best research from just one firm. Part of the job of the prudent adviser is to keep abreast of what's being written in the top financial publications (*Wall Street Journal, New York Times, Barron's, Investors Business Daily, BusinessWeek, Forbes, Kiplinger's Personal Finance,* leading investment newsletters, web sites, and so on).

There is always an abundance of information out there that is not covered by the research department of a particular firm but that would be of keen interest to its clients. They will not hear about it unless the adviser makes it his business to stay broadly informed. If the outside research conflicts with in-house recommendations, that's all the more reason for presenting both to the customer. After exposing the differing opinions, the adviser can make a case for his own bottom-line recommendation and then let the customer make up his own mind.

> "The single most important lesson that I've learned in 48 years in this investment business is that thinking is no substitute for taking action. Thinking is just rehearsing. You must learn to act."
>
> —*Richard Russell*

When I broke into the securities business with Merrill Lynch, I was struck by the fact that most customers based their investment decisions on advice from the one firm. I thought the investor would be helped by broader exposure and so I started the *Dick Davis Digest,* which provided a cross section of professional opinion. Brokers from different firms were among our best customers. They used the *Digest* to supplement their own firm's research. Since market wisdom is not confined to one source, the enlightened adviser will go wherever necessary to find it.

Part Two

OKAY, SO WHAT DO I DO WITH MY MONEY?

Chapter 6

Active versus Passive Investing

I f you've read everything up to this point, I'm pleased. It means that all the important stuff that has stuck in my brain over the years is now lodged in your brain. I hope it'll stick. I believe it will save you heartache and money. Some readers may have come directly to this bottom-line advice section of the book and skipped the preceding chapters. I urge you to start from the beginning. The upcoming recommendations will be far more meaningful if you've digested what's gone before. If you want the maximum effect of a 10-day diet, you don't start on the fifth day.

For most of the twentieth century, *investing* meant buying stocks and bonds. Mutual funds entered the mix in the 1980s. Today we have more mutual funds than we have listed common stocks. Index funds and exchange-traded funds (ETFs) have become so popular that it seems they've been around forever. The first index fund was introduced in

1976 by John Bogle at Vanguard and the first ETF listed in 1993, but it's only been the last decade or so that they've been widely embraced by Wall Street.

Like many others smarter than me, I'm a big fan of indexing and believe it should play a major role in the holdings of most investors. It is the twenty-first century way of buying stocks and bonds. However, I believe most everyone should have some portion of their equity money invested outside the index field. Choices include actively managed mutual funds such as target funds, monitored portfolios, alternative investments, and individual stocks.

The 80-20 Solution

How much of your money should be used to *settle* (accepting whatever the market gives you via passive indexing) and how much should be used to *reach* (trying to top the market's results via elite performers and your own stock picking) depends on your individual circumstances. A reasonable starting point for the broad range of investors might be 80 percent passive and 20 percent active. These numbers will vary considerably, depending on age, investment goals, risk tolerance, level of investment experience, emotional temperament, available reading time, and so on.

This part of the book is divided into two major sections. The first deals with passive buy-and-hold investments (the 80 percent portion). Featured are model portfolios of diversified, low-cost mutual fund index funds and ETFs along with the recommended allocation for each component.

The second section is about active investing—the attempt to outperform the market in one of two ways. One is by having someone else do the decision making for you; the other is by doing it yourself. In the former category, we feature some of the best-performing mutual funds over the long term. Also included are systems and monitored portfolios that have produced outstanding results over time. All choices are grouped under the heading "active investing" even though it is someone else, usually a professional, that is being active, not you.

In the do-it-yourself category, I am confident that what you've read in this book will give you an edge. To tilt the odds further in your favor, you'll find a compilation of my favorite sources of investment wisdom. Exposure to these insights will better prepare you to compete with the best stock

"The dumbest reason in the world to buy a stock is because it's going up."

—*Warren Buffett*

pickers in the world. I believe it is healthy and instructive for most investors to engage in some form of active investing. Doing it yourself can be the most challenging, the most exciting, and the most rewarding way to go, both financially and emotionally. But for most, the odds of success in any form of active investing are less than in indexing—which is why I favor index funds and ETFs for most of your money.

When Dumb Money Stops Being Dumb

In recommending market-cloning index funds, I am mindful that they will never be popular with some investors. Indexing represents an unnatural surrender of ego. The same human nature that makes most of us ill-equipped emotionally to succeed in the market also makes most of us think we are far better investors than we are. If indeed, only 20 percent of investors outperform the S&P 500 Index, invariably we think of ourselves as part of that 20 percent, not only this year but every year. The use of indexing is seen as throwing in the towel, an act of submission incompatible with the confidence that we can do better than our neighbor.

Warren Buffett, by contrast, sees throwing in the towel as an enlightened move. In 1993 he wrote, "By periodically investing in an index fund, the know-nothing investor can actually outperform most investment professionals. Paradoxically, when 'dumb' money acknowledges its limitations, it ceases to be dumb" (BerkshireHathaway.com, Warren Buffett's Letter to Berkshire Shareholders, 1993).

In this "recommendation" part of the book, I'm following the same formula I used in the *Dick Davis Digest* newsletter. For 25 years, the masthead of that publication has carried these words: "Investment ideas from the best minds in Wall Street." In the "Passive Investing" section, I select index fund portfolios recommended by some of the smartest, most successful investors I know. In the "Active Investing" section I spotlight an elite group of mutual funds and monitored portfolios that have risen above their peers. The combination of mostly passive and some active strategies represents the best answer I know to the all-important question: "Now that I've been forewarned and forearmed by the preceding chapters, what exactly do I do with my money?"

I offer a selection of model portfolios because it would be presumptuous to offer just one, although that's all that may be required. Keep in mind, none of what follows applies to the short-term trader. That's a whole other book written by someone far more nimble than me. These are strictly long-term recommendations.

An Unequivocal Conclusion

During my years in radio, TV, newspapers, and writing a newsletter, I never recommended stocks personally. Nor have I since my semiretirement, not even to close friends and family. I never had the necessary conviction. But now I do—at least to the point of recommending individual portfolios, if not specific stocks. It's one of the reasons for the book.

Like so many others who have been around the market for a long time, I've come to the unequivocal conclusion that most of the money of most investors belongs in index funds. The portfolios presented in the following pages are ones that I'm comfortable with. Some will fit your personal situation better than others, depending on the variables we've mentioned like age, objectives, and risk tolerance. But one thing applies to them all: Just like stocks, it is important to buy index funds and mutual funds at a reasonable price. That's easier to do if you buy only 25 percent or 50 percent of a position at one time or if you use dollar cost averaging.

The broadest index funds are supposed to mirror the overall market. For decades, the expression *the market* referred to the Dow Jones Industrial Average. It is still the oldest and most popular index. However, since it has only 30 stocks, the performance of the broad general market is usually measured by the S&P 500 Index. When the question is asked, "What kind of return does the stock market throw off?" the answer is usually "Around 10 percent," which refers to the 10.4 percent average compounded annual return including dividends of the S&P 500 since 1926 (Ibbotson Associates, Chicago). There's only one way to lock in that return and avoid being in the majority group of underperformers and that's to buy only the S&P 500 Index itself and hold on to it for what could be a long, long time.

The ability to buy 500 stocks in just one security didn't exist in my father's time. Today, it's done routinely via a traditional mutual fund or an ETF. As a practical matter, however, besides dealing with the boredom, it's a difficult strategy to implement for three reasons.

Drawbacks of Owning Just One Major Index

First, few of us have the patience to hold on to a laggard performer, especially when other sectors of the market are doing well. Historically the S&P 500 has done poorly for long stretches at a time (although its decades-long upward bias is clear). It took nine years after its 1973 high for the S&P 500 to reach that level again. If the gurus are correct and we're faced with narrow-moving, trading-range markets, those drought periods could occur even more frequently.

S&P Index holders who bought at the March 24, 2000, bull market high of 1527 had to wait seven years before that mark was topped. With so many market sectors posting huge gains during that period, it is likely that only the most disconnected and/or disciplined stayed with the index. According to John Bogle, Vanguard's index fund pioneer, only some 20 percent of those who buy the S&P 500 are long-term investors. It's hard to recommend a market approach (buying only the S&P 500) that is so difficult to implement.

The second obstacle to a single focus on the S&P 500 is the always-difficult job of buying low. If you're going to go with just one index, the proper entry level becomes magnified in importance. The third negative is the fact that the S&P 500 represents a bet on one sector of the market—namely, the large capitalization stocks. Going into 2007, that bet had been a long-term loser. Small caps had outperformed big caps for the seventh year in a row. However, in fairness to the venerable S&P 500 Index, it's also true that anyone who bought the index at its March 2000 high but continued to buy it regularly as it plunged 50 percent to its October 2002 low, came out ahead in far less than seven years. The boring, methodical process of dollar cost averaging once again paid off. Princeton's professor of economics, Burton Malkiel, believes the S&P 500 will continue to be the preeminent index of choice for the core of an equity portfolio for the next 50 years (*Barron's,* May 28, 2007).

At some point, large cap stocks such as those in the S&P 500 and the Dow Jones Industrials will return to favor. However, a diversified list of index funds (including large caps) rather than just one overall market index is likely to produce a happier result. That's why the following pages feature

> "By day we write about 'Six Funds to Buy Now!' By night we invest our own money in sensible index funds. Unfortunately, pro–index fund stories don't sell magazines."
>
> —*Anonymous* Fortune *magazine writer*

portfolios of various asset classes, not just one broad-based index. It's an approach that reduces risk and enhances performance potential. Instead of matching the market, we're using diversified index funds to beat it.

Here's a thumbnail overview of what's included on passive and active investing beginning here and continuing through Chapter 9.

Passive Investing—An Overview
- Index funds: The 17 most important things to know
- Model index fund portfolios
  - Most popular asset classes
  - Twenty-eight model index fund portfolios

Active Investing—An Overview
- Life cycle/target funds
- Mutual funds
  - The 20 most important things to know including outstanding funds and elite managers.
- Stocks: The 12 best places to go for ideas.

Passive Investing—An Overview

Four out of five investors will do worse than the S&P 500 Index this year. At least that's what's commonly reported. I get the feeling that the 80 percent failure figure has been reported so often over the years, it's simply accepted as gospel.

Some studies I've seen put the underperformance percentage at an even higher rate. Paul Farrell, in a February 4, 2006, MarketWatch.com column, wrote: "The S&P 500 beat 97 percent of mutual fund managers for a 10-year period ending October 2004. In two 30-year studies, the S&P 500 outperformed 97 percent and 94 percent of the managers. And only 12 percent of the top 100 managers repeated." And these were professionals. Let's be conservative and use the word *majority,* meaning that over half of investors will underperform the S&P 500 over time. That's still a telling statistic.

The reason for such a high failure rate is both psychological and financial. As discussed earlier, most of us are inclined by temperament to make the wrong moves in the market. In a well-known study by Boston-based research firm Dalbar, Inc., that covered a 20-year period, the average equity investor earned an average 2.5 percent annually (less than inflation) compared to the 12.2 percent earned by the S&P 500 Index investor during that same period. That's a dramatic difference. The main reason: the strong tendency of stock investors to buy high and sell low.

How about the portfolio managers of mutual funds? Why do studies repeatedly show that over the long haul, index funds perform better than thousands of other competing traditional mutual funds? The answer is management fees and trading costs. Index funds simply mimic an index. They always have lower fees and expense because they don't have to pay high-priced managers; their trading activity is limited so their commission costs are low. That cost efficiency represents an almost insurmountable advantage over actively managed funds.

Making Sure Someone's at the Party

Cornell-based retirement specialist Robert Julian conducts workshops for 401(k) participants and puts out an especially informative monthly newsletter, *Your Retirement* (RetirementPlanningConsultants.com). He is a strong advocate of index funds as the means of building a retirement nest egg. In a July 18, 2007 telephone interview from his home in Ithaca, New York, he says, "Returns from index funds are predictable. . . . You will earn the rate of return provided by the stock market. With index funds, you capture the entire return of each asset class. By using index funds, you use a simple, time-tested, low-cost, easy-to-understand, do-it-yourself, low stress, uncomplicated approach to building your nest egg. Your low-maintenance portfolio does not require worrying about your investments on a day-to-day basis."

Index funds have surged in popularity for another reason—their ability to capture moves in individual sectors of the market. There is usually a bull market going on somewhere, even in range bound or declining markets. (Exception: A killer bear market with blood in the street offers no place to hide.) Index funds offer a convenient way to profit from individual sector strength. All that's necessary is to be right on the sector, not on any one stock.

The leadership of the market is always changing. It's one of the few market events we can anticipate with certainty. What we don't know is which groups will be the next leaders. That's why diversification makes so much sense. If we spread out enough, we're sure to have someone at the party.

The index fund is the ideal tool to deal with the certainty of sector rotation. That's reflected in the widespread use of indexing to structure diversified portfolios. Whatever the investment style (growth, value, big cap, small cap, etc.), asset class (stocks, bonds, real estate, commodities, foreign, etc.), or sector (pharmaceuticals, technology, retail, etc.), there are hundreds of index funds to choose from, and new funds continue to proliferate. Thus, despite their short existence, index funds have quickly evolved into more than just a vehicle to mirror the overall market. In fact, only a small percentage of index funds today are designed to clone the market.

> "Pundits who make a business out of making predictions mostly are no better than the rest of us. The only difference is that they get paid for their bad judgment."
> —*Unknown*

Pie Slices Keep Getting Thinner

Not only are most index funds benchmarked to a slice of the pie rather than the pie itself, the slices are getting thinner and thinner. Vanguard's John Bogle is a strong critic of the fragmentation going on in the index world. In remarks before a group of security analysts in San Francisco, he pointed out that sector ETFs are largely used by traders for short-term speculation. The traditional index fund, the S&P 500 that he originated more than 30 years ago, was designed for long-term *investing*, not short-term speculation. It was diversified and risk averse whereas sector funds are narrowly based and risky. And the S&P 500 index fund that he pioneered guaranteed its owner would earn a fair share of the stock market's return. "The investor who *trades* ETFs—and especially sector ETFs—has nothing even resembling such a guarantee" (vanguard.com, view Bogle speeches, *What's Happened to the Mutual Fund Industry?,* October 2006).

In his latest book, *The Little Book of Common Sense Investing* (John Wiley & Sons, 2007), Bogle is even more direct. Pointing out that the expense ratios in sector ETFs can run three to six times the level of the lowest-cost, broad-based index funds, he reaches this definitive conclusion: "Sector ETFs as a group are virtually certain to earn returns that fall well short of those delivered by the stock market." Summing up, the father of index funds defends his progeny vehemently: "The exchange-traded fund is a traitor to the cause of classic indexing. I urge intelligent investors to stay the course with the proven strategy. While I can't say that classic indexing is the best strategy ever devised, our common sense should reassure you that the number of strategies that are worse is infinite."

Bogle's criticism is aimed mostly at speculators who use index funds as short-term trading vehicles. He would likely have less objection to using broader market sectors and asset classes in a diversified, long-term, buy-and-hold portfolio. In fact, in *The Little Book* he says, "Broad-based ETFs are the only ones that can replicate, and possibly even improve on the classic index fund."

I believe that by picking the right combination of uncorrelated "bigger slices," staying with them, and rebalancing periodically, an investor can largely eliminate the trading risks Bogle refers to. It's my strong sense (perhaps colored by wishful thinking) that, over time, such a balanced portfolio has excellent prospects of outperforming the S&P 500 or Total Stock Market Index. That's why 28 such portfolios are featured in the following pages.

No Longer a Matter of Settling

The perception continues to persist that those who buy index funds are "settling" for whatever the market does. That is no longer the case. We have to adjust our thinking to these four realities:

1. The term *passive* investing, as it was meant originally, applies today to only the broadest of indexes like the S&P 500, the Wilshire 5000, the Total Stock Market Index, and so on. They represent a handful of the index fund universe.

2. The proliferation of specialized index funds reflects the desire of investors to have different ways of doing better than the market. Buying index funds is no longer synonymous with mediocrity and compromise. Instead, it represents the use of risk management, non-correlation, and diversification to achieve superior results.

3. The reason why individualized index funds are still classified as "passive" investments, even though they represent a chosen market niche, is because their objective is no more than to mirror their particular benchmark. They still clone an index but it's more narrow. There is little or no active management imprint, although this is likely to change soon.

4. Not enough time has elapsed to definitively conclude that a diversified mix of customized index funds will, indeed, outperform the broad general market. However, it makes sense that a diversified portfolio of asset classes that have a history of recurring market leadership but that have little or no representation in the S&P 500 (like small cap value and REIT stocks) will outperform that index over time. Some of the portfolios featured in Chapter 7 have allegedly outperformed the S&P 500 over specified time periods. Successful back-testing is no insurance of continued success but, if accurate, is certainly a comfort factor.

Moderating the Market's Sting

The buy-and-hold model portfolios featured in this section, then, are low-worry, low-maintenance, and low-cost ways of investing for the long term. Yes, they'll go up and down just like any investment, but the frequent independence of their various components will moderate the sting of the market's extremes. When bought at reasonable levels with a commitment to the long term and rebalanced periodically, they are the best choice for overcoming the vagaries of the market and out-performing the majority of investors.

Interestingly, institutions, not individuals, were the first big fans of index funds. Quick to recognize their flexibility, professional money managers used them for hedging, arbitrage, program trading, and other sophisticated strategies. Individual investors gradually joined the ranks as it became apparent that indexing represented a new way to play the game. What was not possible for most of the twentieth century was now easily doable. My father loved the market (which triggered my interest), but if he thought the market was going higher, there was no S&P 500 or total market index for him to buy. If he liked the oil or utility groups he had to single out a Standard Oil of New Jersey or Consolidated Edison rather than an all-encompassing energy or utility fund. (And if he bought 500 shares, he paid hundreds of dollars in commissions, not $5.)

It behooves investors today to take advantage of these major new tools for reducing risk and creating wealth. As the word spreads about the unique features of index funds—their low costs, tax efficiency, flexibility, liquidity, diversification, simplicity, and transparency—their use by individuals may rival that of institutions. The way that ETFs, for the first time, open up access to huge areas of the market with the purchase of just one security is a powerful magnet.

Part of the appeal is psychological. Being able to own all U.S. stocks with just one ETF, or all stocks in the world outside the United States, or all bonds in the United States, or all bonds outside the United States, or the 25 largest companies in China, and so on, just sounds like a smart, safe, uncomplicated way to go.

Growth will likely accelerate with the passage of enough time to prove convincingly that one can invest passively in a diversified list of index funds and still be in the top 20 percent that outperform the market. The almost $500 billion in assets held by some 600 ETFs is increasing by leaps and bounds every day.

There's plenty of room for growth. Vanguard's founder John Bogle estimates that maybe 20 percent of the U.S. stock market is indexed. Exchange-traded funds of various kinds represent almost half of the daily volume on the American Stock Exchange but they still represent only around 5 percent of total mutual fund assets. Future historians will likely look back

> "Building a portfolio around index funds isn't really settling for average. It's just refusing to believe in magic."
> —*Bethany McLean*

on the early twenty-first century as the beginning stage of the climb of indexing, and especially ETFs, to a dominant role in implementing the investment strategies of America's investors. An important catalyst will likely be the increasing use of ETFs in the nation's 401(k) plans.

Index Funds: What's Most Important To Know

This section on passive investing is not meant to be a primer on index funds. There are thousands of web sites, not to mention books and news-letters, all devoted exclusively to explaining the ins and outs of index funds and ETFs. Some of the more helpful sites on the Internet include:

Amex.com
BillCara.com
DFAus.com (Dimensional Fund Advisors)
ETF-reader.com
ETF.seekingalpha.com
ETFcentral.com
ETFconnect.com
ETFdigest.com
ETFexpert.com
ETFguide.com
ETFinvestmentoutlook.com
ETFscreen.com
ETFzone.com
Finance.yahoo.com/etf
Fool.com (The Motley Fool)
IFA.com (Index Fund Advisors)
Indexchange.com
Indexfunds.com
Indexinvestor.com
Indexuniverse.com
iShares.com
JournalofIndexes.com
Moneycentral.msn.com
Morningstar.com
Nasdaq.com
Powershares.com
Sectorspdr.com
SmartMoney.com
XTF.com (XTF Advisors)
Morningstar's *ETFInvestor* newsletter (available at Morningstar.com)

Notable books on index funds and ETFs include *The Exchange Traded Funds Manual* by Gary L. Gastineau (John Wiley & Sons, 2002); *Exchange Traded Funds: An Insider's Guide to Buying the Market* by Jim Wiandt (John Wiley & Sons, 2001); *All About Exchange Traded Funds* by Archie Richards Jr. (McGraw-Hill, 2002); *The ETF Book: All You Need to Know about Exchange Traded Funds* by Richard Ferri (McGraw-Hill, 2006); *Power Investing with Basket Securities: The Investor's Guide to Exchange-Traded Funds* by Peter W. Madlem and Larry Edwards (CRC, 2001); *Index Funds: The 12-Step Program for Active Investors* by Mark T. Hebner (IFA Publishing, 2005); *Getting Started In Exchange Traded Funds* by Todd Lofton (John Wiley & Sons, 2007); *Exchange-Traded Funds for Dummies* by Russell Wild (For Dummies, 2006); *Investing with Exchange-Traded Funds Made Easy* by Marvin Appel (FT Press, 2006); *Index Mutual Funds* by W. Scott Simon (Namborn, 1998); *Index Your Way to Investment Success* by Walter R. Good and Roy W. Hermansen (Prentice Hall, 1999); and *The Unbeatable Market* by Ron Ross (Ross, 2002).

Whether you select one or a combination of the index fund portfolios featured in the following pages, or put together one of your own, you will likely own it for a long time. That's why it makes sense to check out some of these suggested sources and get a good solid background in the basics of indexing. However, if you're allergic to homework, the following is a digest of what I think are the most important facts about index funds for you to know. They should help in evaluating the model portfolios.

The Big Picture

If you get involved with index funds at all, you should be aware of the big picture and where you are in that picture. Index funds come in two basic forms. There are those offered by conventional mutual funds which are bought and sold at their end-of-the-day net asset value. Vanguard is the pioneer and dominant player. The other index funds are traded on a listed exchange, which is why they're called exchange-traded funds. They can be bought and sold anytime during trading hours like any other security (most are on the American Stock Exchange, some on the NYSE, a few on NASDAQ). Unlike traditional mutual funds, ETFs can be sold short (offering protection in a bear market) and traded using stop-loss and limit orders and options in some cases.

More money is put into index funds via Vanguard and other traditional mutual fund families than via ETFs. In fact, ETFs represent only a tiny fraction of the $11 trillion total mutual fund industry. There are some 13,000 mutual funds and only some 600 ETFs (but a lot more to come). However, their small relative size is misleading and belies their importance.

There is widespread duplication of index funds. If a particular type of index fund is available as a conventional mutual fund, a similar type fund will be trading as an ETF. For example, there are hundreds of large cap mutual funds spread out over hundreds of mutual fund families, but there are also over 100 large cap ETFs. There is likely to be much less duplication among the increasing number of small, specialized sector funds.

The ETF business is dominated by a few financial organizations or sponsors. Biggest, by far, is Barclays Global Investors (iShares) with State Street Global Advisors (SPDRs and streetTRACKS) a distant second. Other players include the Vanguard Group (ETF, formerly VIPER), Amvescap (PowerShares), Merrill Lynch (HOLDRS), Bank of New York (BLDRs), Rydex Fund Group, PowerShares Group, ProFunds Group (ProShares), and WisdomTree, among others.

There are some 600 exchange-traded funds and the list keeps growing. About 150 were introduced in 2006 alone and almost 400 were in registration on August 30, 2007. The *AAII Journal of American Association of Individual Investors,* in an especially well-organized guide to ETFs (October 2006), divides the ETF universe into 13 major categories, shown in Table 6.1. The comprehensive survey provides 15 pieces of information on each of some 300 exchange-traded funds. Included are average daily volume, asset size, one-year total return, risk grade, expense ratio, high, low, and inception date. Because ETFs are being introduced at such an explosive rate, the numbers in the right-hand column in the table will be quickly outdated. This 26-page guide to the ETF universe is published in October every year in the monthly *AAII Journal.* If you're interested in getting a complete, easy to understand overview of ETFs, this issue alone is worth the annual $29 subscription fee.

So much for the big picture. For you to make an informed judgment about whether to invest in an index fund portfolio, you should

Table 6.1   The ETF Universe, as Categorized by AAII (as of September 15, 2006)

Category*	Number of ETFs in Each Category**
Broad-Based/Large-Cap ETFs	49
Broad-Based/Mid-Cap ETFs	24
Broad-Based/Small-Cap ETFs	20
Broad-Based/Micro-Cap ETFs	4
Broad-Based/Specialty ETFs	4
Broad-Based/Specialty/Dividend Focus ETFs	13
Sector ETFs (listed by 13 sectors)*	108
Foreign/Global ETFs	14
Foreign/Regional ETFs	19
Foreign/Country ETFs	27
Foreign/Sector ETFs	5
Foreign/Currency ETFs	7
Fixed Income/Bond ETFs	6

*The 13 sectors include biotechnology, consumer, energy, financial, health, industrial, materials, natural resources—gold and commodities, real estate, technology, telecommunications, transportation, utilities.
**Some of these numbers may already have doubled.
Source: AAII Journal.

be aware, at the very minimum, of the following important facts. Since I'm recommending that most of your money go into index funds, I want to make sure you know just what's involved, both good and bad.

"Seek to become average. This is a hard resolution to live up to because we've been told since birth—who wants to be average. But, in the world of investing, being average (investing in index funds) means you are one of the best students in the class."

—*Robert R. Julian*

Final Index Insights

1. Rebalancing Is Important But the Timing Is Tricky Building a portfolio involves a few basic steps: picking those areas of the market you want represented, deciding how much you want to invest in each, and selecting one or two index funds for each segment. Once that's done, there's only one other thing to do: Rebalance your holdings periodically.

Rebalancing is the process of buying and selling portions of your portfolio in order to set the weight of each asset class back to its original state. "An unbalanced portfolio is dangerous at any time," says columnist Jim Jubak of MSNMoney.com ("Turn Short Term Fear into Long Term Profit," June 1, 2006). Because it forces you to buy low and sell high, rebalancing is a means of controlling risk.

It's also a process that's in harmony with a basic market truism: After going to extremes, there's a tendency for things to even out over time. Richard Russell, the market-savvy veteran and editor of *Dow Theory Letters,* says, "The surest rule in the stock market is the rule . . . called 'regression to the mean.' What performs very well doesn't do so forever. It reverts back to middle ground. And what acts poorly gets better in time" (Marketwatch .com, Mark Hulbert, "Regression to the Mean," May 9, 2006).

The gray area in rebalancing is when to do it. In theory, doing it methodically every year, or every six months or two years, is the best way to go because it removes all the guesswork and emotion. It makes it a strictly mechanical process. However, if a sector reemerges after being depressed for a long time, waiting before trimming back may make sense.

Wall Street Journal columnist Jonathan Clements says, "If a market segment is bouncing back after a rotten stretch, don't rebalance every year. Instead, hold off rebalancing for two or three years so you can capture more of the rebound" (WSJ.com, "Rebalancing Act," December 21, 2005). Investment adviser William Bernstein of North Bend, Oregon, agrees. He is quoted in the *Wall Street Journal* column just cited, "There's significant evidence of momentum in asset class returns, so you don't want to rebalance too often." And Ronald Roge, head of the Bohemia, New York wealth management firm, R.W. Roge & Co., says, "Unless a category is more than 5 percent out of whack, I'd just keep an eye on it" (NCTimes.com, "Asset Allocation Important for 401(k) Performance," March 11, 2006). You might want to raise the 5 percent figure to, say, 20 percent, if the category is just a small part of your portfolio.

Finally, count John Bogle among the rebalancing naysayers. He conducted two studies, one going back 20 years, the other going back to 1826. In both cases, the differences between rebalancing and not rebalancing were minor. Bogle concludes that statistics cannot validate rebalancing. Perhaps a big gain in weighting may call for action but, "there's no reason to slavishly worry about small changes in the equity ratio. There's certainly nothing the matter with doing it, although I don't do it myself" (SeekingAlpha.com, "Vanguard's Jack Bogle on Rebalancing: Don't!," July 16, 2007).

Ability to Act Decisively Is Key As a practical matter, there are probably few investors who actually rebalance. I'd guess that maybe half who set up portfolios will rebalance at least once, but three or five years after that, there'll only be a handful who continue to follow through. Obstacles include lethargy, the inclination to avoid paying commissions on trades, taxes on capital gains, and the reluctance to sell what's working and buy what's not working. However, the biggest deterrent is uncertainty.

There is never a time when the course of action is clear. Influenced by greed and fear, there is always the feeling that what's high can go higher and what's low can go lower, so why not wait? Investors are often guilty of procrastination (which is certainly understandable since we're mostly guessing anyway). Talk to any broker and he'll tell you the most common customer response to his recommendations is, "Let's watch and see what happens." A universal trait of successful traders is the ability to take action, to make a decisive move, even if it's the wrong one.

Because it's easier to implement, it's probably best to go with the strictly mechanical, no-judgment-required approach to rebalancing, especially if you have a long period of time to make it work. Richard Ferri, author of *All About Asset Allocation* (McGraw-Hill, 2005), offers this incentive: "By taking some money out of things that did well and putting it into things that were down, you'll pick up 1 percent more on your equity portfolio per year over the long term. That's a good deal."

Remember, when you rebalance you're not getting rid of your winners, only a small portion of them. You're still left with most of your position. If you feel strongly that you're selling or buying too early, you can compromise. Stop putting new money in the overweighted sector but don't sell it; commit new funds only to the underweighted sectors. Finally, if there's a significant change in your personal lifestyle that involves your ability to assume risk, feel free to adjust your original weightings accordingly.

2. Buy Low Goes for Index Funds, Too "Buy low" is a rule that applies to index funds as much as it does to any other security. When putting together an index fund portfolio, the objective is to buy each component at a reasonable price. That rules out buying the entire portfolio all at once. At any given time, some asset classes will be fully priced based on their historical range, others will be bargain priced, and most will be somewhere in between. Ideally, each component would be bought while it's depressed and before it returns to favor. That's what money managers were trying to do in 2005 and 2006 when they shifted from the hot, overextended small caps into the neglected, overdue large caps.

The problem is that oversold and overbought sectors of the market often become even more extended and stay that way for a long time. Unless you have a rare talent for timing the market or an inordinate amount of luck, the best approach is to accumulate a position in pieces over time. Even better would be a long-term program of dollar cost averaging. In the best of all worlds, the index fund you buy would stay depressed, giving you ample time for accumulation, and then move sharply higher. At the April 2004 Berkshire Hathaway annual meeting, Warren Buffett suggested to shareholders that if they invested in a very low expense index fund and averaged in over 10 years, they'd do better than 90 percent of those who put all their money in at one time.

Three years later, he again emphasized the importance of buying shares gradually. He told CNBC anchor Liz Claman in a May 7, 2007, interview that for most people, buying cheap index funds is the best way to invest in the stock market. "Keep accumulating regularly over time. If you do, you won't buy at the bottom, but you won't buy it all at the top either."

3. "Hold On" Is the Key Although index funds are popular with traders, the model portfolios featured in this book are offered primarily as a buy-and-hold strategy. The best way I know for most investors to deal with the unpredictable ups and downs of the market and come out a winner is to gradually accumulate a diversified list of low-cost index funds, rebalance periodically, and hold on.

The "hold-on" part is the key. Almost any reasonably conceived market strategy, if you stay with it long enough, is likely to work out. The index fund approach makes the "hold on" part less stressful. Broad-based indexes insure that you will do no worse than the market, while a smartly diversified portfolio offers the promise of doing better than the market over time.

There are many market approaches that sound great in theory but break down when it comes to their practical application. Human nature gets in the way. We're asked to do things that run counter to our natural disposition. Index fund investing is not without its behavioral challenges (the need for patience, commitment, and lack of ego) but, relatively speaking, it is among the more doable strategies. Other than periodic rebalancing, the portfolio, once in place, requires minimum maintenance. The important maintenance is the taking care of your personal health. That's what will insure long-term success.

> "Nobel Prizes have been awarded to academics for their analysis of how stock markets work. Their findings are not based on a need to earn a commission or sell you an IPO. More than a hundred years of academic research has concluded that index funds are an investor's best investment."
> —*Mark Hebner*

4. Low Expenses Are Key to Fund Performance There is one dominant theme that cuts through all the research on index funds: The reason why passively managed index funds outperform most actively run funds over the long term is because of their lower costs. Actively managed funds have much higher rates of turnover, which means higher trading costs. They also incur other annual expenses such as management fees as well as advertising and distributions costs, which can eat up the return of the active investor over time. The result is that passively run index funds outperform actively managed funds in nearly every investment category over almost all time periods. It's a trend that is likely to continue as long as funds are weighted down by the expenses of active management.

In the 1996 Berkshire Hathaway annual report, Warren Buffett said, "Most investors . . . will find that the best way to own common stocks is through an index fund that charges minimal fees. Those following this path are sure to beat the net results (after fees and expenses) of the great majority of investment professionals." Vanguard founder and index fund pioneer John Bogle believes that instead of trying to pick the mutual fund with the best return, investors should be looking for the fund with the lowest expenses. Invariably, the difference in performance between active managers and indexes over the long term is similar to the difference in expense levels.

In a revealing piece in the April 2005 Morningstar publication *Fund Investor,* Russell Kinnel, director of research at Morningstar, seconds Bogle's opinion that expenses are a more reliable forecaster of fund performance than past returns. He reports that a randomly selected fund with a five-year return that ranks in the *worst* 25 percent but with expenses also in the lowest 25 percent is likely to do better than a fund with a five-year return in the top 25 percent but with expenses also in the highest 25 percent. Kinnel concludes, "Higher expenses don't get you better management."

The performance of bond funds and money market accounts is especially sensitive to in-house expenses since yields within different types of bond groups are roughly similar. The lowest-cost funds in each category outperform with regularity. It should also be noted that in the low return environment widely forecast in the years ahead, keeping expenses down becomes even more important.

There are other debilitating costs outside those incurred by the funds themselves that deflate investor results. The stellar returns touted by traditional mutual funds are not real returns in the real world because they don't take into account the taxes and commissions that have to be paid by the investor (index funds, by contrast, seldom distribute capital gains). Nor do mutual fund ads recognize the long-term, eroding effect of inflation. If they did, returns would have to be adjusted significantly lower.

5. Allocation of 15 Percent or 30 Percent? It Doesn't Matter That Much If you put together your own diversified, index fund portfolio, you'll have to decide what percent should be allocated to each asset class. If you use one of our model portfolios, that decision is already made. You may want to tweak the model depending on your age, your tolerance for risk, your income requirements, and so on. But it's important to realize that there is no magic allocation formula.

Even the professionals are making educated guesses. Veteran *Wall Street Journal* columnist Jonathan Clements says, "Whenever somebody asks me how much to allocate to a particular sector, I usually respond that, within reason, it doesn't much matter.... Whether you allocate 15 percent or 30 percent of your stock portfolio to foreign markets probably won't make a whole lot of difference over the next 30 years, provided you stick with your target percentage....What counts is commitment" (*Wall Street Journal,* December 11, 2005).

Investing always involves uncertainty; broad diversification is your best defense. Own a little bit of everything and portfolio volatility will shrink.

6. Grow Your Portfolio through Automatic Investing Once you have your portfolio in place, a good way to make it grow is to invest a fixed amount every month or every two or three months. Making automatic investments over time allows you to reap the benefits of dollar cost averaging (see Chapter 4).

This can be done through company-sponsored 401(k) plans or through a mutual fund company. For example, you can authorize a fund to make monthly withdrawals from your checking account and invest the money in a particular mutual fund or funds. Many fund families have no-fee automatic investment plans (AIPs). Because you pay a commission every time you buy or sell an exchange-traded fund, they don't qualify for no-fee AIPs. But you can use AIPs to build an index fund portfolio if you use traditional mutual index funds rather than ETFs. If you choose index funds from different fund families, you may have to open more than one AIP account.

It's true that you have no control over external market forces, but you *can* control the spending of your money. A program of forced savings (along with any automatic dividend reinvestment plan) makes you less vulnerable to the randomness of the market.

7. Three Best Asset Classes for Spreading Risk The purpose of asset allocation is to reduce risk by exposure to uncorrelated asset classes. When one class goes down, the other goes up. However, there are few things about investing that are black and white. Correlations are constantly shifting. What worked 10 years ago may or may not work in the next 10 years or it may just work sometimes.

Richard Ferri's book *All About Asset Allocation* was published by McGraw Hill in the fall of 2005. In a May 24, 2006, interview on Smart Money.com, Ferri, president of Portfolio Solutions in Troy, Michigan, said, "The idea of the book is simply that you have a little bit everywhere and once a year, on your birthday or after New Year's, you rebalance your portfolio. You get it back to your original targets. Correlations fluctuate. You don't know what's going to happen to energy, to tech, to bonds, to emerging markets. You do know that in the long run everything regresses to the mean over your lifetime" (meaning that what goes up or down a lot eventually returns to the middle).

In conducting his research, Ferri found that three segments of the market were especially effective in reducing risk and increasing long-term returns. Small cap value stocks, micro cap stocks, and REITs are three asset classes that deviate substantially from the performance of the total stock market and make a portfolio more efficient.

Robert Arnott also has three favorite asset classes to protect a portfolio from a uniform decline, but they're different from Ferri's choices. Arnott, chairman of Pasadena, California–based Research Affiliates and manager of the Pimco All Asset Fund (PASAX), is probably best known as the creator of the increasingly popular fundamentally based or enhanced ETF, as opposed to the traditional capitalization weighted index fund.

In a *Barron's Online* interview (April 20, 2007), Arnott was asked, "What are the best assets for investors to diversify their traditional stock and bond portfolios?" His answer: "I'd pick three asset classes. I'd start with commodities, which are negatively correlated with mainstream stocks and bonds. They aren't necessarily a brilliantly attractive play for high returns, but they are going to reduce the volatility [of the overall portfolio]. The second is TIPS [treasury inflation protected securities] and the third are international bonds in their home currency [which provide defense against the tumbling dollar]. These are three asset classes that most investors have far too little invested in."

8. Dispelling Confusion about Some Major Indexes The S&P 500 Index, a proxy for the mostly big cap leaders of American industry, is the most popular benchmark with index fund buyers. There are over 30 S&P 500 index funds with at least a 10-year history. Companies like Barclay's, Black Rock, Dreyfus, Fidelity, Schwab, Wells Fargo, and others, all offer their own version. Some are traditional mutual funds, others are ETFs. Each one is a separate entity but they all do the same thing, which is to track the 500 stocks in the S&P 500 Index. Easily the biggest is a mutual fund. It's the $118 billion Vanguard 500 Index Fund (symbol VFINX). It's also the oldest, launched by John Bogle in 1976.

In the ETF field, the biggest S&P 500 index fund is the $58 billion SPDR Trust Series I (Symbol SPY), started in 1993 by State Street. It was the first ETF. But the biggest ETF overall (always subject to change) is Vanguard's $89 billion Total Stock Market ETF (symbol VTI). Vanguard used to call its ETFs *VIPERs*. Vanguard's Total Stock Market Index ETF tracks a benchmark index (MSCI U.S. Broad Market Index) that includes over 3,700 stocks that measure the performance of the overall U.S. stock market, all in one security. Incidentally, the firm of Morgan Stanley has put together lots of benchmark indexes, which is why you see the letters MSCI (Morgan Stanley Capital International) in so many fund titles.

The biggest index funds are not the most heavily traded. That distinction belongs to the NASDAQ 100 Trust (symbol QQQQ, curiously called "triple Qs"). It's an ETF that tracks the 100 largest nonfinancial companies listed on the NASDAQ with a heavy focus on technology companies. It is a favorite of speculators who want to trade the high-tech sector and is usually at or near the top of the daily American Stock Exchange most active list. In 2006 the three most actively traded securities on the big U.S. exchanges were the ETFs that matched the S&P 500, the NASDAQ 100, and the Russell 2000 indexes.

The NASDAQ 100 is often confused with the NASDAQ Composite. They are both important but for different reasons—one as a 100 stock ETF, the other as a 3,000 stock major index. The nickname for the NASDAQ 100

"The vast majority of investment returns can be attributed to an asset allocation decision. Putting the asset classes together to form a portfolio that meets your goals is where the bulk of the heavy work should be done.... Unless you still believe in the tooth fairy, you will want to select an index fund for every asset category."

—*Frank Armstrong III*

ETF, the "triple Qs," is a household name among traders because of its huge daily volume. The NASDAQ Composite, on the other hand, is famous because, along with the Dow Jones Industrial Average and the S&P 500 Index, it is one of the three most widely followed stock market indexes in the world. It represents over 3,000 domestic and international common stocks listed on the NASDAQ. Because it includes many high-tech and smaller cap stocks, it is the more volatile of the three major indexes. There is an ETF that tracks the NASDAQ Composite (symbol ONEQ) but it is not widely traded.

9. ETFs Are Not Always the Right Choice In most cases, ETFs enjoy a competitive advantage, expense-wise, over index funds sold by traditional mutual fund families. According to Sonya Morris, Editor, *Morningstar ETF Investor* (April 2007), "The typical diversified large-cap index fund charges .57 percent while its ETF counter-part costs just .20 percent. The typical closed-end bond fund costs 1.20 percent which is significantly more expensive than the median bond ETF, which charges just .15 percent."

There are some exceptions—mutual funds whose expense ratios are the same or less than ETFs. Vanguard Group, the pioneer and longtime leader in low-cost funds, has been challenged by other funds like Fidelity with expense ratios on some index funds below that of Vanguard. To cover all index fund bases, more fund families are introducing ETFs to complement their existing index mutual fund lineup. (Vanguard has 28 and will soon have over 30 ETFs, for example).

There are other areas in which mutual funds have an edge over ETFs. Some traditional index mutual funds have managers, and a particularly skilled one can make a difference. Vanguard's S&P 500 Index Fund in the hands of savvy veteran Gus Sauter, for example, has been able to outperform its ETF equivalent.

In the May 7, 2007, CNBC appearance already cited (also reported that day on MarketWatch.com), Warren Buffett weighed in on the ETF versus traditional index funds debate. "I have nothing against ETFs, but I really think an index fund that just charges a few basis points for management is pretty hard to beat. You put it away, you have nobody encouraging you to trade it next week or next month. . . . Your broker isn't going to be on you."

ETFs have been criticized for overspecialization with the introduction of more and more subsectors. Vanguard's John Bogle, as mentioned earlier, is one of the more vocal critics of customization. As the slices of the pie become thinner and thinner and the focus narrower, the risks become greater. If diversification reduces risk, concentration does the opposite. This is not to say that speculation, per se, is bad. Our markets could not function as we know them without risk-takers. But it's important that a person buying a speculation be aware that he's speculating (more risk), not investing (less risk). There's nothing wrong with speculating as long as you do it with money you can afford to lose.

The commission cost of buying and selling ETFs is a major negative for anyone trading or accumulating them on a regular basis. The frequent index fund buyer can limit expenses by using no-load mutual funds instead. Another option for the active ETF trader is the Foliofn web site (foliofn.com). It permits dozens of trades for a flat yearly fee. There are other web sites such as sharebuilder.com, buyandhold.com, and mystockfunds.com, which cater to investors who want to buy ETFs on the cheap.

Overall, aside from the transaction cost disadvantage of frequent small purchases of ETFs, the two forms of index funds are similar, especially when dealing with the broad-based indexes. In a cover story in the June 2007 *AAII Journal*, "Face-Off: Mutual Funds versus ETFs," John Markese concludes by saying, "In the index arena, avoid getting caught up in the mutual fund versus ETF debate. Instead, concentrate on creating a diversified portfolio and applying appropriate portfolio weightings for your time horizon, risk tolerance, and portfolio goals. And then turn to either mutual funds, ETFs, or a combination—it really makes no difference."

10. The Two Kinds of Sector Funds The ability to buy a whole sector of the market with one security is a valuable tool. But there are two basic types of sector funds and it's important to know the major difference between them. One involves active management, the other is unmanaged.

Mutual fund sector funds consist of a representative group of stocks within the sector and are actively managed. Stocks are bought and sold within the portfolio. The fund itself is bought and sold at its daily closing net asset value (NAV). Fidelity dominates the field with some 43 sector funds which it calls "Select."

ETF sector funds, by contrast, mirror a fixed group of stocks from a particular sector. The group or basket is called a *benchmark index*. Since ETFs simply clone a static benchmark, they require no active management. Competition and ingenuity will undoubtedly lead to actively managed ETFs in the future. Like all ETFs, sector ETFs are bought and sold on an exchange during trading hours for a commission.

11. Index Fund Portfolios Good Choice for 401(k)s About half of America's 95 million investors own stock by virtue of their 401(k) plans. From all accounts, the performance of 401(k) plans over the years has been less than stellar. Reasons cited include the lack of time, interest, and sophistication on the part of the employee; poor guidance; lethargy; insufficient information; and limited selection.

A portfolio of diversified funds may be one way to improve that performance. Unfortunately, the choice of funds in many 401(k)s is limited. If your plan selection includes enough index funds to use some of the model portfolios suggested here, I would give that serious consideration providing you will be investing for a long time. If you do not have the index funds called for in the model portfolio (or an equivalent substitute), perhaps you can ask the provider to expand the list. Hopefully, in the future, 401(k) providers will sharply increase the number of index funds available to the employee. Also needed is an annual automatic, computer-generated rebalancing service as well as some way of getting around the problem of commission costs for ETFs.

An investment retirement account (IRA) permits you to buy anything you want, so that's another way to go. The reason to favor a 401(k) is the "matching funds" feature. Not all plans have it but in those that do, the corporation will match the employee's contribution up to a maximum percentage of salary. If the employee doesn't take advantage of the offer, it's free money thrown away.

Exchange-traded funds are seldom used in 401(k)s because of the commission costs. However, no-load index mutual funds are entirely suitable. Indeed, Vanguard's S&P 500 Index Fund (VFINX) is probably the most widely held security in America's 401(k)s. (A quick way of distinguishing an ETF from an index mutual fund is by its symbol—the former has three letters, the latter five letters.) Whether you use index funds in your 401(k) or not, the most important thing is to commit long-term to a monthly (or some other time interval) investment. It's difficult to build net worth unless the sums deposited are of some substance and are continuous.

12. In the Short Run, Active Can Top Passive Management There are periods of time when actively managed funds outperform index funds. Daniel Boone, adviser to the Calvert Social Investment Equity Fund, looked at rolling five-year periods going back to the early 1930s. He found that the S&P 500 has had 10 five-year stretches of losses. But these cycles have had a limited life. Kunal Kapoor, former director of fund analysis for Morningstar, was quoted in the July 7, 2004, *Wall Street Journal,* saying, "You can carve out periods where index funds trail actively managed funds, but over long periods they trump actively managed funds because of their lower costs and less frequent trading."

Let's say you *do* succeed in choosing an active manager who tops his benchmark. What are the chances that he will repeat this the next year and the year after that? Only one fund out of more than 13,000 mutual funds was able to beat the S&P 500 Index for 15 straight years (1991–2005) and that's Bill Miller's Legg Mason Value Trust. No other fund has come close to that streak. (Of course, Miller had down years, but not down as much as the S&P 500. And if measured by other than the calendar year, his streak would have ended sooner.) Economist and financial columnist Ben Stein sums it up: "The people who can beat the broad market indexes consistently are like hen's teeth." (*New York Times,* February 27, 2005).

It bears repeating that for investors to match the superior performance of index funds over long periods of time, they must own them over the same long period of time. There is often a big discrepancy between a fund's published returns and those of the fund's owner. The difference is that the fund's results reflect a long string of full-year returns. The smaller return of the investor reflects the tendency to exit the fund when it's low and enter when it's high, as reported in the

> "Most of the mutual fund investments I own are index funds, approximately 75 percent."
> —*Charles Schwab*

aforementioned Dalbar study. The bottom line: To benefit fully from everything index funds have to offer, they must be bought at a reasonable price and held for a long time.

13. ETFs: Small Part of a Giant Industry In size, the ETF business is a small fraction, less than 5 percent, of the total mutual fund industry, and the ratio will likely stay that way, despite the expected growth in indexing. The reason is that mutual funds are aggressively sold by an army of salespeople. Exchange-traded funds are not; their growth will come as a result of the inherent advantages they enjoy over mutual funds, namely costs, tax efficiency, liquidity, convenience, and so on.

It is because of these advantages that the index fund portfolios featured in this book consist mostly of ETFs. Until a lot more people in Wall Street can make a lot more money pushing ETFs, the huge, $11 trillion dollar mutual fund industry will continue to be dominated by traditional, non-ETF funds.

14. Should Index Funds Give More Weight to Capitalization or Fundamentals? There is an ongoing debate within the index community as to whether capitalization-based or fundamentally based indexes will perform better over time. Until recently, indexes like the S&P 500 were unchallenged. In a cap-weighted index, stocks with greater market values have greater sway over the index's performance.

Now, people like Robert Arnott of Research Affiliates in Pasadena, California, with Wharton Finance professor Jeremy Siegel, hedge fund guru Michael Steinhardt, and former SEC Chairman Arthur Levitt (the latter three with WisdomTree Investments) have introduced index funds with a different focus. It is their contention that expensive stocks are given too much influence and cheaper stocks too little influence in a capitalization-weighted index. Instead, they believe an index fund with weighting based on fundamentals such as earnings, book equity value, free cash flow, sales, and high dividend yield (Siegel's favorite metric) will outperform the S&P 500.

Dimensional Fund Advisors (DFA), out of Santa Monica, California, also offers index funds with a different twist. For the past 25 years, DFA has sponsored funds that resemble the S&P but with a strong tilt toward smaller, value stocks. Because it has performed well, DFA can afford to be independent. You can only buy DFA index funds through a financial planner who is on its approved list.

Vanguard's index maven, Gus Sauter; John Bogle, founder of Vanguard Group; and Burton Malkiel, economic professor at Princeton, are not persuaded. They believe deemphasizing the importance of a stock's capitalization (the amount of stock a company has outstanding times its price per share) in favor of a company's fundamentals will give too much weight to small cap value stocks. They point out that the superior performance of small value stocks may not last indefinitely and that running a fundamentally based fund is likely to require higher fees, costs, and taxes and incur higher turnover rates.

Since fundamentally based index funds are relatively new, it will take the passage of time to see how they will perform. Columnist Jonathan Clements says that even if fundamental indexing proves to be a superior strategy, traditional index funds "will remain what they have always been: a superior way to beat most active investors" (*Wall Street Journal,* May 5, 2007).

15. Sideways Markets Limit Appeal of Buy-and-Hold Indexing

Many of the best minds in Wall Street, everyone from Warren Buffett to John Bogle and Burton Malkiel to Jonathan Clements, have forecast modest gains for the stock market in the next 5 to 10 years. It's a viewpoint supported by history.

Lengthy bull markets in the past, such as we had from 1982 to 2000, have been followed by extended periods of sideways movement. After the bull market that preceded the 1929 crash, it took the Dow 25 years to 1954 to make a new high. The next long bull market was followed by 17 years of sideways movement (1965 to 1982). And after the historic 18-year bull market that peaked in early 2000, it took close to 7 years for the Dow to reach a new high. Admittedly, the steady climb in the Dow and the S&P 500 in the second half of 2006 and the first half of 2007 surprised the "range-bound" forecasters, who had to keep stretching their "range." The NASDAQ, however, probably because it was so super-extended before the bubble burst in 2000, is still far below its peak.

The market's volatility is also well below its highs. We have had nowhere near the wide swings we experienced in the 1980s and 1990s. For the most part, moves have been gradual though 2007 did see a marked increase in volatility. The broad consensus continues to call for relative sideways action for a while, perhaps a long while. If that's true, it would seem to favor the nimble buy-and-sell investor over the buy-and-holder. (Regardless of how flat the overall market, there are always individual stocks in their own bull markets.)

If forecasts of modest gains in the market prove prescient (and they may prove too cautious) and there is no sweeping uptrend, it follows that proper diversification is more important than ever. The right mix of asset classes or sectors is key to capturing whatever it is the market has to give. If there is no rising tide to lift all boats, it's crucial to be in the right boat.

Indexing a diversified portfolio relieves the pressure of having to choose the right sector. It's true that a sideways or downward market may put a lid on gains from a buy-and-hold index approach. However, a well-bought, well-thought-out mix of asset classes should provide some exposure to the better-acting segments of the market. This, in turn, will limit the downside risk to the overall portfolio.

The universality of the forecast for single-digit market gains makes it suspect. With 2007 being the third and historically strongest year of the four-year presidential cycle, we may or may not see a sustained move higher. Regardless, at some point, we will again resume an ongoing, durable bull market, and when we do, index funds, by definition, will participate fully, as they have in the past. Like any long-term approach, it's the passage of time that makes it work.

16. The Psychological Benefits of Asset Allocation The following are three basic truths that I've discussed in some detail: (1) Some asset classes act directly opposite other asset classes more often than not; (2) some asset classes outperform their opposites (small caps over large caps) for a long time; and (3) out-of-favor groups will always return to favor in time.

The efficacy of buying an index fund portfolio spread over different asset classes is based on these truths. Instead of tying your fortunes to just one group or style or class and waiting until it regains popularity, owning an entire diversified portfolio permits asset allocation to perform its risk-balancing function over time. Some part of the portfolio will always be doing well or relatively well in all but no-escape bear markets.

It is this security against blanket erosion that makes a carefully selected diversified portfolio psychologically comforting. You may have lost a close ball game but you scored some runs. The despair of total defeat has been avoided. And it's a long season.

17. No Coincidence: The Best Minds Favor Indexing The list of seasoned, savvy market veterans who are on record favoring index funds as opposed to actively managed funds is long and illustrious. It includes everyone from John Bogle to Anthony Tobias, Warren Buffett to William Bernstein, David Swenson to Paul Merriman, Larry Kudlow to Jonathan Clements, and many, many more. It cannot be coincidence that such a diversified pool of stock market brainpower coming from all corners of the investment universe all come to the same conclusion.

When asked the eternal question, "What's the best way to make money in the stock market?" their unequivocal answer, at least with part of your money, is "Index funds." And as the years pass, we hear more and more stories about leading investment gurus quietly buying index funds for their own retirement.

I could also compile a list (though not as impressive) of *anti*-indexers. Indexing, after all, is only one of many market approaches, as discussed in Chapter 4. Other options, if applied consistently, may produce better results, but for most investors with most of their money the odds favor indexing as the best way to go.

I like Burton Malkiel's approach. The Princeton economics professor and author of the classic *A Random Walk Down Wall Street* (W.W. Norton, 2003) is a strong advocate of index funds. About 80 percent of his personal retirement money is invested in index funds. But according to John Wasik's column on Bloomberg.com (May 3, 2004), "Malkiel also likes to pick a few individual stocks for fun." I take the same approach in this book.

> "If we knew what we were doing, it wouldn't be called research."
> —*Albert Einstein*

Chapter 7

Passive Investing

Twenty-Eight Model Index Fund Portfolios

This chapter features a number of model portfolios for you to consider. Certain asset classes are included in most of the portfolios. Starting in the 1990s, there has been a dramatic move to expand the three basic asset classes—stocks, bonds, and cash—to five: stocks, bonds, cash, real estate, and commodities. To complement the "big five," the surge of ETFs has added many other popular asset classes. What's more, each class is divided into increasingly narrow segments, much to the delight of traders and the consternation of traditional indexers.

Setting the Table

There are only so many basic, all-encompassing asset classes. Each is likely to show up in most broadly diversified index fund portfolios. Here are a few salient points about each of the most popular categories and why you might want to include them in your portfolio. These brief comments are not meant to substitute for the voluminous explanatory material on each asset class that is just a click away on the Internet.

Total Stock Market

John Bogle, who founded the S&P 500 Index Fund over 30 years ago, believes the Vanguard Total Stock Market Index Fund (VTSMX) is a better choice than the S&P 500 for investors seeking an all-in-one-stock fund. The VTSMX tracks the MSCI U.S. Broad Market Index of close to 4,000 stocks. It includes nearly all publicly traded domestic stocks—large, small, growth, and value—in a single mutual fund. Because it spans the entire domestic stock universe, it has a small to mid cap bias. Its performance would likely be negatively affected by disenchantment with small caps.

Small Cap

Small capitalization stocks have had a long run. They've been among the market leaders since 2000. They have outperformed for other long periods of time. According to Chicago-based research firm Ibbotson Associates, small caps have outperformed large cap stocks by an average two percentage points a year (12.67 percent vs. 10.4 percent) over the past 80 years ending in 2005.

A recent study by the Schwab Center for Investment Research concludes that investors able to hold assets for 20 years or more would get their best returns from small cap stocks. Part of the reason is their anonymity. More than half the companies with market caps below $250 million have zero research coverage (according to Alex Paris, Barrington Research, Chicago), which creates opportunity for well-chosen small companies.

Foreign

More than 75 percent of all publicly traded companies are located outside the United States. They can be accessed by some 800 mutual funds and over 100 ETFs, all dedicated to investing abroad.

Even though the United States has the largest stock market capitalization in the world by far (Japan and Britain are distant runner-ups), it has not ranked as the world's top-performing market for over 10 years. In fact, in the four years 2002–2005, according to Morgan Stanley's country index of nine developed countries (United States, Japan, Britain, Germany, France, and so on), the annual return of the United States ranked dead last for three years and next to last in one. Says veteran money manager Peter Bernstein, "I would have no more than half my assets in the U.S. if I was starting fresh" (WealthTrack.com, May 26, 2006).

Periods of decline in the U.S. dollar translate into high prices in the euro, the yen, and others, and help buyers of foreign stocks. The most widely used proxy for foreign stocks among ETFs is the Morgan Stanley Capital International—Europe, Australia, Far East (MSCI—EAFE), symbol EFA. This is an index of 1,000 stocks encompassing all markets other than the United States. Like small caps, REITS, and emerging markets, foreign stocks have had a long period of outperforming the Dow. Analysts generally suggest putting 15 to 35 percent of a portfolio in foreign stocks and bonds.

Widely read columnist Jonathan Clements points out that, although U.S. and foreign stocks often rise and fall at the same time, foreign stocks have easily outperformed the overall U.S. stock market over the past five years. "Foreign shares account for more than half of the world's stock market value, so they deserve a permanent place in your portfolio. Consider earmarking 20 percent or 30 percent of your stock portfolio for foreign shares—and then stick with your target percentage, come what may" ("Stormy Markets: Foreign Stocks Often Offer a Safe Harbor," *Wall Street Journal,* April 4, 2007).

> "The twenty-first century is going to be the century of China. They call themselves communists but they are among the world's best capitalists. The single best advice I can give you is to teach your children and grandchildren Chinese."
>
> —*Jim Rogers*

Real Estate Investment Trusts

Real estate investment trusts (REITs) have a good record of low correlation with other asset classes, which is why, along with their outperformance, they are included in so many diversified portfolios. Traditionally bought for high income, the yields on REITs have come down as their stock prices have gone up. The group enjoyed a run of six straight years going into 2007. Unlike most groups whose components move more or less together, different types of REITS (mortgage, office building, shopping mall, hotel, etc.) often go their own way.

Large Cap

The S&P 500 and Dow Industrial averages consist mostly of big cap stocks. So, by definition, when the major averages are at the forefront of sweeping, sustained bull markets, the large caps do well. Each year since the 2000–2002 bear market ended, Wall Street forecast a return to favor of the big caps. Each year, through 2006, that expectation proved premature. They've done okay but have been decisively outperformed by small caps and many other asset classes.

In the meantime, profits have continued to grow steadily. Earnings of the 500 large cap companies in the S&P 500 Index rose by double digits for a record 17 quarters ending in 2006. Many of the large blue chips have more than doubled their profits over the last five to seven years. Yet some stock prices were below where they were before the turn of the century. That stored-up value is likely to be recognized sooner or later. Wall Street has been repeatedly wrong in calling for a resurgence of the big quality names, but at some point, it will be right.

Bonds

Bonds, stocks, and cash are the three cornerstones of most portfolios. Bonds are traditionally bought for income and safety, not growth. Typically, we allocate more to bonds as we get older because they are less speculative than stocks. Their main appeal in a portfolio is the balance they provide. When stocks zig, bonds zag—not always, but often. The reason is that bad news on the economy is usually negative for stocks but positive for bonds. When stocks collapsed in the 2000–2002 bear market, bonds did well.

Unless held to maturity, bonds are not risk-free. Their performance is tied to the trend of interest rates, which is totally unpredictable. When rates go down, bonds go up, and vice versa.

Because of their stabilizing influence on a portfolio, everybody except the very young should probably own some bonds. The best vehicles are no-load, low-expense mutual funds or ETFs. Roughly in order of safety are short-term U.S. Treasuries, TIPS (described later in this section), quality corporate bonds, closed-end bond funds, high-yield junk bonds, foreign bonds, and emerging market debt. (Municipal bonds pay tax-free income and appeal to high tax bracket investors.)

The key to the performance of a bond fund is the degree to which it controls expenses. For example, Vanguard's bond index mutual funds have an attractive annual expense ratio of 0.2 percent or less, meaning just $0.20 of each $100 invested goes to expenses. More and more ETF bond funds are being launched, led by Barclays with 16 and growing.

Commodities

Once considered too volatile and speculative for the average investor, commodities are found in more and more diversified portfolios. The reason: As we move ever closer to becoming a global economy, it is becoming increasingly difficult to find asset classes that move contrarily. In a flat world the trend is toward *more* correlation among financial assets, not less. But commodities continue their mostly independent ways.

A sustained uptrend in commodities frequently spells trouble for stocks, bonds, and for the U.S. dollar. Rising commodity prices fuel inflationary expectations, which often act as an anathema to both stocks and bonds. A study supervised by analyst Barry Bannister of Stifel, Nicolaus & Co., found that over the past 130 years, commodities and stocks have alternated performance leadership in regular cycles averaging about 18 years. Thus the addition of commodities to a portfolio adds a measure of protection and balance over time. Taking on specific risk reduces overall risk.

Commodity guru Jim Rogers, who, unlike many other talking heads on TV, actually made money following his own advice, believes we are in a golden age of hard material investing fueled by rapidly rising global demand, especially in China and India (*BusinessWeek,* January 25, 2006). He thinks it could last another decade and has moved to Singapore to be closer to the action.

Gold, perhaps the most glamorous of the commodities, has hundreds of years of history of being noncorrelated with financial assets.

It is often used as a hedge against inflation and as a safe haven in times of geopolitical unrest. If the consensus forecast of an ongoing decline in the dollar is correct, gold should benefit from its natural bias to move opposite the greenback. Bulls on gold also believe the long 22-year decline in the yellow metal (1980–2002) augurs well for a sustained recovery.

Emerging Markets

As the name implies, emerging markets (also called developing markets or Third World markets) such as Brazil, Russia, India, and China are less seasoned and more volatile than developed countries such as the United States, Britain, Japan, Germany, and France. Unlike more mature economies, the huge demand for goods and services from emerging economies like China and India present the potential for both high profit and high risk. China and India together have almost half the world's population. You might be hard pressed to present a well-diversified portfolio without their inclusion.

Emerging markets were star performers for four years before experiencing a serious setback in 2006. Because it is an unseasoned, volatile, and risky asset class, allocations in most portfolios are modest. However, youthful populations, a wealth of natural resources, and enormous pent-up demand bodes well for these markets in the future.

Treasury Inflation-Protected Securities (TIPS)

U.S. Treasury bonds that are bought for protection against inflation are a popular choice in a diversified portfolio. When and if inflation heats up, stocks are likely to suffer, but TIPS should do well.

The yield on TIPS has two components—a low, fixed, semiannual coupon rate, and an annual addition to the principal based on the rise in the consumer price index. Unlike other bonds, the coupon rate is applied to the inflation-adjusted principal, not to par (100 or 1,000). That means if inflation goes up, both your interest return and principal go up each year. If inflation goes down, you can't receive less than par at maturity.

Like all bonds, TIPS will go down when interest rates go up, and interest rates usually go up with rising inflation. But the decline in the value of the bond should be more than offset by the annual inflation kicker.

Remember, the relentless rise in prices that we all see in the real world (food, gas, drugs, etc.) is not reflected in the lower numbers the government uses to measure inflation.

TIPS are a bet on rising inflation, which has been a recurring phenomenon in our history, but not so in the recent past. Because TIPS are U.S. Treasury bonds and involve minimum risk (only if sold before maturity), they are considered a relatively conservative "sleep at night" investment. Launched in 1997, TIPS are issued in 5-, 10-, and 20-year maturities. Individual bonds can be bought directly from the government (www.TreasuryDirect.gov), or a basket of TIPS can be bought via some two dozen mutual funds and a few ETFs.

Dividends

Over the past 80 years, the S&P 500 has delivered a 10.4 percent annualized return, 40 percent of which is attributed to dividends, according to Standard & Poor's. Dividends are a big deal because in an era of expected single-digit returns, a healthy dividend means a lot of the work is done. Lower-yielding stocks with steadily increasing dividends generally outperform higher-yielding stocks that do not grow their dividend.

Investing in stocks that pay rising dividends and then reinvesting those dividends unleashes the power of compounding. University of Pennsylvania professor Jeremy Siegel, perhaps the most vocal proponent of dividend investing, says, "Dividend payers that trade at reasonable valuations are the stocks that did the very best for investors over the long run. . . . I can't emphasize enough the importance of dividends and reinvesting those dividends" (Money.CNN.com, November 30, 2004).

You can buy a collection of dividend-paying stocks via both mutual funds and ETFs and ask the broker to reinvest your dividends. The most popular ETF is iShares Dow Jones Select Dividend Index (DVY). It follows an index of 100 stocks that have increased their dividends over at least the past five years without paying out more than 60 percent

> "Understanding where 'value' exists, is the winning strategy over the long term."
>
> —*Jeffrey Saut*

of their earnings to do it. The SPDR Dividend ETF (SDY) focuses on 50 companies that have raised their payout every year for at least 25 years.

(A select list of blue-chip companies have upped their dividend for 40 to 50 years in a row, including Procter & Gamble, 3M Company, Colgate, Coca-Cola, Kellogg, and Johnson & Johnson.)

Final Portfolio Housekeeping

The particular index funds selected to represent the preceding asset classes in our model portfolios are mostly ETFs but some are traditional mutual funds. Each one has a symbol. Put the symbol in the "quote" box on your favorite investment web site and you will access extensive fundamental and technical information about each fund. You can also get background information about the portfolio itself, including its track record, by typing in a search box the names of the originator of the portfolio or the sponsoring organization.

In case you should want to substitute a different index fund for the one that's recommended, you can go to many of the ETF sources listed in Chapter 6 for a master list to choose from; AAII.com might be a good place to start. The model portfolios presented in this chapter include the picker's first choice in that asset class, but there are usually other candidates that may prove almost as good, just as good, or better. Of course, where there is one dominant fund in the field, it makes things easier. You will note that many of the portfolios include the same names. If you put together your own portfolio, be sure to consider these favorites.

A few of the portfolios that follow contain only suggested asset classes and not specific funds. I believe these bare-bones portfolios have value because the choice of asset class is more critical than the choice of the fund within that class. In fact, it's probable that the single most important part of investing is the process of dividing our money among asset classes. Once we have the right mix, most everything else should fall into place in time.

"Buy and Hold" But with a Wrinkle

The recommended models are long-term, all-weather, buy-and-hold portfolios—but with a wrinkle. That wrinkle is the need to rebalance when one asset class gets out of whack. As discussed earlier, that may not happen for a long while. Yes, it would be great not to have to do anything. You can get away with an absolutely do-nothing approach if you hold CDs or bonds to maturity or hold target retirement mutual funds, or if you buy the right individual stock or mutual fund and hold it long enough. But when it comes to a portfolio of different uncorrelated parts, performance is likely to be hurt if action (rebalancing) isn't taken from time to time.

When I was publishing the *Dick Davis Digest,* each issue contained many stock recommendations. I knew some would work out and others wouldn't. This is different. I believe that over time, any of the following diversified index fund portfolios will do well. Since they are all carefully balanced among key asset classes, the difference in future performance is likely to depend less on the particular portfolio chosen and more on the prices paid for its components.

In that regard, please review the comments on the importance of buying index funds at the right price and suggestions on how to do that. And remember, after you buy whatever it is you're buying, it will invariably go lower. So expect it and don't let it upset you. And don't be too disappointed or dissuaded if your portfolio treads water or underperforms for extended periods. It's frustrating but it's an unavoidable part of the process.

I have not included past performance results for each portfolio. You can obtain updated numbers in an Internet search. Because there are always variables and different interpretations, I am skeptical about the accuracy of published performance results. Show me five independent researchers and I'll show you five different statistical conclusions. Show me one statistic in a widely read, respected column and I'll show you that exact same statistic repeated by many other writers glad not to have to do the original work (sometimes I'm one of the many). Suffice it to say, these portfolios are from responsible sources with alleged results that consistently match or, in most cases, outperform the overall market (S&P 500) because of the diversity of asset classes.

Nothing Is Forever

It goes without saying (okay, not the best expression for an author) that the following model portfolios are not *equally* suitable for all investors. We all have different ages, incomes, risk tolerances, target goals, investment skills, and so on. "One size fits all" does not apply, but a diversified list of index funds probably comes as close as you can get. Why? Because, whatever your risk profile, you'll likely want to include the core holdings of U.S. stocks, foreign stocks, and U. S. bonds.

The authors of some of these portfolios may be making changes in their holdings in the future. Please check the web sites involved to keep updated. Nothing is forever, not even a buy-and-hold portfolio.

I believe that in selecting portfolios, the idea that *simpler is better* applies most of the time. There are many model index fund portfolios out there promoted by brokerage firms, investment newsletters, and financial web sites. However, most require frequent revisions. The sales pitch is that close monitoring in response to changing market conditions enhances performance. That may or may not be true. What's certain is that the more stripped down the content (as long as it includes the basic three cornerstones of U.S. stocks, foreign stocks, and U.S. bonds), the fewer the decisions, the lower the costs, and the easier it is to understand, implement, and measure, all of which increases the odds that you will stay with your portfolio. That's key. Stick-to-it-tiveness is what makes this strategy work.

Finally, to keep things in perspective, each of the portfolios that follow is special. It is not a routine recommendation but, instead, it is the author's ultimate solution to the quest for the perfect portfolio. Each is a distillation of a lifetime of looking and learning. Reduced to a few index fund names, the portfolio may appear run-of-the-mill. It's easy to forget the implied message from the author of each of these portfolios: "After long years of experience in the investment business, I believe passionately and irrefutably that buying this list of securities is the very best thing you can do with your long-term money."

> "Smart people don't wait for luck to make them wealthy. Every day, they cultivate habits and follow rules that others don't. If you want to be wealthy, live below your means. Pay yourself first and build wealth, not a lifestyle that saddles you with expenses."
>
> —*Paul Merriman*

Paul Farrell: Lazy Man Portfolios

Paul B. Farrell, based in Arroyo Grande, California, has been a financial columnist for MarketWatch.com since 1997. He has published more than 1,400 columns and nine books including *The Lazy Person's Guide to Investing* (Warner Business Books, 2004). Farrell says that after 10 years of column writing, he has learned two things from the 40,000 or so e-mails he has received from readers: save regularly and invest lazily (MarketWatch.com, Paul Farrell, May 21, 2007). He is the leading exponent of the "lazy portfolio" approach to investing. The specific portfolios featured here are not his but he is largely responsible for their wide exposure.

The lazy man's portfolio is a fixed, diversified, buy-and-hold group of low-cost, no-load index funds. The number of funds in each portfolio varies from 2 to 11, some ETFs but mostly conventional index mutual funds. Though some of the portfolios have only a few funds, careful selection results in broad market exposure. They're called "lazy" because they are easy to understand and implement and because they require low to zero maintenance. Despite their simplicity, they are credited with consistently outperforming the broad general market over the past one, three, and five years (the performance results of the lazy man portfolios are usually compared to that of the S&P 500 Index). The combination of performance and simplicity is appealing to even the most sophisticated investors.

Charles Kirk, the most consistently successful trader I know (see Chapter 5), writes on his web site (TheKirkReport.com, February 13, 2007):

> Within my own long-term retirement accounts, I've put together what is known as a "lazy man's portfolio." I'm a huge advocate for using this type of approach to long-term investing. I think the lazy portfolio approach is the very best way to go for the vast majority of investors. It's a strategy that keeps it simple, has low overhead costs, and is diversified and tax-efficient. Many of the portfolios have been properly back-tested and produced excellent returns. I believe that if you don't incorporate some variation of the lazy portfolio strategy in your own approach, you are short-changing yourself and your financial future. My suggestion: Develop a few model portfolios of your own based on the various lazy portfolios but suited to your needs and track them closely for a couple of years. If you do this, as I have, I think you'll come to value their performance.

Kiss Your Broker

Paul Farrell is a strong advocate of passive investing. He says, "Kiss your high-cost broker or financial adviser goodbye, and manage your own money using low-cost index funds. . . . Lazy portfolio balanced asset allocation strategies have proven to be solid performers in both bull and bear markets, often besting the benchmark indexes by healthy margins" (MarketWatch.com, March 27, 2005, and July 18, 2006).

Farrell tracks six and sometimes seven lazy portfolios: the Couch Potato Portfolio, the Margaritaville Portfolio, the No-Brainer Portfolio, the Coffeehouse Portfolio, the Ted Aronson Portfolio, the Second-Grader's "Starter" Portfolio, and the Yale Portfolio. Each one is highlighted in the following pages. Go to MarketWatch.com and read Paul Farrell's columns of July 9, 2007, September 10, 2007, and any subsequent updates for complete details and latest performance results of all the lazy man portfolios.

Farrell added a new lazy portfolio in his MarketWatch.com column of February 20, 2007 ("Youth Movement"). He calls it the Second-Grader Starter Portfolio (see Table 7.1). Kevin Roth, an 8-year-old second-grader, got started in the market with the help of his financial planner father, Allan (Colorado Springs), and a gift from his grandmother. Kevin invested the $3,000

> "Great management can't always cause a stock to go up, but bad management will nearly always cause a stock to go down."
>
> —*Mark Sellers*

minimum in each of three Vanguard index mutual funds. According to back-testing data compiled by Morningstar and reported by Farrell, the

Table 7.1   Second-Grader Starter Portfolio*

Asset Allocation	Name of Fund	Symbol
60%	Vanguard Total Stock Market Index	(VTSMX)
30%	Vanguard Total International Stock Index	(VGTSX)
10%	Vanguard Total Bond Market Index	(VBMFX)

*If exchange-traded funds are preferred, replace the above with the following three ETFs: Vanguard Total Stock Market Index (VTI), iShares MSCI EAFE International Index (EFA), and iShares Lehman Aggregate Bond Index (AGG).

simple, no-frills, three-fund portfolio outperformed the S&P 500 over the 5- and 10-year periods ending December 31, 2006.

Twenty-Eight Model Index Fund Portfolios

1. Scott Burns: Couch Potato Portfolio

Scott Burns (scottburns.com) is a seasoned, widely read, and widely quoted financial writer. He was the financial editor for the *Boston Herald* and then the *Dallas Morning News,* the latter for 21 years till he retired in late 2006. Based now in Santa Fe, New Mexico, he continues to write a twice-weekly nationally syndicated column on investing and personal finance, something he's been doing for over 30 years. He's also the chief investment strategist for Asset Builder, Inc. and co-author of *The Coming Generational Storm* (MIT Press, 2004).

Burns originated the Couch Potato Portfolio in 1991 with just two mutual index funds—the S&P 500 Index and the Total Bond Market index. Later, he replaced them with the Total Market Index fund and a TIPS index fund (see Table 7.2). Says Paul Farrell, "The Couch Potato Portfolio is so simple it's shamelessly embarrassing. Just two funds in a 50/50 asset allocation." For the younger or more aggressive couch potato, Burns offers the same two funds but with a 75 percent stock and 25 percent bond allocation.

Burns stresses the importance of low fees and expenses and favors Vanguard. His approach is based on the premise that gains in bonds will offset some of the losses in stocks (as they did in the 2000–2002 market collapse), thereby reducing volatility and risk.

Table 7.2 Couch Potato Portfolio

Portfolio Allocation	Name of Fund	Symbol	More Aggressive
50%	Vanguard Total Stock Market Index Fund	(VTSMX)	75%
50%	Vanguard Inflation-Protected Securities Fund	(VIPSX)	25%

He describes returns over the past 5, 10, and 15 years as "solid" with some periods showing losses. He recommends rebalancing on an annual basis.

A Challenge to Wall Street In a March 15, 2006, interview on AllThingsFinancialBlog.com, Burns said, "The Couch Potato Portfolio offers a simple challenge to all the purported brain power on Wall Street. It produces a good return by being incredibly cheap to manage—20 basis points or less—and by being something you can do while making your fifth margarita. If you can fog a mirror and divide by two with the help of an electronic calculator, you can manage a Couch Potato Portfolio. As a result, normal people who don't care about investments can manage their own money without having to help someone on Wall Street make his Mercedes payment."

Burns started the Margarita Portfolio in early 2004 in honor of the other Buffett, singer Jimmy. Like the drink, it's made with three equal parts: one-third U.S. stocks, one-third international stocks, and one-third U.S. bonds (see Table 7.3).

In recent years, Burns has conceded that a slightly more diversified portfolio is apt to produce a higher risk-adjusted return over time. To that end, he's added a four-fund, a five-fund, and a six-fund portfolio, each the same as the one before it plus one new fund (see Tables 7.4 through 7.6). He calls them building-block portfolios. The new funds he's added to enhance potential returns include an international bond fund, an REIT, and an energy fund. For further details,

> "Living with an error is a far greater mistake than making one in the first place."
>
> —*Larry Swedroe*

Table 7.3   Margarita Portfolio

Portfolio Allocation	Name of Fund	Symbol
33.3%	Vanguard Total Stock Market Index Fund	(VTSMX)
33.3%	Vanguard Total International Stock Index Fund	(VGTSX)
33.3%	Vanguard Inflation-Protected Securities Fund	(VIPSX)

Table 7.4 Four Square Portfolio

Portfolio Allocation	Name of Fund	Symbol
25%	Vanguard Total Stock Market Index Fund	(VTSMX)
25%	Vanguard Inflation-Protected Securities Fund	(VIPSX)
25%	Vanguard Total International Stock Index Fund	(VGTSX)
25%	American Century International Bond Fund	(BEGBX)

Table 7.5 Five Fold Portfolio

Portfolio Allocation	Name of Fund	Symbol
20%	Vanguard Total Stock Market Index Fund	(VTSMX)
20%	Vanguard Inflation-Protected Securities Fund	(VIPSX)
20%	Vanguard Total International Stock Index Fund	(VGTSX)
20%	Vanguard REIT Index	(VGSIX)
20%	American Century International Bond Fund	(BEGBX)

Table 7.6 Six Ways from Sunday Portfolio

Portfolio Allocation	Name of Fund	Symbol
16.65%	Vanguard Total Stock Market Index Fund	(VTSMX)
16.65%	Vanguard Inflation-Protected Securities Fund	(VIPSX)
16.65%	Vanguard Total International Stock Index Fund	(VGTSX)
16.65%	Vanguard REIT Index	(VGSIX)
16.65%	American Century International Bond Fund	(BEGBX)
16.65%	Vanguard Energy	(VGENX)

including returns, check out scottburns.com, "another happy year for sloth and passivity," December 23, 2006, and any updates.

2. Bill Schultheis: Coffeehouse Portfolio

Bill Schultheis, 47, a broker for 13 years with Smith Barney, is currently a money manager for Pacific Asset Management in Seattle, Washington. He created the Coffeehouse Portfolio in a 1998 book, which he revised in 2005 (*The Coffeehouse Investor,* Palouse Press).

Schultheis' buy-and-hold index fund portfolio is 40 percent bonds and 60 percent stocks. For the bond portion, he uses an intermediate-term bond index fund. The stock portion is divided equally into six asset classes: large cap, large cap value, small cap, small cap value, international, and real estate. That's seven funds in all. Schultheis favors the Vanguard family of low-cost, no-load index mutual funds, rather than ETFs, to build his portfolio.

Says Paul Farrell, "The Coffeehouse Portfolio is so simple, boring, and effective that commission brokers hate it. It's a winner in bull and bear markets and it wins with no trading, no rebalancing, no tinkering with asset allocations. Set it and forget it! It is clearly one of the safest of the 'Lazy Portfolios' we've been tracking" (MarketWatch.com, January 18, 2005; December 26, 2005).

Farrell is a strong proponent of index mutual funds over ETFs because brokers' commissions on the latter "can kill returns." However, if you're a buy-and-holder and not a trader and if you use low-commission, online, discount firm web sites like Foliofn.com, then ETFs, with their other advantages, become doable. With that in mind, Farrell offers an alternative Coffeehouse Portfolio. It consists of seven Barclays iShare ETFs that track the same indexes as the seven mutual funds.

Get On with Your Life Here's what Bill Schultheis says about his own brainchild (www.CoffeehouseInvestor.com, 2005):

> There is nothing special about index funds. They just happen to be the most effective way to capture the entire return of an asset class in a cost-efficient, tax-efficient manner. . . . The seven index fund Coffeehouse Portfolio . . . has dramatically outperformed Wall Street's beloved blue chips the past seven years. . . . As for the three low-cost ETF portfolio, it's likely to outperform anything your stockbroker throws at you over the next 10 years. Forget about hedge funds, gold and commodity funds and all those other newfangled ETFs that have come on the market. Stick with the simple three-fund portfolio and get on with your life. . . . There will come a time when our simple approach to building wealth underperforms, or even generates a negative return for 12 months or more. That will be the time . . . to stay the course.

Schultheis's three-fund portfolio is outlined in Table 7.7. For
the past seven years, his seven-
fund portfolio (Tables 7.8 and

"Being bearish or cautious always
sounds smarter than being bullish."
—*Bill Miller*

7.9) has benefited from its value and small cap bias. Though that's not
likely to last indefinitely, he suggests weakness could present a buying
opportunity.

Table 7.7   Bill Schultheis' Three ETF Fund Portfolio

Asset Allocation	Name of Fund	Symbol
33.3%	Vanguard Total Stock Market	(VTI)
33.3%	iShares International MSCI EAFE Value	(EFV)
33.3%	iShares Lehman Aggregate Bond	(AGG)

Table 7.8   Coffeehouse Portfolio

Portfolio Allocation	Name of Fund	Symbol
40%	Vanguard Total Bond Index	(VBMFX)
10%	Vanguard 500 Index	(VFINX)
10%	Vanguard Value Index	(VIVAX)
10%	Vanguard Small Cap Index	(NAESX)
10%	Vanguard Small Cap Value Index	(VISVX)
10%	Vanguard Total International Stock Index	(VGTSX)
10%	Vanguard REIT Index	(VGSIX)

Table 7.9   Alternate Coffeehouse Portfolio Using ETFs

Portfolio Allocation	Name of Fund	Symbol
40%	iShares Lehman Aggregate	(AGG)
10%	iShares S&P 500	(IVV)
10%	iShares S&P 500/Barra Value	(IVE)
10%	iShares Morningstar Small Core	(JKJ)
10%	iShares Russell 2000 Value	(IWN)
10%	iShares MSCI EAFE	(EFA)
10%	iShares Dow Jones US Real Estate	(IYR)

3. William J. Bernstein: No-Brainer Portfolio

Portland, Oregon–based Dr. William Bernstein, 58, is probably best known as the author of the widely quoted *The Four Pillars of Investing* (2002). He also wrote *The Intelligent Asset Allocator* in 2000 and *The Birth of Plenty* in 2004—all three books are published by McGraw-Hill. He and Susan Sharin offer financial advice to high net worth individuals (www.efficientfrontier.com).

Dr. Bernstein belies the perception that doctors make poor investors. His portfolio was labeled a no-brainer by Paul Farrell because, as a neurologist, he has "a unique understanding of the workings of the brain." Bernstein's simple formula is to put 25 percent in each of four Vanguard index mutual funds. He favors mutual funds over ETFs and selects Vanguard because "they are no-load with low expenses and diversified across thousands of stocks and fixed-income securities."

Bernstein also offers an expanded nine-fund portfolio, sometimes called the No-Brainer Coward's Portfolio. It uses a total market index instead of the S&P 500 Index; divides the international allocation among European, Pacific Rim, and emerging markets; and adds a real estate component. The tilt is more toward value than growth. For the bond portion, his overriding principle is to select short-term (five years or less) high-grade bonds.

Chimpanzees Throwing Darts In *The Four Pillars of Investing* (Chapter 13, "Defining Your Mix"), Bernstein says an adequate portfolio needs to contain only three broad asset classes: U.S. total stock market, international stocks, and short-term U.S. bonds (see Tables 7.10 and 7.11). "If over the past 10 or 20 years, you had simply held a portfolio consisting of one quarter each of indexes of large U.S. stocks, small U.S. stocks, foreign stocks, and high-quality U.S. bonds, you would have beaten over 90 percent of all professional money managers and with considerably less risk."

Bernstein stresses that his approach requires sticking with it. It also calls for adjusting positions so as to keep the overall allocation constant. Bernstein claims that by balancing once a year, portfolio return can be enhanced by about 0.5 percent to 1 percent over time.

Though his approach is conservative, Bernstein pulls no punches in his criticism of the Wall Street establishment. In *Four Pillars of Investing* he

Table 7.10   Basic No-Brainer Portfolio

Asset Allocation		Symbol	Alternates for Taxable Accounts	
25%	Vanguard 500 Index	(VFINX)		
25%	Vanguard Small Cap Index	(NAESX)	Vanguard Tax Managed Small Cap	(VTMSX)
25%	Vanguard Total International Stock	(VGTSX)	Vanguard Tax Managed International	(VTMGX)
25%	Vanguard Total Bond Market	(VBMFX)	Vanguard Short Term Bond	(VBISX)
			Or	
			Vanguard Short Term Investment Grade	(VFSTX)

Table 7.11   No-Brainer Coward's Portfolio

Portfolio Allocation		Symbol	Alternates for Taxable Accounts	
40%	Vanguard Short Term Investment Grade	(VFSTX)		
15%	Vanguard Total Stock Market	(VTSMX)		
10%	Vanguard Value Index	(VIVAX)		
10%	Vanguard Small Cap Value	(VISVX)		
5%	Vanguard Small Cap Index	(NAESX)	Vanguard Tax Managed Small Cap	(VTMSX)
5%	Vanguard REIT Index	(VGSIX)		
5%	Vanguard European Stock	(VEURX)		
5%	Vanguard Pacific Stock	(VPACX)		
5%	Vanguard Emerging Markets Stock	(VEIEX)		

includes a chapter titled "Your Broker Is Not Your Buddy," which includes this unambiguous advice: "Under no circumstances should you have anything to do with a 'full service' brokerage firm." Nor is he subtle when commenting on the performance of portfolio managers: "We are looking at the proverbial bunch of chimpanzees throwing darts at the stock page. Their success or failure is a purely random affair. Ninety-nine percent of fund managers demonstrate no evidence of skill whatsoever." Thus Bernstein's strong bias for indexing.

He believes the specific index funds you buy are not that important: "Find the right mix of foreign and domestic stocks and bonds and your choice of individual securities becomes almost irrelevant in the long run."

> "It's not that I am so smart; it's just that I stay with problems longer."
>
> —*Albert Einstein*

4. Ted Aronson Portfolio

Ted Aronson, 54, heads the Philadelphia value-oriented firm Aronson+ Johnson+Oritz (AJOParners.com) which manages some $27 billion in tax-exempt institutional funds. He also actively manages two mutual funds, Quaker Small-Cap Value Fund I (QSVIX) and HighMark Large-Cap Value Fund (HMIEX). Both he and his partners have most of their personal retirement money (not taxable) in the two funds. But all of his and his mother's taxable money is in Vanguard no-load index funds. Specifically, Aronson's personal family portfolio is invested in 11 Vanguard index mutual funds which are allocated 40 percent domestic equities, 30 percent foreign stocks, and 30 percent fixed income (Table 7.12). It is this list of 11 funds that Paul Farrell includes in his collection of lazy man portfolios.

He does so enthusiastically. Farrell is a fan of Aronson because of his excellent performance and unusual candor. Aronson has been a chartered financial analyst and fund manager for over three decades. Unlike most of America's 75,000 money managers, he believes managers should share some of their clients' risks, and so he offers to tie his fees to performance in both good and bad markets. He is also the rare exception in his willingness to reveal the exact portfolio in which he invests his personal funds. TheStreet.com has called Aronson "the world's most honest money manager."

At MarketWatch.com (September 14, 2004 "Being Ted Aronson" and January 11, 2005 "Laziest Portfolio 2004 Winner"), columnist Paul Farrell says, "It's important for every American investor to understand Ted's super-simple portfolio. Remember, there are absolutely no actively managed funds in his lazy portfolio. . . . He doesn't sell or trade, he just

Table 7.12   Ted Aronson Portfolio

Asset Allocation	Name of Fund	Symbol
U.S. Stocks 40%		
5%	Vanguard Total Stock Market Index	(VTSMX)
15%	Vanguard 500 Index	(VFINX)
10%	Vanguard Extended Market Index	(VEXMX)
5%	Vanguard Small Cap Growth Index	(VISGX)
5%	Vanguard Small Cap Value Index	(VISVX)
Foreign Stocks 40%		
20%	Vanguard Emerging Markets Stock Index	(VEIEX)
15%	Vanguard Pacific Stock Index	(VPACX)
5%	Vanguard European Stock Index	(VEURX)
Fixed-Income Bonds 20%		
10%	Vanguard Inflation-Protected Securities	(VIPSX)
5%	Vanguard High Yield Corporate	(VWEHX)
5%	Vanguard Long Term U.S. Treasury	(VUSTX)

keeps adding new money to rebalance and maintain the designated asset allocation. . . . Aronson is a brilliant fund manager with a reputation for absolute integrity."

Aronson himself says, "The good results of my portfolio are driven by the focus on international stocks. Vanguard does the heavy lifting by providing capital market returns at rock bottom cost" (MarketWatch .com, "Lazy Portfolios Outrun S & P 500," January 16, 2006). Here, then, is where all the Aronson family (taxable) money goes. For further details on his investment approach and why he makes the portfolio allocations shown in Table 7.12, see Jonathan Burton's interview with Aronson (MarketWatch .com, "Matchless Match," January 3, 2007).

> "Having been in the stock market for more than four decades, I believe that the best time to invest for those with a long-term horizon is when they have the money."
>
> —*Shelby M. C. Davis*

5. David Swensen Portfolio

David Swensen, 53, is the longtime manager of Yale University's $18 billion endowment fund, which trails only Stanford in total assets.

Originally from Wisconsin, he has been the chief investment officer for Yale since 1985 when he was hired at the age of 31. Prior to that he received his PhD in economics at Yale and worked for six years on Wall Street at Salomon Brothers and Lehman Brothers. He currently teaches classes at Yale on investing and institutional money management.

But his main job is to allocate assets and pick the right asset managers for Yale's big endowment portfolio. (Yale uses more than 100 outside managers to invest its endowment money.) One of his selection criteria: Does the manager have a lot of his own money in the fund?

During the first 20 years of his stewardship he averaged annual returns of over 16 percent, a remarkable record. In the fiscal year ending June 30, 2006, the return was an eye-popping 22.9 percent. *New York Times* reporter Joseph Nocera labels him "the best manager of institutional money in the U.S." (August 13, 2005). Vanguard founder John Bogle calls him an "investment genius" and Jack Meyer, former manager of Harvard's endowment, says, "I think David is the best in the business."

Swensen has been able to achieve his extraordinary results by using alternative investments unavailable to the individual investor. They include oil and gas, real estate, timberland, private equity, exotic foreign securities, and hedge funds. He invented what has become known as "The Yale Model," a mechanism for multi–asset class investing that is used worldwide.

Swensen became so convinced of the "nearly insurmountable hurdles confronting ordinary investors" that he felt compelled to write a book explaining in detail the plight of the investor and his only way out. In a review in *Barron's* (November 1, 2005, page 50), Martin Fridson describes *Unconventional Success* (Free Press, 2005) as "refreshingly truthful."

Swenson urges his readers to give up illusions of beating the stock averages. He says most of Wall Street's actively managed funds are motivated by greed, which corrupts their behavior. His sharpest criticism is directed at mutual funds that charge big fees but fail to deliver market-beating returns. "Overwhelmingly, mutual funds extract enormous sums from investors in exchange for providing a shocking disservice. . . . You lose by playing their rules."

Plain Vanilla Portfolio Swensen's attack on the Wall Street establishment and defense of the little guy is not an original theme. Back in

Table 7.13   David Swensen's Portfolio

Asset Allocation	Name of Fund	Symbol
U.S. Stocks 50%		
30%	Vanguard Total Stock Market Index	(VTSMX)
20%	Vanguard REIT Index	(VGSIX)
Foreign Stocks 20%		
15%	Vanguard Developed Markets Index	(VDMIX)
5%	Vanguard Emerging Markets Stock Index	(VEIEX)
U.S. Bonds 30%		
15%	Vanguard Short Term Treasury Index	(VFISX)
15%	Vanguard Inflation Protected Securities	(VIPSX)

1975, Charles Ellis sounded similar warnings in *Winning the Loser's Game* (McGraw Hill). Vanguard's John Bogle has been fighting the good fight on behalf of the individual investor for decades. In his book *The Battle for the Soul of Capitalism* (Yale University Press, 2005) Bogle argues that the rewards for fund managers are vastly disproportionate to those of the funds' investor owners.

The way out for investors, according to Swensen, is the use of low-cost index funds. To be successful, the individual investor must avoid actively managed funds completely. Instead, the basic prescription is an indexed portfolio spread over three core investment categories. He identifies these as stocks (both domestic and foreign), bonds (treasuries and TIPS), and real estate. (See Table 7.13.) Swensen believes that for most individual investors, including many wealthy people, this type of plain-vanilla portfolio is the only way to go to achieve decent returns. He favors the use of Vanguard mutual funds with their rock-bottom fees but concedes that there are also some ETFs that provide low-cost, tax-efficient diversification.

Swensen is a strong proponent of consistent portfolio rebalancing. He believes each asset class should comprise at least 5 to 10 percent of the total to have any impact, and that no asset class should exceed 25 to 30 percent. The portfolio in Table 7.13 comes from his book, *Unconventional Success*. In it you will find full details on Swensen's index fund approach

> "It's amazing how little people understand about the market, even professionals.... There are no experts. Most commentators are just that."
>
> —*Laszlo Birinyi*

and his stinging condemnation of Wall Street. *Newsweek* (August 22, 2005) says of the book, "This is not only investing made easy, it's investing made smart." And Vanguard's John Bogle adds, "This is elegantly simple advice in a wonderful book that will change the way you think about mutual funds."

6. Ben Stein

Los Angeles–based Ben Stein, 62, may be as close as we can get to a twenty-first century renaissance man. His father, economist Herbert Stein, was the chairman of the Council of Economic Advisors for Presidents Nixon and Ford. But Ben's talents go far beyond economics. He is a lawyer, teacher, economist, TV personality, movie actor, comic, speechwriter, scriptwriter, and financial columnist. He shares his insightful investment commentary regularly via articles written for Yahoo! Finance online and the Sunday *New York Times* Business Section. He is also the author of some 25 books, mostly on personal finance. Titles include *How Successful People Win* (Hay House, 2006) and *Yes You Can Still Retire Comfortably* (New Beginnings Press, 2005). For details on all his books and recent columns go to benstein.com.

Stein admits to being "far too timid to handle anyone's money but my own. If I had a bad month and a widow called me in tears, I would probably jump off a tall building" (*Barron's*, July 10, 2006). But like all very smart people, Stein has other very smart people giving him input. He has co-authored a number of his books with Phil De Muth and consulted with Ray Lucia, both of whom he calls "brilliant" financial managers.

Stein is a fan of indexing. His approach is based on the fact that "over long periods (very long periods, to be sure), indexes beat all but the very best and rarest stock pickers" (*Barron's*, July 10, 2006). In his column on Finance.Yahoo.com ("Investing Strategies for the New Year," January 8, 2007), he highlights two long-term themes and recommends an index fund portfolio that will benefit from them.

The first theme is Stein's expectations for the decline of the dollar:

> It may have pauses and eddies, but for the long run the decline
> in the dollar is going to continue. The United States is import-
> ing so much more than we export that the world is awash in the

dollars we've created to pay for them. As when all commodities are in surplus, their price goes down.

Stein points out that Europe and many emerging market countries in the Far East are running trade surpluses with the United States, which causes their currencies to appreciate against the dollar.

> The simple, sensible way to play this is to buy the index funds of the major foreign industrial powers in Europe, Australia and the Far East known as the EFA. The EFA allows investors to bet that these economies will strengthen and that corporate profits there will rise. But most important of all is that their currencies, especially the Euro, will strengthen against the dollar.

A Long-Term Sure Thing The second theme is the favorable outlook for the world's emerging markets. Stein says that the index funds of the emerging markets "allow investors to bet on continuing success in China, India, Brazil, Russia, Thailand, the Philippines, Mexico and many other countries. Index funds also allow investors to bet that the currencies of these countries will continue to rise against the dollar. This seems like a sure thing, and in the long run it is."

With these themes in mind, Stein constructs an index fund of six components (Table 7.14). He suggests about 15 percent in EFA but as high as 25 percent if you have a very long-term horizon; about 10 percent into emerging markets but "the ride can be bumpy"; about 30 percent into a total stock market index "which covers a very large swath of the market

Table 7.14 Ben Stein's Long-Term Portfolio

Portfolio Allocation	Name of Fund	Symbol
15%–25%	iShares MSCI EAFE Index	(EFA)
10%	iShares MSCI Emerging Markets Index, or	(EEM)
	BLDRS Emerging Markets 50 ADR Index	(ADRE)
30%	Fidelity Spartan Total Market Index, or	(FSTMX)
	Vanguard Total Stock Market ETF	(VTI)
10%	iShares Cohen & Steers Realty Majors	(ICF)
10%	iShares Russell 2000 Value Index	(IWN)
15%	Cash	

and allows for major diversification in one purchase" (he recommends putting some of the 30 percent in a broad stock market index–based variable annuity but only after shopping "extremely thoroughly"); about 10 percent into REITs, "which may be high but pay a good dividend: they'll probably stall for a while and then go up in the future; about 10 percent into small cap value which are unlikely to repeat 2006's gains for a while but, historically, are a fine place to be in the long run; about 15 percent in cash against a rainy day . . ."

Stein sums up his overall approach, "Get the broadest possible market indexes. Spread yourself out over large and small caps. Have a large dollop of the developed foreign and a goodly chunk of the developing market. Yes, it'll be a rocky ride in China and Brazil, but over long periods you'll do great" (finance.yahoo.com, March 2, 2007).

What about investing in a market that's high by historical standards? Says Stein, "I wouldn't let that stop me from buying. . . . Barring some awful act of terrorism, a national disaster, or a catastrophic failure of monetary policy, . . . in 20 years it will be much higher. You'll be sorry if you didn't buy in 2007—and keep on buying. If the market falls, just keep on buying. When the prices fall is when you get the real bargains" (Finance.Yahoo.com, "Investing Strategies for the New Year," January 8, 2007).

Ben Stein's Two-Fund Retirement Portfolio with Staying Power With the help of his financial guru pal, Phil DeMuth, Stein has constructed a retirement portfolio that deals with the scary prospect of running out of money before you die. Says Stein, "I don't just like high-dividend stocks, I love them. Long-term careful studies show that over lengthy periods, high-dividend stocks have better total return than either low- or no-dividend stocks, or the broad market generally."

With that in mind, Stein proposes a stripped-down, super-simplified, streamlined portfolio of just two higher-dividend-paying ETFs (Table 7.15). After thorough

> "Ultimately, the economy and profits determine what the stock market does, and there's nothing in the history of the past half century or so to suggest the economy or profits would be much different no matter which party is screwing up the government."
> —*Alan Abelson*

Table 7.15   Ben Stein's Two-Fund Retirement Portfolio with Staying Power

Asset Allocation	Name of Fund	Symbol
50%	StreetTRACKS Wilshire REIT	(RWR)
50%	iShares Dow Jones Select Dividend	(DVY)

testing, Stein and DeMuth conclude that for someone who lives 30 years after retirement withdrawing 4 to 5 percent annually and who compounds the balance, this portfolio would present almost no risk of running out of money. Instead, after 30 years the nest egg would multiply substantially. For further details go to Ben Stein's January 9, 2006 column on Finance. Yahoo.com ("A Retirement Portfolio With Staying Power").

7. Jim Cloonan (American Association of Individual Investors)

The individual investor anxious to learn has no better friend than the American Association of Individual Investors (AAII). It's an independent nonprofit association out of Chicago whose only agenda is to help the investor succeed. Its funds are limited and, therefore, so is its marketing, but it is a quality organization that turns out a quality product.

It does so through its publications, web site, educational software, national conference, and a chain of local AAII chapters across the country. Its outstanding monthly magazine, the *AAII Journal,* is included in the basic $29 annual membership. The giveaway price makes AAII a screaming buy.

With Maria Crawford Scott as its longtime editor, the *AAII Journal* is a special publication. It has a knack of selecting timely subjects that cry out for explanation in understandable language. It does so with the help of some of the best minds in Wall Street who contribute regularly. Among its most valuable features are the comprehensive 20- to 30-page "Guides," updated annually, on such topics as top mutual funds, top web sites, ETFs, discount brokers, taxes, and so on. Popular with readers are its model portfolios for stocks, mutual funds, and ETFs, which are monitored on an ongoing basis. Most widely followed is its Shadow Stock Portfolio. Initiated in 1993, it focuses on the less-explored micro cap value sector of the market and has compiled an outstanding record.

AAII also offers over 50 screens and a monthly stock advisory newsletter is based on the four screens that are working the best at the time, called the *Stock Superstars Report*. Whether an investor is a novice or a veteran, AAII is an invaluable resource.

It is the genius, passion, and entrepreneurial spirit of Chicago native James Cloonan, PhD, 76, that has fueled the growth of AAII. After doing some teaching, financial consulting, and heading a brokerage firm, Cloonan founded AAII in 1978. He believed that individual investors could outperform the popular averages if they had access to effective, unbiased investment education and the dedication to use it.

Helping investors achieve performance are Cloonan's model Shadow Stock and Mutual Fund portfolios, which are featured in the *Journal* as teaching tools. Committed to helping investors effectively manage their own assets for almost 30 years, AAII Chairman Cloonan continues to write articles for his 150,000 subscribers. The president of AAII is 20-year veteran John Markese, PhD, who also writes for the *Journal* on a broad range of investment topics and is often quoted in the financial press.

Many, Many More ETFs to Come In the August 2006 *Journal* (pages 19–22), James Cloonan introduced an experimental model portfolio of ETFs which we feature on these pages (see Table 7.16). However, it's important to first read Cloonan's explanation. It is an example of his precise, lucid, careful approach. He puts himself in the shoes of the investor and goes from there.

Table 7.16   AAII Model ETF Portfolio

Portfolio Allocation	Name of Fund	Symbol
20%	First Trust Dow Jones Select Micro Cap Index	(FDM)
20%	Power Shares FTSE RAFI US 1000	(PRF)
20%	Rydex S&P Mid Cap 400 Pure Value	(RFV)
20%	Rydex S&P Small Cap 600 Pure Value	(RZV)
20%	iShares Cohen & Steers Realty	(ICF)
Optional:		
	iShares Lehman 1–3 Year Treasury Bonds	(SHY)

This portfolio focuses on low-cost, smaller-cap, value oriented ETFs; the individual funds were selected to work as a portfolio. The model consists of four stock funds, one REIT and one short-term Treasury fund. . . . The latter two should be considered optional and would be used to control risk through diversification. Since every investor has a unique risk situation, the use of these two funds would vary. . . . I want to emphasize that the portfolio is experimental and the extent to which it succeeds won't be known until there is more history. . . . My choices were made from existing ETFs. It is a "modern" portfolio. I do not like cap-weighted funds because the largest capitalization stocks dominate the fund. . . . There are literally thousands more ETFs coming to market. . . . If new ones have advantages, I will make changes to the model. . . . If you choose to follow this portfolio with your own real money, please keep in mind that the portfolio is experimental and do so with only a small up-front amount at this point.

Interestingly, Cloonan has this to say about the future of ETFs: "There will be thousands of ETFs before long (now around 600), many of which will be virtual duplicates. Some will likely disappear because of lack of investor interest. When the smoke has cleared several years from now, ETFs may have as many investment dollars as conventional index mutual funds." Cloonan points out that his model ETF portfolio is "very long term," which is why the short-term bond index is "optional."

Go to AAII.com for details and updates. While there, check out AAII's Shadow Stock and Mutual Fund model portfolios. Both have excellent track records. The man behind them, James Cloonan, also put together the model in Table 7.16, which was initiated as of April 1, 2006.

> "The real measure of your wealth is how much you'd be worth if you lost all your money."
> —*Unknown*

8. *Burton Malkiel*

Who is the most famous person to teach at Princeton University? Main Street would likely answer Albert Einstein, but Wall Street would probably vote for the widely influential Burton Malkiel, currently a professor of economics at Princeton. Malkiel is a passionate proponent of the efficient market hypothesis (EMH). It's a theory that contends that stock prices reflect all publicly available information rapidly and, for the most part, accurately.

Malkiel believes that because it is so extremely difficult to outguess the collective wisdom of the market, investors are far better off in low-cost index funds. Picking stock winners, he contends, is more erratic than systematic. The randomness of the process insures that out of, say, 10,000 portfolio managers only a handful will beat the market year after year after year, and who they are is unknowable beforehand. There are always outperformers but the list looks different each year.

Though understandably not a favorite with the stock-picking Wall Street establishment, Malkiel's views are endorsed by a large cadre of the industry's leading thinkers. His message has undoubtedly helped to fuel the dramatic growth of indexing.

Before joining the Princeton faculty, Burton Malkiel, 75, had a varied career in finance. After receiving his MBA from Harvard and his doctorate from Princeton, he worked in the investment banking department of Smith Barney. He later served as a member of the President's Council of Economic Advisors and dean of the Yale School of Management (Harvard, Yale, Princeton—not bad). Malkiel has served on the boards of several corporations including Prudential Financial and, not surprisingly, the bastion of index funds, Vanguard (interestingly, John Bogle, a Princeton graduate, founded Vanguard in 1974, the year after Malkiel published *A Random Walk Down Wall Street*).

Rarely is a man's national reputation identified so closely with a single book. Mention the name Burton Malkiel and invariably *A Random Walk Down Wall Street* (W.W. Norton, 2007, 9th edition) comes immediately to mind. Attesting to its durability and influence, there have been nine updated editions since 1973, the latest just published. (In the 9th edition, Malkiel has added chapters on behavioral finance and investment for retirement.) The book's enduring appeal may be due partly to Malkiel's engaging style of writing but it is mostly because the book convincingly and lucidly gives investors a successful way to deal with an unpredictable market. *A Random Walk Down Wall*

Street is an investment classic because its message has stood the test of time. Over the years, the experience of investors has corroborated the truth of Malkiel's ideas.

Same Opinion as 30 Years Ago, Only Stronger You might think that with all the changes that have occurred in Wall Street the past three decades, and especially with the plethora of new financial instruments now available to the investor, Malkiel's views would also change. Not so. He says, "The message of the original edition was a very simple one: Investors would be far better off buying and holding an index fund than attempting to buy and sell individual securities or actively managed mutual funds. . . . Now, over thirty years later, I believe even more strongly in that original thesis."

Malkiel also sticks by what is probably his most widely quoted proposition: "The basic thesis of earlier editions was that the market prices stocks so efficiently that a blindfolded chimpanzee throwing darts at the *Wall Street Journal* can select a portfolio that performs as well as those managed by the experts. . . . Through the past thirty years that thesis has held up remarkably well. More than two-thirds of professional portfolio managers have been outperformed by the unmanaged S&P 500 Index." Malkiel today explains that the chimpanzee metaphor should not be taken literally. The better analogy, he says, is to throw a blanket over the stock pages and opt for a diversified basket of low-cost index funds.

The use of the S&P 500 Index is one area where Malkiel *has* modified his views. He says, "I now believe that if an investor is to buy only one U.S. index fund, the best general U.S. index to own is the broader Dow Wilshire 5000 stock index (WFIVX)—not the S&P 500." Malkiel gives two reasons—the popularity of the S&P 500 can lead to its components being overpriced, and the S&P 500 doesn't include enough smaller stocks. "Seventy-five years of market history confirm that, in the aggregate, smaller stocks have tended to outperform larger ones."

On the all-important subject of risk tolerance, Malkiel reduces it to basics: "It has become increasingly clear to me that one's capacity for risk-bearing depends importantly upon one's age and ability to earn income from non-investment sources. . . . The risk involved in most investments decreases with the length of time the investment can be held."

Table 7.17   Burton Malkiel: Asset Allocation for Different Age Groups

Age	Stocks[1]	Real Estate[2]	Bonds[3]	Cash[4]
Mid-twenties	65%	10%	20%	5%
Late thirties to early forties	55%	10%	30%	5%
Mid-fifties	45%	12.5%	37.5%	5%
Late sixties and beyond	25%	15%	50%	10%

1. Mid-twenties through mid-fifties: good representation in U.S. smaller growth companies; also, international stocks including emerging markets; late sixties: primarily high-quality U.S. stocks with some smaller growth companies.
2. Portfolio of REITs or real estate fund.
3. Zero coupon Treasury bonds; no-load GNMA funds or no-load high-grade bond fund; some TIPS; if bonds are to be held outside of a tax-favored retirement plan use tax-exempt bonds.
4. Money market fund or short-term bond fund (average maturity 1 to 1½ years).

Malkiel provides a model asset allocation life-cycle guide for different age groups (pages 350–351 of *A Random Walk Down Wall Street*). He also spotlights a specific Index Fund Portfolio for Aging Baby Boomers (page 362). He is careful to point out, however, that "no guide will fit every individual case. Any game plan will require some alteration to fit the individual circumstances."

Burton Malkiel: Life Cycle Investment Guide Malkiel believes foreign exposure is important. "A portfolio that is diversified internationally will tend to produce more stable returns from year to year than one invested only in domestic issues. . . . As investors age, they should start cutting back on riskier investments and start increasing the proportion of the portfolio committed to safer bonds and stocks that pay generous dividends such as REITs. A general rule of thumb for many investors is to make the proportion of bonds in one's portfolio almost equal to one's age." Recently Malkiel conceded that, due to longer life expectancy, the stock allocation for late sixties and over should be raised from 40 to 50 percent ("stocks" include REITs). See Table 7.17.

Burton Malkiel: Index Fund Portfolio for Aging Baby Boomers (Mid-Fifties) Regarding this portfolio (see Table 7.18), Malkiel says:

> Those who are not in their mid-fifties can use the same selections and simply change the weights to those appropriate for

their specific age group. . . . Those willing to accept more risk in the hope of greater reward could cut back on bonds. Those who need a steady income for living expenses could increase their holdings of real estate equities, which provide somewhat larger income. . . . I am assuming here that you hold most, if not all your securities in tax advantaged retirement plans. If not, you may prefer tax exempt bonds and tax managed index funds. . . . Since I am a director of Vanguard, I have included a number of non-Vanguard funds for you to choose from.

Malkiel's book provides additional information on these funds (all conventional mutual funds, not ETFs) plus an explanation of the role of tax managed funds.

Previously I have maintained that the oft-heard advice to investors—"do your homework"—is mostly meaningless. Instead of studying financial ratios and 10-Ks, I've suggested spending the time reading the great insights from the great books. A select group of investment classics have endured

> "If stock market experts were so expert, they would be buying stocks, not selling advice."
>
> —*Unknown*

Table 7.18   Burton Malkiel: Index Fund Portfolio for Mid-Fifties

Allocation	Asset Class	Name of Fund (Percentage)
5%	Cash	Fidelity Spartan Money Market Fund, TIAA-CREFF Money Market Fund, Vanguard Prime Money Market Fund, or a short-term bond fund (average maturity 1 to 1½ years)
37.5%	Bonds	Vanguard Total Bond Market Index Fund (32.5%) Treasury Inflation-Protected Securities (5%)
12.5%	Real Estate Equities	Vanguard REIT Index Fund
45%	Stocks	U.S. Stocks—Fidelity Spartan, T. Rowe Price, or Vanguard Total Stock Market Fund (34%) Developed International Markets—Fidelity Spartan, Dreyfus, or Vanguard International Index Fund (7.5%) Emerging International Markets—Vanguard Emerging Market Index Fund (3.5%)

because they truly enlighten. A productive way to do your homework is to take a *Random Walk* with Burton Malkiel.

9. John Bogle

In my opinion, the two people who have done the most for the individual investor in this country are Louis Rukeyser and John Bogle. Rukeyser educated investors for 32 years via his weekly TV show *Wall Street Week*. Bogle has championed the rights of the investor for most of his 56-year career.

When he was 22 years old in his senior year at Princeton, Bogle wrote a thesis arguing for low-fee mutual fund investing. Today, at the age of 78, more than half a century later, Bogle is still pounding the table on the issues that matter most to him—low fees, buy-and-hold investing, index funds, corporate abuse, and investors' rights.

Bogle's life exemplifies the very qualities he advocates for investors—conviction, commitment and persistence. "Press on" is his mantra. He warns that a well-diversified, low-cost portfolio of index funds doesn't provide insurance against rough seas. Like Rudyard Kipling ("If you can keep your head when all about you/are losing theirs . . ."), Bogle exhorts index fund investors to steel their resolve, stay the course, and then "be confident of earning a fair share of whatever long-term returns the market may provide" (remarks before Financial Analysts of Philadelphia, February 15, 2001).

Perhaps what is most impressive about Bogle is his ability to maintain such a high level of intensity, passion, and energy. His unwavering dedication to putting the odds in favor of those who *buy* Wall Street's products rather than those who *sell* them is reflected in a prodigious outpouring of words and opinion. His many articles, op-ed pieces, speeches, interviews, and books are carefully documented and archived on the Internet (johncbogle.com).

Because of his keen mind, his vision, his integrity, and his achievements, Bogle has attained a stature in the financial community few enjoy. This, despite the easy-to-understand opposition of the $11 trillion mutual fund industry. Accused by Bogle of not representing the best interest of their clients, mutual fund leaders sarcastically label him "Saint Jack" and strongly disagree with his mantra for passive investing.

The Wall Street marketing machine may disagree with Bogle but it's my guess that he is *respected* by friend and foe alike.

In doing my research on Bogle, the descriptive words that kept recurring were *pioneer, legend, revolutionary, tireless champion, titan of our age, fearless crusader, icon of indexing, father of index funds,* and *conscience of the mutual fund industry.* All this may or may not be a little much, but there's no doubt that millions of mutual fund investors are in his debt.

In a *Wall Street Journal* interview (March 7, 2007), columnist Jonathan Clements writes, "When it comes to the big issues, Jack Bogle is almost always right." In the Clements article, Bogle reveals a change in his thinking. He is now more partial to foreign stocks, partly because he sees a weakening of both the U.S. dollar and our position in the world community. He recommends up to a 20 percent allocation, equally divided between developed and emerging markets. Like so many other gurus, Bogle forecasts modest market returns in the decade ahead, averaging around 7 percent.

$20 Million versus $20 Billion Bogle was born in Montclair, New Jersey, in 1929. He attended Blair Academy, Princeton (magna cum laude in economics), and University of Pennsylvania. In 1951 he joined Wellington Management Company and later became its chairman. In 1974 he founded Vanguard Group in Valley Forge, Pennsylvania, which grew to become the second-largest mutual fund company in the world (next to Fidelity) and the undisputed leader in low-cost index funds.

He introduced the first index fund in 1976, the Vanguard 500 Index Fund which buys and holds the stocks that make up the S&P 500 Index. It has over $120 billion in assets. (Today, over 30 other mutual fund families have S&P 500–based index funds that are 10 years old or more). Bogle served as Vanguard's chief executive until 1996 and senior chairman until 2000, when he literally stepped down (his new office is one floor below where he was) to become president of the Bogle Financial Markets Research Center.

In 2004, *Time* magazine named him one of the world's 100 most powerful and influential people. In 1999 *Fortune* magazine designated him as one of the investment industry's four "giants of the 20th century." A complete list of all his awards, honors, and recognitions would fill pages.

What I think is particularly revealing is Bogle's personal financial rewards as compared to those of the head of Fidelity. It tells us a lot about just how much money can be made by selling mutual funds. Vanguard is an ultra cost conscious fund that's owned by its fund holders. Fidelity is a conventionally structured fund company whose profits accrue to its private owners. Founded in 1946 by Edward Crosby Johnson II, Fidelity has been around a lot longer than Vanguard. Even so, the difference in personal fortunes is striking. *Fortune* (January 20, 2003) estimated Bogle's net worth at around $20 million. *Forbes* (September 21, 2006) assigned a net worth of over $20 billion to the Johnson family, $7.5 billion to Edward Johnson III (77) and $13 billion to his daughter, Abigail (45).

In addition to his articles and speeches, Bogle has written six books, the most recent being *The Little Book of Common Sense Investing: The Only Way to Guarantee Your Fair Share of Stock Market Returns* (John Wiley & Sons, 2007). It is a concise summary of why the long-term investor should buy index funds. In his book *The Battle for the Soul of Capitalism* (Yale University Press, 2005), he focuses on the decline of business and ethical standards in corporate America, in investment America, and in mutual fund America. Other titles include *Bogle On Mutual Funds* (McGraw-Hill, 1993), *Common Sense on Mutual Funds* (John Wiley & Sons, 1999), *John Bogle on Investing: The First 50 Years* (McGraw-Hill, 2000), and *Character Counts: The Creation and Building of The Vanguard Group* (McGraw-Hill, 2002).

You Can Own the Sun When asked in an interview what the long-term investor should do and why, Bogle answered:

> Index the market, capture the market's return, get costs out of the system, be bored to death and have a comfortable retirement. . . . Talk to any Nobel laureate who has ever won the economics prize and he is going to tell you to index. Ask college professors of finance what they do and they'll say, "I index." . . . But we can't crank this "low return to the financial system, high return to the investor" into the mainstream of American

investing, because we have dreams of glory. We all think we're above average, and we have a mutual fund industry that has become a giant marketing system where the idea is to bring in the most money by fair means or foul.

(Interview on Frontline/PBS, February 7, 2006;
available at PBS.org)

Bogle is widely quoted because his advice is so sensible and because he speaks so often (about 60 speeches a year), a reflection of his fervor for indexing. In a speech where he compared superstar portfolio managers to comets that shine brightly in the heavens and then fade, Bogle said:

> So here is my simple conclusion: If you can't foretell the future, diversify. Stop taking your chances with comets that are all too often disguised as stars. Go right to the center of the universe and own the sun. If you can't consistently switch back and forth from growth to value (or large cap to small cap) at or near the half-dozen or so inflection points that will occur during an investment lifetime, just own the entire U.S. stock market. Own the stocks of every public corporation in America, weighted by their market capitalizations, and hold them forever—Warren Buffett's favorite holding period. . . . Owning the U.S. stock market for a lifetime through a low-cost, highly tax effective all-market index fund should pose extremely limited risk for those who have the courage to stay the course. I believe it is the ultimate winning strategy for the long term."

(Speech for Financial Analysts of Philadelphia,
February 15, 2001)

Bogle lives in Bryn Mawr, Pennsylvania, and is a twin, a squash player, and a philanthropist. He has long had a genetic heart condition and received a heart transplant in 1996. He has six children and 12 grandchildren who keep him busy setting up trusts. His son, John Jr., has his own investment firm in Wellesley, Massachusetts. He manages the Bogle Small Cap Growth Fund, which Morningstar calls one of its "favorites." It's the only mutual fund with the Bogle name.

For further information on Bogle himself and his speeches, articles, and books, put "John C. Bogle" or "Bogle Financial Markets Research Center" in a search box on your computer. You can also go to http://www.johncbogle.com. For a truly inspiring message, check out his October 23, 2006, speech, "The Battle for the Soul of Capitalism," delivered before the students of Immaculata University in Pennsylvania.

> "If you don't feel comfortable owning something for 10 years, then don't own it for 10 minutes."
> —*Warren Buffett*

John Bogle's Personal Holdings Why list John Bogle's personal holdings (Table 7.19)? The fund selections and asset allocations of a wealthy but still working 78-year-old man hardly qualify as a model portfolio for the typical investor. It's likely that what's right for you will be different from what you see here. But that doesn't mean you can't benefit from Bogle's thinking. If your portfolio includes a total market fund or a TIPS fund or a growth and income fund, you could do worse than own the same one that Bogle owns. You'll be following the judgment of the savviest of veterans who has spent a lifetime immersed in the world of index funds. Everyone in Wall Street espouses the virtues of transparency. Few apply it to their personal holdings. It behooves us to take advantage of Bogle's forthrightness.

Bogle's personal holdings reflect a special set of beliefs. He is committed to index funds but not to ETFs (Vanguard has close to 30 of them; see his Immaculata speech and his latest book, *The Little Book of Common Sense Investing,* for his views on ETFs). He prefers a total market index to the S&P 500 because of its broader coverage. He strongly favors capitalization-weighted, all-market funds over those that are fundamentally weighted. Although most are passively managed, he *does* own some actively managed or "enhanced" index funds, slightly tilted toward value and smallness. These include legacy funds like Wellington, Wellesley and Windsor which he has owned from the beginning. His largest single investment, as befits his conservatism and tax bracket, is Vanguard Limited-Term Tax-Exempt.

Like many investors, Bogle's holdings are divided between a tax-sheltered retirement plan and taxable accounts. Table 7.19 is a composite.

Table 7.19 John Bogle's Personal Holdings (Partial List)

Asset Allocation	Name of Fund	Symbol
60% Bonds	Vanguard Inflation-Protected Securities	(VIPSX)★
	Vanguard Intermediate Term Bond Index	(VBIIX)
	Vanguard Limited Term Tax Exempt	(VMLTX)
	Vanguard Intermediate Term Tax Exempt	(VWITX)
	(½ bonds, ½ stocks) Vanguard Tax Managed Balanced	(VTMFX)
40% Stocks	Vanguard Total Stock Market Index	(VTSMX)
	Vanguard 500 Index	(VFINX)
	Vanguard Extended Market Index	(VEXMX)
	Vanguard Tax Managed Capital Appreciation	(VMCAX)
	Vanguard Growth & Income	(VQNPX)
	Vanguard Prime Cap Fund	(VPMCX)
	Vanguard U.S. Growth	(VWUSX)
	Vanguard Explorer	(VEXPX)
	Vanguard Wellington	(VWELX)
	Vanguard Wellesley Income	(VWINX)
	Vanguard Windsor	(VWNDX)

★Every Vanguard Fund has an "Admiral" class, which offers slightly less expense but requires cash and longevity minimums. Bogle owns the Admiral class in each of his funds. These symbols represent the more widely held non-Admiral class.

Sources: "John Bogle Walks The Talk" by Dawn Smith (SmartMoney.com, 11/22/00); "An Inside Look at Jack Bogle's Portfolio" by Sue Stevens (Morningstar.com, 04/06/06); and a personal interview (12/07/06).

His combined asset allocation is about 60 percent bonds and 40 percent stocks. Ten years ago he was about 25 percent bonds and 75 percent stocks. Bogle's sizable holdings are an example of the good things that can happen when someone invests regularly in common stocks over many years. Bogle started in 1951 putting $37.50 each month (15 percent of his $250 monthly salary) into his company's tax-deferred retirement plan and, as his income grew, he stayed with it.

Vanguard Star Fund (VGSTX): A Fund of Funds Only one of Vanguard's more than 150 mutual funds (outside of its stable of life cycle/target retirement funds) is a fund of funds. It's called the Star Fund

Table 7.20 Vanguard Star Fund (VGSTX) Asset Allocation as of 12/31/06

Asset Class	Allocation
Short-term reserves	5.6%
Bonds	34.0%
Stocks	59.8%
Other	.5%

Vanguard Star Fund: Fund Holdings	
Name of Fund	Portfolio Allocation
Vanguard Windsor II Fund	16.25%
Vanguard Long Term Investment Grade Fund	12.32%
Vanguard GNMA Fund	12.42%
Vanguard Short Term Investment Grade Fund	12.30%
Vanguard Windsor Fund	8.87%
Vanguard PRIMECAP Fund	6.85%
Vanguard U.S. Growth Fund	6.86%
Vanguard Morgan Growth Fund	6.91%
Vanguard International Value Fund	6.36%
Vanguard International Growth Fund	6.38%
Vanguard Explorer Fund	4.31%
Other	.17%
	100.00%

(see Table 7.20). It consists of 11 other Vanguard funds—a diversified, low-cost group of funds that are roughly 60 percent stocks and 40 percent bonds. It could easily qualify as a model buy-and-hold, core portfolio.

It is actively managed with a track record going back to 1985. Says Morningstar, "With its small cap and international exposure, Star represents exceptional diversification in one package with strong returns and modest risk. It is a great option for the one-stop, hands-off investor" (Morningstar.com, September 18, 2006).

> "Whenever you find that you are on the side of the majority, it is time to reform."
>
> —*Mark Twain*

10. Charles Kirk

You've already read the comparison of Charles Kirk and Jim Cramer (Chapter 5), so you know that Kirk is near the top of my "people I most admire" list. He excels in four areas: (1) He has an uncanny feel for the market, which has produced an amazing (I use the word seldom) track record; (2) he is totally committed to perfecting his trading skills, working tirelessly to learn more and do even better; (3) he has a passion to share his insights with his readers in hopes of making them better traders, and has turned down lucrative money management opportunities so he can "follow his bliss" (Joseph Campbell); (4) he is modest, low-key, and quick to give credit to others, qualities more likely to be found in his hometown of Hugo, Minnesota, than on Wall Street.

Kirk's award-winning web site, TheKirkReport.com, is a financial blog with postings throughout the day. It's designed primarily for traders for whom it is a valuable resource. But his observations about investing in general, his long lists of links to all kinds of interesting stock market–related information, and his monthly Q&A sessions in which he responds candidly to subscriber questions and interviews leading professionals, make his web site as helpful as any out there for all investors.

In the November 2005 Q&A session, Kirk explained his approach: "Trading is my primary focus. So, over the past few years I've developed what I call a passive-aggressive retirement portfolio. It is passive in that I don't trade or actively manage it more than the absolute minimum, and it is aggressive because I've set the allocation so that I think it will produce significant returns on a consistent basis. So far it has done just that." The portfolio is actually a composite of the retirement accounts of both himself and his wife. Most retirement holdings are in Roth IRAs and represent roughly half of their assets (the other half is committed to trading). See Table 7.21.

It's interesting that someone as involved and as successful in the world of short-term trading invests half his money long-term. Says Kirk, "Few realize how complex the market really is. . . . There are always things to worry about as an investor, but, unlike traders, long-term investors have a key advantage—time. . . . Time heals all wounds, even those caused by inevitable recessions and bear markets." I am pleased that Kirk's long-term investment approach mirrors that advocated in this book—approximately 80 percent invested passively in index funds and 20 percent in actively managed vehicles.

Table 7.21   Charles Kirk: Target Long-Term Passive-Aggressive
Retirement Portfolio

Asset Allocation	Name of Fund	Symbol
U.S. Equities 40%		
10%	Rydex S&P Equal Weight	(RSP)
10%	Vanguard Value ETF	(VTV)
10%	Power Shares Zacks Micro Cap	(PZI)
10%	Vanguard Small Cap Value ETF	(VBR)
Foreign Equities 40%		
10%	iShares MSCI EAFE Index	(EFA)
10%	iShares MSCI EAFE Value Index	(EFV)
10%	Vanguard Emerging Markets Stock ETF	(VWO)
10%	WisdomTree International Small Cap Dividend	(DLS)
Sector Based ETFs 10%		
5%	PowerShares Water Resources	(PHO)
5%	StreetTRACKS Gold Shares (or possibly other sectors)	(GLD)
Individual Stocks 10%		
10%	(Target is 5 to 10 positions)	

"I'll Let You In on a Secret" Kirk's basic trading philosophy revolves around independence—doing your own homework, learning to think for yourself, and not relying on the opinion of others. He believes a retirement portfolio should be customized according to age, temperament, investment goals, skill levels, and financial circumstances. That's why, in revealing his personal holdings to his subscribers, he says, "No one should consider this a buy list of any sort." I include it with our other model portfolios because I believe it is impossible not to learn from the thinking of very, very smart people. (Check out his multiyear record). Not to mention that this portfolio is a living and breathing one, not theoretical. Just be sure to keep in mind the differences between Kirk's situation and your own.

Before we focus on Kirk's holdings, here's another plug for the lazy man portfolio concept (TheKirkReport.com, November 2005, Q&A). Kirk's strong endorsement shows how open he is to the ideas of others, despite his own expertise:

> My retirement portfolio is based, in part, on variations of the
> lazy portfolio approach advocated by others (Scott Burns,

William Bernstein, Bill Schultheis, Ted Aronson, David Swensen, Frank Armstrong, and Ben Stein). . . . If you don't have the inclination, desire or skills to pick good stocks/sectors, a basic lazy portfolio is a very smart way to go. And I'll let you in on a little secret—these portfolios will out-perform everything you'll find out there if you stick to them. In fact, I'll go so far as to say that over the long term, if you set up your portfolio in this (lazy man) manner, you'll beat 98% of the pros out there—including yours truly. Yes, it really is that simple."

In his retirement portfolio, Kirk maintains an 80/20 exposure. The 80 percent is in market-matching indexed positions. The remaining 20 percent is in more aggressive positions—individual stocks and sector-based ETFs—that have the potential for higher long-term rewards. By October 2006, he sharply reduced his individual stock holdings from 48 to 15 with plans to cut the total to 10. Not all are long-term holds.

Kirk doesn't hesitate to sell weaker stocks but he holds on to his good performers. "Letting winners run is a key strategy in long-term investing," he says. Kirk also uses stops religiously, for long-term positions as well as short-term, the placement depending on the volatility of the security.

Keep Your Powder Dry The primary objective of his retirement portfolio is to "stay up and slightly beat the overall market as measured by the S&P 500." As for structuring the portfolio, what's paramount to Kirk is keeping it simple and easy to manage, especially in light of his time constraints. With that in mind, he is in the process of streamlining his portfolio. Because he is impressed with some of the new ETFs available, he will add a few good ones (PowerShares and WisdomTree) to beef up his performance potential.

When will he do his selling and buying? Not surprisingly, Kirk uses technical tools to guide him. Specifically, he sells when his screens, charts, and gut tell him the market is overbought and buys when the market is oversold. Using the combination of various sentiment factors and moving averages, Kirk tries to put fresh cash to work in the portfolio at times when the majority of investors are selling. And when the market heats up, he'll take some money off the table. For example, in late October 2006, with the market on a three-month hot streak and the

Dow topping 12,000 for the first time, Kirk said he was comfortable raising cash and being patient for new opportunities. Similarly, on February 26, 2007, the day before the sharp 416-point one-day plunge in the Dow, Kirk titled his blog, "Keep Your Powder Dry" and advised subscribers he was 100 percent in cash.

Selling strength and buying weakness is a fine approach if you have a feel for the market like Charles Kirk. Dollar cost averaging would likely be a safer, more effective, and less stressful strategy. Even Kirk, who tries to time the market, concedes that dollar cost averaging will work for most investors. However, commission costs become a factor when steadily buying an ETF. So buying the ETF's equivalent in a conventional no-load mutual fund or using a low-commission online broker like Foliofn.com are ways to make dollar cost averaging doable.

In terms of long-term investments, Kirk focuses on companies that he thinks will be the major beneficiaries of future dominant trends, such as the growing need for clean water (water covers 70 percent of the earth's surface but only 3 percent is drinkable). In an April 10, 2007, posting, he writes about another enduring theme: "Clean energy in any form, including nuclear and solar, is a theme that will continue to remain in favor for the foreseeable future, so long as there is concern about global warming and increasing demand for energy. I don't see how either issue is going away any time soon. Like the water plays, I think we're only in the beginning stages of the trend."

Table 7.21 shows what Kirk's retirement portfolio will look like when he has finished implementing his planned target allocation. To see his retirement portfolio before these adjustments, go to TheKirkReport.com, November 2005 Q&A. To get a complete explanation for the updated 2007 portfolio presented here, check out his October 2006 Q&A. Go to his site for ongoing updates of his holdings. Table 7.21 is his planned target allocation—all ETFs.

Kirk does not include a fixed-income class but says he'll always have varying amounts of cash sitting in interest-earning money markets because of rebalancing, stops going off, waiting for weakness to buy, and so on.

> "Trying to minimize taxes too much is one of the great causes of really dumb mistakes in investing."
> —*Charlie Munger*

11. Jonathan Clements

London-born, Cambridge-educated, and Metuchen, New Jersey–based Jonathan Clements, 44, is one of the nation's premier financial journalists. He has written the *Wall Street Journal's* popular "Getting Going" personal finance column since October 1994. His books include *You've Lost It, Now What? How to Beat the Bear Market and Still Retire on Time* (Penguin Group, 2003). Prior to joining the *Journal* in 1990, he covered mutual funds for *Forbes*.

Clements' clipped but lucid writing style uncomplicates the complicated and delivers provocative thought and opinion. He is a stalwart champion of index funds. "Reams of statistics prove that most of the mutual fund industry's stock pickers fail to best the market. . . . Want surefire stock market winners? Index funds are as close as you will ever get" (*Wall Street Journal,* "Hang Tough," June 5, 2005).

Clements follows his own advice. In his *Wall Street Journal* September 15, 2004, column, "Eating His Own Cooking," he tells how he invests his own money. "In addition to college funds for my two kids, I have seven other accounts where I am investing for the long haul. All seven accounts are invested entirely in mutual funds, mostly index funds." He recommends three core funds and says that's really all you need. "Despite its delightful simplicity, I can't recall ever meeting an adviser who uses the three fund mix. In part, I suspect, advisers feel that to justify their fees, they have to advocate more complex portfolios."

When asked to assess his contribution to his millions of readers in a February 10, 2006, interview with AllThingsFinancial.com, Clements answered, "My greatest value lies in providing readers with the reassurance that, yes, saving diligently and diversifying with index funds really is the best long run strategy." I believe Clements is one of our most insightful writers on the financial scene, which is why he's quoted so often in this book.

Jonathan Clements' Three-Fund Global Portfolio Clements writes, "Despite the trend toward increasing complexity, all you really need to build a globally diversified index portfolio are three funds: a 'total market' index fund that tracks the broad U.S. stock market, a foreign stock index fund and a bond index fund. [Table 7.22] shows a

Table 7.22 Jonathan Clements' Three-Fund Global Portfolio

Asset Allocation	Name of Fund	Symbol
45%	T. Rowe Price Total Equity	(POMIX)
40%	T. Rowe Price U.S. Bond	(PBDIX)
15%	T. Rowe Price International Equity	(PIEQX)

simple three-fund portfolio built with T. Rowe Price Group funds. But you can put together a similar mix at Fidelity Investments, Charles Schwab, Vanguard or Barclays iShares ETFs" (*Wall Street Journal,* June 15, 2005). The percentage allocations are from his *Wall Street Journal* column of March 11, 2007.

Jonathan Clements' Expanded Portfolio Clements also confesses to being "intrigued by a growing array of smaller asset classes which can goose long run returns" but he would still have 70 to 80 percent of his portfolio in the three core holdings just mentioned. In a June 4, 2006, *Wall Street Journal* column, he suggests eight asset classes with specific fund candidates. However, you'll note in the following portfolio Clements assigns a percentage allocation to only five of the eight asset classes. In his own portfolio he has 25 percent earmarked for bonds but expects to increase that to 35 to 40 percent by retirement.

When Clements makes suggestions, they are just that; they are not rigid and they include numerous alternatives (see Table 7.23). "The precise percentages are not as important as the willingness to stay with them." In his September 17, 2006, *Wall Street Journal* column, Clements reiterates his strong support of the three-core-fund portfolio ("in a sea of index funds, a core triumvirate") but does acknowledge the new breed of fundamentally based index funds. He

> "When a fellow says it ain't the money but the principle of the thing, it's the money."
>
> —*Kim Hubbard*

says, "I am not going to object too strenuously but I wouldn't stray too far from a market-weight approach." If you do, Clements warns of possible bigger tax bills, higher costs, and greater risks, especially with the highly specialized industry sector funds that can boom and bust and take decades to recover.

Table 7.23   Jonathan Clements' Suggested (but not etched in stone)
Eight Asset Class Index Fund Portfolio

Allocation	Asset Class	Name of Fund	Symbol
	U.S. Stocks		
25–30%	Foreign Stocks	Fidelity Spartan International,	(FS1IX)
		T. Rowe Price International Equity, or	(PIEQX)
		Vanguard Total International Stock	(VGTSX)
	High Quality U.S. Bonds		
	Inflation- Indexed Treasury Bonds	Fidelity Inflation-Protected Bond, Vanguard Inflation-Protected Securities, or www. TreasuryDirect.gov	(FINPX) (VIPSX)
5%	Gold	American Century Global Gold	(BGEIX)
5%	REITs	Vanguard REIT Index	(VGSIX)
5%	Commodities	Pimco Commodity Real Return Strategy "D"	(PCRDX)
5%	Emerging Markets	Vanguard Emerging Markets Stock Index	(VEIEX)

12. Paul Merriman

Paul Merriman, 64, has been managing money for clients since 1983 when he founded the investment advisory firm Merriman Capital Management in Seattle, Washington. He is one of the nation's leading authorities on mutual funds. His thinking is accessible through his web site FundAdvice.com, his radio broadcast, workshops, videos, and his book, *Live It Up Without Outliving Your Money: Ten Steps to a Perfect Retirement Portfolio* (John Wiley & Sons, 2005).

Throughout his career, Merriman has pounded the table on the crucial importance of asset allocation. "Your choice of asset classes has far more impact on your results than any other investment decision you can make. . . . It's far more important than exactly when you buy and sell those assets and much more important than finding the very 'best' stock, bond or mutual fund" (FundAdvice.com, "The Ultimate Buy-And-Hold Strategy," February 22, 2007).

How do you know which asset classes to choose? Regarding stocks, he writes on FundAdvice.com, "Researchers have found that over long periods of time, the best returns are likely to come from having just the right balance of large-cap and small-cap stocks, value stocks and growth stocks, U.S. stocks and international stocks." As for bonds, he makes this observation:"The 60/40 split between equities and bonds is the way large institutional investors traditionally allocate their assets. The equities provide growth while the bonds provide stability and income. It's not the right balance for all investors. Many young investors don't need any bonds in their portfolios. And many older folks may want 70 percent in bonds or more. But the 60/40 ratio is nevertheless a very good long-term investment mix. It's the industry standard and that's what we'll use."

Merriman recommends a wide range of model buy-and-hold portfolios on his web site. He uses mostly traditional, no-load, index mutual funds but also includes an all-ETF portfolio. Some are balanced portfolios, others are all stocks. For each type, the investor has a choice of an all–Vanguard fund portfolio or all Fidelity or all T. Rowe Price. Since Schwab offers funds from many families, the Schwab portfolio also includes non-Schwab funds.

Merriman's preferred mutual fund manager, however, is Dimensional Fund Advisors (DFA), at DFAUS.com, a favorite of many investment advisers because of its outstanding track record and impressive board of

Table 7.24 Paul Merriman: Balanced Buy-and-Hold Portfolio (Schwab)

Portfolio Allocation	Name of Fund	Symbol
6%	Schwab 1000	(SNXFX)
6%	Soundshore Fund	(SSHFX)
6%	Schwab Small Cap Index	(SWSMX)
6%	Heartland Value Plus	(HRVIX)
6%	Cohen Steers Realty Shares	(CSRSX)
6%	Schwab International Index	(SWINX)
6%	Dodge and Cox International Stock	(DODFX)
6%	Lazard International Small Cap Open	(LZSMX)
6%	Tocqueville International Value	(TIVFX)
6%	American Century Emerging Market	(TWMIX)
20%	American Century Government Bond	(CPTNX)
12%	American Century Short-Term Government	(TWUSX)
8%	American Century Inflation-Adjusted Bond	(ACITX)

directors (which includes Rex Sinquefield, Eugene Fama, and Roger Ibbotson). The drawback is that DFA does not deal directly with the individual investor but is available only to institutional investors and the clients of a select list of financial planners and investment advisers.

Tables 7.24 through 7.27 are four of Merriman's recommended buy-and-hold model portfolios. Two of them are broken down by asset class

Table 7.25 Paul Merriman: ETF Balanced Buy-and-Hold Portfolio

Portfolio Allocation	Name of Fund	Symbol
6%	S&P 500 SPDRs	(SPY)
6%	Vanguard Value ETF	(VTV)
6%	iShares Russell Microcap Index	(IWC)
6%	Vanguard Small Cap Value ETF	(VBR)
6%	Vanguard REITs Index ETF	(VNQ)
6%	iShares MSCI EAFE	(EFA)
6%	iShares MSCI EAFE Value Index	(EFV)
12%	WisdomTree International Small Cap Div Fund	(DLS)
6%	Vanguard Emerging Market ETF	(VWO)
20%	iShares Lehman 7–10 year	(IEF)
12%	iShares Lehman 1–3 year	(SHY)
8%	iShares Lehman TIPS Bond	(TIP)

Table 7.26 Paul Merriman: Ultimate Buy-and-Hold Portfolio

Portfolio Allocation	Type of Fund
40%	Short/Intermediate Term Bonds
6%	S&P 500 Index
6%	U.S. Micro Cap
6%	U.S. Small Cap Value
6%	U.S. Large Cap Value
6%	REITs
6%	International Large Cap
6%	International Large Cap Value
6%	International Small Cap
6%	International Small Cap Value
6%	Emerging Markets

Table 7.27   Paul Merriman: Perfect 401(k) Plan

Fixed Income	Broadly diversified bond fund, or Guaranteed Income contract fund
Equities	At least one low-cost index fund in each of the following asset classes:
Portfolio Allocation	**Type of Fund**
10%	U.S. large cap stocks
10%	U.S. large cap value stocks
10%	U.S. small cap stocks
10%	U.S. small cap value stocks
10%	U.S. real estate stocks
10%	International large cap stocks
10%	International large cap value stocks
10%	International small cap stocks
10%	International small cap value stocks
10%	Emerging markets stocks

only; the other two include both asset class and the specific funds recommended within each class. Go to FundAdvice.com for further explanation and details, including back-tested annualized returns and latest updates.

Paul Merriman's Ultimate Buy-and-Hold Portfolio

"We don't use the word *ultimate* lightly. We don't claim this is the best investment strategy in the world. But it's the best one that we know. . . . I believe almost every buy-and-hold investor can use it to increase returns and reduce risk. . . . It is easy to apply using low-cost, tax-efficient, no-load index funds. . . . The Ultimate Buy-and-Hold Strategy creates a sophisticated asset allocation model with worldwide diversification and the addition of value stocks and small-cap stocks to a traditional large-cap growth stock portfolio. . . . We did not invent this strategy. It evolved from the work of many people over a long period, including some winners and nominees of the Nobel Prize in economics" (FundAdvice .com, March 28, 2006).

Paul Farrell includes this portfolio as one of his featured Lazy Portfolios. Check out his column "Lazy Portfolios 2Q update" (MarketWatch.com, July 9, 2007) for the latest tweaking in Merriman's 11 fund Ultimate Portfolio.

Paul Merriman's Perfect 401(k) Plan

Most 401(k)s fall far short of the following ideal plan. Too often they contain actively managed funds with high expenses and sometimes with sales loads. . . . Few plans offer all the essential asset classes. . . . You can try to persuade the trustees of your plan to offer better options. . . . Among the keys to success are the following: contribute as much as you can regularly; *manage your risk by adjusting the bond part of your portfolio (less risk equals more bonds);* keep your expenses low; invest in index funds that own small companies, value stocks and foreign companies and remember the most popular, well-known and "safest" companies don't make the best long-term investments.

(paulmerriman.com, July 21, 2005)

For anyone looking for 401(k) guidance, there's little you won't find at the web site 401kHelp .com, a service of Merriman Capital Management.

> "If past history was all there is to the game, the richest people would be librarians."
>
> —*Warren Buffett*

13. Timothy Middleton

Based in Short Hills, New Jersey, Timothy Middleton writes a widely read weekly column for MSNMoney.com focusing mostly on mutual funds. He also does commentary on CNBC's *Squawk Box* and WCBS radio in New York City. He was a former mutual fund columnist for the *New York Times* and authored "Abreast of the Market" for the *Wall Street Journal Europe*. A financial journalist for over 25 years, he was twice nominated for the Pulitzer Prize in investigative journalism. His profile of Pimco's Bill Gross, *Bond King,* was published by John Wiley in 2004.

Middleton is one of a band of bold writers who are willing to recommend stocks, funds, model portfolios, and so on, knowing they're going to have to revisit those recommendations, right or wrong, in future columns. In addition to the buy-and-hold portfolios recommended here, he also monitors an all-ETF portfolio that he started in November 2003. It can't be labeled "buy-and-hold" because he tweaks it regularly. But he tells his readers exactly when, what, and why, so everything is transparent. Go to MSNMoney.com and put "Middleton" in the search box for the current status of his monitored ETF portfolio.

Timothy Middleton's Four–Sector Fund Buy-and-Hold Portfolio Middleton believes that a portfolio that is hostage to the S&P 500 is a recipe for red ink. "There's nothing wrong with the S&P 500 index unless you think it can be the foundation of your financial future. It can't. It can only play a supporting role. If you want to build a portfolio you won't have to touch for the next 25 years, buy sector funds that invest in financial services, health care, leisure and technology" (Timothy Middleton, MSNMoney.com, August 16, 2005). Middleton recommends accessing these favorite four either through sector mutual funds (Fidelity is the leader along with Rydex, ProFunds, and others) or ETFs. See Tables 7.28 and 7.29. (The latter uses the same sectors as Table 7.28.)

Timothy Middleton's Monitored ETF Portfolio The all-ETF portfolio shown in Table 7.30 was launched in November 2003. It has compiled a good track record. But, unlike the two preceding portfolios, this is not a buy-and-hold ensemble. Middleton tweaks this portfolio from time

Table 7.28   Middleton: Four-Fund Buy-and-Hold Portfolio via Mutual Funds

Portfolio Allocation	Name of Fund	Symbol
25%	Fidelity Select Financial Services	(FIDSX)
25%	Fidelity Select Health Care	(FSPHX)
25%	Fidelity Select Leisure	(FDLSX)
25%	Fidelity Select Technology	(FSPTX)

Table 7.29   Middleton: Four-Fund Buy-and-Hold Portfolio via ETFs

Portfolio Allocation	Name of Fund	Symbol
25%	Vanguard Financial ETF	(VFH)
25%	Health Care SPDR	(XLV)
25%	PowerShares Leisure & Entertainment	(PEJ)
25%	iShares Goldman Sachs Technology	(IGM)

Table 7.30 Middleton: Monitored "Play It Safe" Portfolio

Portfolio Allocation	Name of Fund	Symbol
13.5%	S&P 500 Spiders	(SPY)
12.7%	PowerShares FTSE RAFI US 1000	(PRF)
9.8%	NASDAQ 100 Trust	(QQQQ)
10.9%	iShares Russell 2000	(IWM)
5.9%	iShares Goldman Nat Resources	(IGE)
20.1%	iShares MSCI EAFE	(EFA)
9.9%	iShares Lehman Aggregate Bond	(AGG)
4.9%	iShares C & S Realty	(ICF)
12.2%	Schwab Investors MMF (Money Market)	

to time when he believes changes should be made. Changes, and the reasons for them, are explained in his column, so it's easy to follow.

> "Wall Street's favorite scam is pretending luck is skill."
> —*Ron Ross, PhD*

Check out the rationale behind the holdings in Table 7.30 and a track record update at MSNMoney.com ("A Play-It-Safe Portfolio for 2007," December 26, 2006).

14. Frank Armstrong III

Frank Armstrong is an independent investment adviser. His financial planning firm, Investor Solutions, is located in Coconut Grove, Florida. His book, *The Informed Investor: A Hype-Free Guide to Constructing a Sound Financial Portfolio* (American Management Association, 2002) is included on a list of 11 books labeled by *BusinessWeek Online* as all-time "Must Reads for Investors." On that list he joins such heavyweights as Benjamin Graham, Burton Malkiel, Jeremy Siegel, Andrew Tobias, and Phillip Fisher. The book's back cover says, "Armstrong detests Wall Street's steep commissions and high fees. He offers no-nonsense advice for evaluating mutual funds . . ."

Armstrong uses his index fund expertise in the supervision of 401(k) plans. He has created a series of what he calls life-cycle strategies for his clients. These range from 100 percent equities for youthful employees to 40 percent equities/60 percent fixed income for those approaching retirement. He is a strong believer in international exposure and also

Table 7.31   Frank Armstrong's Ideal Index Fund Portfolio

Portfolio Allocation	Name of Fund	Symbol
31.00%	Vanguard Total International Stock	(VGTSX)
30.00%	Vanguard Short-Term Bond	(VBISX)
9.25%	Vanguard Small Cap Value	(VISVX)
9.25%	Vanguard Value	(VIVAX)
8.00%	Vanguard REIT	(VGSIX)
6.25%	Vanguard Small Cap Growth	(VISGX)
6.25%	Vanguard 500 Index	(VFINX)

overweights small and value stocks because studies have shown they outperform large-growth companies over long periods.

Like Paul Merriman, Armstrong favors the use of index funds from the exclusive firm Dimensional Fund Advisors (DFA) for his clients. These funds are only available to institutions and clients of approved financial advisers. However, when asked by MSNMoney.com columnist Timothy Middleton to put together a portfolio of publicly accessible funds designed to deliver the best returns with the least risk, he came up with the seven funds shown in Table 7.31.

Armstrong says this is as close to an ideal portfolio as you can get using widely available index funds. (Although he is a DFA fan, he will often use index mutual funds or ETFs if he can get the same coverage at a lower cost.) Says columnist Timothy Middleton, "You can put this mutual fund 'smoothie' in the freezer and take it out years later, and it will still be fresh" (Timothy Middleton, MSNMoney.com, October 11, 2005). The only variable in this portfolio would be the percentage of bonds (30 percent) versus stocks. The more risk averse, the higher the percentage of bonds. For more about Armstrong and his approach to investing, see InvestorSolutions.com.

> "You can learn from your mistakes but it's better to learn from someone else's mistakes."
> —Warren Buffett

15. Jim Lowell

Jim Lowell is a leading expert on the subjects of the Fidelity family of funds and exchange-traded funds. He is a prolific and fluent writer. He is the ETF columnist for *Forbes* magazine and a monthly columnist for Marketwatch.com. He's been giving independent advice on Fidelity funds since 1998 in his monthly newsletter, *Fidelity Investor*. He is also the editor of two ETF publications, *The Forbes ETF Advisor* and *The ETF Trader* from Marketwatch. He is the author of *Smart Money Moves* (Penguin, 2000), *Investing from Scratch* (Penguin, revised December, 2006), and *What Every Fidelity Investor Needs to Know* (John Wiley & Sons, 2007). Working out of Needham, Massachusetts, Lowell also lectures on philosophy and religion and is an avid sport fisherman.

Writing in a Marketwatch.com column titled "Spring Portfolio Planting," he says, "To help you sow the seeds of growth for your own portfolio harvest, I'm presenting a diversified portfolio of exchange-traded funds. I'm not simply a believer in the principle of diversification, but an active personal and professional proponent of it.... Once sown, the seeds of this eight ETF portfolio ought to

> "If you don't know who you are, the stock market is an expensive place to find out."
> —*George Goodman*

provide growth for many seasons to come." With the emphasis on growth, Lowell includes only stocks and no bonds in this particular portfolio. See Table 7.32, and go to the Marketwatch.com (April 3, 2006) web site for further details.

Table 7.32 Jim Lowell: The Sower's Growth Portfolio of Eight ETFs

Big-Caps	40%	Symbol
10%	Diamonds Trust	(DIA)
15%	iShares DJ U.S. Total Market	(IYY)
7.5%	Fidelity NASDAQ Composite	(ONEQ)
7.5%	Power Shares Dynamic Market	(PWC)
Mid-Caps	**15%**	
15%	Mid Cap SPDR Trust	(MDY)
Small-Caps	**10%**	
10%	iShares Russell 2000	(IWM)
Foreign	**35%**	
25%	iShares MSCI EAFE	(EFA)
10%	iShares MSCI Emerging Markets	(EEM)

16. Andrew Tobias

I am a big fan of Andrew Tobias, 60, often called the dean of U.S. personal finance writers. He is a very smart man, as modest as he is bright, who uses insight, humor, and engaging prose to convey rock-solid guidance on all things money related. T.S. Perić, the editor of *Managing Small Business,* says, "If financial advice is what you're looking for, Tobias is the king."

When students ask me what one investment book they should read, my unhesitating answer is Andrew Tobias' *The Only Investment Guide You'll Ever Need* (Harcourt Books, paperback, revised 2005). It's on most lists of top 10, must-read investment books and, over the years, has sold over a million copies. An entertaining, fun read (the dedication reads, "To my broker—even if he has, from time to time, made me just that"), it combines simplicity and wisdom. In both his *Guide* book and his web site (AndrewTobias.com), Tobias offers sound, perceptive advice that's easy to digest because it's served with such a light touch. On the subject of investing, if my opinion differs from Tobias, I have serious second thoughts.

An MBA from Harvard, Tobias has written articles for most of the nation's major business publications. He's also authored some dozen books including three that made the *New York Times* best-seller list. Subjects of his books include the Revlon story, auto insurance reform, and the youth-targeted marketing of tobacco companies. His daily column on AndrewTobias.com deals mostly with three subjects: money, gay issues, and national politics (he's been the treasurer of the Democratic National Committee since 1999 but admits having quite a few Republican friends).

Three-Hundred-Pound Jockeys A recurring theme on his web site is his strong belief that investors should opt for index funds, assuming they should be in the market at all. Aiming to keep it simple, he believes diversification can be achieved with just a few index funds. He believes they should be bought on a dollar-cost-averaging basis and rebalanced periodically.

Writing about their competitive advantage, he says index funds are like "thoroughbreds with 20 pound jockeys on their backs when all the other horses in the race have 100, 200 and even 300 pound jockeys. . . . I think most people should do most of their stock market investing via a steady program of buying U.S. and international index funds, month in and month out, leaving, at most, a relatively small kitty to be managed on your own, whether it be for the tax control it gives you ... or for the sheer fun of it." (AndrewTobias.com, February 17, 2005). Tobias is partial to Vanguard index funds. "Low expenses and low tax exposure all but guarantee you will do better than most of your friends who try harder."

Andrew Tobias' The Only Investment Portfolio You'll Ever Need "The simplest way to outperform most amateurs and professionals in most years—especially after tax considerations are included—is to buy an index fund with a very low expense ratio, like the two Vanguard index funds described below: one that owns practically the entire U.S. stock market and one that does the same for the rest of the planet." (*The Only Investment Guide You'll Ever Need,* page 267).

Tobias is also a strong believer in TIPS as protection against future inflation. In a column titled "Where to Put Your Money Now" (AndrewTobias.com, August 16, 2004), he reveals that he owns TIPS in his own retirement plan as "a long-term core holding." In his book he gives a lucid explanation of all the fine points involved in owning TIPS (pages 84–86). He says, "The Vanguard Inflation-Protected Securities fund is a solid choice for TIPS," but offers an ETF, the iShares Lehman TIPS Bond Fund as a possible alternative.

His bottom-line advice to investors: "If you're in it for the long haul, investing something every month via one or two or three Vanguard index funds, keep it up. And hope the market goes *down,* so you can buy future shares at cheaper prices." Tobias doesn't specify allocation percentages. (As a daily reader of his web site, I get the feeling, and it's only a guess, that he would be comfortable with one-third in each fund, perhaps shifting to a 50-25-25 allocation [50 percent TIPS bonds] as retirement approaches.) See Table 7.33.

> "In investing, what is comfortable is rarely profitable."
> —*Robert Arnott*

Table 7.33   Andrew Tobias' Simple But Far-Reaching Monthly Accumulation Portfolio

Fund	Symbol
Vanguard Total Stock Market Index Fund	(VTSMX)
Vanguard Total International Stock Index Fund	(VGTSX)
Vanguard Inflation-Protected Securities Fund	(VIPSX)

17. *Standard & Poor's* **The Outlook**

Probably the surest test of the value of a service or product is its staying power. By that measure, *The Outlook* must be doing something right. It's been dispensing advice weekly for 79 years, making it the oldest investment newsletter in the country (Babson–United ceased publication in 2001; Richard Russell's *Dow Theory Letters,* launched in 1958, is the oldest written by one person).

The Outlook is owned by Standard & Poor's, best known for its widely followed market indexes, its bond and stock rating services, and as a provider of independent investment information. Research from Standard & Poor's is often featured on *BusinessWeek Online* (BusinessWeek .com) because both S&P and *BusinessWeek* are owned by the same company, McGraw–Hill.

The March 21, 2007, issue of *The Outlook* spotlights a model ETF portfolio of eight funds (see Table 7.34). The S&P investment policy committee monitors the asset allocations in the portfolio on an ongoing basis. Not surprisingly, the U.S. stock portion of the portfolio mirrors three different Standard & Poor's indexes. The balance of the portfolio, foreign stocks and bonds, are represented by six Barclays ETFs known as iShares. For further information on the model ETF portfolio go to www.outlook.standardandpoors.com. The 16-page *Outlook* is published four times a month ($298 per year; (800) 852-1641).

Table 7.34 Standard & Poor's Model ETF Portfolio

	U.S. Stocks	**40%**	
34%	Large Cap Blend	S&P 500 SPDR	(SPY)
4%	Mid Cap Blend	S&P 400 Mid Cap SPDR	(MDY)
2%	Small Cap Blend	iShares S&P Small Cap 600	(IJR)
	Foreign Stocks	**20%**	
13%	International	iShares MSCI EAFE	(EFA)
3%	Japan	iShares MSCI Japan	(EWJ)
4%	Emerging Markets	iShares MSCI Emerging Markets	(EEM)
	Bonds	**25%**	
20%	U.S. Debt	iShares Lehman Aggregate	(AGG)
5%	U.S. Short-Term Debt	IShares Lehman 1–3 Year Treasury	(SHY)
	Cash	**15%**	
15%		U.S. 6-Month Treasury Bills	

Accompanying the model portfolio is this reminder from *The Outlook* on the importance of rebalancing:

Many investors dislike rebalancing because it means selling winners and buying losers. But S & P believes that is the wrong way to think about it. Rebalancing is a way to force yourself to sell high and buy low, the primary tenet of successful investing.... We advise rebalancing all of your investments at least once a year.

> "Whatever your opinion, you can always find an historical analogy to support it."
> —*Unknown*

18. John Wasik

John Wasik is one of the nation's leading personal finance journalists. He's won numerous awards for his columns and investigative reporting. He lectures, guests on radio and TV, and writes books, 10 in all. They include *The Kitchen-Table Investor* (Owl Books, 2001), *The Bear-Proof Investor* (Owl Books, 2002), and *The Merchant of Power,* a profile of Sam Insull (Palgrave Macmillan, 2006). A resident of Lake County, Illinois, Wasik is probably best known for his weekly personal finance column for *Bloomberg News* which reaches some 400 newspapers on five continents.

On the day he turned 50, July 2, 2007, Wasik wrote the following on Bloomberg.com: "My goal is to set aside 15 to 25 percent of my gross income every year (he has 2 daughters under 12) ... my speculative, high-rolling days are behind me ... I'm interested in beating inflation with a mostly passive diversified portfolio. My inflation hedge is a position in TIPS (Treasury Inflation Protected Securities) and commodities through the Pimco Commodity Real Return Strategy Fund. . . . I try not to pay more than .50 percent annually in management expenses."

John Wasik's Autopilot Nano Investment Plan In a column titled "Stop Worrying and Download the Nano Investment Plan" (www.bloomberg.com, January 2, 2006), Wasik writes:

"What's tiny about the Nano plan are the expenses, the number of funds in it and the amount of brainpower and emotional energy

"The key to understanding financial markets is the unexpected.
We expect all swans to be white
and are shocked when a black
swan swims by. In spite of the
empirical record, we continue to
project into the future as if we
were good at it."
— *Nassim Nicholas Taleb*

you need to keep it running
in all kinds of market cycles. In
short, it pretty much runs itself,
but you have to give it a jump-
start. The Nano plan employs
just a handful of index or
exchange-traded funds to cover
virtually the entire world of
bond and stock markets. . . .
They provide a neat, tidy pack-
age. (Disclosure: I own several of these funds in my retirement portfolio) . . . The following [Table 7.35] is a streamlined Nano plan where
a conservative, boiler plate allocation would be 20 percent in each
fund. . . . Those close to retirement might want to take less risk and
have less in stocks and more in inflation-protected securities,
or TIPS."

19. Richard Jenkins

Richard Jenkins is editor-in-chief of MSNMoney.com, one of the biggest and most popular investment web sites. Prior to joining MSN
Money in 1996, he spent 17 years at newspapers in southern California,
including a stint as news editor of the business section of the *Los Angeles
Times*. Popular MSN Money columnists who work under Jenkins
include Jim Jubak, Jon Markman, Liz Weston, M. P. Dunleavey, and Tim
Middleton.

On March 15, 2004, Jenkins started an all-ETF portfolio for investors with relatively small amounts of money to invest. His approach is to

Table 7.35 John Wasik's Nano Investment Plan

Portfolio Allocation	Name of Fund	Symbol
20%	Vanguard Total Stock Market Index ETF	(VTI)
20%	Vanguard Total International Stock Index	(VGTSX)
20%	Vanguard REIT ETF	(VNQ)
20%	iShares Lehman TIPS Bond	(TIP)
20%	iShares Lehman Aggregate Bond	(AGG)

Table 7.36   Richard Jenkins' (MSN Money) $100 a Month
                 Simple ETF Strategy

Portfolio Allocation	Name of Fund	Symbol
33%	Vanguard Total Stock Market ETF	(VTI)
25%	iShares MSCI-EAFE	(EFA)
17%	iShares Lehman Aggregate Bond	(AGG)
17%	iShares Dow Jones U.S. Real Estate	(IYR)
8%	iShares Dow Jones U.S. Basic Materials	(IYM)

put as little as $100 a month in one of five diversified ETFs and then rotate to the others each month (the same strategy works for any amount of money). See Table 7.36.

Conventional wisdom is to avoid ETFs if you're buying them often and use index mutual funds instead because one charges commissions and the other doesn't. However, Jenkins gets around this by using Sharebuilder.com, an online broker that charges very low commissions with no minimum account size. Jenkins describes step-by-step the mechanics involved in his simple but apparently effective approach to successful investing. He includes examples of what your portfolio will look like after years 1 and 2 under certain scenarios. For complete details go to MSNMoney.com and search for "Start investing with just $100" (no date given). The following are excerpts from that article.

> The costs are low enough to make investing in small amounts practical, if not cheap. . . . Put your first $100 in a broadly diversified ETF that represents the entire stock market. Every month after that continue investing as much as you can, rotating your purchases among the 5 ETFs until you reach your target percentage for each one. Concentrating your purchase in a single ETF each month minimizes your commission costs. In the first year, commissions reduce the overall return by 4%, but that cost drops to 2% in the second year, 1.3% in the third year and 0.8% by the fifth year.

> Once your portfolio reaches a total value of at least $25,000— and it will—you'll want to switch your commodity allocation to PIMCO Commodity Real Return Strategy fund (PCRDX,

minimum initial investment $2,500) which more accurately captures the returns of the commodities futures market than a collection of stocks can.... The following portfolio puts extra weight on U.S. and foreign stocks where most of your growth is likely to come.... Bonds, the fixed-income asset class, give your portfolio extra stability in rough markets.... In fact, it's during bear markets that asset allocation really makes a difference.

Rebalancing should be done at least once a year. The basic idea is to keep your allocation close to the target by adding new money, rather than selling your winning funds which will generate a taxable profit. Add each month's $100 investment to whatever asset class is farthest below your target allocation. If they're all about equally in line, than start rotating through each of the five as you did in the beginning.... Succumbing to the temptation to guess what the next hot asset class will be is your surest ticket to mediocre returns. The key to success is discipline. Stick with your $100 monthly investment and this portfolio is likely to outperform the vast majority of mutual funds over the long haul.

> "What we have learned from history is that we haven't learned from history."
> —Benjamin Disraeli

For follow-up information go to MSNMoney.com and put "ETF expert portfolio" in the search box.

20. Kiplinger

The Washington D.C.–based Kiplinger organization has been publishing personal finance advice and business forecasts for over 80 years. Its stable of products includes magazines, newsletters, books, web sites, and software. Probably its two best-known publications are *The Kiplinger Letter* and *Kiplinger's Personal Finance* magazine (formerly *Changing Times*). The *Letter* dates back to 1923 and features business, economic, and political forecasts. The magazine, launched in 1947, attempts to provide its readers with the information they need to make smart decisions about their money. Apparently they've succeeded since *Personal Finance* is still going strong after 60 years. Like *Forbes*, the Kiplinger franchise is a family affair; Knight Kiplinger is the current editor-in-chief.

Table 7.37   Kiplinger's Five-Fund ETF Portfolio for Growth

Asset Allocation	Type of Fund	Name of Fund	Symbol
40%	Large U.S. Stocks	iShares S&P 500, or	(IVV)
		iShares Russell 3000	(IWV)
20%	Small U.S. Stocks	iShares Russell 2000	(IWM)
15%	Diversified Foreign Stocks	iShares MSCI EAFE	(EFA)
5%	Emerging Market Stocks	iShares MSCI Emerging Markets	(EEM)
10%	Corporate Bonds	iShares Corporate Bond	(LQD)
10%	Money Market Fund		

Table 7.38   Kiplinger's Five-Fund ETF Portfolio for Income

Asset Allocation	Type of Fund	Name of Fund	Symbol
30%	Large U.S. Stocks	IShares S&P 500, or	(IVV)
		IShares Russell 3000	(IWV)
10%	Small U.S. Stocks	IShares Russell 2000	(IWM)
10%	Diversified Foreign Stocks	IShares MSCI EAFE	(EFA)
25%	Corporate Bonds	IShares Corporate Bond	(LQD)
25%	Short-term Treasury Bonds	IShares Lehman 1–3 Year Treasury	(SHY)

In an article titled "Get Going with Exchange Traded Funds" (Kiplinger.com, March 22, 2005), contributing editor Erin Burt extols the virtues of ETFs versus actively managed funds. "Only 4 percent of stock funds beat Standard & Poor's 500 index over the past decade." In addition to being vehicles for one-stop diversification, Burt lists the following advantages of ETFs as the reason for their dramatic increase in popularity: rock-bottom fees, lower taxes, immediacy of execution, transparency, and the opportunity ETFs give to sell short, buy on margin, place stop-loss and limit orders, and, in some cases, trade options.

Burt presents two sample ETF portfolios. The one for growth (Table 7.37) is for investors with a time horizon of at least 5 to 10 years. The one for income (Table 7.38) is for investors who

> "The essence of effective portfolio construction is the use of a large number of poorly correlated assets."
>
> —*William Bernstein*

are more risk-averse or seeking more income. She advises rebalancing when allocations get out of whack.

21. Morningstar: Don Phillips and Sue Stevens

Morningstar is a household name among investors even though it's been around for less than 25 years. Joe Mansueto, a former securities analyst, founded the company in his Chicago apartment in 1984. At that time, outfits like Standard & Poor's and Value Line were providing independent research reports on stocks, but not on mutual funds. Morningstar filled that void with analysis of individual mutual funds. That analysis featured two proprietary tools that have become closely identified with the Morningstar brand—the one to five star rating system and the nine-square style box.

The star rating is designed to give investors a quick take on how a mutual fund has balanced risk and return in the past relative to other funds in the same category. The style box is a visual snapshot of the type of securities held by the fund. Each of the three major styles—value, growth, and blend—are broken down into large cap, small cap, and mid-cap. The result is a nine-square box with one of the squares filled in to designate the fund's style.

Although best known as the authority on mutual funds, Morningstar has expanded its services. It now does for stocks what it does for mutual funds, covering 1,800 companies in 100 industries. It also offers investment consulting, retirement planning, and independent research via the Internet, software and a host of monthly publications. The latter include Morningstar *Fund Investor, Stock Investor, ETF Investor, Dividend Investor,* and the annual bible of the mutual fund industry, the 605-page *Morningstar Funds 500.* Its most far-reaching tool for the individual investor is the web site, Morningstar.com, one of the nation's premier investment web sites, with more than 3.6 million registered users.

Morningstar Five-Star Team   The most visible member of the Morningstar management team is Don Phillips, managing director and editorial voice of the company. Phillips is the go-to guy when the financial media wants insightful commentary on the latest developments in the mutual fund industry. With the company over 20 years, he was Morningstar's first mutual fund analyst and helped develop their signature style box and rating systems. Also widely quoted on the subject of mutual funds are research directors Russell Kinnel and Christine Benz. Less visible is the founder and CEO Joe Mansueto, but he owns roughly 70 percent of the stock (as of December 2006). The company went public in May 2005 (MORN), at $18.50. At an April 2007 price of $53, Mansueto's holdings were worth over $1.5 billion.

As part of its financial planning services, Morningstar offers model portfolios designed for both workers and retirees. Behind this effort is Sue Stevens whose articles on personal finance appear regularly on Morningstar.com. Stevens is obviously qualified to do her job as director of financial planning. She has an MBA from the University of Chicago, CPA (certified public accountant), CFA (chartered financial analyst), CFP (certified financial planner), and her own financial planning firm. She is also editor of Morningstar's latest monthly newsletter, *Morningstar Practical Finance*.

In an article titled "How to Build a Great Portfolio for Your Working Years" (Morningstar.com, August 17, 2006), Stevens suggests four sample portfolios: two conservative, one aggressive, and the one for moderate risk featured in Table 7.39. In another column titled "Model Portfolios for Retirees" (Morningstar.com, June 15, 2006), Stevens suggests five model portfolios, each one based on a different retiree life expectancy. The time horizons range from less than 10 years to 20 years or more. The portfolio shown in Table 7.40 is for retirees with a life expectancy of at least 15 years. Stevens uses both ETFs and index

Table 7.39 Morningstar Model Portfolio for the Working Years—Moderate Risk

Portfolio Allocation	Name of Fund	Symbol
5%	Vanguard Prime Money Market	
30%	I-Bonds (TreasuryDirect.gov)	
25%	iShares S&P 500	(IVV)
20%	iShares Russell Midcap Value	(IWS)
10%	Vanguard Small Cap ETF	(VB)
10%	Vanguard Total International Stock	(VGTSX)

Table 7.40 Morningstar Balanced Portfolio for Retirees

Stock Total			**50%**
10%	Large Value	T. Rowe Price Value,	(TRVLX)
7%	Large Blend	Vanguard Total Stock Market ETF, or	(VTI)
		iShares Russell 1000 Value	(IWD)
10%	Large Growth	Fidelity Blue Chip Growth or	(FBGRX)
		T. Rowe Price Growth Stock	(PRGFX)
10%	Mid/Small Cap	Fairholme or	(FAIRX)
		Royce Value	(RYVFX)
8%	Foreign	Dodge & Cox International Stock or	(DODFX)
		Vanguard Total International Stock	(VGTSX)
2.5%	Real Estate	T. Rowe Price Real Estate or	(TRREX)
		Vanguard REIT ETF	(VNQ)
2.5%	Precious Metals	No specific fund named	
Bond Total			**45%**
20%	Short to Intermediate Term	Vanguard Short Term Bond or	(VBISX)
		Vanguard Short Term Investment Grade or	(VFSTX)
		Fidelity Short-Intermediate Municipal Income	(FSTFX)
15%	Inflation Indexed	I Bonds (for taxable accounts) or	
		Vanguard Inflation-Protected Securities (for tax-deferred accounts)	(VIPSX)
5%	High Yield	Vanguard High-Yield Corporate or	(VWEHX)
		T. Rowe Price Tax Free High-Yield or	(PRFHX)
		Loomis Sayles Bond	(LSBRX)
5%	Foreign	T. Rowe Price International Bond	(RPIBX)
Cash and Cash Equivalents			**5%**

mutual funds in her portfolios. For her additional model portfolios, and for most everything there is to know about mutual funds, go to Morningstar.com.

Morningstar Moderate Risk Portfolio for Workers Says Stevens, "A moderate portfolio uses a mix of 5 percent cash, 30 percent fixed income, and 65 percent stocks. We've used an inflation-protected bond, an I-Bond, for the fixed-income portion of this portfolio. It's a type of U.S. savings bond (see TreasuryDirect.gov on the Web). If you are investing in a tax advantaged account like an IRA, you could use a Treasury Inflation-Protected Securities (TIPS) fund instead."

Morningstar Balanced Portfolio for Retirees Says Stevens, "Is your life expectancy at least 15 more years? Do you want to beat inflation by at least 3 percentage points per year? Could you tolerate it if your portfolio value declined in some years? Will you have other sources of retirement income, like a pension? If this describes your situation, a Balanced Portfolio might be right for you." See Table 7.40.

> "Just because prices are more reasonable than they were doesn't mean they're reasonable."
> —*Geoffrey Colvin*

22. J. D. Steinhilber

J. D. Steinhilber, 36, eats, lives, and breathes ETFs. In 2001, he founded AgileInvesting based on his conviction that index funds combined with disciplined asset allocation produce superior investment results. Based in Nashville, Tennessee, his firm manages client portfolios using a pure ETF approach.

As a recognized authority on ETFs and ETF portfolio strategies, his articles are featured in major business publications, investment web sites, and in his own newsletter on ETF investing. He is a regular contributor to SeekingAlpha.com, an award winning web site originated by David Jackson that has some 200 financial writers as active contributors. Jackson says one of his favorites is J. D. Steinhilber: "His work stands out for its quantitative rigor. We particularly like his comparative analysis of asset classes."

In a July 4, 2006, posting on SeekingAlpha.com, Steinhilber updates the three model ETF portfolios which he monitors periodically. (See Table 7.41.) He uses the same index funds for all three portfolios—conservative growth, moderate growth, and aggressive growth. Only the percentage allocations change. To get updates

> "It ain't the things we don't know that get us in trouble. It's the things we know that ain't so."
> —*Artemus Ward*

Table 7.41 J.D. Steinhilber: Three Model ETF Portfolios

		(1) Conservative Growth	(2) Moderate Growth	(3) Aggressive Growth
Large Cap Blend	(IVV)	15%	15%	20%
Large Cap Growth	(IVW)	5%	10%	10%
Mid Cap Blend	(IJH)	0%	0%	5%
Health Care Sector	(IYH)	5%	5%	5%
U.S. Equity		**25%**	**30%**	**40%**
Developed Markets	(EFA)	7%	7%	10%
Emerging Markets	(EEM)	0%	5%	5%
Pacific Region	(VPL)	5%	5%	5%
Int'l Equity		**12%**	**17%**	**20%**
Total Equity		**37%**	**47%**	**60%**
Min–Max Range		**30–70%**	**40–85%**	**50–95%**
Money Market		22%	17%	14%
Short Term Treasuries	(SHY)	25%	20%	15%
Diversified Bonds	(AGG)	10%	10%	5%
Fixed Income		**57%**	**47%**	**34%**
Min–Max Range		**25–70%**	**10–60%**	**5–50%**
Precious Metals	(GLD)	3%	3%	3%
Energy Master Ltd Ptnrs.	(KYN)	3%	3%	3%
Alternative Investments		**6%**	**6%**	**6%**
Min–Max Range		**0–15%**	**0–15%**	**0–15%**

and further information from J. D. Steinhilber go to his web site, AgileInvesting.com (also SeekingAlpha.com).

23. Carl Delfeld

Carl Delfeld, 49, is an expert in the international investment arena and uniquely qualified to put together a global portfolio. His more than 20 years in the investment business have included positions as an international banker, a consultant on Asian investment to the U.S. Treasury, an international economist for the U.S. Senate, and a director of the Asian Development Bank in Manila where he led missions to a dozen Far East countries. He has held investment banking positions in London, Tokyo, Hong Kong, and Sidney. He was a Japanese government scholar at Keio University in Tokyo and taught international business at the University of Colorado.

Currently, Delfeld is president of Chartwell Partners, a global investment advisory firm based in Colorado Springs, Colorado. He believes investors need a global approach when building a portfolio. "It makes about as much sense to invest in only one country as it does to invest in only one company or one industry. I believe the United States is the best country in the history of the world. The fact remains, however, that not once in the past 10 years has it been the world's top-performing stock market" (ChartwellAdvisor.com, *Why A Global Investment Perspective Is Essential*).

Delfeld specializes in ETFs, which he calls "a great core investment tool. They offer a low-cost, tax-efficient, transparent and diversified way to build an S&P 500–beating global portfolio." He shares his ETF and global expertise via his e-book, *The New Global ETF Investor;* his column in *Forbes Asia;* his monthly ETF newsletter; and his web sites, ChartwellAdvisor.com and the recently introduced ETFXray.com.

Perhaps Delfeld is best known for the performance of his six model global portfolios. Two are conservative: "Core Conservative" and "Gone Fishing" (see Table 7.42). The other four are growth portfolios for the more adventuresome: "Global Opportunity," "International Opportunity," "Asian Opportunity," and "New Venture." Each of the six portfolios has a cash component and contains between 9 and 13 ETFs. Go to ChartwellAdvisor .com for details on all six portfolios including Delfeld's insights into ETF investing, the track record of his models, and the latest updates.

Table 7.42   Delfeld's Gone Fishing Portfolio

Portfolio Allocation	Name of Fund	Symbol
5%	iShares Gold	(IAU)
5%	iShares Pacific Ex-Japan	(EPP)
10%	iShares Lehman 1–3 Year Bond	(SHY)
5%	iShares Select Dividend	(DVY)
10%	iShares G S Natural Resources	(IGE)
10%	iShares Lehman Aggregate	(AGG)
10%	iShares Europe, Asia, Far East	(EFA)
5%	iShares Emerging Markets	(EEM)
10%	iShares S&P Global 100	(IOO)
15%	iShares TIPS Bond	(TIP)
5%	Silver ETF	(SLV)
10%	Cash	

Carl Delfeld Gone Fishing Portfolio   Delfeld believes ETFs present investors with the best tools to build a "Gone Fishing" type portfolio because they are low cost and tax efficient. Here's how he describes this portfolio, which he changes from time to time: "The Gone Fishing Portfolio is a simple, yet well-diversified ETF starter portfolio with a low expense ratio. It is appropriate for long-term growth investors and can easily be adjusted to meet specific goals, risk tolerance and time frame. . . . It is a diversified, conservative portfolio that will protect your capital so you'll always have time to fish all day long" (Forbes .com, April 20, 2006). See Table 7.42.

> "In the investment business there's a fine line between being early and being wrong."
> —*Bill Nygren*

24. David Jackson

David Jackson is an achiever. Following his graduation from Oxford University and the London School of Economics, he worked in technology venture funding and then five years as a technology analyst for Morgan Stanley. After a stint at managing money, he launched his initial web site, TechUncovered.com, which morphed into SeekingAlpha .com in early 2004. ("Alpha" represents performance over and above that of the general market.)

In just a few years, SeekingAlpha.com has become the largest network of stock market blogs, opinion, and analysis. It has over 200 contributors, mostly finance professionals, submitting wide-ranging articles. Features on the web site include a daily one-page summary of the *Wall Street Journal,* a weekly *Barron's* summary, and hundreds of conference call transcripts.

In September 2006, SeekingAlpha.com received an infusion of cash from the venture capital firm Benchmark Capital. The money helped to fund a new venture with the world's largest investment web site. Yahoo! Finance agreed to use SeekingAlpha content. Typing a stock symbol in the Yahoo! quote box produces a page of information that includes, under the heading "Financial Blogs," any comment on that stock from SeekingAlpha. Exposure on Yahoo! is a big step forward for both SeekingAlpha and its content providers.

David Jackson specializes in ETFs. His commentary on the subject of ETFs is thoughtful, lucid, thorough, organized, and articulate. If you limit yourself to one research source for ETFs, go to SeekingAlpha.com and type "ETF investing guide" in the search box. Jackson makes it easy by providing a "One-Page Summary of the Entire Guide." He favors the use of an online brokerage account where the trading costs of managing the portfolio are low. He is a strong believer in rebalancing as a means of reducing risk and forcing a buy low, sell high trading discipline (see his "Rebalancing Rules").

Investors Overestimate Need for Advice   As for the basic problem of whether to use traditional index mutual funds or ETFs, his advice is hardly wishy-washy: "The specific index funds you choose should be determined by two factors—cost and ease of management. . . . The key question for individual investors is: What instruments can I use that (a) minimize my costs and (b) maximize the ease with which I can rebalance my portfolio while minimizing taxes? The answer, I think, is clear: For individual investors, ETFs win outright because you can easily find numerous alternatives for tax loss selling to offset rebalancing gains, you can use limit orders to help rebalance, and ETFs are intrinsically more tax efficient."

Here's how Jackson sums up his feelings about indexing: "Most wealthy investors overestimate their need for investment advice. Management of a core portfolio of 8 to 12 ETFs in an online account is easy

Table 7.43   David Jackson: Low-Maintenance Five-Fund ETF Portfolio

Name of Fund	Symbol
iShares Dow Jones U.S. Total Market Index Fund	(IYY)
iShares MSCI EAFE Index Fund	(EFA)
Vanguard Emerging Markets	(VWO)
streetTRACKS Wilshire REIT Index Fund	(RWR)
iShares Lehman Aggregate Bond Fund	(AGG)

and not time consuming and likely provides better diversification and overall performance than most high net worth financial services using individual stocks and mutual funds."

Jackson assembles a core ETF portfolio of 10 ETFs. However, in terms of simplicity and ease of management, he believes a portfolio of only five ETFs may even be better. So he spotlights the low-maintenance portfolio in Table 7.43, about which he says, "It has a slightly higher cost and lower flexibility but it still offers the same diversification, reduced risk, reduced fees, and tax benefits of the larger portfolio."

David Jackson's Low Maintenance Five-Fund ETF Portfolio Jackson does not include percentage allocations. He feels that each investor's situation is unique and requires individual tweaking. The myriad of personal circumstances (age, finances, risk tolerance, goals, etc.) preclude any type of generalization. However, he does feel the five carefully selected ETFs in Table 7.43, allocated according to individual need, effectively fulfill the requirements of a core portfolio.

David Jackson 10-Fund Core Portfolio For those who prefer a wider selection of funds to cover the U.S. stock market and the U.S. bond market, Jackson offers his core portfolio (Table 7.44). In a lucid explanation of the rationale behind its construction, Jackson details the advantages of buying funds that split the U.S. stock market into market cap groupings versus buying a single total market index fund. He concludes:

> "There are two requirements for success in Wall Street. First, you have to think correctly and second, you have to think independently."
> —*Benjamin Graham*

Table 7.44 David Jackson: Ten-Fund ETF Core Portfolio

Name of Fund	Symbol	Market Sector
iShares S&P 500 Index Fund	(IVV)	Large cap U.S. stocks
iShares S&P Mid Cap 400 Index Fund	(IJH)	Mid cap U.S. stocks
iShares Russell 2000 Index Fund	(IWM)	Small cap U.S. stocks
iShares MSCI EAFE Index Fund	(EFA)	Large cap foreign developed market stocks
iShares MSCI Emerging Markets Index Fund	(EEM)	Large cap emerging market stocks
streetTRACKS Wilshire REIT Index Fund	(RWR)	Real estate investment trust index fund
iShares GS $ Investop Corporate Bond Fund	(LQD)	U.S. corporate bonds
iShares Lehman 1–3 Year Treasury Bond Fund	(SHY)	U.S. short-term government bonds
iShares Lehman 7–10 Year Treasury Bond Fund	(IEF)	U.S. long-term government bonds
iShares Lehman TIPS Bond Fund	(TIP)	U.S. government inflation-protected bonds

"That's it. You have ten index fund ETFs from which to construct an ultra low cost, diversified portfolio. Three index funds cover the U.S. stock market, two funds cover non-U.S. stocks, four index funds cover the bond market, and one the real estate market." For the complete story go to SeekingAlpha.com, "ETF Investing Guide: Understanding the 'Core Portfolio,'" (July 1, 2006).

25. Larry Swedroe

Investment adviser Larry Swedroe, 55, is one of the heroes of the world of indexing. He is among the strongest, most persuasive and articulate champions of passive investing and asset allocation. He was among the first to publish a book that explained the merits of indexing in layman's language.

Based in St. Louis, Missouri, Swedroe has been a principal and director of research at Buckingham Asset Management for the past 11 years. Previously he worked as vice chairman for Prudential Home Mortgage and for Citicorp as a regional treasurer. Swedroe has written extensively on the passive asset class investment approach. His insightful commentary has been featured on national TV and quoted in the financial media.

He has written five books, including *What Wall Street Doesn't Want You To Know* (Truman Talley Books, 2001), *Rational Investing in Irrational Times* (Truman Talley Books, 2002), *The Successful Investor Today* (St. Martin's Griffin, 2003), and co-authored *The Only Guide to a Winning Bond Strategy You'll Ever Need* (Truman Talley Books, 2006). But his best known work, on most must-read lists of investment books, is the classic *The Only Guide to a Winning Investment Strategy You'll Ever Need*. Originally published by Dutton in 1998, it was updated and rereleased by St. Martin's Press in 2005.

In his book, Swedroe explains how the principles of modern portfolio theory (MPT) and efficient markets hypothesis (EMH) provide a road map to a long-term winning investment strategy. Modern portfolio theory, developed by Harry Markowitz in 1952, states that the risk in a portfolio of diversified stocks is less than the risk inherent in any one of the stocks, provided the right combination of noncorrelated stocks is chosen. According to the theory, it's possible to construct an "efficient frontier" optimal portfolio that offers the maximum possible expected return for a given level of risk.

The efficient market hypothesis, created by Eugene Fama in the 1970s, is a theory that states that beating the market is highly unlikely because at any given time the market reflects all the relevant information available. The market is "efficient"—it represents the best estimate of the correct price, which means a search for undervalued stocks or an attempt to predict market trends is likely to prove unproductive. (Both theories are controversial and widely debated on Wall Street.)

How Do You Know How Much Risk to Take? Vanguard founder John Bogle says, "Swedroe takes MPT . . . out of the realm of academia and into the real world of investing." Indeed, Swedroe supports his conclusions with extensive scholarly research but he is able to explain statistics simply and understandably. Part of Swedroe's book deals with how to build a globally diversified model portfolio and then how to maintain it through rebalancing and tax management. He discusses various risk factors and how they impact returns. He performs a special service for investors by helping to answer the sticky question, "How do we know just how much risk we can take?" Swedroe makes it easy by breaking down risk into three components:

1. Your *willingness* to take risk—in other words, the fortitude and discipline to stick with your strategy.
2. Your *ability* to take risk—how long a time frame you're working with, the stability of your earned income, and your need for liquidity.
3. Your *need* to take risk—the rate of return required to achieve your financial objectives.

This type of helpful analysis is found throughout the book.

Swedroe explains that active buying and selling stocks is what Wall Street wants but that it's a loser's game for the individual investor. Instead, he favors no-load, low-cost passive management via index mutual funds and ETFs. He advocates broad diversification across U.S. stocks, international stocks, and U.S. bonds. In *The Only Guide*, he distills his ideas in a number of featured sample portfolios both for tax-deferred (401(k) and IRA) and taxable accounts. Included is the track record of various asset classes over a 31-year period. For the fixed-income portion of his models, he recommends high-grade (AA or better), short-intermediate term bonds (1 to 5 year) and TIPS (treasury inflation-protected securities). About his models Swedroe says, "These are only samples in the sense that they are good starting points to consider. How much you allocate to each asset class is a personal decision." See Table 7.45.

For fresh insight into why index funds are a clear choice over active investing, and for access to his other model portfolios, check out his book, *The Only Guide To A Winning Strategy You'll Ever Need*, and BAMServices.com.

Table 7.45   Larry Swedroe: Model Portfolio Allocations

	Conservative	Moderate	Moderately Aggressive	Highly Aggressive
Equity	40	60	80	100
Fixed Income	60	40	20	0

Table 7.46 Larry Swedroe: Stock Portion of Model Portfolio

Portfolio Allocation	Name of Fund (Symbol)
17.5%	Vanguard S&P 500 Index (VFINX) or iShares S&P 500 Index (IVV)
17.5%	iShares S&P Mid Cap 400 Value Index (IJJ)
17.5%	Vanguard Tax Managed Small Index (VTMSX) or iShares S&P Small Cap 600 Index (IJR)
17.5%	iShares Small Cap 600 Value Index (IJS)
70%	**Total U.S.**
20%	Vanguard Tax Managed International Index (VTMGX)
10%	Vanguard Emerging Market Index (VWO)
30%	**Total International**

> "Success is a lousy teacher. It seduces smart people into thinking they can't lose."
>
> —*Bill Gates*

Larry Swedroe: Sample Portfolio for Taxable Accounts— Equity Portion The model in Table 7.46 is the *stock* portion of the portfolio. It represents 40, 60, 80, or 100 percent of the portfolio, depending on which of the four risk levels applies (refer to Table 7.45).

26. Steven Schoenfeld

Steven Schoenfeld, 44, is a heavyweight in the world of indexing—the professional's professional. If someone is called to speak to the most sophisticated investment managers on the subject of indexing opportunities in the global marketplace, it's likely to be Steven Schoenfeld. His long list of credentials explains why; currently, he's chief investment officer in charge of quantitative global investments for Northern Trust. This involves management of some $220 billion in index and enhanced index strategies. Before that he was founder of Global Index Strategies, a San Francisco–based consulting firm; chief investment officer for Active Index Advisors; and for six years, a managing director at Barclays Global Investors, where he focused on global index-based strategies including iShares ETFs.

Prior to Barclays, Schoenfeld structured the first emerging market index funds for the International Finance Corporation (IFC), an arm of the World Bank. He was a Fulbright scholar in economics at the National University of Singapore and later spent three years at the Singapore Exchange trading Japanese stock index futures. He is the founder of the web site IndexUniverse.com, a rich source of information on all aspects of index-based investing, now headed by Jim Wiandt.

Isn't "Active Indexing" an Oxymoron? Schoenfeld has written a number of books. His most prestigious and influential work is *Active Index Investing* (John Wiley & Sons, 2004), a 670-page, 31-chapter tome that's been described as "the essential book of indexing" and "a must-have desk reference." Isn't "active index" an oxymoron? No, says Schoenfeld. His book is filled with creative ways to enhance performance using index funds. Away from the world of indexing, Schoenfeld enjoys sailing, skiing, hiking, and participating in public policy and politics.

In Chapter 30 of *Active Index Investing,* Schoenfeld focuses on the "four key axioms for long-term investment success." They are (1) Build a diversified asset allocation; it's what matters most; (2) use a risk budget framework to choose managers/approaches for each asset class; (3) be disciplined about rebalancing; (4) rigorously control costs and taxes—the things you can always control.

The portfolio in Table 7.47 is found on the next two pages. It appears on pages 612–613 of Schoenfeld's book and is reproduced on SmartMoney.com. It was updated on October 14, 2006. Go to ActiveIndexInvesting.com for more on Schoenfeld and his book.

> "You've got to think about big things while you're doing small things, so that all the small things go in the right direction."
> —*Alvin Toffler*

27. Dr. Marvin Appel

There is a perception that doctors make poor investors. If true, Dr. Marvin Appel, 45, is an obvious exception. He is both an MD (with

Table 7.47 Steven Schoenfeld's Model ETF Portfolio for Three Levels of Risk

Asset Class	Type	Name of Fund	Symbol	Conservative	Moderate	Aggressive
U.S. Equities:	Large Cap (choose one)	iShares Russell 1000	(IWB)	15%	30%	35%
		iShares S&P 500	(IVV)			
		SPDR 500	(SPY)			
		Vanguard Large Cap	(VV)			
	Mid/Small Cap (choose one)	iShares Russell Mid Cap	(IWR)	10%	15%	20%
		iShares S&P Mid Cap 400	(IJH)			
		Mid Cap SPDRs	(MDY)			
		Vanguard Mid Cap	(VO)			
		iShares Russell 2000	(IWM)			
		iShares Small Cap 600	(IJR)			
		Vanguard Small Cap	(VB)			
International	Developed	iShares MSCI EAFE	(EFA)	5%	8%	15%
Equities:	Emerging	iShares MSCI Emerging Markets	(EEM)	—	2%	5%

Table 7.47 (*continued*)

Asset Class	Type	Name of Fund	Symbol	Conservative	Moderate	Aggressive
Fixed Income:	Short Term	iShares Lehman 1–3 Year Treasury Bond	(SHY)	15%	5%	—
	Long Term	iShares Lehman 20+ Year Treasury Bond	(TLT)	15%	10%	5%
	High Yield	iShares iBoxx $ Invest Grade Corp Bond	(LQD)	10%	5%	5%
	TIPS	iShares Lehman TIPS Bond		15%	10%	—
Alternatives:	REITS	Dow Jones U.S. Real Estate	(IYR)	10%	10%	10%
	(choose one)	iShares Cohen & Steers Realty Majors	(ICF)			
		streetTRACKS Wilshire REIT Fund	(RWR)			
	Commodities:	PowerShares DB Commodity Index	(DBC)	5%	5%	5%
	(choose one)	Tracking Fund				
		iShares GSCI Commodity-Indexed Trust	(GSG)			

Source: *Active Index Investing* by Steven Schoenfeld. Copyright © 2004. Reprinted with permission of John Wiley & Sons, Inc.

an inactive practice) and a money manager/technical analyst. A Harvard graduate, he received his training in internal medicine at Massachusetts General Hospital and in anesthesiology at Johns Hopkins. He also did data analysis work at M.I.T. and has a PhD in biomedical engineering. He has applied his expertise in computer research and mathematical modeling to stock market analysis, asset allocation, and most recently to the field of ETFs. Dr. Appel has his own money management firm, Appel Asset Management in Great Neck, New York. He is editor of the respected and durable investment newsletter *Systems and Forecasts,* founded by his father, Gerald, in 1973.

Dr. Appel's latest book, *Investing with Exchange Traded Funds Made Easy* (Prentice-Hall, October 2006), bears this subtitle: "Higher Returns with Lower Costs—Do It Yourself Strategies Without Paying Fund Managers." The book explains how ETFs work and what they can and cannot do. Subjects covered include how to choose between growth and value ETFs and how to establish an ETF asset allocation strategy.

In Chapter 7, Dr. Appel explains how to use ETFs to build a "one-decision" ETF portfolio (Table 7.48). He says, "The goal is to offer the best possible investment that requires only a minimal time commitment. I call it the One-Decision Portfolio because after you adopt the following asset allocation, all that is required from you in the future is a few minutes work once each year to maintain the specified program."

Dr. Appel recommends a 50 percent stock, 50 percent bond/cash allocation, "a mix that has been far safer than stocks alone and far more profitable than bonds alone." In the equity portion, he focuses on three areas—REITs, small cap value, and S&P 500—because "historically they have had a

Table 7.48 Dr. Marvin Appel's One-Decision Portfolio

Portfolio Allocation	Name of Fund	Symbol
20%	S&P 500 Depository Receipts or	(SPY)
	iShares S&P 500 Index Fund	(IVV)
20%	iShares Cohen and Steers Realty Majors Index Fund	(ICF)
10%	iShares Russell 2000 Value Index Fund	(IWN)
20%	iShares Lehman Aggregate Bond Fund	(AGG)
30%	Cash (90-day U.S. Treasury bills or highest-yielding money market fund or bank C.D.)	

Source: *Investing with Exchange Traded Funds Made Easy: Higher Returns with Lower Costs—Do It Yourself Strategies Without Paying Fund Managers* (Prentice-Hall, October 2006).

relatively low correlation with each other. As a result, diversification among these three areas, historically, has been effective at reducing risk." The income portion consists of 60 percent cash and 40 percent intermediate-term bonds. The funds in the portfolio all have low expense ratios.

Dr. Appel back-tested his five-component portfolio to 1981 with positive results. Check out his book, his personal web site (AppelAsset .com), and/or the article "The One-Decision ETF Portfolio" on the SeekingAlpha web site (http:// ETF.seekingalpha.com/article/ 22048) for details, including reasons why he omits international exposure.

> "The best time to panic is generally before everybody else does."
> —*Unknown*

28. XTF

XTF LP (eXchange Traded Funds) is a young but aggressive New York–based firm that deals exclusively with the creation and marketing of ETF portfolios (XTF.com). Only in existence since 2000, it has already made an impact because of its innovative moves to design customized portfolios to fit any customer profile from most conservative to most aggressive.

There are those who believe that indexing is only in the beginning stages of a mushrooming industry. These visionaries see millions of Americans using new ETF products, even more than individual stocks, to implement a broad range of investment strategies and styles. If there is any truth to this, a pioneering firm like XTF using its proprietary research and a rapidly expanding line of ETF portfolio offerings is likely to be among the leaders of the advance.

XTF has assets under management approaching $300 million and offers 20 all-ETF portfolios, but expects to offer a lot more. It has two kinds—there are 11 what it calls "tactical" portfolios which are fine-tuned according to the investor's risk tolerance. It does this by adjusting the exposure to stocks in 10 percent increments. The 11 portfolios range from 100 percent equity and 0 percent fixed income to 100 percent fixed income and 0 percent equity. Each portfolio is named according to the amount of equity exposure. For example the "ETF 70" portfolio is composed of 70 percent equity ETFs and 30 percent fixed-income ETFs.

XTF also offers a second kind of ETF portfolio. In the third quarter of 2006 it introduced seven target date portfolios at mostly five-year intervals, 2005 through 2040. Each portfolio's asset mix becomes more conservative with the passage of time. Young investors who choose the "ETF 2040" start out 100 percent in equities. At age 65, they'll be 50 percent in equities and 50 percent in bonds, and 20 years past retirement they'll maintain a 20 percent equity and 80 percent bond and real estate allocation. Recently, XTF has added two specialty ETF funds to its lineup—a sector rotation fund and a country rotation fund. It has also entered the 401(k) market with mutual funds of ETFs.

In addition to adjusting for the investor's risk tolerance, XTF adds another customized feature to its portfolios. It will adjust the percentage allocation of components within a portfolio at any time they believe conditions in the economy or the stock and bond markets call for it. Says XTF, "We may overweight or underweight a particular asset class

Table 7.49   ETF 50 (50% Equity, 50% Income)*—One of 11 Tactical ETF Portfolios from XTF

Equities 50%

19%	U.S. Large Cap	State Street SPDR	(SPY)
17%	International Equities	iShares MSCI EAFE	(EFA)
8%	U.S. Mid Cap	Vanguard Mid Cap ETF	(VO)
6%	U.S. Small Cap	iShares Russell 2000	(IWM)

Fixed Income 50%

10.8%	Intermediate Term U.S. Treasuries	iShares Lehman 7–10 Year	(IEF)
10.8%	Short Term U.S. Government	iShares Lehman 1–3 Year	(SHY)
6.9%	Long Term U.S. Treasuries	iShares Lehman 20 Year	(TLT)
5.9%	Investment Grade Corp. Bonds	iShares iBoxx Corp. Bond	(LQD)
4.9%	U.S. Treasury Inflation-Protected Securities	iShares Lehman TIPS Bond	(TIP)
9.8%	U.S. Real Estate	Vanguard REIT Index	(VNQ)
1.0%	Cash	90 day Treasury Bills	

*As of 12/31/06, XTF made a tactical move to increase its equity exposure in this portfolio from 50 percent to 70 percent. That means that each of the allocation percentages shown above for the four equity funds were raised 20 percent and the allocation numbers shown above for each of the fixed income funds were reduced by 20 percent. Check out the "ETF 50" profile on XTF.com for the exact numbers and any updates.

based on a series of market, fundamental, technical, and risk factors. We do this to enhance the return and lessen the risk of each portfolio."

Says Chairman Sander Gerber, "I passionately believe that educating investors about the potential of ETFs and giving them access to professional-grade portfolio management will ultimately make a huge difference in their lives."

For background information on Chairman Sander Gerber, CEO Michael Woods (formerly managing director at Legg Mason), and their management team, as well as full details on all 18 portfolios, including hypothetical returns since 1990, go to XTF.com. The model portfolio in Table 7.49 is one of 11 XTF tactical ETF portfolios.

APPENDIX: In addition to this chapter's 28 model portfolios, you might want to check out another lazy portfolio. It's put together by Marketwatch columnist Paul Farrell using fundamentally-based Wisdom Tree Funds based on Professor Jeremy Siegel's research (Marketwatch .com, Paul Farrell, April 2, 2007, "Weighting Game"). Also, for a subscription fee, Morningstar's newsletter, *ETF Investor* monitors two model ETF portfolios each month. One is the long-term oriented Hands-Free Portfolio, the other the more active Hands-On Portfolio.

Finally, there's the personal portfolio of Less Antman, a California-based CPA and investment adviser. He is quoted often by his friend Andrew Tobias (AndrewTobias.com) who labels Antman estimable and profoundly wise. Read Antman at simplyrich.com and you'll likely be impressed. He's superbright, candid, and engaging. In his newsletter of July 30, 2007, he reveals his and his wife's long term portfolio. It consists of six asset classes and nine ETFs. It's unlikely your situation is the same as Less' but you can learn a lot from him. For further explanation, details, and updates go to simplyrich.com.

> "Success in business or investments requires desire and energy. Any I.Q. over 125 is wasted."
> —*Warren Buffett*

Chapter 8

Active Investing with Mutual Funds

For most of the history of the securities markets, almost all investing was active. There was no means of buying the performance of the total market or a sector of the market. Investors bought individual stocks and mostly held on to them, hoping for a good return from appreciation and a substantial dividend. They didn't think of themselves as "active" investors because there was no other kind.

What's more, *active* was a poor choice of words since the average holding period was many years. Today, stocks on the New York Stock Exchange are held for an average of less than a year. Short-term traders, both individual and institutional, are a growing market force while long-term buy-and-holders are playing a lesser role.

Common stocks are still the favorite vehicle of active investors. In the past few decades, however, mutual funds and life-cycle/target funds have been widely promoted as a way to beat the market. These next two chapters are devoted to active investing. This chapter focuses on life-cycle funds and mutual funds. Chapter 9 deals with common stocks.

Ways for Do-It-Yourselfers to Outperform the Market: Introduction

I believe most investors should invest most of their money in index funds. The previous chapters have explained why and how. But even the most die-hard proponents of indexing—people like John Bogle and Burton Malkiel—set aside a portion of their own money for active investing.

This section deals with money that's invested *outside* of indexing; I've suggested a mix of about 80 percent indexing and 20 percent active but the numbers can vary. Strongly risk-averse investors may opt for 100 percent indexing. Investors with more time, more money, more risk tolerance, and more savvy may allot more than 20 percent to active management. As I have suggested, there are situations where the risk of financial loss by do-it-yourselfers is more than offset by the benefits of social and emotional fulfillment.

The 20 percent devoted to trying to beat the market is the fun part of investing. Unlike indexing, matching wits with the best investors in the world and coming out a winner—even if it's only once in a while—can be fulfilling. And it can keep you coming back for more. This is not about short-term trading. The orientation is still longer term. With the active 20 percent, the focus is more on capital gains (one to three years or longer).

For the 100 years before indexing became popular, *all* investing was active. There was no vehicle for buying the total stock market or the S&P 500. The goal of the individual investor was simply to earn a good return. For most of the twentieth century an average annual gain of around 15 percent was the widely accepted objective of Wall Street professionals. So 15 percent was the mythical benchmark used by investors to measure their performance.

Today, the climate has changed to one of low interest rates and range-bound markets. The broad consensus has lowered the expected average annual return to single digits. But the challenge is still there.

Stocks Are Always More Popular than Index Funds

Every year there's a long list of individual stocks, mutual funds, investment advisers, and monitored portfolios that dramatically outperform the market.

The list looks a lot different each year but nevertheless, in good or bad markets, there are always big winners. Instead of single-digit returns, the names at and near the top of the list sport gains of 15 to 25 percent and more. The challenge for the investor is to match the results of these elite performers. It's difficult to do, especially since luck plays such a big role. But there are ways to better the odds.

The purpose of this section is to do just that—to point your actively managed money in the right direction. I explore those avenues that, in the past, have led to outstanding performance. In the process I spotlight some of the top-performing actively monitored portfolios, individual advisers, and proven market systems. Since mutual funds are often winners one year and losers the next, I address the challenge of picking the most consistent mutual fund performers.

As for picking individual stocks, everything in this book up to the section on indexing is aimed at improving your stock market skills. Why is so much of the book devoted to stocks and active investing when that only represents 20 percent of my suggested mix? Because far more people buy stocks than index funds, because there's much more to learn about active than passive investing, and because the challenge of buying and selling stocks has a much broader appeal than buying and holding index funds.

Since this is the part of the book devoted to active investing, I touch briefly on stocks once again. This time the focus is on what I believe are the best places to find good stock buying ideas and the most productive type of homework you can do to achieve success.

The specific active approaches discussed in these remaining three chapters all have one thing in common—an impressive track record. Being aware of what has worked best in the past is a far more reliable approach than "this time it's different." Of course, not all of these active investing options will repeat their past success. But given time, many will. As always, the longer you stay with any of these strategies, the greater your odds for success.

Running a Four-and-a-Half-Minute Mile

A word about sector funds. They are not included in this active investing section, but they could be. There has been an explosion of new, ultraspecialized, niche, sector funds. They are mostly used by speculators who are betting that that particular slice of the market will outperform the popular indexes. In that sense, even though sector funds involve an index, their index is so narrowly based that they must be considered an active choice, and a risky one. As the slices of the pie get smaller and smaller, the risks increase. For example, there are 18 HealthShares ETFs, most devoted to stocks of companies targeting a particular ailment such as heart disease, cancer, diabetes, or eye disease. And there were 22 separate state-specific ETFs in registration in July of 2007, each containing 50 stocks of companies based in a single state. We prefer to use the broader sector funds in our index portfolios as vehicles for achieving diversification, balance, and risk reduction.

For most investors, over the long term the odds favor indexing over active investing. Financial columnist Andrew Tobias puts it this way (andrewtobias.com, May 8, 2006): "Can you beat the market? Mostly, I think: no. You can't. Most mutual fund managers don't (especially after accounting for fees, let alone taxes). Most pension fund managers don't. Most brokers don't. Most individual investors don't. But there's a difference between don't and can't. Most can't, any more than most can run a four and a half minute mile. But some can . . . " This section tries to put you in the group that can.

The current market climate provides special incentive for active investors. The consensus view that we will see no more than modest, single-digit gains on average in the years immediately ahead may or may not prove correct. If true, however, the desire to try and outperform a sluggish market should be even more compelling.

> "We all know that active management fees are high. Poor performance does not come cheap."
> —Rex Sinquefield

Life-Cycle/Target Retirement Funds

"Keep it simple" is usually a winning formula. There's no better example than what's happening in the all-in-one fund business. Life-cycle or target retirement funds represent a single-fund solution to all of the investor's needs. It's the closest thing the $11 trillion mutual fund industry has to a maintenance-free retirement fund. Introduced in 1994, the growth of these funds has been explosive, especially in recent years. According to the Investment Company Institute, assets surged 63 percent in 2006 alone, reaching a total of $110 billion. As of year-end 2006, over 30 mutual fund families offered 210 life-cycle funds, most of them less than three years old. Because they are being offered by more and more employers and because of the widespread appeal of the "having to do nothing" approach to investing, growth is likely to accelerate.

Each life-cycle fund is a *fund of funds,* meaning it invests in a diversified list of other mutual funds. For the investor, it's a simple process. Pick out one of a host of mutual fund families and invest regularly in its target fund that comes closest to your planned retirement date (for example, Fidelity Freedom 2030, Vanguard Target Retirement 2025, or T. Rowe Price Retirement 2040). These one-stop-shopping packages include various asset classes, mainly U.S. stocks, foreign stocks, bonds, and cash. The percentages allocated to each asset vary depending on when you plan to retire. As you move closer to your retirement date, the fund shifts assets away from more volatile stock investments into more stable income-producing ones like bond funds. The fund manager makes all the decisions for you.

How wise or effective those decisions will prove to be is unknowable. There are no long track records. What *is* knowable is that many investors are happy to shift the decision-making responsibility. They are often overwhelmed by the range of options available. A one-step solution that removes all worries about complex choices, asset allocations, and periodic rebalancing offers instant appeal.

Seventy-six million American baby boomers will enter retirement over the next two decades. Already burdened with career and family responsibilities, the nation's workforce has been especially receptive to a decision-free, one-stop approach to their investment problems. An instant hit among owners of 401(k) plans, a growing number of plans designate life-cycle funds as the choice (default option) for employees who fail to indicate a preference.

Retirement Will Last 20 to 30 Years on Average

Recent legislation is likely to accelerate the use of life-style/target retirement funds among the nation's 47 million 401(k) holders. In August 2006, Congress passed pension reform legislation giving companies the green light to add automated features to their savings plans. This enables companies to automatically enroll the 21 percent of eligible employees who don't join their 401(k) plan (the employee has the option to refuse, but once enrolled, most stay in). The employee is usually assigned a conservative investment option but the range of choices is expanding. The new law also gives financial firms greater latitude in offering advice. In recent years, the trend has been more and more away from the traditional company pension plan (defined benefit plan) and toward 401(k) and IRA plans (defined contribution plan). The new Pension Protection Act of 2006 will accelerate the trend toward defined contribution investing.

One note of caution to owners of 401(k) plans. In a 02/25/07 article titled, "Don't Let an Automated 401(k) Lull You to Sleep," *New York Times* reporter Paul Lim says, "It's folly to think that you can literally set your retirement plan in your 20s or 30s and forget it until you retire." He warns that most employees who are automatically enrolled will stick with the rate of savings that the plan selects for them, and it's not likely to be enough. Financial planners suggest a savings rate of 15 to 25 percent is necessary, depending on age, to prepare adequately for retirement.

Criticized for being too conservative, most life-cycle funds have decided to retain most of their equity exposure in the later years instead of trimming back. Critics were concerned that reduced growth potential might result in insufficient funds to deal with rising post-retirement expenses and longer life. The average life expectancy for Americans who are 65 has increased to almost 85 with a 25 percent probability of living beyond 92 (men) and 94 (women). That means a retirement of some 20 to 30 years on average, and it could extend a lot further in the not too distant future.

With retirement years lasting so much longer, the industry consensus is that new retirees should maintain a stock allocation of perhaps 50 to 60 percent. For investors starting out and up through about the age of 40, most fund families allocate some 90 percent of the life-cycle portfolio to stocks. Two different target funds with the same retirement date can have very different allocations. Some are more aggressive than others and some have fewer expenses than others. Also, some deal with the long-term risk of inflation by owning Treasury inflation-protected securities (TIPS) and others do not. All funds, however, provide extended life-cycle coverage

beyond retirement. Income funds are offered for 5, 10, up to 30 years past
retirement to go with stock holdings. Almost all fund families maintain
stable exposure to international stocks, even after retirement.

The three biggest players in the life-cycle field are Fidelity, Vanguard,
and T. Rowe Price but there is a growing list of others. The terminology
used to label these all-in-one funds can be confusing. In addition to life-
cycle and target retirement funds there are also balanced funds, asset allocation funds, and lifestyle funds. The main difference is that the latter
group do not make age-related shifts in asset classes. However, some are
divided into conservative, moderate, and aggressive portfolios, and it's up
to you to switch if and when your tolerance for risk changes.

"I Don't Like Life-Cycle Funds"

What's the downside to life-cycle/target funds? For one thing, they are
relatively unseasoned and untested. It will take years to establish a track
record. Other objections are voiced by stock market trader/blogger Charles
Kirk (TheKirkReport.com, Q&A, October 2006): "I don't like life-cycle
funds. In my experience, they underperform, they are too conservative,
they're not very tax efficient, and I think allocation should be determined
by more than just age. . . . You need to take an active role with your money.
No one is going to defend your best interests the way you can."

In a perfect world, knowledgeable investors would take charge of
their own investments and make wise decisions. In the real world, I
believe a buy-and-hold life-cycle/target fund is a viable option. The
gradual transition from aggressive to conservative over the preretire-
ment years would seem a valid concept, one that would not likely be
implemented by the average investor. The attempt by target funds to
allocate and shift assets effectively is just that—an attempt. But as
imperfect as it might be, results are likely to better those of most
nonprofessionals. There are also psychological benefits. An anxiety-
free, homework-free, decision-free approach, even if misplaced, has a
money value.

What you can do to help make a life-cycle approach work is to select
a fund with low expenses (0.2 percent to 2 percent is the normal range)
and one that fits your risk profile (more stocks means more risk and more
growth potential; more bonds means less risk and less growth).

One caveat: Retirement planning experts say it's important that a life-cycle/target fund represent all, or almost all, your holdings. This is so the allocation percentages customized to your target date will not be upset by investments outside the fund. Investing only in a target fund, then, is a sensible alternative to, say, building an index fund portfolio. (Of course, none of this works unless the investor keeps his commitment to making regular contributions.)

Investing in only one life-cycle/target fund is fine but I don't think it's an ironclad rule. I'm not sure that asset classes have to be that fine-tuned. An overweighting or addition of an asset class can turn out to be a good thing as well as bad. One option is to let the target fund represent some 80 percent of your holdings with the other 20 percent invested on your own. To help you with the latter, read

> "In selecting mutual funds, outperformance does not predict future outperformance. Low expenses and low turnover are much more predictive of future results."
> —*Robert Bingham*

on. (The Internet is a rich source of information on life-cycle funds. For an excellent overview, including comparisons of the plans offered by Vanguard, Fidelity, T. Rowe Price, and Alliance Bernstein, see the cover story in the January 2007 *AAII Journal*.)

Mutual Funds: 18 Key Points

There are over 13,000 mutual funds. That's far more than the total number of stocks on the New York Stock Exchange. So far in this book, I've focused on passively managed index mutual funds and exchange-traded funds—a very small part of the $11 trillion dollar mutual fund universe. All the other funds, both stock and bond funds, are actively managed. Their performance is measured against a benchmark index of similar holdings. Unlike index funds, however, they attempt to do better than the benchmark through superior stock-picking techniques.

Some of these funds have outperformed over a long enough period of time to conclude that there's more involved than luck. This elite group of top performers may be a good starting place for long-term investors looking to narrow the field. Those with a shorter time frame may focus instead on those asset classes and/or sectors with the alleged brightest current prospects.

Trying to pick a few mutual funds out of 13,000 is a daunting task. How to go about it—what to do and what not to do—is the subject of millions of words in thousands of books, articles, and web pages. Research never hurts and it's good to be informed because being aware can mean fewer mistakes. But as you know from my previous remarks on the exaggerated value of stock-specific homework, I see little correlation between great preparation and great results when it comes to buying securities. You're simply dealing with too much that is imponderable, unknowable, and fortuitous. Checking out the performance of a fund manager is likely to be time better spent than studying statistics.

As with stocks, however (and remember, an equity mutual fund is no more than a portfolio of stocks), the longer you own the fund, the greater the chance that the reason you bought it will have a chance to come into play. Illustrating just how difficult it is to pick mutual funds, none of the three model portfolios offered by Morningstar's "Fund Investor" (Morningstar is considered the leading authority on mutual funds) has been able to beat its benchmark. (Admittedly, the five-year measuring period—November 2001 to November 2006—may be too short for a fair evaluation.)

This section is not meant to be a primer on mutual funds. All you need to know and much more is available in a myriad of sources on the Internet. Type "mutual funds" in a search box and you'll be inundated. Every major investment web site has a learning center. If, however, you do little homework, the following represents what I believe are the important essentials about mutual fund investing. Kathy Yakal, former investment web site columnist for *Barron's,* says (January 8, 2007) that her five favorite mutual fund web sites are Morningstar.com, AOL.com, SmartMoney .com, MoneyCentral.msn.com, and finance.yahoo.com/funds.

1. Picking a Fund

Studies have shown conclusively that most actively managed funds underperform the broad market over time. That makes picking the right fund at the right price critical (although luck is still your best ally). All other things being equal, invest with the fund that shows it cares about its long-term shareholders. This is manifest, in part, by the fund limiting the number of shareholder trades, charging redemption fees to those who sell in the first two or three months, not pushing class B shares, closing funds to new investors when money starts pouring in, and by managers owning a significant dollar amount of their own fund. Other important factors in choosing an actively managed fund include low annual expenses, low portfolio turnover, no or low load or sales commission, and continuity of talent (managers responsible for the track record still at the helm).

Whitney Tilson, columnist for *Motley Fool,* says (December 2006), "To select good mutual funds, I suggest adopting a contrarian mind-set: Look for sectors that are out of favor and have under performed, and stick to funds run by proven value-oriented managers."

2. Can This Year's Hot Funds Repeat?

Mutual fund companies will typically gloat about a good track record in their advertising. It's okay to be proud of what you've accomplished, but in the investment business everyone knows past performance is no guarantee of future results. Psychologically, I am more comfortable buying a fund that has done well than one that has done poorly. But it's a gray area.

The prevailing wisdom is not to chase last year's winners. However, momentum often propels top-performing groups from one year into the next—and then the next after that. Such action is consistent with the concept of the durability of major trends. My sense is that more often than not, immediate past performance is an unreliable guide, but there are enough exceptions to make the rule a shaky one.

> "Chasing stellar performers has been the best way to underperform any market throughout history."
> —Charles Kirk

3. Difficult to Stay on Top

A top-performing 20 to 25 percent average annual return over a 15-year period can be due to a few years of spectacular gains. Hidden during some of the other years may be big losses. A Standard & Poor's study (standardandpoors.com, August 16, 2006) shows how difficult it is for funds to stay on top. In the five years ended June 30, 2006, just 1.12 percent of large cap funds were able to stay in the top 25 percent every year for five years. And over the same five-year period, only one fund out of all the mid cap and small cap funds measured was able to maintain its top-quartile ranking.

Your Retirement newsletter (RetirementPlanningConsultants.com, January 2006) reports the results of another performance study: "Only one in every 10 top-performing mutual funds in a given year stays in the top 25 percent for the next two years. (Listed as common characteristics of the repeat elite are longer manager tenures, lower expense ratios, and minimum losses in bear markets.)" Clearly, the ability of funds to perform at a high level is rarely sustainable.

Perhaps we attach too much importance to winning streaks. In his "Fund Watch" syndicated column (February 17, 2007), Chet Currier of *Bloomberg News* writes, "Past performance always matters; you don't buy a fund without looking at its record. Among other things you want to see evidence of how the manager has fared in both good times and not so good. That doesn't warrant making a fetish of consistency. Since market conditions are constantly shifting, it figures that every so often even the most skillful manager is going to be zigging when the market zags." (Twenty-nine years a columnist, Currier died July 29, 2007.)

4. You Don't Have to Be Smart

Buying a fund for capital gains (one to three years) involves more guess-work than taking a long-term position. It's pretty much a call on which currently popular asset classes/groups will continue their winning ways or which out-of-favor funds are about to emerge. Is the six-year uptrend in small cap value stocks about to end? Will the laggard big caps finally come to the fore? It's a timing problem.

When you invest for the long term you don't have to be that smart, especially if you dollar-cost-average. Since *all* classes and groups eventually return to favor, even if you're wrong with your timing, the passing years will bail you out. And the mechanics of accumulating funds on an ongoing basis couldn't be easier. Most mutual funds offer automatic investment plans; money is withdrawn from your bank account every month and invested directly in the funds you choose.

5. No-Loads Make Cents

As long as mutual funds are sold by commission salesmen, load funds will remain popular. All other things being equal, however, no-load funds are likely to perform better.

If you're considering a load fund, it makes sense to find a no-load fund with similar style, performance, and risk and save the load charge. Sheldon Jacobs, editor of the *No-Load Fund Investor,* has been working with mutual funds for 27 years. He simply says, "There's always an equal or better no-load." Of course there are always exceptions, the most notable being the American Funds family. Despite a 5.75 percent load, it owns 6 of the 10 biggest funds in America (*Barron's,* March 12, 2007, page 42), including the world's largest, Growth Fund of America (AGTHX). Why? Because American's performance has been excellent and has more than offset the load, and because it is aggressively sold.

6. Keep Expenses Low

Expenses matter over the long term; all other things being equal, cheaper is better. John Markese, president of the American Association of Individual Investors, says, "If the expense ratio of a stock fund is approaching 1.5 percent or a bond fund 1.0 percent, think twice before investing. Such fees can be a costly drag on long-term performance" (AAII.com, "What Every Investor Should Know About Mutual Funds"). Morningstar's Christopher Davis adds: "Focus on funds that keep turnover low, keep tax efficiency in mind, and have expense ratios below 1 percent a year, though even cheaper is better" (yahoofinance.com, June 6, 2006).

> "In general, a manager's fee and not his skill, plays the biggest role in performance."
>
> —*Eugene Fama*

7. How Do You Sleep at Night?

If you're putting together your own portfolio of mutual funds instead of using a model, how do you determine the proper mix of asset classes? Janet Brown, editor of *NoLoad Fund*X,* ranked by Hulbert as one of the top-performing mutual fund newsletters over the past 20 years, says, "The two most important things to consider are your investment time horizon and your tolerance for risk. Your time horizon is simply when you'll need the money; risk tolerance is another way of saying, 'How do you sleep at night when the market is in a tail spin?'" (Noloadfundx.com,

June 2006). The asset mix used in some of the 28 model portfolios in Chapter 7 should serve as a helpful guide.

8. Why Fund Investors Do Poorly

I've made this point before but it bears repeating here. When measuring the annual return of a mutual fund or an index, the time period used is January 2 to December 31. If you own a fund and expect your return to be the same as the fund's, the holding period has to be the same.

But typically money pours into a mutual fund when it's strong and near its top and gets withdrawn when it's weak and near its bottom. Rarely does the shareholder buy on January 2 and sell on December 31 (nor should he, necessarily). The result is a sometimes-substantial difference between the published return of a fund and the usually lower return of its shareholders.

This suspected difference in performance was verified by the results of the well-known Dalbar study to which I referred earlier. Published in 2003, it showed that for the 19 years 1984–2002, the average equity fund investor earned a paltry, less-than-inflation 2.57 percent annually, compared to 12.22 percent for the S&P 500 Index. This is incontestable proof of the consistently poor timing of fund holders. Says superstar Bill Miller, manager of Legg Mason

> "There is a huge discrepancy between a mutual fund's return and the return of the average investor in that fund."
> —*Frank Armstrong III*

Value Trust, "The biggest problem that people have isn't selecting the right money managers. It's the way they change managers all the time in response to fluctuations of short-term performance" (CNNMoney.com, "Bill Miller: What's Luck Got to Do with It?," July 18, 2007).

9. Hard to Find a Sleeper

The knock against buying a big mutual fund that owns a large cross section of the stock market is that it is unlikely to outpace the market since, in effect, it *is* the market. Instead, why not buy a small overlooked fund with a good track record? In an era of instant communication where little goes unreported, such sleepers are few and far between.

10. Random Is What's Certain

The probability that this year's top performing fund managers will achieve similar results next year is small. With each succeeding year, the chances of a streak continuing become less and less. If 1,000 people flip a coin and 10 of them get heads 10 times in a row, the chances of the same 10 people doing the same thing on the next time around are remote.

Buckingham Asset Management's Research Director Larry Swedroe says, "There's no persistence of performance beyond what can be expected randomly." Wood Asset Management's Robert Stovall adds, "It's just not true that you can't beat the market. Every year as many as one-third of the fund managers do it. Of course, each year it's a different group." And the *Wall Street Journal's* Jonathan Clements puts it even more succinctly: "Past performance is a lousy guide to future results"(September 10, 2006).

11. Morningstar

This section on mutual funds, as bare-bones as it is, would be incomplete if it didn't mention Morningstar. It behooves investors with an interest in mutual funds to access Morningstar.com, the nation's dominant provider of mutual fund information. It purports to have detailed analyst reports on over 2,000 mutual funds and data on 13,000. It's monthly newsletter, *FundInvestor,* features articles like "Nimble Funds with Room to Grow," "Buying a Good Manager's Weakest Fund," "Is Small Really Beautiful" and "Managers Who Put Their Money Where Their Mouth Is" as well as monitored lists of favorite funds and ETFs. The annual 600-page *Funds 500* is the bible in the industry and a valuable reference. It offers full-page reports on the 500 largest and most popular mutual funds, with statistics on each fund going back 12 years.

12. Compounding

Let your mutual fund dividend and share distributions accumulate. The compounding effect is your best friend. A modest return becomes a large return overall if you let compounding work its magic over many years. Richard Russell, who has been writing the *Dow Theory Letters* newsletter since 1958, calls the compounding interest tables the "Money Bible, the royal, safe, sure road to riches that anybody can travel."

William O'Neil, publisher of *Investor's Business Daily,* explains in his book, *How to Make Money in Stocks* (McGraw-Hill, 2002) how easily a 25-year-old can become a millionaire. All he has to do is invest $1,720 each year till he's 65. O'Neil is assuming an annual rate of return of 11 percent, only a shade higher than the 10.8 percent average annual return (including dividends) of the S&P 500 since 1957. By age 65, the 25-year-old has invested a total of $68,800 (40 years × $1,720) but with interest earning interest for 40 years, it's now worth $1 million. Discount broker Charles Schwab points out that for every five years you wait to start investing, you'll have to put aside twice as much annually to reach $1 million.

13. Mutual Fund Negatives

Just as with stocks, there's always a column B (negatives) about a fund and about buying mutual funds generally. If you're a buyer because you feel the positives outweigh the negatives, it's still wise to be aware of the negatives. It's the best way to avoid unpleasant surprises.

Here's a negative view from professional trader Charles Kirk (TheKirkReport.com): "Most funds underperform the market over the long term so I've always opted for passive index funds and ETFs. Mutual fund investing takes a tremendous amount of research and diligence because you not only have to worry about finding the right fund, but you have to monitor the fund managers and keep a close eye on the expenses they charge you for running the fund. I have better uses for my time."

Former Merrill Lynch security analyst and *Slate* columnist Henry Blodgett said in a December 1, 2004 column, "According to study after study, the vast majority of fund managers can't generate enough extra performance from active management to offset the costs of their efforts (including salaries, bonuses and fund company profits). . . . They collect huge active management fees even when performance stinks. . . . Your odds of picking a market-beating fund are somewhere between one in six and one in 30 (roulette-like); the fund industry's chance of collecting big fees, meanwhile, is 100 percent"

Don't let criticism of the mutual fund industry's greed and self-interest, as valid as it may be, deter you from buying carefully selected funds, especially if your positions are long-term. With the leadership of Jack Bogle and others, reforms will come and the best interest of shareholders will be better served. An $11 trillion, 13,000-fund industry isn't all bad. Thumb through a chart book of mutual funds and you'll see some beautiful long-term uptrends that'll still look pretty good after fees. Money will continue to be made in mutual funds. We have to deal with an imperfect world.

14. More Juice with Sector Funds

The powerhouse in the field of sector funds is Fidelity. It has a stable of 43 sector mutual funds covering all segments of the stock market. Sector funds have appeal because they provide the answer to investors who are more positive on a group than the overall market but not certain which stock in the group to pick.

With sector funds, the investor can be aggressive with a portion of his portfolio in an attempt to juice returns. Mutual fund sector funds like those from Fidelity are actively managed. The manager is trying to outperform a benchmark index. By contrast, the rapidly expanding list of ETF sector funds are clones of the related index and, therefore, require no active management. Both types of sector funds are speculative, the degree of risk depending on the nature and narrowness of the sector.

15. Monitored Mutual Fund Portfolios

A monitored mutual fund portfolio with a good track record is a viable investment option. Most such portfolios are found in mutual fund newsletters and on their corresponding web sites. Some newsletters have been around well over 25 years and their recommended portfolios sport impressive returns (although some of the good numbers result from big gains in the earlier years).

The attraction of these portfolios is their transparency and ease of execution. It's your portfolio and you do the buying and selling but the newsletter tells you what to buy and sell and when. Performance results and updated developments on the portfolio are published monthly, and often sooner, on the web site. The downside is that the investor is obliged to buy *all* the funds in the model portfolio and make all the recommended changes if he's to match the record of the model. Most newsletters feature three or four model portfolios, each representing a different risk level—income, growth, aggressive growth, and so on.

Most investment newsletters are stock oriented, but some focus exclusively on mutual funds. Mark Hulbert (*The Hulbert Financial Digest*) tracks the performance of both, including over 100 mutual fund letters Some of the mutual fund portfolios with the best long-term track records, adjusted for risk, according to Hulbert, are offered through these news-letters: *NoLoad Fund*X* (Janet Brown), *No Load Fund Investor* (Mark Salzinger/Sheldon Jacobs), *Market Timer* (Bob Brinker), *Equity Fund Out-look* (Thurman Smith), *No-Load Mutual Fund Selections & Timing* (Stephen McKee), *Timer Digest* (Jim Schmidt), and *Fidelity Monitor* (Jack Bowers).

There are at least six news-letters that focus exclusively on the Fidelity family of 220 retail mutual funds. Each newsletter is independent of Fidelity and offers three or four monitored portfo-lios that consist only of Fidelity funds. The advantage, of course, is that the limited focus gives news-letter editors Eric Kobren, Jim Lowell, Jack Bowers, Donald Dion Jr., Mark Grimaldi, and others an inti-mate knowledge of all things Fidelity, including their fund managers. Newsletter editors Dan Wiener and John Harris do the same thing with Vanguard, featuring all Vanguard fund model portfolios. The Vanguard universe contains over 130 funds including ETFs.

> "A mutual fund that's performed badly in the short and medium term will almost always perform badly in the longer term, too. Losers over one, three and five years are also likely to become losers over 10 years."
>
> —*Roy Weitz*

16. Outstanding Individual Funds

Sometimes a particular mutual fund excels for so long, it demands attention. The conservative T. Rowe Price Capital Appreciation Fund (PRWCX) hasn't had a single losing year since 1990. That's 16 consecutive years of positive returns through December 31, 2006. No other equity fund has gone as long without reporting a loss.

The FPA New Income Fund (FPNIX), co-managed by Robert Rodriquez and Tom Atteberry, is an intermediate-term bond fund that hasn't had a losing year in 22 years. Bill Miller's Legg Mason Value

Trust (LMVTX) topped the S&P 500 for 15 straight years, 1991–2005. No other fund has come close.

We may hesitate to buy star funds like these because we're afraid that as soon as we buy, the streak will stop. Sure enough, in 2006, Bill Miller's 15-year run ended. Some were relieved. They saw it as inevitable and, now past, a good reason to buy the fund.

The average annual return for Miller's large cap Legg Mason Value Trust over the 15-year run was 16.44 percent. Interestingly, *Barron's* (January 9, 2006) compiled a list of 19 mutual funds that did better than Miller over that same 15-year period, averaging annual gains of 16.5 to 20 percent. Many of the 19 funds made the list because of the popularity of small over large and value over growth during that time span. Unless that popularity persists, it's questionable whether the elite 19 funds will outperform Miller over the next 15 years.

When looking for a mutual fund to buy, here are some things, other than exceptional long-term performance, that would get my attention:

- If someone for whom I have a high regard reveals his personal hold-ings, I pay heed. For example, I have great respect for the judgment of syndicated financial columnist Humberto Cruz, who has been writing about mutual funds for decades. Factual, objective, and devoid of hype, he rarely mentions securities by name. In his May 20, 2003, column he identified eight mutual funds that he owned at that time, namely, Ariel, FAM Value, Muhlenkamp, Oakmark Equity and Income, Royce Total Return, Third Avenue Value, T. Rowe Price Capital Appreciation, and Vanguard Wellington.
- When I learned that savvy billionaire financier George Soros was the biggest investor in Robert Olstein's "Financial Alert Fund," it caught my attention (Bloomberg.com, April 7, 2005).
- I also took note when seasoned fund analyst and editor Dan Wiener ("The Independent Adviser for Vanguard Investors") picked Vanguard Health Care (VHCIX, $25,000 minimum) as his one favorite fund and said he owns it for his kids (MoneyShowDigest .com, January 29, 2005).
- Sometimes a write-up on a fund in a responsible, no-hype publi-cation is so impressive and the statistics so striking, it can't help but get the juices flowing. In the annual *Funds 500* for. 2005 (page 161), Morningstar discusses Fidelity Spartan Municipal

Income Fund (FHIGX) and its manager: "Christine Thompson was our fund manager of the year in 2003 but her success is so consistent, she could easily be a contender every year. She's compiled a remarkably solid record both long-term and short-term. We don't use the word 'remarkable' lightly. This fund and its manager inspire tremendous confidence." Adds *Barron's* in a bullish profile titled "Muni Queen" (April 23, 2005), "In the 10 years just completed, Thompson finished way ahead of the pack, outstripping 96 percent of her group." Write-ups like these in leading publications that have no agenda pique my interest.

17. Elite Fund Managers

If roughly 80 percent of fund managers fail to beat the overall market over time, we're talking here about the other 20 percent. The membership of the elite 20 percent club is constantly changing. Those that manage to stick around for a while usually do so because they're in a hot group that stays hot.

Most managers are trend followers. They almost have to be to keep their job. Going against the trend can sometimes be rewarding but it increases risk and the chances of being wrong. Some, however, have enough confidence in their judgment to make bold moves in volatile sectors. If they're right and their big bet pays off, they end up on the "best manager of the year" list. Seldom do managers make the list without reaching. As Morningstar's Don Phillips says, "You can't beat the market unless you're willing to do something different" (*Barron's*, January 9, 2006). Of course, if they outperform with any regularity, and it becomes apparent that they're bringing something special to the table, their status is elevated to superstar.

Because there are so many random circumstances that can influence performance, lists of best fund managers have limited value. Nevertheless, it can be reassuring to know that your fund manager is recognized as one of the best at what he does. There are a number of publications that publish annual "best" surveys. *BusinessWeek Online* (businessweek .com) features its "Standard & Poor's/*BusinessWeek* Excellence in Fund Management Awards." Winners have to survive a rigorous set of high standards going back over the past five years.

In the *BusinessWeek* survey, the mutual fund universe is divided into 24 categories. Of the 24 winning managers in 2007, only three have won in each of the past five years (2003–2007). They are Bill Miller and Nancy Dennin for Legg Mason Equity Value (LMVTX), Jeffrey Gundlach and Philip Barach for TCW Total Return Bond (TGLMX), and the team that manages Growth Fund of America (AGTHX). Close behind is Dan Fuss for Managers Bond (MGFIX), who won in each of the past four years. Finally, there were three managers who made the winner's circle in each of the past three years: Robert Smith for T. Rowe Price Growth Stock (PRGFX), Bill Gross for Harbor Bond (HABDX), and the team that manages Dodge & Cox Income (DODIX).

Exclusive Group of Repeat Performers *Barron's,* working with Value Line, publishes a list of the top 100 fund managers each year in mid-August. In the 11th annual survey, in 2006, a total of 3,344 equity funds were screened going back 10 years. There were seven managers ranked in the top 10 for both 2005 and 2006 (both lists dominated by growth and foreign equity funds): Bruce Berkowitz, Kenneth Heebner, Charles de Vaulx, Daniel LeVan, Thomas Callan, Neil Hennessy, and Robert Gardiner. Some of the other well-known names that repeated both years were Bill Miller, John Buckingham, Ron Baron, Mario Gabelli, Louis Navellier, Joel Tillinghast, William Danoff, and Chris Davis.

Russell Kinnel, Morningstar's director of mutual fund research and editor of its "FundInvestor" is careful to title his list "Ten of the Best ..." rather than "The 10 Best ..." because he says, "there are other great managers" (Morningstar.com 10/23/06). Kinnel says he favors managers with longer track records. His elite 10 are Will Danoff; Joel Tillinghast; Bob Rodriguez; Saul Pannell; Mason Hawkins and G. Staley Cates (Longleaf Partners); Bill Miller; Brian Rogers; Marty Whitman; and Howard Schow, Theo Kolokotrones, and Joel Fried (Vanguard Primecap).

Some other names that kept recurring in my research on the top fund managers include David Dreman, John Calamos, Wallace Weitz, Richard Aster, Jeff Cardon, Sam Isaly, Gus Sauter, Tom Marsico, Bill Nygren, Robert Olstein, Arnold Van Den Berg, Ed Owens, John Keeley, David Williams, Ron Muhlenkamp, Robert Torray, John Montgomery, and Richard Cunniff.

Cream Rises to the Top Most fund managers are consistent in their approach. If their focus is on small caps and/or value, they don't shift when the spotlight is elsewhere. They wait patiently, knowing their day will come. That means that lists of best managers over 1-, 3-, 5-, and 10-year periods mostly reflect the funds that were in the sweet spot during those time periods. When evaluating managers the comparison should be apples to apples. Most noteworthy are fund managers who outperform others in the same group with some consistency.

We may not be able to quantify the reasons for superior performance but we know it when we see it. And if it recurs over long periods of time, we can mostly eliminate luck from the equation, just as we do with poker players who keep reaching tournament finals or jockeys who keep winning races. Whether it's the mutual fund manager, the poker player, or the jockey, luck always plays some role. Given enough time, however, allowing for some lesser performances along the way, the cream rises to the top.

> "The search for funds that will significantly exceed market returns is one in which past performance has proven of virtually no predictive value; it is a loser's game."
> —*John Bogle*

18. Top 10 Lists

Every January, lists of the best-performing mutual funds for the previous year are featured in the media. Seldom do winners repeat. Even if a group stays hot, the names at the top usually change. Since they cover only a one-year time span, the lists have little more than curiosity value. More meaningful are 3-, 5-, and 10-year results. *Barron's* is one of the few publications that goes back 15 years and, each quarter, ranks the top 20 performers. (Morningstar goes back 12 years with annualized returns in its *Funds 500* and 10 years online). Says Steven Goldberg on Kiplinger.com (May 2006), "Although past results don't ensure future results, you can't ignore them. A fund's long-term performance (10 years or more) compared with other funds that invest in the same types of securities reveals plenty."

There are extenuating circumstances that can dilute the significance of long-term rankings. Funds that hold volatile stocks, fewer stocks, or fewer industries take on more risk and thus position themselves for possible outperformance. Smaller funds and narrow sector funds, especially, are capable of extraordinary gains, so much so that they can mask lots of poor years for a long time. Also clouding the picture is the likelihood of a management change along the way. Today's management may have little to do with yesterday's performance. Overall, the conditions that nurtured superior results years ago may simply not exist today.

Twice a year Standard & Poor's measures the consistency of top mutual fund performers over three and five consecutive years, noting that "Very few funds manage to consistently repeat top 25 percent performance, a sobering reminder of the risks of chasing past performance" (Standardandpoors.com, "Mutual Fund Performance Persistence Scorecard, August 15, 2006). Standard & Poor's does reveal the characteristics common to those who have compiled winning streaks. Most important is the manager's long years of experience. Other shared attributes of outstanding track record holders are low expense ratios and diversified holdings.

Bad Funds Usually Stay That Way Investors with a bargain mind-set may be tempted to scan the names near the bottom of the performance list for possible buys. The rationale is that what falls must rise. Applied to an entire group, that may be true. Applied to a single fund acting worse than its peers, that's likely to be a flawed strategy. Studies have shown that more often than not, a bad fund continues to be a bad fund.

Most major financial publications publish lists of "Best Mutual Fund Performers." Among the more widely followed are those appearing in *Forbes* (annual honor role of great funds), *Barron's, BusinessWeek, Money,* the *Wall Street Journal,* Morningstar, *AAII Journal, Kiplinger,* and so on. All include the top three-to-five-year performers; many extend coverage to 10 years and a few to 15 or 20 years.

Then there are the many financial writers who feature their personal favorites for the long term. Veteran columnist Scott Burns (MSNMoney.com) is typical. In an article titled "The Top Funds for the Next 20 Years" (April 3, 2006), he says, "There is a handful of funds that have been consistent top performers for long enough that we can conclude their managers know how to do the right thing and keep doing it. Here are three balanced funds that may be top-ranked when they put up their 20-year numbers: Leuthold Core Investment, T. Rowe Price Capital Appreciation, and Value Line Income & Growth."

Best Returns over the Past 10 to 15 Years For what it's worth, there are five funds that appear on both the 10-year and 15-year list (through September 29, 2006) of the 20 best mutual fund performers, according to *Barron's* quarterly survey (October 9, 2006, page L21). That feat has been accomplished by Bruce Fund, Fidelity Select Brokerage, Calamos Growth A, BlackRock Global Resources Inv A, and Vanguard Health Care. What kind of return was needed to get on these elite lists? The top 20 funds on the 10-year list ranged between 16.5 percent and 22.7 percent, average annual return; for the 15-year list the range was 15.7 to 18.7 percent.

How can we best use lists of top-performing mutual funds? It would seem prudent to give new managers and new funds on one-, two-, and three-year lists time to prove themselves. John Markese, president of the American Association of Individual Investors, says, "At least a three year performance history that can be compared to the performance of funds with similar investment objectives and assumed risk is indispensable to evaluate a fund manager or a fund. Consistently favorable performance relative to a peer group of funds over different market environments proves no guarantees of future performance, but it is infinitely better than nothing" (AAII.com).

Some investors buy funds on the basis of impressive 5- and 10-year track records but then sell their position after only 12 months of disappointment. Before you buy, it's important to be aware of just how badly the fund has performed and for how long during that 5 to 10 year period. Once you know the bad as well as the good, when the bad comes, you'll at least know it's happened before. What's more, preknowledge of sharp declines in the past will enable you to make a more informed decision—do you have the temperament to hold on during rough times?

When top funds slump, it's the norm, not the exception. The investment advisory firm of Litman/Gregory Analytics in Orinda, California, found that almost all fund managers with good long-term track records have gone through stretches of underperformance lasting three years or longer (*Wall Street Journal,* November 19, 2006).

A Deliberate, Not Random, Walk Down Wall Street The fact that so few funds are able to stay in the top half of their group for three- and five-year periods would seem to support the case for passive investing. On the other hand (when writing about stocks, there's always an "other hand"), a 15-year streak of beating the S&P 500 (Legg Mason Value Trust) or a 16-year streak of never having a down year despite bear markets (T. Rowe Price Capital Appreciation) supports the active investing thesis that homo sapiens *is* capable of taking a deliberate rather than random walk down Wall Street. There are likely others of rare ability who also consistently beat the market, but they work anonymously and we never hear about them. And, of course, there is the handful of inaccessible superstar hedge fund and endowment fund managers who, reportedly, rack up extraordinary gains year after year that we can only read and salivate about.

So much for our capsule discussion of mutual funds. Remember, my purpose is to suggest ways of investing that portion of your money (about 20 percent) not devoted to indexing. So far, I've covered target retirement funds and mutual funds. In the following pages I touch on a number of other ways to go for the active investor. Whatever the investment vehicle, chances are, as an active investor, your holding period will be more capital gains oriented (one to three years) than buy-and-hold oriented. Under this shorter-term scenario, picking the right asset class or sector group at the right time is more important than choosing the right individual fund or fund manager.

> "On average, there is no relationship between a fund's good past investment record and its future returns."
>
> —*Joel Greenblatt*

Chapter 9

Active Investing
with Stocks

Like most strong proponents of indexing, I believe the investor should own some securities outside of index funds. I'm suggesting a roughly 80/20 percent split, the 20 percent devoted to active rather than passive investing. So far, I've discussed two outlets for active investors: life-cycle/target retirement funds (they're for buy-and-holders but actively managed) and mutual funds. A third choice, the most popular one, is buying and selling stocks for capital gains (one to three years or longer). Part One of this book has prepared you for executing this third choice. It's the most challenging and the most fun part of investing. Instead of a professional fund manager, you're making the decisions on your own.

This chapter deals exclusively with ways to generate stock ideas. Specifically, I highlight some of the best places to look for buy candidates. Since there are countless sources of stock ideas, the following list must be limited.

Newsletters

As the former editor of the *Dick Davis Digest* investment newsletter, I can discuss this subject with some perspective.

There are two reasons to buy an investment newsletter: profitable investment ideas and savvy market insights. The better letters provide both, some provide neither. To compete with the vast amount of information available on the Internet, a viable newsletter must bring something special to the table. That special quality is usually a distinctive market approach, wise and insightful commentary, and/or the engaging personality of the editor. An outstanding track record helps a lot but is not essential.

Fortunately, Mark Hulbert (*Hulbert Financial Digest*) provides an objective service for measuring the performance of some 200 newsletters. His records go back to 1980. In his newsletter, his web site (markhulbert .com), and his frequent columns on MarketWatch.com and the *New York Times,* Hulbert, 51, has done a yeoman's job in making the highly diverse newsletter industry more useful, meaningful, and understandable.

In my mutual fund discussion I listed the top fund newsletters. In the stock field, Hulbert says the letters with the best long-term performance are, in order, *The Prudent Speculator* (John Buckingham), *Value Line Investment Survey* (Harvey Katz), *The Chartist* (Dan Sullivan), *Dow Theory Forecasts* (Richard Moroney), *Louis Navallier's Emerging Growth, Growth Stock Outlook* (Charles Allmon), and *Investment Quality Trends* (Kelley Wright). But these are not the only newsletters that merit consideration. There are others (many on the Internet) that have good track records. And still others have loyal subscribers because they bring something special to the table—often the unique perspective, style, or personality of the editor.

Some investment newsletters recommend individual stocks, others offer monitored portfolios of stocks, and some do both. Hulbert's rankings are based on the performance of individual portfolios. Buying a portfolio that has been highly ranked over a period of time is a viable option for the active investor. But if he wants to emulate future performance, he must buy all the stocks in the portfolio, make all the changes as they're called for, and then hope past performance continues. Investors with a shorter time horizon might consider the 68 market timing letters, which Hulbert also ranks (The top three through September 30, 2006, include *Medical Technology Stock Letter* (John McCamant), *Bob Brinker's Marketimer,* and *The Granville Market Letter* (Joseph Granville). Those interested in short-term trading should also explore the wealth of information available on TheKirkReport.com and BrettSteenbarger.com.

One Man's Commitment: A Newsletter Every Three Weeks for 50 Years

Durability is the surest evidence of excellence in a newsletter. Why do subscribers renew year after year after year? Richard Russell has been writing his *Dow Theory Letters* for almost 50 years. Talk about commitment (he's never once skipped a letter). Because he writes with clarity and wisdom, has an engaging style, and has been through all the wars, investors want to keep abreast of his thinking.

There are other veterans with loyal followings. You cannot read Richard Moroney, Louis Navalier, Kelley Wright, Joe Granville, Paul Merriman, John Buckingham, Charles Allmon, Dan Sullivan, Harry Schultz, Jim Stack, Tom Bishop, Bernie Schaeffer, James Dines, Doug Fabian, Jim Oberweis, Michael Burke, John Dessauer, Paul Desmond, Mark Skousen, Norm Fosback, Tom and David Gardner, Peter Eliades, Richard Band, Gerald Appel, George Putnam, Donald Rowe, Robert Prechter, Stephen Leeb, and Sheldon Jacobs, without benefiting from their many years of experience and seasoned perspective. Search their names on the Web and you'll access their newsletters.

The newsletter business is easy to get into, but it is extremely competitive with a high casualty rate. Any subscription letter that's still around after 8 to 10 or more years must have something special going for it. It's usually a particular talent of the writer. With that in mind, here are some additional names of investment newsletter writers that have passed the difficult time survival test. These names, along with those in the preceding paragraph, and those that I have unintentionally overlooked, represent a rich source of stock ideas and market insight:

Adrian Day, Jeff Hirsch, Bob Carlson, Max Bowser, Robert Brinker, Stephen Todd, Timothy Lutts, Tobin Smith, John Mauldin, Arch Crawford, Roger Conrad, Frank Curzio, Dennis Slothower, Thomas Herzfeld, Howard Ruff, John McCamant, Michael Murphy, Martin Weiss, Bert Dohmen, Richard Young,

Jim Lowell, Eric Kobren, Dan Wiener, George Gilder, Todd Harrison, Russell Kinnel, Irwin Yamamato, Janet Brown, Curtis Hesler, Stephen McKee, P. Q. Wall, Neil George, Laszlo Birinyi Jr., George Dagnino, Richard Schmidt, Sy Harding, Jim Schmidt, Irwin Yamamoto, John Bollinger, Mary Anne and Pamela Aden, Bill Mathews, Richard Lehmann, Walter Frank, Jim Collins, Gregory Spear, and Mark Leibovit.

There are hundreds and hundreds of newsletters, many that recommend stocks but not portfolios, that are not followed by Hulbert. One way of getting a good overview is by accessing DickDavisDigest.com (the *Digest* is an excellent compilation of recommendations from a wide range of newsletters; it is in its 26th year of publication; I no longer have an affiliation). Another option is Steven Halpern's guide to financial newsletters, TheStockAdvisors.com. (Steve was my first hire in 1983 and assistant editor at the *Digest*. He and Carla Neufeld were major contributors to the early success of the *Digest*. He's written a book on newsletters, created the first online financial newsletter, and is as knowledgeable as anyone on the subject. I owe a lot to Steve.)

To stay competitive, most print newsletters also have a web site and some are only available on the Web. In the latter category, one of the most popular is John Mauldin's free weekly E letter, "Thoughts from the Frontier," with an estimated weekly readership of over one million (2000wave.com). Mauldin has attracted a sophisticated readership based on the breadth of his writing. He is the author of *Bull's Eye Investing* (2004), *Just One Thing* (2006), and *The Millennium Wave* (2008), all published by John Wiley & Sons.

If a particular investment newsletter piques your interest, always ask for a free sample before subscribing. An updated directory of all 200 newsletters covered by Hulbert with their cost and toll-free number is at MarketWatch .com/news/newsletters/ newsletters.asp.

> "Invest only money you won't need to touch in the next year or three. You don't ever want to be in a position where you're selling because you have to, only because you want to."
>
> —*Andrew Tobias*

The following are a few widely read newsletters. It's only a tiny sampling. As we have detailed, there are a great many others that are well established and highly regarded.

The Prudent Speculator *(prudentspeculator.com)*

This is a value-oriented monthly service with three weekly hotlines. According to Hulbert it is ranked number one within 10-, 15-, 20-, and 25-year periods ending October 31, 2006. Average annual gains during those periods ranged from 16 percent to 24 percent. Like all highly ranked services, it has had bad years along with the good. Its best year produced a 101 percent return while its worst year showed a 50 percent loss.

The Prudent Speculator (TPS) was founded in 1977 by Al Frank, who invested as a hobby while teaching. The stocks he bought and sold in *TPS* were his own. He looked for out-of-favor, undervalued stocks and, if necessary, held them six to eight years. Frank died in 2002 and John Buckingham, 42, who had been co-manager, has been in charge ever since. It's an example of a benign change in management.

TPS runs four portfolios. The oldest and biggest one, inherited from Frank, holds well over 100 stocks. As a teacher, Al Frank had a modest income so he used margin to maximize his returns. *TPS* still uses margin but only negligibly.

Value Line

Founded in 1931 by Arnold Bernhard, and a public company since 1983 (VALU), Value Line is best known for its stock ranking system. It covers some 1,700 stocks and each one is ranked for "Timelines" (probable market performance over the next 6 to 12 months) and "Safety." Stocks are ranked 1 to 5 for Timelines and there are always 100 stocks ranked 1. Additions and deletions are made weekly. It is this group of 100 stocks ranked 1 for Timelines, launched in 1965, that has compiled an impressive record.

For much of the past 25 years, *The Value Line Investment Survey* has been at or near the top of the Hulbert rankings for long-term risk-adjusted performance. Its average annual gain for the 25 years through October 31, 2006 is 13.5 percent. Warren Buffett says, "I don't know of any system that's as good" (ValueLine.com).

The brains behind the ranking system is Sam Eisenstadt, 83, who has been with the company over 60 years and is still active. He's been described as an unassuming, brilliant statistician who resisted pressures during bad markets and stayed with his system. The problem for the individual investor is that the Value Line Timelines system, assuming it continues to perform, requires the purchase of 100 stocks plus weekly changes. An option would be to buy a new ETF, the PowerShares Value Line Timelines Select Portfolio (PIV), or the closed-end fund, First Trust Value Line 100 Fund (FVL), although performance results are likely to differ from the benchmark.

Value Line is widely used as a source of research and reference and is found in most libraries. Each weekly issue brings a full-page report and long-term chart on about 130 stocks, updated in rotation every 13 weeks. Value Line also publishes six other newsletters including ones on mutual funds, convertibles, options, and special situations.

The AAII Journal

I have already written about the American Association of Individual Investors in the section on model index fund portfolios (Chapter 7). I mention it again because its newsletter, the monthly *AAII Journal*, is an especially valuable resource for the do-it-yourself investor. Few if any newsletters offer the same combination of quality research and affordability ($29 per year). It monitors three model portfolios which it claims are more for guidance and instruction than actual purchase (which is why they're not followed by Hulbert). Managed by the chairman of AAII, savvy veteran James Cloonan, updates on the activity in all three portfolios are provided regularly on AAII.com and the *AAII Journal*.

The six-fund model ETF portfolio was discussed in Chapter 7 (Jim Cloonan: AAII). The four-year-old model Mutual Fund Portfolio consists of 10 diversified no-load mutual funds that meet stringent requirements. The 14-year-old Shadow Stock Portfolio of micro cap value stocks is Cloonan's pride and joy. A recent review revealed holdings of 33 stocks and a 10-year average annual return as of October 31, 2006, of 19 percent. All stock purchases must meet strict criteria and stocks are sold if specific standards are not maintained. It is an actual portfolio with real dollars invested. Cloonan says he expects occasional poor years when large cap and growth are market leaders but, in any event, he plans to stay with small cap and value.

Another national organization devoted to investor education that's been around since 1951 is NAIC, the National Association of Investors Corporation. It has its roots in over 13,000 small, local investment clubs. They are supported by regional chapters that hold seminars on long term-investing. The cohesive factor that holds it all together is their excellent

> "Anchoring yourself to a stock can be a fast trip to the bottom. Stocks don't always get back to even."
>
> —*Kevin Gahagan*

monthly magazine, *Better Investing* ($22 for new subscribers), edited by Adam Ritt. For a list of benefits that go with an annual $79 membership, see betterinvesting.org.

Standard & Poor's **The Outlook**

The nation's largest independent financial research firm is best know to investors for its S&P 500 Index, its bond and stock ratings, and its monthly stock guide. It also puts out a weekly investment newsletter, *The Outlook,* that's been around for 79 years. Perhaps it's best known for its stock appreciation ranking system (STARS) which separates its universe of 1,600 stocks into five categories. The highest-rated category are those 125 stocks assigned a "5" ranking, which means the highest potential for appreciation over the next 12 months. All five-star stocks are strong buys and are expected to outperform the S&P 500 Index by a wide margin. They've done just that over the past 17 years, posting average annual gains of 5 to 7 percent above the major market indexes, according to *The Outlook.*

In addition to its Focus Stock of the Week, *The Outlook* recommends nine monitored portfolios. The Platinum portfolio consists of stocks with both a five-star ranking and a "5" fair value rating. It also runs a portfolio of stocks it considers most undervalued, a model ETF portfolio, and a Top 10 portfolio consisting of five-star stocks with the best total return opportunity. Also available: a capital appreciation portfolio, a small/mid cap growth portfolio, a "Power Picks" portfolio, an industry momentum portfolio, and a high yield portfolio.

InvestingInBonds.com

This is a web site, not a newsletter. It covers the important subject of bonds, which we haven't addressed other than their inclusion in our model index fund portfolios. Bonds are key to a diversified portfolio because they provide balance, relative safety, noncorrelation, and income. As we get older and our investment objectives focus more on reducing risk and generating income, bonds may represent most or even all of our holdings.

This is an outstanding, all-inclusive web site with an excellent tutorial section. From a practical point of view, I believe the three most important things to know about bonds are these:

1. The direction of interest rates is even more unpredictable than stocks. That means that unless you hold bonds to maturity (and few long-term buyers do), there is risk of loss. There's even risk if you hold bonds to maturity. In a period of rising inflation, the dollars you redeem will have lost value.
2. In most cases, the longer the maturity, the greater the yield and the greater the risk. Short term means short risk.
3. If the prevailing yield is 5 percent on a 10-year bond and you're offered 6 percent there's a reason—and it's not because you've found a hidden gem. It's because, in some way, there's more risk involved (which salesmen often adamantly deny). The market is all-knowing.

There is little transparency in the buying and selling of bonds. The spread between bid and ask is mostly a gray area to the retail investor. Because spreads and mark-ups can vary widely, two firms can sell the same bond at the same time at different prices. Now, however, thanks to the Bond Market Association and its web site, the retail bond buyer is far less in the dark. In February 2005, InvestingInBonds.com brought the $44 trillion dollar debt market into the twenty-first century by providing real-time prices (within 15 minutes of the trade) for all three bond markets— municipal, corporate, and U.S. government. Before buying, you can now check out the latest trades in your bond, and after buying, you can see your actual trade and how the price compares with what others paid before and after you. As a result, you can make better decisions and be more assured of receiving reasonable prices from your broker.

Sooner or Later, Everybody Buys Bonds In addition to real-time prices, InvestingInBonds.com provides a wide range of helpful services. You can get detailed information on a particular bond including its full trade history. There are constantly updated summaries of what's happening in the bond markets as well as extensive graphs and screens. InvestingInBonds.com is among the very best sites for bond education. It starts with basics for the newcomer and covers all levels of expertise including information on mortgage-backed securities and zero-coupon bonds. It discusses such pertinent subjects as making decisions on what bonds to buy, how best to buy them, how long to hold them, and when to sell them.

Sometime during an investor's life, later if not sooner, bonds become an important component of a strategically balanced portfolio. Usually an index fund—Total Bond Market Index Fund (VBMFX) or an iShares Lehman Aggregate Bond Fund (AGG)—is the popular choice because it provides wide diversification without having to select individual bonds. The same advantage is offered by a wide variety of mutual fund bond funds and listed closed-end bond funds.

A note of caution regarding the latter: Closed-end bond funds, both corporate and municipal, often use leverage (borrowed money) to increase their return, but that can backfire. It's best to buy a leveraged closed-end bond fund in a climate of flat or declining interest rates. If rates go up, a leveraged bond fund will suffer an exaggerated decline.

If, for whatever the reason, you decide to buy individual bonds, a familiarity with InvestingInBonds.com can only help. Other excellent bond web sites include Yahoo! Bond Center (bonds.yahoo.com) and BondsOnline.com.

> "I'd be a bum on the street with a tin cup if the markets were always efficient."
>
> —*Warren Buffett*

"My One Favorite Stock" Lists

The financial media is replete with lists of favorite stocks. Almost every major publication and web site columnist spotlights a list of "favorite stocks for next year." More meaningful is the narrowing down to just *one* favorite stock.

For example, out of 1,600 stocks covered by Standard & Poor's research analysts, 40 are selected each year for the Power Picks portfolio. The 40 stocks represent the single best idea from each of 40 analysts and are published on *BusinessWeek Online*. When an industry analyst who only covers a limited number of stocks and knows them all like the back of his hand says, "This is the one stock I would buy," and knows he's on record with that stock for the following 12 months, I believe it carries more thought and conviction than a routine recommendation.

In January each year, the *Dick Davis Digest* surveys some 50 of the nation's leading market letter writers and publishes their single favorite stock for the coming year. The *Dick Davis Income Digest* does the same thing in the fixed-income field and publishes a "my single best idea" list for generating income and appreciation. Similarly, Steve Halpern, each January, surveys the nation's leading advisors and publishes their one favorite conservative and speculative stock on his web site, TheStockAdvisors.com.

Finally, for many years, *Institutional Investor Magazine,* later followed by the *Wall Street Journal,* publish each October the results of a comprehensive survey to pick the best analysts on Wall Street. One is called the All-American research team, the other the All-Star team. The winning analysts are chosen by the institutions that use their research and are deemed to be the very best within their industry. The competition is keen and winners sometimes get salary increases or bonuses. The published results often include mention of the top analysts' favorite stock(s) within each industry. In looking for stocks, we could do worse than checking out the best ideas from the best analysts.

Being aware of the top analysts in each industry can help in another way. Let's say you want an opinion on Pfizer and the survey names Mr. So-and-So as the number one pharmaceutical analyst. You call the local branch of the analyst's firm. Ask the broker to contact his research department for an opinion on Pfizer from Mr. So-and-So. Why should the local broker do that? Because you tell him that if you act on the information, you'll open an account through him. If you do take action, keep your promise.

Piggybacking the Masters

"We can't own their brains but we can own their stocks." That's the thought process—identify the most successful investors of our time and the stocks they're buying; then buy the same stocks.

It can work if you have patience, since these are often long-term positions. Then again, it may not work, partly because your cost price is likely to be different, but mostly because the stock may prove to be a dud. The best investors in the world are the first to admit they make mistakes. They just make them far less frequently than others. So the odds are with you if you're willing to hold. The odds are better if you duplicate all the guru's moves rather than just one or two.

The reputations of the world's elite investors are sometimes built on the dramatic gains in stocks bought a long time ago. New purchases made in today's range-bound markets are unlikely to show the same explosive growth, or at least not unless held for a long, long time. It's not that the master has lost his touch. It's just that the markets are very different and, more than ever, time is needed to produce results. John Templeton, one of the world's most successful investors, said in 2005, "In all my 92 years, I've never seen a time when it was so hard to find a bargain" (TempletonPress.org, November 28, 2005).

Nevertheless, news of a stock purchase by a superstar investor often has a marked immediate impact. On April 9, 2007, it was announced that Warren Buffett had bought more than 10 percent of Burlington Northern, making him the railroad company's largest stockholder. The stock reached a high that day of 93.22, up over 10 points on the day. Trading in the stock was more than three times the average daily volume.

The Internet has made it easy to track the stock picks of the elite investors. GuruFocus.com, for example, reports the latest buys and sells of 32 members of what it calls its "Guru Hall of Fame." Included are Warren Buffett, George Soros, David Dreman, Edward Lampert, Ken Fisher, Marty Whitman, David Swensen, Joel Greenblatt, Ken Heebner, and Michael Price. The web site lists the complete portfolio and latest commentary from each guru. Both AAII.com and Stockpickr.com also follow the portfolios of selected gurus. Moneyshow.com and SeekingAlpha.com spotlight the top picks of the top newsletter writers, among others.

John Reese takes piggybacking one step further. On his web site, Validea.com, he creates a hypothetical portfolio of stocks that he believes would have been bought by some dozen investment legends. He has developed a buy and sell strategy for each of these gurus based on their published writings. He monitors the portfolios and tracks their performance. Legends include Warren Buffett, Peter Lynch, Benjamin Graham, Ken Fisher, Martin Zweig, *The Motley Fool,* David Dreman, James P. O'Shaughnessy, William O'Neil, Joseph Piotroski, and John Neff, among others.

Own the Stocks Owned by the Most Top Funds

Another variation of piggybacking is a *Forbes* system that has compiled a good track record in its short history. *Forbes* screens for the best-performing funds run by the most experienced managers and then identifies the stocks that are held by the highest number of those elite funds. *Forbes* determines the best long-tenured managers by zeroing in on those who have beaten their peer group in 1-, 3-, 5-, and 10-year time periods. Funds that trade a lot are eliminated. Forbes.com runs its "Picks of the Pros" screen every January when it comes up with its new, "most-widely-held by the best funds" 10-stock portfolio. Says *Forbes,* "The thesis is simple. If a lot of smart guys like the same stock, it must be worth holding." (Forbes.com, January 9, 2006).

Morningstar adds still another twist to the piggyback theme. They start with a group of 20 top-performing investment managers and select stocks that are owned by many of them but that also pass two Morningstar tests: They must be rated five-star, and they must have a high expected average annual return over the next three years. Eleven stocks passed these three tests as of the start of the second quarter of 2007 (Morningstar.com, March 30, 2007): Tyco, Wal-Mart, Dell, Berkshire, Time Warner, American Express, Sprint Nextel, Expedia, Johnson & Johnson, Anheuser-Busch, and Pulte Homes. When a stock is reduced to a three-star rating, it is dropped from the list.

> "I'd be happy if 60 percent of my ideas turned out winners."
> —Peter Lynch

Within the 9,000 hedge fund community, there is a small group of superstar managers, people like George Soros, James Simons, Ed Lampert,

Carl Icahn, and Bruce Kovner. They operate largely in secrecy and are mostly inaccessible. Their funds are closed to all but the super wealthy. Their exploits however, have been widely reported. Firms like Goldman Sachs publish reports that list the stocks favored and avoided by hedge funds. By looking at the top holdings of the most successful funds, the investor can put together a best ideas portfolio without paying management fees.

Steven A. Cohen, 50, has been called the hedge fund king. His $11 billion hedge fund, SAC Capital Partners, has allegedly shown annual average gains of a remarkable 36 percent since its inception in 1992. One of his funds requires a minimum of $25 million to join plus a 3 percent management fee, 35 percent performance fee, and a three-year lock-up period. Those fees resulted in earnings of more than $1 billion to Cohen in 2005 alone. *Forbes* reports his net worth at $3 billion, making him the 85th richest man in America. He has paid as much as $137 million for one painting.

If that kind of consistent investment success triggers your curiosity, how do you find out what stocks Cohen owns and his latest purchases? One source is Stockpickr.com which has thousands of portfolios in its database constantly updated. Here, for example, is part of what it says about Steven Cohen: "He is probably the best trader ever. His hedge fund contains billions of his own money. . . . Known primarily as a short-term trader, in recent years he's been taking longer-term positions. Here are details on some of his main holdings including five new positions." (Hedge fund managers must file a 13-F report of their U.S. equity holdings within 45 days of the end of each quarter.)

Let Buffett Do the Research for You

When star money manager Bill Miller buys a stock, he's using his fund's money, not his own. Few fund managers reveal how they invest their own money. Warren Buffett does. In the 2005 annual report of Berkshire Hathaway (page 75), Buffett says he has about 99 percent of his net worth in the stock of Berkshire Hathaway (BRK) (over time he will be donating some 85 percent of his fortune to charity, mostly to the Bill and Melinda Gates Foundation). He's not uncomfortable owning only one security because BRK itself is a diversified portfolio of many stocks.

So, because of Buffett's candor, you can own the exact same stocks owned by, arguably, the most successful investor of our time. Just buy and hold the following 49 stocks in the BRK portfolio (as of March 31, 2007). They are listed in order of the weight they have in the portfolio (percent of total assets). The top four stocks—KO, AXP, WFC, and PG — represent over 50 percent of the portfolio (Table 9.1).

Table 9.1   Berkshire Hathaway Portfolio*

Symbol	Company	Symbol	Company
KO	Coca-Cola	GE	General Electric
AXP	American Express	FDC	First Data
WFC	Wells Fargo	STI	SunTrust Banks
PG	Procter & Gamble	AMP	Ameriprise
MCO	Moody's	IRM	Iron Mountain
JNJ	Johnson & Johnson	LOW	Lowes Cos.
BNI	Burlington Northern	WU	Western Union
WSC	Wesco Financial	GCI	Gannett
PLC	Tesco	TMK	Torchmark
BUD	Anheuser-Busch	HD	Home Depot
WPO	Washington Post	UPS	United Parcel Service
COP	ConocoPhillips	WLP	WellPoint
PKX	Posco	PTR	PetroChina
UNP	Union Pacific	SVM	Servicemaster**
WTM	White Mountain Ins.	UNH	United Health Group
WMT	Wal-Mart	SNY	Sanofi-Aventis
USB	US Bancorp	IR	Ingersoll-Rand
USG	USG Corp	HRB	H&R Block
MTB	M&T Bank	CMCO	Comdisco Holdings
ASD	American Standard Co.	PIR	Pier 1 Imports
NKE	Nike		Tesco PLC (Britain)
NSC	Norfolk Southern		Kingfisher PLC (Britain)
TYC	Tyco		Iscar Metalworking (Israel)
CMCSA/ CMCSK	Comcast		Posco (South Korea)
COST	Costco		

*As of March 31, 2007; stocks listed in order of percentage weight in the portfolio. See May 21, 2007 Morningstar article on Berkshire's portfolio—Justin Fuller spotlights Morningstar's seven favorites in the portfolio: Johnson & Johnson, Wal-Mart, Wesco Financial, US Bancorp, Western Union, United Parcel Service, and Procter & Gamble.
**To be acquired by Clayton, Dubilier & Rice, a private equity firm.
***In the second quarter of 2007, Berkshire added Bank of America (BAC), a small position on Dow Jones (DJ) and sold H&R Block and Pier 1.

In a March 2, 2007, guest appearance on CNBC–TV, veteran money manager Harvey Eisen (chairman, Bedford Oak Partners), talked about Berkshire Hathaway's stock holdings. He advised viewers to make it easy for themselves and simply buy Buffett's favorite stocks: "Arguably, the world's greatest investor has done all the research for you."

Berkshire reports its holdings to the SEC (13–F) at the end of every quarter. The portfolio is very concentrated with the top four stocks accounting for over 50 percent of the total value. That means you only need to buy four stocks to own half of what Buffett owns. Keep in mind, however, that his holding period is "forever" and that his cost price on these securities, because he's held them forever, is extremely low. The weighting of foreign stocks in his portfolio is not known. To keep updated go to GuruFocus.com, Stockpickr.com, edgar-online .com, or Morningstar.com.

Virtual Investing

Some advisers suggest practicing the buying and selling of stocks on paper before committing real money. The idea is that you can learn about the market and about yourself without the risk of loss. We could certainly learn more, especially about ourselves, if we risked real dollars, but even in a fictional setting, there's a lot to be learned. Ken Kam and his web site, Marketocracy.com, make it especially easy.

San Mateo, California–based Marketocracy invites the public to create their own virtual portfolio with $1 million of virtual cash. The make-believe portfolios operate under the same SEC rules followed by mutual fund managers and performance is tracked in real time. There are some 100,000 amateur investors in 130 countries who have set up portfolios for free, and trade with a fake million dollars. Everyday Marketocracy updates the percentage gain/loss in each portfolio so the owner can compare performance with the major indexes. Those that rank among the best 100 on a long-term basis, three to five years, earn some real prize money. For a fee, there is access to the holdings and latest trades of the top 100 portfolios.

Kam says his mission is to find the best investors in the world. He contends that no investor is good in all sectors of the market and that his web site gives members a chance to find out just where their strengths are. His message is a simple one: "Find out how good you are, for free." For do-it-yourself investors, Marketocracy looks like a good place to learn and discover talent—or lack of it.

There are other fantasy investment sites that give you play money to practice your trading skills without risk. These include Young Money's Fantasy Stock Market (at YoungMoney.com), Investopedia's Stock Simulator (simulator.investopedia.com), Virtual Stock Exchange from MarketWatch, and Stock Trak (stock-trak.com), among others.

> "Anytime anybody offers you anything with a big commission and a 200-page prospectus, don't buy it."
>
> —*Charlie Munger*

Stock Screens

When looking for stock ideas, stock screens can be a big help. They act as filters, scanning a database of thousands of securities and coming up with a list of stocks that have just the qualities you want. The screening tools found on financial web sites feature long lists of financial criteria such as P/E ratios, profit margins, and growth rates. You can select one or more of these indicators, choose a desired range and click "search." The more restrictive your parameters, the smaller the list of candidates.

For example, let's say you're looking for drug companies that are listed on the NYSE with a P/E ratio under 20, earnings growth of at least 10 percent over the past four years, and profit margins of at least 12 percent. Before computers, this would have taken forever. Run a screen and it's instantaneous.

Let's say you come up with five stocks. That in itself should not be considered a buy list. You don't buy stocks based on statistics alone. But you have narrowed the field to a group of stocks you may want to watch or run further screens on. At the end of the day, you may end up buying a stock for reasons that will never show up on a screen. The process, however, will make you better informed and that's rarely a negative.

Screening can help both the least and the most sophisticated investor. The former may simply want to focus on the highest-yielding stocks with rising earnings, stocks that have been up at least six days in a row, the strongest stocks in the strongest groups, or the most profitable companies with low P/Es. The seasoned investor may be more interested in those stocks that have broken out of their 200-day moving average or show a minimum cash flow growth over the past five years.

Separating the Wheat from the Chaff

In the "Tools" section of some web sites there are screens with as many as 150 categories or metrics. The possible combinations are endless. And the results of these combinations can themselves be further combined, refined, and expanded, and on and on. For example, you may want to find out which utility stocks are yielding over 4 percent and going ex-dividend within 60 days, and then which of those are growing the fastest, and then which of those, if any, are being accumulated by the top 50 hedge funds. Or you may want to look for the strongest stocks in the weakest groups and then which of those are trading with P/E multiples near their historic lows.

Many web sites do the screening for you. They create innovative screens and then track the candidate stocks, often with impressive results. For example, one of AAII's many screens is called "Up 5% Earnings Revisions." It is a simple concept but has produced excellent returns. The screen looks for companies that have announced significant (5 percent or more) upward revisions in their annual earnings estimates. Historically, in a slowing economy, investors have rewarded such companies with higher share prices. This tendency is reflected in the excellent track record for this screen. AAII also offers screens that track portfolios based on its interpretation of the investment strategies of leading professionals including Buffett, Dreman, Graham, Lynch, Neff, O'Neil, Templeton, and Zweig. Performance results for each of its 50 investment strategy portfolios are updated monthly.

Some of the more popular online screening tool web sites include BusinessWeek, MSN Money, Yahoo! Finance, Morningstar, and SmartMoney. Charles Kirk's two favorite screeners are Reuters'"Power-Screener" and "Stock Investor Pro" from AAII (both charge a fee). Kirk gives subscribers access to many of the screens he uses for his personal investing and trading.

Screening is not the end-all and be-all for selecting stocks. Statistical or quantitative factors can't provide you with information about upcoming products, pending lawsuits, or a possible recession. But if you're doing your own research, screens can be a good place to start. They'll save you time and narrow your options. The screen results may or may not affect your final stock selection, but separating the wheat from the chaff definitely gives you a leg up.

> "The best stocks over the next 20 years will be stocks no one knows about today. Use stock screens to ferret out the unknown and undiscovered."
>
> —*Charles Kirk*

Brokerage Focus Lists

Almost all major brokerage firms publish an ongoing "favorite stocks" list. The performance of the list is especially important to the firm, not only for bragging rights but also for its use in marketing. To the investor, especially those who facetiously claim to use analyst stock picks as contrary indicators, a list of favorite stocks is yawn-inducing at best. Interestingly, the results of a recent study show the firm ranked highest in focus list performance uses technology not analysts, to pick stocks.

For more than a decade, Chicago-based Zacks Investment Research has compared the performance of focus lists from 12 major Wall Street brokerages over one-, three-, and five-year periods. Zacks puts a stock in a theoretical portfolio when the broker adds it to its "best idea" list and deletes it when the broker removes it. *Barron's* reports the rankings twice a year. For both the three- and five-year periods ending June 30, 2006, Charles Schwab is the winner.

Schwab uses a quantitative system to select 100 stocks for its Equity Model Portfolio. It starts with 3,200 stocks, which are ranked weekly according to 18 factors. Included are such metrics as free cash flow, sales to assets ratio, capital expenditures, stock buybacks, short selling, stability of revenues, and price momentum (*Barron's*, November 27, 2006). The success of its approach (three times its nearest five-year competitor) may be due, in part, to its strictly statistical model, which stays away from analysts' judgment calls like earnings forecasts. Other firms that have ranked high in three- to five-year performance are Goldman Sachs and Morgan Stanley.

As with all model portfolios, if you want to duplicate its performance, you have to buy every stock (the average focus list holds 20 to 30 issues), add and delete when told, hold for three to five years, and hope history repeats itself. One reason to follow such a buy-and-hold strategy, according to Zacks Research, is that the average return of the 12 brokers lists of "best ideas" has easily beaten the S&P 500 index for both three- and five-year periods (*Barron's,* September 25, 2006).

Stock-Picking Columnists

There is an unending flow of stock recommendations coming from a host of financial columnists. Most every investment-oriented newspaper, magazine, and web site has its own staff of armchair analysts. Those with the biggest following are those who have been around the longest, work for the biggest publications, and avoid really big mistakes. The veteran columnist becomes a veteran because he helps readers the most, by adding to either their understanding or their pocketbook. To stay in business, it helps to recommend more winners than losers. More and more writers are tracking their own performance.

The columnists for MSNMoney.com, for example, like Jim Jubak, Harry Domash, Jon Markman, and others, typically give themselves a report card. So do the stock pickers for *Barron's, Forbes,* and others. My hat's off to anyone who makes recommendations in print and then, voluntarily, revisits them later on. It's the type of transparency that should be commonplace, not only in the press but also on TV (with the help of visual aids). As it is, the talking heads on television get a free ride.

Among the more noteworthy stock-picking columnists is John Dorfman (age 60). President of Thunderstorm Capital, a money management firm in Boston, Dorfman recently retired as a columnist for Bloomberg.com after nine years. Previously he was a journalist for the *Wall Street Journal.* Like everyone else, Dorfman picked losers, but on balance, his portfolios did very well over the years (the Robot Portfolio, the Bunny Portfolio, etc.).

He is disarmingly candid. "Here's a look at my triumphs and tragedies" he titles one of his columns. "Anyone who followed my advice to buy Invacare, maker of wheelchairs, must feel like calling for one now. . . . The performance of the eight stocks I recommended back in September has been awful . . ." (His triumphs more than offset his losses). In his "disclosure note" at the end of his column he stretches transparency to the limit: "I own Boston Scientific for two clients, Stone Energy for one. My wife owns Exxon Mobil, as does one client" (Bloomberg.com, November 14, 2006).

What I Learned after Writing a Column for Nine Years

John Dorfman is now focused on his investment firm, Thunderstorm Capital. Here are some excerpts from his final column (Bloomberg.com, February 13, 2007):

> I'd like to highlight lessons that emerged from writing the column in the past nine years. (1) Out-of-favor stocks are the best road to capital gains. The results of the hypothetical portfolios published in this column have deepened my long-standing conviction that a value style is the wisest investment course. . . . (2) Don't be swayed by what Wall Street analysts say. From 1998 through 2006 I tracked the annual performance of the four stocks analysts most loved (those with unanimous "buy" recommendations for a large number of analysts) and the four they most hated (those with a high percentage of "sell" recommendations). Over the nine years from 1998 through 2006, the stocks the analysts loved posted an average annual loss of 3.7 percent. The despised stocks did better, down 0.2 percent annually. Neither group beat the overall market. . . . (5) Predicting the markets with consistency is extremely difficult. I've learned to take all market predictions, including my own, with a grain of salt. . . . (7) High valuations alone aren't a good reason to sell a stock short. . . . (8) High profits alone are no reason to invest in a stock."

Boston-based Dorfman can be reached at jdorfman@thunderstorm capital.com.

A complete list of stock-picking columnists would be too long. The following is a small sampling of some of the more seasoned, widely read writers who could well prove a fertile source of stock ideas: David Dreman, Laszlo Birinyi, John Rogers, Ken Fisher, and Jim Grant (all do eight columns a year for *Forbes*); James Stewart, Roger Lowenstein, and Eric Savitz (*SmartMoney*); Alan Abelson, Andrew Bary, Michael Santoli, and Shirley Lazo (*Barron's*); Marshall Loeb, Herb Greenberg (MarketWatch.com), Jason Zweig (*Money*), Jim Cramer (TheStreet.com), Andrew Tobias (andrewtobias.com) and Harry Newton (TechnologyInvestor.com). There are many others equally popular.

Two of the aforementioned columnists have unique credentials. Alan Abelson is 82 years old and has been with *Barron's* for over 50 years, formerly as editor. His weekly column, "Up and Down Wall Street" (he focuses on the "Down" part) has been in the forefront of financial journalism for decades. Few have his ability to put words together as cleverly or as effectively. In the tradition of the most artful wordsmiths like William Buckley, Louis Rukeyser, George Will, William Safire, and others, Abelson can write stinging sarcasm, belly-laugh humor, or compelling logic with equal dexterity. He is known for his strong bearish bias and thus performs a valuable service. First, he is a source of badly needed balance in times of euphoria, and second, he is a major builder of the "wall of worry" that bull markets need to climb.

Richest Financial Columnist in America

If he's not the wealthiest financial columnist in America, Ken Fisher, 56, has to be close. In 2006, *Forbes* ranked him the 297th richest man in America with a net worth of $1.3 billion. That doesn't come from writing eight columns a year for *Forbes*. It is the result of a combination of extremely aggressive marketing of his money management firm and a good track record. Fisher is unusual, not only for his unconventional views but because he backs up his massive self-promotion with solid performance. Exposure of his "Portfolio Strategy" column in *Forbes* for 22 years and his numerous articles and books have given him an effective platform to grow his business. Fisher Investments in Woodside, California, has a reported $35 billion of assets under management (go to Stockpickr.com for a list of his latest holdings).

Fisher comes by his investment acumen naturally. His father, Philip Fisher (who died in 2004), was a legendary buy-and-hold investor best known as a mentor of Warren Buffett and the author of the investment classic, *Common Stocks and Uncommon Profits* (John Wiley & Sons, 1958, updated 2003 by his son).

Ken Fisher is a student of behavioral finance. In his recently published *The Only Three Questions That Count* (John Wiley & Sons, 2006), he advises not to get suckered into believing falsehoods just because everyone else believes them. He counsels investors to avoid regret and instead embrace mistakes and learn from them. And he says you should act on ideas that you think are true but that everyone else thinks are crazy.

I should also mention that *Forbes* columnist Jim Grant is among the nation's leading authorities on the tricky subject of interest rates. Candidates for the "big three" in that field would likely be Bill Gross, the "bond king" from Pimco; Martin Barnes, the longtime editor of the prestigious monthly newsletter *The Bank Credit Analyst;* and Jim Grant.

> "In my personal portfolio I have 97 stocks. I don't care how well you think you know a company, anything can happen."
> —*John Buckingham*

After an eight-year stint writing "The Current Yield" column in *Barron's,* Grant launched *The Interest Rate Observer* in 1983. With a contrarian, value bias, Grant writes with prescience, insight, and wit and is a favorite of the institutions. That's why he's able to get $850 a year for his 12-page, 24 times a year newsletter. Grant describes his publication this way: "Without bragging, we like to think we are the financial information medium that least resembles CNBC" (grantspub.com).

The CAN SLIM Approach: William O'Neil

A few investment strategies made popular by a particular individual have caught on. One is called CAN SLIM®, a system for selecting stocks devised by William J. O'Neil, 74, founder and publisher of *Investors Business Daily®* (*IBD®*). O'Neil launched *IBD* in 1984 to promote the virtues of CAN SLIM and aggressively market it through seminars and workshops. He believes his system gives the investor an opportunity to succeed on his own without Wall Street research or professional help, providing he does his homework and has the right temperament.

O'Neil studied the characteristics of 600 of the biggest stock market winners from 1953 to 2001. The result: CAN SLIM, an acronym for what O'Neil found to be the seven common attributes of all great performing stocks *before* they make their big price run-ups. O'Neil is looking for potential "ten baggers," stocks with the potential to soar at least 10 times in value. Candidates must meet these seven criteria:

Current quarterly earnings per share up at least 18 to 20 percent, year over year.

Annual earnings up 25 percent or more for each of the last four or five years.

New products or services or management fueling growth and not cost cuts; stock at or near a new high.

Supply and demand reflects small or reasonable number of shares outstanding and rising volume as the price moves up.

Leading stock—that is, one of the top two or three stocks in a strong industry group that show a high relative strength ranking.

Institutional ownership—stocks held by a minimum of 10 institutions with ownership by mutual funds increasing.

Market direction—Dow, S&P, and NASDAQ should be in a confirmed uptrend since three out of four stocks follow the market's overall direction.

The system is explained in detail on the *Investors Business Daily* web site (investors.com, "Learning Center") and in O'Neil's book *How to Make Money in Stocks: A Winning System in Good Times or Bad* (3rd edition, McGraw-Hill, 2002). O'Neil is a strong advocate of cutting losses quickly by selling any stock that falls 8 percent below the purchase price, with no exceptions.

Some characterize CAN SLIM as momentum investing, buying high and selling higher, but O'Neil takes exception. He says what the system does is identify companies with strong fundamentals—big sales and earnings increases which are a result of unique new products or services—and encourages buying their stock when they emerge from price consolidation periods or bases and before they advance dramatically in price (see Wikipedia's article, "CANSLIM"). It is an excellent tool for active investors looking for growth stocks.

Human Nature Gets in the Way

The knock on CAN SLIM is the same as on most theoretically sound systems: Execution requires robot-like, not human, qualities. It calls for a commitment to study and monitor watch-lists and charts. The data on stocks that meet the criteria has to be reviewed frequently to ensure accurate entry and exit timing.

In a revealing article in the March 5, 2006, *Los Angeles Times,* journalist Thomas Kostigen wrote about his own pursuit of CAN SLIM, including his attending monthly meetings. The sessions are held for O'Neil devotees in the United States and five other countries. Kostigen solicited comments from fellow attendees: "CAN SLIM calls for investors to be patient and to buy only at the most opportune moment. Human nature gets in the way." Said another, "How many people can take time out of their busy lives to pore over stock charts and stare at the computer all day?" How did the *Los Angeles Times* writer's attempt to follow the system work out? "In the end, it was like a diet. CAN SLIM proved just too rigorous to stick with over time."

On the other hand, the CAN SLIM portfolio selected by the independent American Association of Individual Investors led all of its other model portfolio screens in 2005 and produced excellent results in the previous seven years. In the *AAII Journal* (April 2003), analyst John Bajkowski wrote, "CAN SLIM has been one of the most consistent and strongest performing stock selection systems during both bull and bear markets." Of course, the proprietary screens used by AAII may vary from other CAN SLIM screens. Since some of the basic criteria that must be met is less than definitive, there can be different interpretations. The metrics used to determine the "direction of the market," for example, or "significant growth" or "strong volume" can vary according to interpretation and so, therefore, can the screens used and the results attained. Some may find Mike Gibbon's subscription service, breakoutwatch.com, helpful: It identifies stocks that it believes are technically ready to breakout.

Followers of CAN SLIM find it helpful to subscribe to *Investors Business Daily* since it supplies information required for CAN SLIM analysis. The newspaper also features the "100 IBD" list. It's a weekly computer-generated list of its 100 highest-rated stocks (strong price

performance and superior earnings). Investors.com also provides
subscribers with a weekly CAN
SLIM Select screen. It includes
the top 100 candidates that fit its
criteria, including stocks not far

> "We have never really seen a
> great five year investment that
> doesn't give you another oppor-
> tunity to get back in."
> —*Duncan Richards*

from their 52-week high. It's a popular source of stock ideas for traders.
Although the *Wall Street Journal* has some 10 times more paid circulation
(2,068,439 vs. 214,059 for *IBD* on March 31, 2007; Audit Bureau
Circulation), *Investors Business Daily* is a favorite of more sophisticated
investors, especially those that are technically oriented.

The Magic Formula: Joel Greenblatt

Another investment strategy that has sparked interest is Joel Greenblatt's
magic formula. It's a value approach to investing that was introduced
with the publication of *The Little Book That Beats the Market* (John Wiley
& Sons, 2005). An attention-getting title, a unique format (the book is
indeed little at 5 × 7 inches and 155 pages), a simple, engaging writing
style, a positive review in the *Wall Street Journal* along with other mostly
enthusiastic reviews, and a Foreword by the dean of financial writers,
Andrew Tobias, resulted in an immediate best seller.

Joel Greenblatt, 49, is the founder and managing partner of Gotham
Capital, a hedge fund that alleges 40 percent annualized returns since its
inception in 1985. Says Tobias in the foreword he wrote for *The Little
Book* ... , "I've known Joel for decades. He is really smart ... really successful (I mean really successful).... His success has come from shrewd
investing (not from selling books)."

An MBA from the Wharton School, Greenblatt founded a bond
firm and a web site for professionals called the Value Investors Club. He
was chairman of Alliant Techsystems, a major supplier of ammunition to
the U.S. government. He is currently an adjunct professor at the Columbia University Graduate School of Business where he teaches a course
called "Value and Special Situation Investing." His philanthropy is aimed
at the education of children in New York City. He has five children and
says this book was inspired by the desire to teach them how to make

money for themselves in terms that an 11-year-old can understand. The investment gene runs in his family; his younger sister, Linda, is also a New York hedge fund manager.

What's unusual about Greenblatt is that he is one of the few authors who write about how to make a lot of money investing who has actually *made* a lot of money investing. To the extent that his success on Wall Street came from following the same advice he gives his readers, his book takes on added credibility.

Defining What's Good *and What's* Cheap

The idea behind *The Little Book* is a simple one: Invest in good companies when they're cheap. Generally, good companies do not come cheap but there are always some that do. Greenblatt tells you how to spot them by explaining exactly what's *cheap* and what's *good*.

> **"Cheap" stocks** are based on earnings yield that is the inverse of P/E (price to earnings). It's simply last year's earnings divided by the stock's market capitalization. A stock with a high earnings yield is one that earns a lot relative to its price—in other words, it's inexpensive, just as a low P/E stock is inexpensive.
>
> **"Good" stocks** are based on return on capital, which is a measure of efficiency. A company that generates a high return on invested capital is one whose stores or factories earn a lot relative to the cost of building them.

It's not enough to buy at a cheap price. It has to be a good company at a cheap price.

Greenblatt says if we buy companies that have *both* a high earnings yield and a high return on capital we can make a lot of money. His magic formula uses a database of 3,500 of the largest listed U.S. companies. Each company is assigned a ranking from 1 up to 3,500. The company with the highest earnings yield is ranked 1, the lowest is ranked 3,500th. The company with the highest return on capital is ranked 1, the lowest is ranked 3,500th. The magic formula combines the rankings. The companies that have the lowest combined totals are the best companies to own. A company that is ranked 8th cheapest and 13th for return of capital would have a score of 21. The magic formula says to buy the 25 to 30 stocks with the lowest scores, hold them for one year (or, for tax reasons, just under a year for losses and just over a year for winners), and then replace them with new candidates.

To make it easy, Greenblatt generously created a free web site so readers can get the names of the latest stocks that the formula is picking (the 3,500 stock database required is expensive). Go to MagicFormulaInvesting.com for a daily updated list of the highest-ranked stocks under the magic formula. During the first year, buy five to seven stocks every few months until you reach 20 to 30 stocks (equal dollar amounts in each stock). Sell each stock after holding it for one year. Replace sold companies with an equal number of new selections. (To minimize commissions you can use foliofn.com, buyandhold.com, sharebuilder.com, etc.) Continue this process for at least three to five years, regardless of results. Otherwise, Greenblatt believes you're likely to throw in the towel before his magic has had a chance to work.

Have Faith When the Market Says You're Wrong

The reason why stocks selected by the magic formula are selling at depressed levels, Greenblatt concedes, is because their earnings prospects are poor. The magic formula doesn't factor in estimated future earnings, only last year's earnings. That's why the system often doesn't work for one, two, or even three years in a row. Since initial purchases are staggered, it means you may be forced to keep buying losing stocks every few months for years. The magic formula requires faith that you are right when the market is saying you're wrong. Of course, that applies to value investing in general. Out-of-favor stocks can stay unloved for a long time, which can be stressful and draining on the holder.

Greenblatt says, "It either makes sense to buy above average companies at below average prices or it doesn't. If it does, it means you'll need a 3 to 5 year period to bear that out."

Greenblatt promises his readers that with patience the results of his system will "beat the pants off even the smartest professionals." He has back-tested the magic formula for 17 years (1988–2004) with outstanding results versus the S&P 500 and an equal-weighted market index. However, some critics claim the methodology used in the back-testing was flawed and that matching past performance 30 percent-plus numbers in the real world is unlikely (*Barron's*, March 27, 2006). Others criticize the sheer number of trades that have to be made each year, as well as the commissions and close monitoring involved. Ronald DeLegge, editor of ETFguide.com, refers to Greenblatt's "sophomoric assumption that the investing masses can somehow duplicate his track record by reading his book. In theory it should work. In real life it doesn't."

Most reviews have had a positive bias. It's hard to argue against buying above-average companies at below-average prices. The consensus is that the jury will be out for another 5 to 10 years but that the patient investor who has the conviction and discipline to do all he's supposed to do is likely to beat the averages over time.

A recurring theme throughout this book is the terrible difficulty of making money in the stock market. (That's why I recommend a diversified, low-cost portfolio of index funds for most of your money.) Joel Greenblatt believes "most people have no business investing in individual stocks on their own." That's why he advocates a magic formula and a way to implement it. As a practical matter, the number of people who actually follow this system over a long period of years is not likely to be much greater than the number of investors who put $1,000 into Microsoft 30 years ago and have $50 million today. But I could be wrong.

Unlike other gurus, Greenblatt deserves points for acknowledging, up front, that human nature is likely to derail attempts to stay with the program long-term. That's why he doesn't worry about too many people following his formula at the same time, forcing prices higher. They simply won't be around that long. But that doesn't cool Greenblatt's

> "When the market has hit bottom after a long decline, i.e. the bear market has ended, that is the time when the most reasons are given for why the market will go lower still."
>
> —*Unknown*

passionate belief in the system itself. It's my view that anyone who is very, very smart, very successful, highly regarded by his peers, and who feels so strongly about a way to make money that he writes a book about it for his own kids to follow, deserves serious consideration.

Jeremy Siegel's Dividend Approach

There are other investment gurus with their own systems for outperforming the market. Prominent among them is Jeremy Siegel, 62, a professor of finance at the Wharton School for over 30 years. "Mr. Dividend" has written extensively on why dividend-paying stocks are the investor's best friend. Historically, dividend stocks have been bought for income and safety, not appreciation. But Siegel believes you can buy dividend-paying stocks for growth providing you reinvest the dividends and hold the stocks for a long time.

More than any one point, Siegel keeps pounding the table on the vital importance of reinvesting the dividends (most companies will do that for you). By reinvesting dividends, the investor gains from both the magic of compounding and the accumulation of more shares in down markets. The combination of these benefits is what produces the growth in high-dividend-paying stocks over time. In addition to paying dividends, Siegel favors stocks that represent good quality, good value, and have a wide moat (strong barriers to entry by the competition).

Siegel's most popular books are *Stocks for the Long Run* (McGraw-Hill, 1994; rev. 2002) in which he makes a strong case for long-term investing; and *The Future for Investors* (Crown Business, 2005). The latter is best known for two widely quoted studies that produced unexpected results. The first compares the performance of the original S&P 500 stock portfolio with the continually updated S&P 500 from March 1, 1957 (when the S&P index was initiated) to December 31, 2003. To his surprise, Siegel found that anyone who bought the original portfolio and did nothing but reinvest dividends, outperformed the continually revised index. Why? Because, says Siegel, investors overpay for growth. On average, 20 new stocks are added to the S&P 500 Index each year, and when they're added they're invariably at the top of their game and expensively priced.

In the second study, Siegel compares the performance results of growth-oriented IBM with that of stodgy Standard Oil of New Jersey (later Exxon) for the 53-year period 1950–2003 (later extended to 2005), reinvesting dividends for both stocks. IBM's earnings grew much faster but, at the end of the day, it lagged Exxon's return by a significant amount over the long term. Why the unexpected result? Because IBM consistently sold at a high price due to investor's high growth expectations whereas more modest prospects kept Jersey's price down. Jersey also paid a larger dividend, averaging over a 5 percent yield compared to 2.1 percent for IBM over the 53 years. Jersey's relatively low price and reinvestment of a bigger dividend resulted in the accumulation of more shares. The extra shares were enough to beat out high-powered IBM in the long run.

Dividends Are Great But So Are Index Funds

Despite this evidence of the long-term superiority of high-dividend-paying stocks, Siegel recommends investors put half their money in index funds. Specifically, in order to outperform the modest returns he expects for the overall market, he recommends the allocation shown in Table 9.2 (*BusinessWeek Online*, January 26, 2005).

In selecting stocks, Siegel favors what he calls "corporate El Dorados," the 20 best-performing surviving stocks from the original 1957 S&P 500, all dividend payers. These include stocks like Bristol Myers-Squibb, Coca-Cola, Colgate, Wrigley, Schering Plough, Wyeth, General Mills, Altria, Tootsie Roll, Royal Dutch, PepsiCo, and Abbott Labs.

To access Siegel's latest thinking, check out his monthly columns on Yahoo.com and *Kiplinger's Personal Finance* magazine. To find out what stocks currently meet his criteria, go to JeremySiegel.com ($150 annual subscription). Another option is to buy one of the 37 relatively new fundamentally based ETFs from WisdomTree. Siegel has allied himself with the WisdomTree family of funds as an adviser—not surprisingly,

Table 9.2 Jeremy Siegel Portfolio Allocation

Percentage	Asset Allocation	U.S. or Abroad	Description
50%	Index Funds	U.S.	A Wilshire 5000 based index fund
		International	iShares MSCI EAFE (Europe, Australia, Asia, Far East) (EFA)
50%	Stocks	60% U.S.	Broadly diversified with focus on high-dividend stocks with low P/E ratios. Tilt toward industries that have performed the best over time, including brand name consumer staples, pharmaceuticals, and energy stocks. Without fail, reinvest dividends.
		40% Overseas	In the next 20 to 40 years, a lot of growth expected outside the United States.

Data source: Amey Stone, "Street Wise," *BusinessWeek Online*, January 26, 2005.

since it is a company that sells only fundamentally weighted funds based on cash dividends and other metrics. Siegel is a passionate advocate of fundamentally weighted indexes rather than the traditional capitalization-weighted indexes like the S&P 500.

The Next Wave of Investing

According to his back-tested research, weighting stocks in an index by some fundamental metric—like earnings, sales, and especially dividends—instead of by the stock's total market value (capitalization) will generate higher long-term returns. For example, in a dividend-weighted index, a company that pays out $200 million annually in cash dividends will enjoy twice the weight of a company paying $100 million, regardless of their respective market values.

The debate between fundamentally based and capitalization-based indexers is a heated one. Siegel labels fundamentally weighted indexes "the next wave of investing," ideal for devotees of value investing. Equally passionate in their opposition are such traditionalists as John Bogle and Burton Malkiel.

In assessing Siegel's overall approach, if it is hard to fault a strategy of buying good stocks cheap (Greenblatt's magic formula), it is harder still to criticize a strategy of buying good stocks cheap that pay a nice dividend—especially when, according to Siegel's research, the bulk of the real return on stocks (minus inflation) has come from dividends.

But every market approach has its negatives, and this one has four:

1. Past performance is no guarantee of future results—a point that Siegel readily concedes.
2. Like everything good that happens in the market, success requires lots of time and patience.
3. Reinvesting means not having the dividends to spend even though they're taxable. We may need the extra income.
4. The number of attractive high dividend stocks is shrinking. There are few, if any, quality stocks today like the old Standard Oil of New Jersey that yield 5 percent (the closest may be Altria around 4 percent).

The yield on the S&P 500 at under 2 percent is less than half of what it used to be. Only time will tell if the WisdomTree dividend ETFs, based on Siegel's approach, will outperform the market. Against these negatives, I see one compelling positive: Take almost any well-thought-out approach that's researched and strongly supported by a lot of smart people, and the odds will be in your favor if you stay with it.

> "It's important to keep a company and the stock of that company separate in your thinking. At some point, most shares of good companies get overpriced and become bad stocks and shares of poor companies get underpriced and become good stocks."
> —David Nassar

Private Money Managers

Perhaps the question I've been asked the most over the years is, "Can you recommend a good investment adviser to handle my account?" For the active investor trying to beat the market with other than index funds, a professional money management firm with a good track record is a viable option. There are thousands of such firms. Some specialize in managing certain asset classes, others run a diversified portfolio, but most offer a variety of options. They collect a fee based on the size of the account. What they're selling is advice. You tell them your situation and goals and they build a portfolio or rearrange the one you have. As long as you continue to pay the fee, they continue to monitor your holdings.

An easy way to access a money management firm is through your broker. Managed money or *wrap* accounts have been embraced by Wall Street. The broker shares the fee with the outside manager. Most of the major brokerage firms offer their customers a roster of 100 or more money management firms of every type. Different brokers offer the services of many of the same managers. For example, Davis Advisors, Eaton Vance, Fayez Sarofim, Goldman Sachs, Invesco, Lord Abbett, Neuberger Berman, Renaissance Advisors, Rittenhouse, and other managers are all available to customers of Merrill Lynch, Wachovia, Smith Barney, and other brokers.

A long-tenured broker/salesperson who uses wrap accounts should be able to give you a good referral. He knows firsthand which management firms have performed well for his customers and which haven't. Of course, firms with recent poor performance but solid long-term credentials should not necessarily be ruled out. Their asset class focus may simply be out of favor. An excellent source of information on wrap accounts and the total universe of money management firms is WrapManager.com. Among other services, it provides an alphabetical list of thousands of money management firms and phone numbers.

I have not discussed financial planners because their purview encompasses much more than securities (insurance, mortgages, tax planning, estate planning, retirement planning, etc.). However, a good financial planner can be the source of excellent investment advice. They all have favorite mutual fund families and money management firms that they work with. In many cases, their choice of advisers is the result of a winnowing-out process over the years. That's one reason why the more experienced planner has an edge. Because the financial planner has the complete picture of your situation, he is better able to choose the specific approach of the specific money manager that makes the most sense for you. For more information on financial planners visit the National Association of Personal Financial Advisors (napfa .org) and the Financial Planning Association (FPAnet.org).

Best Web Sites and Blogs

There are many thousands of investment web sites. Every possible investment-related subject is covered in exhaustive detail by multiple sites. The most widely used are the huge, comprehensive, all-purpose sites like MSN Money, Yahoo! Finance, Morningstar, MarketWatch, Bloomberg, Reuters, *BusinessWeek, Wall Street Journal, Barron's, SmartMoney, Motley Fool,* TheStreet, CNN Money, Hoovers, *Forbes,* FinancialTimes, Kiplinger, and so on (add .com to each name). Other web sites take a smaller slice of the investment universe and deal exclusively with such diverse subjects as company filings, insider trading, point and figure charts, short selling, financial statements, mergers, currencies, and 401(k)s. The topics that are covered in this book in a few paragraphs can be found on the

Internet in voluminous detail in specialized sites like Prophet, Valuengine, Zacks, Investinreits, Bigcharts, Gainskeeper, Bankrate, and so on (add.com to each).

In this chapter on active investing, a number of outstanding web sites have already been described. The best way to get an overall picture of just what's out there is to access *Forbes'* annual list of "Best on the Web" awards at Forbes.com. It is an expansive undertaking, with "Investing" only one of many general categories. There are 38 subcategories under the "Investing" umbrella, starting with "Alternative Investing" and ending with "Wall Street Research." There is one winning "Forbes Favorite" web site in each sub-category plus 7 to 15 runner-ups and honorable mentions. For example, in the subcategory, "Stock Picking," *Forbes'* favorite (2006) is ClearStation (clearstation.etrade.com). It's followed by the other picks, MSN Money (MoneyCentral.com/investor), Marketocracy (marketocracy.com), and Reuters Investor (reuters.com/investing), which are followed, in turn, by seven other honorable mention sites.

Another excellent source for ferreting out the best financial sites on the Internet is AAII's annual "Top Web Sites Guide." It's available both in the September *AAII Journal* magazine and on AAII.com. With 27 subcategories it's not quite as far-reaching as *Forbes,* nor does it select one favorite in each sub-category. But AAII's focus is only on investing and its site assess-ments are more detailed. For each "best of the Net" site, there's an explanation of what it likes and what it doesn't like. Under the category "Webcasts," for example (September 2006), it critiques four web sites that offer broadcasts of earnings conference calls, shareholder meetings, and so on. The best are BestCalls.com, BusinessWeek.com, Earnings.com, and InvestorCalendar.com.

> "The scariest and most clueless of all investors are those who talk about the stock market with certainty."
>
> —*Unknown*

100,000 Blogs Added Every Day

Any discussion of web sites is incomplete without acknowledging the increasing impact of blogs (personal diaries updated with posts during the day). We're told there are over 100 million blogs worldwide with some 100,000 added every day. Even at half those figures, the numbers are staggering.

Blogs devoted to investing and finance are everywhere. Many of them are a rich source of stock ideas and learning. The investor benefits from the enormity of the blog universe because those that rise above the intense competition must necessarily be outstanding. The fact is that many investment bloggers are established professionals who write with keen insight and intellect. They include Floyd Norris, Herb Greenberg, Larry Kudlow, Paul Merriman, Mark Cuban, Barry Ritholtz, Brett Steenbarger, Michael Steinhardt, Bernie Schaeffer, and Henry Blodgett, to name a few.

How do you separate the wheat from the chaff in the crowded blog world? Probably a good place to start is with someone else's well-documented "best" list. Kiplinger's *Personal Finance* (October 2006) features "16 Must Read Financial Blogs"; 24/7 Wall St. (247wallst.com, June 17, 2007) spotlights "The 25 Best Financial Blogs"; and TheKirkReport.com lists "The 86 Blogs I Read." Another good jumping-off spot is StockBlogs .com, which claims to be "the largest stock market blog directory." Its best stock blogs are divided into eight categories: general market, technical analysis, fundamental analysis, options, contrary investing, commodities, foreign exchange, and miscellaneous.

A good way to get a sense of the astonishing amount of investment information that can be found on just one page of a blog is to visit BetweenTheHedges.com. If you were to link to every source listed on the home page and then continue linking to sites of interest as they come up, you'd probably stay busy for years. For example, just one of the myriad of links that appear on BetweenTheHedges.com is one that links to over 70 favorite investment blogs.

24/7 Wall Street estimates we're approaching 1 million financial blogs. A tiny sampling of investment blogs I've seen on multiple "best" lists includes the following:

247WallSt.com	BetweenTheHedges.com
Abnormalreturns.com	BigPicture.typepad.com
AntAndSons.com	Billcara.com
BespokeInvest.typepad.com	BioHealthInvestor.com

BlogginWallStreet.com
BloggingStocks.com
Blogs.wsj.com/marketbeat
buttonwood1792.blogspot.com
  (The Kingsland Report)
CarlFutia.blogspot.com
ControlledGreed.com
CrossingWallStreet.com
CXOadvisory.com
DDO.typepad.com (Daily Dose
  of Optimism)
ETFDigest.com
ETFinvestor.com
ETFTrends.com
FinancialSkeptic.blogspot.com
Footnoted.org
Herbgreenberg.com
InternetOutsider.com
InvestmentJungle.com
JeffMathewsIsNotMaking
  ThisUp.com
Minyanville.com
Mymoneylife.blogspot.com
NakedShorts.typepad.com
oldprof.typepad.com (a Dash of
  Insight)
Paul.Kedrosky.com (Infectious
  Greed)

PhatInvestor.com
PoorAndStupid.com
RandomRoger.com
SchaeffersResearch.com
SeekingAlpha.com
SelfInvestors.com
StingyInvestor.com
StockerBlog.com
StockMarketBeat.com
StocksAndBlogs.com
Suite101.com
TheFlyOnTheWall.com
TheKirkReport.com
TheMarketBeat.com
TheStockMasters.com
TickerSense.com
TraderFeed.blogspot.com
TraderMike.net
TraderTim.blogspot.com
WallStreetFolly.com
W-street.com

"The real business of Wall Street often consists of introducing people who shouldn't buy securities to people who shouldn't sell them."
—*Thomas Donlan*

Chapter 10

Conclusion

I n these final pages, I focus on what I hope you will do after reading this book. If I had my druthers, the first thing I'd have you do is read it again, or at least the Introduction and Chapters 3 through 7. Understandably, that's not going to happen. So I end the book with a compilation of the most salient points that I hope you take away from your reading. It's what I feel most strongly about. But first comes a list of 85 great investment books and 100 additional quotations.

Great Investment Books: The Right Kind of Homework

The subject of homework has been discussed before. I revisit it again here to make these two points. First, if your stock goes down, there should be no self-blame because you didn't do the stock-specific research everyone tells you to do. In the vast majority of cases, it wouldn't have made any difference. Second, there *is* something you can do with any homework time you may have that *will* make a difference. Read on.

All the gurus advise investors to do their homework. It's a universal admonition and often well founded. The more you know about what's available and doable in the investment world, the better. Whether it be about 529 college tuition plans, laddering bonds, low-commission web sites, newly introduced ETFs, and so on, the amount of potentially helpful information is endless. But in most cases, the advice "Do your homework" is meant as "Research the stock."

Within this context, I submit (repeating what I have said before) that it may not be the best counsel. On its face, the advice sounds unassailably logical. The problem is that much of the time what's asked is simply not doable. "Do your homework" is one of Jim Cramer's basic rules. On his TV show *Mad Money*, he exhorts his viewers to read annual and quarterly reports, study balance sheets and SEC filings, listen to conference calls, and read all the analyst reports you can. He tells you, before buying a bank stock, to find out its net interest margin; if it's a cable stock, dig out its enterprise value; or if it's a company coming out of bankruptcy, read the bankruptcy trustee's report.

The advice is theoretically sound and obviously well intentioned. Everybody, not only Cramer, urges investors to research their stocks. But as a practical matter, most investors lack the time and most certainly the skill to perform these tasks. They require a level of sophistication that's simply not there. In fairness to Cramer, he does say if you don't have the time or inclination, you should have a professional do the work for you. But what we mostly don't have is the ability. We are not trained to analyze cash flows, inventory turnover, book to sales ratios, or balance sheet footnotes.

And even if we were, even if we were all CPAs, the truth is that even then, such homework might well prove to be useless. If you knew and understood every statistic there was on a company, there is no way you could know how the market will respond to that information. It may act as it has in the past in similar circumstances, or it may not. Or the market may ignore your diligently acquired information and react instead to broader influences unrelated to the company. Or what you've learned through your homework may already be reflected in the price of the stock since multitudes know what you know before you know it.

The knowledge that really counts in the market is the awareness that information, of and by itself, is often meaningless regardless of how assiduously acquired. Scholarship does not ensure investment success.

Money manager Paul Merriman (FundAdvice.com, "Strategic Laziness") says, "There are literally tens of thousands of pieces of data that you might conclude are important to the investment process and potentially important to your portfolio. You could spend all your time finding and analyzing that data, and still not know what to do."

As we have already discussed, the often irrelevance of statistics also applies to "news." If this hasn't happened to you, it will. Your adviser tells you of good things that'll be happening to a company (or you dig up the information yourself). You buy the stock and, happily it goes up. But then it starts to go down and as it goes lower and lower your adviser keeps telling you all the reasons why it shouldn't be. The good news may very well prove accurate: Both you and/or your adviser have done your homework well. But there's a total disconnect between "news" and performance. The result: confusion and frustration.

Studying Tobias or Turnover—It's a No-Brainer

If my premise is correct that most of us are unable to understand and analyze financial data, much less predict how the market will react to it, then I suggest a different homework assignment. *Read the great investment books.* The choice between devoting the three hours or so it takes to read Andrew Tobias's *The Only Investment Guide You'll Ever Need* (Harcourt, Inc., rev. 2005) or using the same time to study stock-specific reports is a no-brainer. If you have the time to do both, that's fine. Reading annual reports and SEC filings may or may not help you succeed as an investor, but reading Warren Buffett's annual letters to stockholders *will* make you a better long-term investor, period. In fact, savvy veteran Harvey Eisen (chairman, Bedford Oak Partners) says, "Put all of Warren Buffett's annual letters to stockholders together and you probably have the greatest book on investing ever written." (Access all annual letters since 1977 at BerkshireHathaway.com.)

Of the millions who have dealt with the market over the past decades, there are a handful of gifted people who are able to see truths that others don't and then articulate them for the benefit of others. As investors, the more wisdom we can soak up from these elite thinkers, the more likely we are to prevail as long-term investors. Throughout this book I have maintained that the best we can do is to try and put the investment odds in our favor. I know of no better way to do that than to be familiar with the best minds of our age. Reading great investment books is the most productive use of your homework time.

There are some who will complain that if stock market experts were so expert, they'd be buying stocks, not selling books. In response, I would make five points:

1. Many do both with equal success. Jim Rogers, Joel Greenblatt, Marty Whitman, Peter Lynch, Martin Zweig, David Swensen, William O'Neil, Jim Cramer, Ben Stein, John Neff, and Ken Fisher are a few names that come to mind. There are many more.
2. Great coaches are rarely great players—yet they help players become great.
3. Most of the investment greats are long-term oriented. A nontrading approach provides ample time to both pursue a career and write a book.
4. Many guru authors have already made their fortune. Their priority is to help others and leave a legacy, not make more money.

> "In the business world, everyone is paid in two coins: cash and experience. Take the experience first; the cash will come later."
> —*Harold Geneen*

5. An author can give all kinds of insightful stock market–related advice without being a great stock picker.

Books That Have Stood the Test of Time

When applied to investment books, the term *classic* is used loosely. Strictly speaking, it should be used only to describe books that have stood the test of time. Only the passing of the years gives us the perspective to qualify an author's views as true wisdom. Exceptions are recent books that are a good bet to achieve classic status in the future because of the stature of the author, the success of his prior books, or the wide acclaim from his peers.

The following list of great investment books was derived mostly from the recommended reading lists of dozens of professional reviewers. The focus is mostly on lists of *all-time* great books, not on *this year's* favorite book. In all cases, the selections that appear in the following compilation are recommended on multiple "best" lists and a few, like *The Intelligent Investor*, *A Random Walk Down Wall Street*, and *The Four Pillars of Investing* are on the majority of lists. Because the focus is on the investment process itself, books about market history and personal finance are not included.

Like all such lists, it does not include some excellent books that have been unfairly overlooked. I arbitrarily picked one of Jim Cramer's best-sellers. I object to the short-term focus, which can discourage long-term strategies. Like his TV show, however, Cramer has enough helpful tips in his books to make them worthwhile reading.

Books are listed alphabetically by title. To get detailed information on any book, including revisions, go to Amazon.com, put the title or author's name in the search box, click on to the book's image, and scroll down.

Some of the sources used to help compile the following list include SmartMoney.com, BusinessWeek.com, Barrons.com, Morningstar.com, about.com, Amazon.com, TheKirkReport.com, TradersLibrary.com, MarketWatch.com, Bloomberg.com, TheStreet.com, InvestorGeeks.com, Telegraph.co.uk, TechnologyInvestor.com (Harry Newton), FinancialSense.com (Jim Puplava), DallasNews.com (Scott Burns), AskHumberto@aol.com (Humberto Cruz), Investopedia.com, HarperBusiness.com, Forbes.com, and the recommended reading lists of authors Bill Schultheis, Burton Malkiel, Frank Armstrong, Larry Swedroe, and others.

25 Books That Appear on the Most "Must Read" Lists

Against the Gods by Peter Bernstein
Annual Letters to Stockholders by Warren Buffett (BerkshireHathaway.com)
The Battle for the Soul of Capitalism by John Bogle
Beating the Street by Peter Lynch and John Rothchild
The Coffeehouse Investor by Bill Schultheis
Common Sense on Mutual Funds by John Bogle

Common Stocks and Uncommon Profits by Philip Fisher

Contrarian Investment Strategy by David Dreman

The Essays of Warren Buffett by Warren Buffett

Fooled by Randomness: The Hidden Role of Chance by Nassim Nicholas Taleb

The Four Pillars of Investing by William Bernstein

The Future for Investors by Jeremy Siegel

The Informed Investor by Frank Armstrong

The Intelligent Asset Allocator by William Bernstein

The Intelligent Investor by Benjamin Graham

The Little Book That Beats the Market by Joel Greenblatt

The Only Guide to a Winning Investment Strategy You'll Ever Need by Larry Swedroe

The Only Investment Guide You'll Ever Need by Andrew Tobias

A Random Walk Down Wall Street by Burton Malkiel

Stocks for the Long Run by Jeremy Siegel

Technical Analysis of Stock Trends by Edwards and McGee

Unconventional Success by David Swensen

The Warren Buffett Way by Robert Hagstrom Jr.

Winning on Wall Street by Marty Zweig

Winning the Loser's Game by Charles Ellis

60 Books That Appear on Multiple "Must Read" Lists

The Aggressive Conservative Investor by Martin Whitman

The Art of Low Risk Investing by Michael Zahorchak

The Automatic Millionaire by David Bach

The Battle for Investment Survival by Gerald Loeb

The Bogleheads' Guide to Investing by Larimore, Lindauer, LeBoeuf, and Bogle

Creating Wealth by Robert Allen

Enhancing Trader Performance by Brett Steenbarger

Fire Your Stock Analyst by Harry Domash

The Fortune Tellers by Howard Kurtz

Freakonomics by Steven Levitt and Stephen Dubner

Getting Rich in America by Lee McKenzie

Global Investing by Roger Ibbotson and Gary Brinson

Hot Commodities by Jim Rogers

How to Make Money in Stocks by William O'Neil

How to Make Money in Wall Street by Louis Rukeyser

Index Mutual Funds by W. Scott Simon

Investing with Exchange Traded Funds Made Easy by Marvin Appel

Investment Illusions by Martin Fridson

The Investor's Guide to Charting by Alistair Blair

It's When You Sell That Counts by Donald Cassidy

Jim Cramer's Real Money by Jim Cramer

John Neff on Investing by John Neff

Just one Thing by John Mauldin

The Lazy Person's Guide to Investing by Paul Farrell

Liar's Poker by Michael Lewis

The Little Book of Common Sense Investing by John Bogle

The Little Book of Value Investing by Christopher Browne

Margin of Safety by Seth Klarman

The Millionaire Next Door by Thomas Stanley and William Danko

The Money Game by Adam Smith

A Modern Approach to Graham and Dodd Investing by Thomas Au

The Motley Fool Investment Guide by David and Tom Gardner

The Neatest Little Guide to Stock Market Investing by Jason Kelly

New Era Value Investing by Nancy Tengler

The New Finance: The Case Against Efficient Markets by Robert Haugen

The New Money Masters by John Train

One Up on Wall Street by Peter Lynch

The Only Three Questions That Count by Ken Fisher

Options for the Stock Investor by James Bittman

Poor Charlie's Almanac by Charlie Munger

Portfolio Theory and Capital Markets by William Sharpe

Reminiscences of a Stock Operator by Edwin Lefévre

Rich Dad Poor Dad by Robert Kiyosaki

Searching for Alpha by Ben Warwick

Secrets for Profiting in Bull and Bear Markets by Stan Weinstein

The Single Best Investment by Lowell Miller

The Smartest Investment Book You'll Ever Read by Daniel R. Solin

The Stock Market Jungle by Michael Panzer

Stock Market Primer by Claude Rosenberg

Straight Talk on Investing by Jack Brennan
The Successful Investor Today by Larry Swedroe
The Terrible Truth about Investing by Temkin, Phillips, and Thomas
The Unbeatable Market by Ron Ross
Value Investing: A Balanced Approach by Martin Whitman
Value Investing from Graham to Buffett and Beyond by Greenwald, Kahn, Sonkin, and van Biema
What Wall Street Doesn't Want You to Know by Larry Swedroe
When to Sell by Justin Mamis
Why Smart People Make Dumb Money Mistakes by Belsky and Gilovich
Yes, You Can Time the Market by Ben Stein
You Can Be a Stock Market Genius by Joel Greenblatt

Sayings and Quotations

I didn't have room in the text for all my favorite quotations so I include the rest of them here. Some may prove valuable takeaways from your reading and some may not. Since I don't know which will and which won't, and since what's memorable to one reader may leave no impression on another, I've included them all. Following the quotations is a summary of what I hope you will take away from this book.

"The truth is independent of how many people believe it."

—*Anonymous*

"I have been covering personal finance for two decades and I am continually amazed by how little I know. My advice: develop a sense of conviction about your profound ignorance. You probably won't have time to wait very long for confirmation."

—*Jonathan Clements*

"A rich man is nothing but a poor man with money."

—*W.C. Fields*

"Making money is hard if you wait till situations are clear to everyone. We are often better served by quick analysis that's 80% right than by slow analysis that is 95% right."

—*Jim Oberweis*

"I have fun being honest about my mistakes. When someone says to me that another advisor never admits mistakes, my stock reply is, 'I guess he doesn't make any.'"

—*John Dorfman*

"It's far better to buy a wonderful company at a fair price than a fair company at a wonderful price."

—*Warren Buffett*

"If you don't stay with your winners, you're not going to be able to pay for your losers."

—*Michael Marcus*

"A good technician gets it right maybe 60% of the time, and a great technician, maybe 61% of the time."

—*Gary B. Smith*

"One lesson I've learned over the years is that mutual fund investors almost always do significantly worse than the funds they own. That lesson is likely to be repeated in ETFs."

—*John Bogle*

"Every day I get up and look through the *Forbes* list of the richest people in America. If I'm not there, I go to work."

—*Robert Orben*

"If I were making the money I could be making in this [securities] business, I just wouldn't like the person I'd have to be."

—*Patrick Geddes*

"When you lose, don't lose the lesson."

—*Charles Kirk*

"Whatever happens in the stock market today has happened before and will happen again."

—*Jesse Livermore*

"Human beings are hardwired to be massively irrational when it comes to financial matters. . . . Even the most brilliant investors only have a few good ideas a year."

—*Whitney Tilson*

"When you look at an investment, always look for the sucker. If you don't see one, it's you."

—*Mark Cuban*

"Like selecting a mate, try to build a portfolio that you can live with for a long, long time."

—*Robert Arnott*

"History doesn't repeat itself, it rhymes."

—*Unknown*

"Investing is the most difficult of sports; nowhere else does one begin a career by opposing the world's most accomplished professionals."

—*Brett Steenbarger*

"The objective of investing is to ride the prevailing bias for all we can get."

—*George Soros*

"Good judgment comes from experience, and experience comes from bad judgment."

—*Dr. Steven Cramer*

"Saving money on a regular basis is the key to financial success. It's so simple—and yet so few people do it."

—*Jonathan Clements*

"You have to learn when to hold and when to fold. Most nonprofessionals leave their winnings on the table, figuring their lucky streak will last. It rarely does. This is not your father's 'buy and hold' world."

—*Harry Newton*

"Bull markets are born on pessimism, grow on skepticism, mature on optimism and die on euphoria."

—*Michael B. Steele*

"When it comes to banking and money, the four most dangerous words in the world are, 'This time it's different.'"

—*Allan Sloan*

"The stock market is filled with individuals who know the price of everything but the value of nothing."

—Philip Fisher

"Stock valuations are based on estimates of unknown future performance and events, so they are always imprecise."

—Henry Blodget

"New opinions are always suspected and usually opposed, without any other reason but because they are not common."

—John Locke

"Money talks—but all mine ever says is good-bye."

—Anonymous

"Rule #1: Never lose money. Rule #2: Never forget rule #1."

—Warren Buffett

"Every time history repeats itself, the price goes up."

—Unknown

"By definition, most people are part of the consensus. But on Wall Street, no one wants to admit it."

—Michael Santoli

"Superior bond funds can be systemically identified based solely on their lower expense ratios."

—John Bogle

"A bull market may be defined as an upward movement in prices causing an investor to mistake himself for a financial genius."

—Unknown

"Stocks often rise because of nothing more than unsustainable momentum. Unfortunately, that momentum lulls investors and even company executives into thinking they're smart, when they're really just parading around the chairs while the music is playing."

—Herb Greenberg

"We must believe in luck. How else can we explain the success of those we don't like?"

—Jean Cocteau

"Of all the speculative blunders, there are few greater than trying to average a losing game (always sell what shows you a loss and keep what shows you a profit)."

—Edwin Lefevre

"On average, America's millionaires go out of business or bankrupt 3.5 times before they reach their goal."

—Unknown

"No trading system, no matter how good, will work if too many people start following it."

—Mark Hulbert

"The long-term history of the market indicates that there is a much greater likelihood that value will outperform growth than the other way around. That to me is a fundamental truth of investing."

—Michael Oyster

"Be extremely skeptical and stay with what you know. The great success stories in life are people who figure out what they know, stay with it, put their eggs in that basket and watch it very carefully."

—Jim Rogers

"Unpopular stocks tend to do better than popular ones because equities advance by exceeding expectations. Lower expectations are easier to exceed."

—John Dorfman

"History should be a guide but not a jailor. There is little permanent truth in the financial markets as change is inevitable and constant."

—Doug Kass

"The market is like a teenage daughter—it does exactly what it wants to do when it wants to do it. . . . Most of the money I've made in the market has been from two things—following the dominant trend and getting ahead of key reversals in stocks and the market."

—Charles Kirk

"The only way to beat the market is not to look like the market."

—Larry Swedroe

"I define high quality companies as those that have barriers to entry, consistent growth over long periods of time, high returns on equity and strong balance sheets."

—Harvey Eisen

"Benjamin Graham looked for stocks with a 'margin of safety' which he likened to a search for dollar bills selling for 50¢. By insisting on a margin of safety before investing, we can often avoid getting burned."

—Unknown

"To steal ideas from one person is plagiarism, to steal from many is research."

—Unknown

"Properly measured, the average actively managed dollar must underperform the average passively managed dollar, net of costs. Empirical analyses that appear to refute this principle are guilty of improper measurement."

—William F. Sharpe, Nobel Laureate in Economics

"Almost everybody has a chance of being right if enough time goes by."

—Unknown

"Stock market returns show a strong tendency to revert to the mean—and that mean, over the long run, is up."

—Burton Malkiel

"Most bad companies stay bad, and most cheap stocks get cheaper. Once you realize that, then you're ready for investing in turnaround situations."

—Charles Kirk

"For every transaction there is a buyer and a seller. Each one thinks he/she is dead right."

—Unknown

"Let your profits run but stop your losses; discipline always trumps conviction."

—Doug Kass

"Markets can remain illogical longer than you or I can remain solvent."

—*Gary Shilling*

"There is only one side to the stock market; it is not the bull side or the bear side but the right side."

—*Jesse Livermore*

"The general investment knowledge of the masses can be written large on the head of a pin."

—*Phil De Muth*

"Suggested disclaimer before introducing an analyst on TV: 'The views expressed may be unfounded, biased, self-serving and completely at odds with your long-term investment success. No due diligence on all past recommendations has been attempted.' "

—*John Merrill*

"If an investment idea sounds too good to be true, it is too good to be true."

—*Burton Malkiel*

"The reason why most mergers don't work long-term is the difference in their corporate cultures."

—*Unknown*

"The investor's only real effective, dependable weapon against the equally dependable perversity of the market is time, and lots of it."

—*Unknown*

"Buy a business any fool can manage, because eventually one will."

—*Warren Buffett*

"All technical teaching systems will work if they have good risk management and if you have the discipline to sell your losers and let your winners ride."

—*John Mauldin*

"It's just not true that you can't beat the market. Every year about one-third of the fund managers do it. Of course, each year it is a different group."

—*Robert Stovall*

"You can only win if someone else loses. If you want to win in the long term, you need to understand the schemes and dreams of your opponent."

—*Jon Markman*

"It doesn't matter how spectacularly a stock has performed, it's where it's going from here that counts."

—*Unknown*

"Today's investors find it inconceivable that life might be better without so much information—that ignoring the vast majority of investment noise might actually improve investment performance."

—*Richard Bernstein*

"The stock market is the only place where the customer will run away from a bargain."

—*Unknown*

"If you want to see the greatest threat to your financial future, go home and take a look in the mirror."

—*Jonathan Clements*

"Few people think more than two or three times a year. I have made an international reputation for myself by thinking once or twice a week."

—*George Bernard Shaw*

"There are, indeed, investment professionals who know that they don't know where the market is headed but their livelihood depends upon appearing that they do know."

—*William Bernstein*

"That men do not learn very much from the lessons of history is the most important of all the lessons that history has to teach."

—*Aldous Huxley*

"Statisticians will tell you that you need 20 years worth of data to draw statistically meaningful conclusions. But after 20 successful years of managing a mutual fund, most managers are ready to retire."

—*Susan Dziubinski*

"When everybody thinks a company is going to strike out, you just need a single to do okay."

—*Richard Bernstein*

"When looking for reasons why overbought markets continue to go up, don't forget the buying of nervous short sellers throwing in the towel and covering their wrong bets."

—*Unknown*

"Reversion to the long-term mean is one of the iron-clad rules of financial markets."

—*James O. Shaughnessy*

"Corporate management infrequently, if ever, view their long-term prospects with suspicion."

—*Doug Kass*

"The market will decide how much profit to give you. But only you can decide how much to limit your loss."

—*Linda Bradford Raschke*

"The essence of investment theory is that being smart is not a sufficient condition for being rich."

—*Peter Bernstein*

"The stock market does its best when earnings and dividends are getting drubbed, and worst when they are zooming."

—*Marty Zweig*

"Just because a stock stops going down does not mean it will automatically start going up."

—*Michael Kahn*

"My definition of a guru is someone who is lucky enough to be quoted in the right publication at the right time saying the right thing."

—*Herb Greenberg*

"Be skeptical of a claim about what works and doesn't work in the investment arena unless it stands up to rigorous statistical scrutiny."
—*Mark Hulbert*

"When asked what he considered man's greatest discovery, Albert Einstein replied without hesitation, 'compound interest.'"
—*Charles Ellis*

"The investor's chief problem—and even his worst enemy—is likely to be himself."
—*Benjamin Graham*

"This message [that attempting to beat the market is futile] can never be sold on Wall Street because it is, in effect, telling stock analysts to drop dead."
—*Paul Samuelson, Nobel Laureate in Economics*

"Life, and the stock market, can only be understood in retrospect but both have to be lived going forward."
—*Soren Kierkegaard*

"In a down market, just keep buying at a measured pace. If the market sinks a lot, buy more. I guarantee you that's how the big boys do it. The little guys sell out at the first sign of trouble—the ones with the private jets hang on."
—*Ben Stein*

"Historical analogies can be deployed to buttress any point of view."
—*Michael Santoli*

"No matter what investment you make, you'll always be able to find some other investment that's doing better. In our view, once you have found the right asset classes and the lowest-cost way to invest in them, your homework is done."
—*Paul Merriman*

"When you have too much money chasing investment ideas, bad things happen."
—*Eric Kobren*

"I believe the great investors—the likes of Warren Buffett, Peter Lynch, and John Templeton—have highly developed stock-market instincts, unlike the rest of us."

—*John Dorfman*

"My definition of a quality stock is a high and stable return and low debt."

—*Jeremy Grantham*

"Cash is a terrible long-term investment and Treasury bonds aren't much better. But in terms of keeping calm in a shaky market so that you can make sensible decisions, there's no substitute for cash."

—*Ben Stein*

"If you will not settle for anything less than your best, you'll be amazed at what you can accomplish in your life."

—*Vince Lombardi*

"The best investors always know where the next party is going to be held. They arrive early and make their exit well before the end."

—*The Economist*

"People somehow think you must buy at the bottom and sell at the top to be successful in the market. That's nonsense. The idea is to buy when the probability is greatest that the market is going to advance."

—*Martin Zweig*

"No piece of news is bullish or bearish until the market calls it."

—*Michael Santoli*

"The biggest mistake in investing is believing the last three years is representative of what the next three years is going to be like."

—*Ray Dalio*

"If you owe the bank $100, that's your problem. If you owe the bank $100 million, that's the bank's problem."

—*J. Paul Getty*

"When a fellow says it ain't the money but the principle of the thing, it's the money."

—*Kim Hubbard*

Wrap-Up: What I Hope You Take Away

I use these final pages to capsulate what I hope you will remember about this book. Unless some of my ideas stay with you, I will have accomplished little. First, an overview of what you've read.

The first half of the book is about the stock market. It includes those opinions that I think will help most to put the odds in your favor. These are strongly held convictions developed over four decades on Wall Street. They cover some controversial issues such as the investor's predisposition to fail, the irrelevance of news, the hogwash of home-work, the curse of being instantly and completely informed, the attitude of infallibility by so many advisers and talking heads on television, the under-appreciated durability of major trends and the seldom acknowl-edged role of pure luck.

The second half of the book addresses the question "What should I do with my money?" The answer is an 80–20 solution: index funds for most of your money, say 80 percent, with the balance going into individual stocks and/or mutual funds. On the passive, index side, 28 model, low-cost, diversified index fund portfolios are spotlighted, each recommended by an authority in the field of indexing. On the active side I cover what's most important to know about mutual funds and the best places to go for stock ideas.

Why is more than half the book devoted to stocks, when only a 20 percent exposure is recommended? Mostly because my background is in stock investing. It's what I know most about. But it's also because buying and selling stocks successfully requires more learning than buy-ing and holding a portfolio of index funds—and because stocks are more challenging, more fun, and more popular.

The advocacy of an index fund approach in this book is shared by many others. Index funds, and especially ETFs, have exploded in pop-ularity the past few years. The investor has been inundated with all things ETF. Growth will continue to be fueled by an ever-expanding flood of new ETFs and the outperformance of the major indexes in years like 2006. Interestingly, however, it is the institutions and traders who account for most of the volume in index funds. The individual long-term investor has yet to fully embrace indexing (although it is becoming increasingly popular in 401(k) plans).

The coolness of investors is likely rooted in human nature. We want more of a challenge than indexing provides. We want to see how we do versus the pros. Amateur golfers or tennis players can't compete against Tiger Woods or Roger Federer. But investors can compete with Warren Buffett. And we're energized by thinking we're better than we are.

A Different Approach

What makes the index approach in this book different? It is the inclusion of a wide variety of professionally recommended model portfolios, making it easy to implement an indexing strategy. The reader is not limited to the recommendations of the author. Instead, he is exposed to a cross section of 28 ready-to-go portfolios, each representing the best thinking of an experienced indexer. Hopefully, these diversified, buy-and-hold portfolios will stimulate participation by long-term oriented investors.

Why do many older professionals use index funds for their own account while younger investors do not? Probably because of the difference in experience. The veteran has been through the wars. He has been humbled. Experience has taught him to respect the unpredictability of the market and the attractiveness of indexing as a way to deal with it. I would like to spare the reader that learning experience, which sometimes can be long, unpleasant, and costly. But we usually have to learn from our own mistakes, not from others'. If, on the other hand, your nonindexing journey turns out to be a positive one, I hope the more than half the book devoted to do-it-yourself (stock market) investing will have made a contribution to your success.

One final point in this overview: This book is not a Stock Market 101 textbook. It covers a wide range of topics but none are treated with the in-depth coverage readily available elsewhere. I use a scattergun approach, picking and choosing only the information that you're likely to use. If surface information is all you'll need, that's all that's there. The contents are far from all-inclusive but I believe it includes everything you need to succeed. It's as if you were attending a university that only offers courses that you can actually use in the real world.

> "What if everything is an illusion and nothing exists? In that case, I definitely overpaid for my carpet."
> —*Woody Allen*

What I Hope Stays with You

- No matter how overextended or overbought the market, no matter how widespread the anticipation of a correction or how badly it's needed, no matter how extensive the warnings of its coming, *when it comes*—when a steep sell-off actually takes place—all the warnings that preceded it are forgotten. Fear, shock, and bewilderment take over. Emotion will always trump reason.
- It is impossible to overstate the importance of luck in investing. So often it is the ignored explanation of why things happen.
- It is certain that there will always be an exact opposite to your opinion held by someone smarter than you.
- The market itself always has the last word. It is the final arbiter.
- The market always goes to extremes in both directions—sometimes to extreme extremes.
- There are always positives and negatives about everything in investing. Negatives are usually given little attention. Seek them out to avoid surprise.
- Entrenched trends tend to go further and last longer than expected. In 2006, REITs advanced for the seventh year in a row and small caps beat large caps for the eighth straight year.
- Almost everything good that happens in the market requires the passage of time.
- Owning noncorrelated assets (ones that go up when others go down) is the key to reducing risk and increasing returns. But asset classes are acting more and more alike, especially in steep sell-offs when protection is needed the most. In a sweeping down market, the asset class that can be depended on most to zig when everything else is zagging is fixed income, especially U.S. Treasuries.
- No-hedge self-confidence sells but is the sign of inexperience. Humility does not sell but is the sign of wisdom.
- What you buy is less important than what you pay for it.
- In choosing between like funds, costs are crucial. Lower expenses can make a surprisingly big difference over time.
- In overextended or overvalued markets, a sell-off is healthy. It's what has to happen before the market can resume its uptrend.
- It is the propensity of human beings to forget past mistakes that enables gurus to build reputations.

- Choosing the right asset class is more important than choosing the right stock.
- When a stock goes down after you buy it or goes up after you sell it, don't feel bad. It always happens.
- Because of lack of money, patience, or brains, many who are in the market should not be.
- Taking losses is inevitable. Taking big losses is unacceptable. It can knock you out of the game. Use stops for protection.
- Manage your stocks like a storekeeper manages his inventory: Hold on to winners and weed out the losers.
- In the stock market you're competing with the sharpest professionals in the world. The only sure way to prevail is to invest long-term.
- Transparency and jail sentences may push corporate corruption below the radar screen, but until greed is no longer part of the human condition, we will always have fraud and cheating in corporate America.
- Maybe 20 percent of investors (both professional and nonprofessional) outperform the market each year, but the names are seldom the same from one year to another.
- We are not emotionally wired for success in the stock market.
- Short-term traders give up a huge advantage—the ability to benefit from the stock market's century-long upward bias.
- You can take almost any successful market strategy, do the exact opposite of what you're supposed to do, and, if you stay with it, achieve equally good results.
- The omnipotence of the market and the supremacy of its agenda are on display every time a stock or the market acts contrary to the news. The message is, "I'm in charge; pay attention." It makes the job of TV news reporters almost irrelevant.
- The price of every stock has an emotional component. It is that portion of the price that is due to hope and fear rather than sales and earnings. It is difficult to measure and easily ignored.
- We may have thousands, not hundreds of ETFs in the future. Unlike today, they may be embraced by the public. ETF and ETF portfolios may be common place in implementing the long-term strategies and investment goals of the individual investor.

- Probably the closest you can come to a sure winner in the stock market is to buy a quality, best-of-breed blue chip at a depressed level and hold for as long as it takes.
- When the market sells off sharply, it is frustrating to hear analysts/ brokers list all the bullish fundamentals, including a healthy economy, and conclude the market is overreacting. While stocks are plummeting, you're told why they shouldn't be. It is a glaring example of the disconnect between the rational thinking of the analyst, the irrational behavior of the market, and the emotional response of the investor. With most steep declines, the market is reacting to excessive evaluation and an uninterrupted rise. The bloodbath will stop when the market decides it has corrected the excesses sufficiently. The news cited as the trigger is usually irrelevant. There is always news to blame—as, for example, the big drop in the Chinese stock market that proceeded the 416-point drop in the Dow on February 27, 2007. If not China, it would have been something else. Why the market chose that day to sell off, no one knows. Attempts by reporters to logically explain the sudden slide reflect a lack of understanding of what they're dealing with.
- If the financial media wanted to be more accurate in reporting why things happen in the market, their DNA would likely prevent it. The broadcast media doesn't have the time and most of the print media doesn't have the space. So the means whereby most investors are informed is structurally incapable of performing responsibly—even if it had the savvy. Not to mention that the monotonous repetition of, "We don't know. The following may or may not be a factor" is not exactly a ratings booster. One better-than-nothing "solution" might be the use of a disclaimer: "The reasons behind the moves in stocks and the stock market are usually many and unknowable. They may or may not include what is discussed here. The influence of the market itself and the emotions of investors are acknowledged but are unquantifiable."

> "You can only expand yourself when you travel outside your comfort zone."
> —*Brett Steenbarger*

The Big Five Ideas

I could go on and on. But if I were forced to narrow the list to the five most important ideas for you to take away from this book, they would be these:

1. Absolutely, positively, no one is right all the time, or anywhere near it. The adviser who speaks with great passion, deep conviction, over-whelming reasoning, and absolute certainty of being right, can be dead wrong. The fact that he genuinely and sincerely believes he's right and that he genuinely and sincerely wants to make money for his client, doesn't make his errors less erroneous. If full disclosure required pundits to reveal all of their past mistakes, there would be no pundits left and the talking heads on television would stop talk-ing. The bottom line: Nobody consistently knows; there are just varying degrees of confusion. Discount any opinion on the market or stocks given categorically without allowing for error.

2. The reason why nobody knows has little to do with human incompetence. It has everything to do with the enigmatic nature of the phenomenon they're dealing with—the stock market itself. It is fantasy to expect anyone to forecast accurately and consist-ently an entity that is unpredictable and unknowable—not to mention arbitrary, contrary, capricious, erratic, mercurial, random, and unfathomable. The color of the market is gray, not black and white. There are few absolutes. Its perverse nature precludes hard and fast rules.

3. If indeed, nobody knows with any consistency because the market is unpredictable, the most effective way to deal with it is by buy-ing the market itself—in other words, index funds. If you diversify and buy index funds of various uncorrelated asset classes as well as the total market, it's possible to do better than the overall market. A sensible approach is to dollar-cost-average, hold, and rebalance periodically. Indexing is not settling for mediocrity. If most investors underperform the market and you match it, or more likely beat it, your performance is superior, not mediocre. Many of the smartest people on Wall Street put their own money in index funds.

4. The most durable of all business-related trends is the stock market's historical upward bias, which has persisted for over a century. It is because of this dependable uptrend that you buy common stocks and that you buy this book. It is because of this underlying positive bent that the appreciation in common stocks has exceeded that of private homes, on average, over the years. And it is the reliability of this upward bias that is the reason why long-term investors can have confidence that their market-cloning index funds will go up over time. The stock market reflects the American economy, which is powered by ingenuity and entrepreneurship. As long as we have a free society that rewards hard work and good ideas with financial gain, the economy will continue to expand (with slowdowns and/or interruptions along the way). Says Burton Malkiel, "I don't think anyone will make money in the long run betting against the inherent strength of the U.S. economy" (*Wall Street Journal*, "Irrational Complacency?," April 30, 2007). Adds Warren Buffett, "I am an enormous bull on this country. America is the most remarkable success story in the history of the world" (Q & A session with shareholders, May 2, 2005, "The Oracle Speaks," Jason Zweig, CNNMoney.com).

5. We know markets will go up over time and that a diversified portfolio of low-cost index funds will ensure participation in that growth. The only important thing left for us to do to make sure we can enjoy the results of our wisdom, patience, and discipline is to stay healthy. A long-term approach requires our being here long-term. As obvious as this may appear, it needs emphasis. What does eating right, exercising, and staying stress-free have to do with successful investing? Everything. The best investment advice you can give or receive is "Stay healthy."

I hope these five basic points will help sustain you in your future investing. Indeed, I hope this book adds something extra to your quest for securing your financial future. More important is the privilege dividend that's distributed to all of us who are concerned about increasing our wealth. In a world where almost half the population earns less than two dollars a day, you have the "problem" of how to invest your money and I have the opportunity to write a book about it. We are truly blessed.

REMINDER PAGE

Long Term Investors, HEAR THIS

If you're in a bad market and it's got you depressed, throw away the Prozac and substitute regular visits to this reminder page.

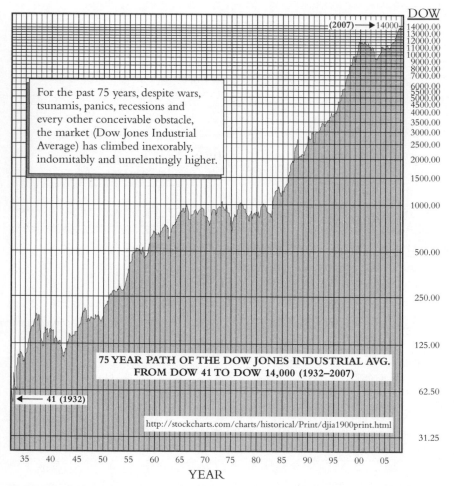

For the past 75 years, despite wars, tsunamis, panics, recessions and every other conceivable obstacle, the market (Dow Jones Industrial Average) has climbed inexorably, indomitably and unrelentingly higher.

75 YEAR PATH OF THE DOW JONES INDUSTRIAL AVG. FROM DOW 41 TO DOW 14,000 (1932–2007)

◄— 41 (1932)

(2007) ——► 14000

http://stockcharts.com/charts/historical/Print/djia1900print.html

YEAR

Source: © StockCharts.com

Index

455